UNTRANQUIL RECOLLECTIONS

UNTRANQUIL RECOLLECTIONS

The Years of Fulfilment

REHMAN SOBHAN

SAGE www.sagepublications.com
Los Angeles • London • New Delhi • Singapore • Washington DC

First published in 2016
This edition published in 2016 by

SAGE Publications India Pvt Ltd
B1/I-1 Mohan Cooperative Industrial Area
Mathura Road, New Delhi 110 044, India
www.sagepub.in

SAGE Publications Inc
2455 Teller Road
Thousand Oaks, California 91320, USA

SAGE Publications Ltd
1 Oliver's Yard, 55 City Road
London EC1Y 1SP, United Kingdom

SAGE Publications Asia-Pacific Pte Ltd
3 Church Street
#10-04 Samsung Hub
Singapore 049483

Published by Vivek Mehra for SAGE Publications India Pvt Ltd, typeset in 11/13 Minion Pro by RECTO Graphics, Delhi and printed at Chaman Enterprises, New Delhi.

Library of Congress Cataloging-in-Publication Data

Sobhan, Rehman, author.
Untranquil recollections : the years of fulfilment / Rehman Sobhan.
pages cm
Includes index.
1. Sobhan, Rehman. 2. Economists—Bangladesh—Biography. 3. Political activists—Bangladesh—Biography. 4. Bangladesh—History. I. Title.
HB126.B263S63 954.9204092--dc23 [B] 2016 2015031717

ISBN: 978-93-515-0986-8 (PB)

The SAGE Team: N. Unni Nair, Saima Ghaffar, Nand Kumar Jha and Ritu Chopra

To my grandchildren, Sahil, Shamil and Samana;
to remind you where it all began.

Bliss was it in that dawn to be alive. But to be young was very heaven.

William Wordsworth's, *The French Revolution as it appeared to enthusiasts at its commencement.*

Contents

List of Abbreviations

ADC	Additional Deputy Commissioner
ADM	Additional District Magistrate
AFP	Agence France-Presse
AJ	Alijoon
AL	Awami League
ASEAN	Association of Southeast Asian Nations
BARD	Bangladesh Academy for Rural Development
BBC	British Broadcasting Corporation
BCL	Bachelor of Civil Law
BCS	Bengal Civil Service
BD	Basic Democracies/Basic Democrats
BEA	Bangladesh Economic Association
BIC	Bangladesh Information Center
BIDS	Bangladesh Institute of Development Studies
BNR	Bureau of National Reconstruction
BPC	Basic Principles Committee
BSF	Border Security Force
BWP	Bangladesh Workers' Party
CA	Constituent Assembly
CENTO	Central Treaty Organization
CIA	Central Intelligence Agency
C-in-C	Commander-in-Chief
CLI	Commerce, Labour and Industries
CM	Chief Minister
CMI	Chr. Michelsen Institute
CMLA	Chief Martial Law Administrator
COP	Combined Opposition Party of Pakistan
CPD	Centre for Policy Dialogue
CPI (M)	Communist Party of India (Marxist)
CRL	Cholera Research Laboratory

CSP	Civil Service of Pakistan
CSS	Central Superior Services
CTC	Calcutta Tramways Company
CUCA	Cambridge University Conservative Association
DAC	Development Advisory Centre
DC	Deputy Commissioner
DHC	Deputy High Commissioner
DIT	Dhaka Improvement Trust
DNF	Dhaka Nawab Family
DSE	Delhi School of Economics
DUCSU	Dhaka University Central Student's Union
EBDO	Elective Bodies Disqualification Order
EPIDC	East Pakistan Industrial Development Corporation
EPIWTA	East Pakistan Inland Water Transport Authority
EPR	East Pakistan Rifles
EPRWP	Eastern Pakistan Rural Works Programme
EPSL	East Pakistan Students' League
EPSU	East Pakistan Student's Union
FA	Football Association Challenge
FIR	First Information Report
FRCS	Fellow of the Royal College of Surgeons
FRU	Forum Research Unit
GHQ	General Headquarters
GOC	General Officer Commanding
HAG	Harvard Advisory Group
HSC	Higher School Certificate
IAC	Indian Airlines Corporation
IAS	Indian Administrative Service
IB	International Baccalaureate
ICI	Imperial Chemical Industries
ICS	Indian Civil Services
IDBP	Industrial Development Bank of Pakistan
IDS	Institute of Development Studies
IFS	Indian Foreign Service
IIE	International Institute of Education
ILO	International Labour Office
IMF	International Monetary Fund

JFK	John F. Kennedy
JMP	Janamaitri Parishad
KDA	Karachi Development Authority
KIT	Karachi Improvement Trust
KSP	Krishak Sramik Party
LFO	Legal Framework Order
LJ	Leslie Jones
LSE	London School of Economics
MAC	Muzaffar Ahmed Chowdhury
MCA	Member of the Constituent Assembly
MCC	Marylebone Cricket Club
MCCI	Metropolitan Chamber of Commerce and Industry
MGM	Metro–Goldwyn–Meyer
MI	Military Intelligence
MIT	Massachusetts Institute of Technology
MNA	Member of the National Assembly
MP	Member of Parliament
MRA	Moral Rearmament
NAP	National Awami Party
NASEP	National Association for Social and Economic Progress
NATO	North Atlantic Treaty Organization
NDF	National Democratic Front
NKVD	Narodnyy Komissariat Vnutrennikh Del
NSF	National Students Federation
NWFP	North-West Frontier Province
PCS	Punjab Civil Services
PEA	Pakistan Economic Association
PECHS	Pakistan Employees Cooperative Housing Society
PFS	Pakistan Foreign Service
PIA	Pakistan International Airlines
PIDC	Pakistan Industrial Development Corporation
PIDE	Pakistan Institute of Development Economics
PL	Public Law
PLO	Palestine Liberation Organization
PM	Prime Minister
PPE	Politics, Philosophy and Economics

PPP	Pakistan Peoples Party
PRC	People's Republic of China
QEH	Queen Elizabeth House
QML	Qayyum Muslim League
ROK	Republic of Korea
RPWP	Rural Public Works Programme
RTC	Round-table Conference
SACEPS	South Asia Centre for Policy Studies
SDO	Subdivisional Officer
SDOP	Subdivisional Police Officer
SEATO	South East Asia Treaty Organization
SP	Superintendent of Police
T&T	Telephone and Telegraph
UDI	Unilateral Declaration of Independence
UN	United Nations
UNESCAP	United Nations Economic and Social Commission for Asia and the Pacific
USIS	United States Information Services
VC	Vice Chancellor
WFP	World Food Programme
WIDER	World Institute of Development Economic Research

Dr Manmohan Singh, *Member of Parliament and former Prime Minister of India*, releasing **'Untranquil Recollections'** in the presence of **Prof Rehman Sobhan**, *author*, **Prof Muchkund Dubey**, *President*, *Council for Social Development and former Foreign Secretary, Government of India*, **Mr Deb Mukharji**, *former Indian High Commissioner to Bangladesh*, **Prof Samiran Nundy**, *Emeritus Consultant, Department of Surgical Gastroenterology and Liver Transplantation, Sir Ganga Ram Hospital* **Dr Srinath Raghavan**, *Senior Fellow, Centre for Policy Research* and **Mr Vivek Mehra**, *MD and CEO, SAGE Publications* at an event held in New Delhi.

Preface

I have lived a reasonably full and eventful life where I have been witness to the historic events that include the birth of the new nation state of Bangladesh. I was, myself, in a modest capacity, involved in some of these events that have provided me with a somewhat closer perspective to reflect on them. While others have also written accounts of these events, whether in memoirs or as history, my own point of departure moves beyond a historical narrative and aims to present my story rather than a history of these events. My story narrates the tale of an ordinary person whose life's journey began from a place where its culmination in my engagement in a political struggle to establish a new country, Bangladesh, appeared highly improbable.

I was raised in a world of privilege and educated in institutions such as St. Paul's School, Darjeeling; Aitchison College, Lahore; and Cambridge University, which catered to the elite and where English was the exclusive medium of instruction. I first came to live in Dhaka in January 1957, at the age of 21. At that time, I could not speak Bangla as I had been raised in a family with little exposure to its rich culture. I could never relish *ilish*,[1] had rarely heard any *Rabindra Sangeet* and could not take inspiration from the poetry of either Tagore or Nazrul Islam. When I landed in Dhaka after three years in Cambridge, I was, true to my upbringing and education, a brown sahib, fit for a career abroad, or in the Civil Service of Pakistan (CSP), or as an executive in the head office of a multinational company located in Karachi.

By the time I departed from Cambridge in October 1956, I had already made the critical decisions that have guided my life over the next 59 years. I chose, quite deliberately, to make my home in Dhaka, which has remained so ever since. I opted for a career as

[1] Ilish is a species of fish in the herring family and a popular food fish in South Asia.

an economist, whether in public service or as a university teacher, and to commit myself to a life of political engagement dedicated, however imprecisely, to the people of a land with which I was completely unfamiliar. Even before I left Cambridge, I had been offered a position as a Reader in economics at Peshawar University, which I turned down because I had decided to work only in what was then East Pakistan, now Bangladesh, and, in consequence, never sought employment anywhere else. At that stage of my life, my adopted homeland was for me, an idea, not a real place. I thus, chose to make my home in Dhaka, not out of the compulsions of circumstance, birth or ancestral inheritance, but as an ideological decision to proclaim myself a Bangali.

This memoir seeks to track the improbable journey of a child born at an elite nursing home in Calcutta, with a British doctor in attendance, to a mother from the Dhaka Nawab Family (DNF) and a father who was a member of the Imperial Police Service of India. The central theme of my story is intended to explain why, how and under what circumstances the great-great-grandson of Nawab Ahsanullah, the son of a police officer who was once a contemporary of Field Marshal Ayub Khan at Sandhurst, would, on 27 March 1971, have his home in Dhaka invaded by an officer and his troops from the Pakistan army with orders to take him into custody on charges of high treason to the State of Pakistan.

In tracing this transformation in the trajectory of my life, I am fortunate in being able to draw upon my exposure to important historical events and some of the great and lesser personalities who contributed to the shaping of these events. As far as possible, I draw upon my own first-hand experiences, as also on the narratives of those whom I trust, who were themselves exposed to these events, which they have narrated through their own memoirs or through conversations with me. On some rare occasions, I draw on works of scholarship on the emergence of Bangladesh that serve to illuminate aspects of my story which were not within my immediate vision.

As may be expected, some discrepancies may be found, as between these narratives, as to dates, logistics, activities and interpretation of events. I leave it to historians to evaluate and reconcile these differences within a more scholarly work, treating our subjective musings as useful intermediate inputs based on first-hand experiences.

My story, as narrated in this book, concludes at the liberation of Bangladesh, when I returned to Dhaka on 31 December 1971 after spending nine months abroad as an envoy for the Government of an independent Bangladesh. At that moment, at the age of 36, I experienced a sense of fulfilment, which I was never destined to experience again over the next 43 years of my life. This story ends at this high moment in my life.

For me and all my generation who participated in or even witnessed the epic struggle, which culminated in the birth of a nation, this journey, with all its ups and downs, was full of excitement and promise where "bliss was it to be alive, but to be young was very heaven." In our uphill journey, our occasional flagging spirits were always recharged by a glimpse of the mountaintop above us which inspired us with the hope that we would eventually attain that summit. That is why I have titled my recollections, however untranquil they may appear, as a memoir of fulfilment.

All those alive today—who, "like Cortez upon a peak in Darien," looked down on the glorious new world of Bangladesh that lay before us at that historic moment in December—will share my sense of fulfilment, so it is better that I end my story on this high note. This high point in our lives should remind the present generation of Bangladeshis that there were moments of infinite possibility in our history, where a generation once believed that a new nation could be built that would give meaning to the lives of the millions who made enormous sacrifices so that we would live as free people in a just society. How far our dreams for a new order were realized within an independent Bangladesh will be narrated by me as part of another, rather less fulfilling, part of my life's story, if divine providence wills that I should live long enough to narrate it.

Acknowledgements

Whatever I have achieved in my life and narrated in this story draws on my engagement with many actors—my parents, my teachers, my students, my academic colleagues, my intellectual and political fellow travellers, my close and trusted friends and above all my immediate family, Salma, Taimur, Babar, Zafar and, now, Rounaq—who have, in various ways and varying degrees, contributed to whatever I have accomplished. The story, itself, draws these actors into my narrative and indicates their various contributions, though perhaps not as adequately as they may deserve.

In the preparation of this memoir, I would like to acknowledge the more specific contributions of particular people. My principal inspiration, critic and editorial adviser in this enterprise has been my wife, Rounaq Jahan, whose intensive reading of my drafts has helped me immeasurably in improving the final text. I have also passed on all or parts of this manuscript to others, some of whom have responded with useful comments that have corrected my history, refreshed my memory or suggested constructive editorial changes. I would, here, particularly wish to acknowledge the detailed and enormously helpful comments by my friend Amartya Sen on my chapter on Cambridge, the inputs on family history shared with me by my brother Farooq Sobhan and my uncle Khwaja Sayeed Shahabuddin whose own memoir provided valuable information on the DNF. My nephew Waliul Haq Khondkar added to my knowledge of my paternal family by presenting me with copies of my grandfather Khondkar Fazlul Haq's treatise on the Khondkars as well as the chapter on our family contributed by Major Walsh in his *History of Murshidabad*.

I have also been benefited by comments provided by my son Zafar; my cousin Kamal Hossain and his wife Hameeda Hossain; my nephew Habibul Huq Khondkar; my lifelong comrades

Nurul Islam, Anisur Rahman and Muyeedul Hasan on the events of 1971 where he played a critical role in parts of my story. Others who have taken the time to read, respond and make constructive suggestions on my account of the Liberation War include David Nalin, William Greenhough, Lawrence Lifschultz and Arnold Zeitlin who were, in various ways, themselves involved in the events of 1971. However, at the end of the day, all my commentators should not feel slighted if their suggestions are not fully reflected in my story, which, after all, remains the ultimate ego trip. In concluding, I would like to register my deep appreciation for the painstaking work but in coping with various logistical constraints, Unni Nair and Saima Ghaffar at SAGE Publications, for the contribution in bringing this work to fruition.

1

Families Inherited and Chosen

Families

The lives of most people are constructed around two families. The families into which they are born and the families into which they marry. Both family lines influence our lives. My own life might have in some measure been influenced, by the ancestral origins of my parents. My father, Khondkar Fazle Sobhan came from Murshidabad and my mother, Hashmat Ara, from Lucknow on her father's side and Dhaka on her mother's side. However, in my own case, my chosen family, largely through the longer and more intimate relations I have had with my wives, Salma Rashida Akhtar Bano and after her passing in 2003, with Rounaq Jahan, have exercised an even more significant role in influencing the course of my life. Where we ourselves choose the person we marry, rather than have our parents make the choice, we are more likely to relate to the person and less to their family. However, the person we choose is also influenced by their family inheritance, so it is not inappropriate to also explore their family lines. For these reasons, I will discuss my family under the two heads 'family heritage' and 'family by choice'.

Family Heritage

I have travelled a long way from my ancestral inheritance. The course of this journey and its improbable trajectory from its origins provide the substance of my memoir. There were two family streams that came together to give me life. My father's side of the family lived in Murshidabad, a district in what is today known as Paschimbongo (formerly West Bengal) in India, located along the banks of the Bhagirathi. In contrast, two separate streams converged to give my mother life. Her father's side of the family originated from the city of Lucknow in the state of Uttar Pradesh in India but later settled in the city of Patna in Bihar. Her mother's side of the family, the Khwajas, originated from the state of Kashmir but migrated for business reasons to Bengal in the 18th century and made their home in the city of Dhaka, now the capital of the independent State of Bangladesh. I am the product of this confluence of families, but since the two family streams were very different in their origins, circumstances and engagement with the world around them, I will discuss them separately.

The Khondkars of Murshidabad

A monograph written by my paternal grandfather, Khondkar Fazlul Huq Siddiqui, in 1926, titled *A Treatise on a Branch of the Khondkars of Fatteh Singh in Murshidabad District*, and another work by a certain Major Walsh, who has included a chapter on the Khondkars in his *History of Murshidabad*, provide considerable detail on our family history. Both publications possibly draw upon two publications by my grandfather's uncle, Dewan Khondkar Fazle Rabbi, the *Origin of the Mussalmans of Bengal*, written in English in 1897, and a related work written in Urdu, *Tusdiqur-Nihad*.

All these works trace the origins of the Khondkars to Arabia, where they reportedly descended from Hazrat Abu Bakr Siddiq, the first caliph of Islam. My grandfather's treatise not only constructs such a family tree but explains in some detail the trajectory of this family over 31 generations from the first caliph down to the generation of my father. I am not qualified to affirm the historical accuracy of my ancestry, which possibly merits further study by historians with a special interest in family lineages.

According to the 'treatise', a branch of our family, in its eighth generation, migrated from Arabia to Persia. An ancestor from the 16th generation of the family, Khwaja Rustam, during the reign of Emperor Akbar in India, moved from Khorasan in Persia to Hindustan, where his son Khwaja Mukhdum Ziauddin Zahid settled in Allahabad. One of his sons, Shah Sheikh Serajuddin, moved to Bengal, where he was appointed *Qazi-ul-Quzzat*[1] during the reign of Sultan Ghiasuddin. His son and their descendants appear to have been men of some spirituality who were revered locally as saints or *peers*, and their tomb in Syed Kulat, adjacent to my ancestral village of Bharatpur in Murshidabad, remains a place of pilgrimage. This tradition of piety extended down to the 24th generation where the tomb of an ancestor, Shah Serajul Arefin, lies within the premises of our family home, Seraj Manzil, in Bharatpur and remains a place of reverence to this day.

This identification with a long tradition of spirituality did not discourage various members of the family from seeking public service in the early years of British rule. But in those days, governance was still practised using Persian, the language of choice of the Mughal State. Family members who were well educated in Persian and Urdu were, thus, in some demand. But English was eventually established as the official language of the State once British rule consolidated itself. All those seeking advancement under the British Raj took to English education where the families of the Muslim ruling elites across India, including in Bengal, tended to lag far behind their peers from other communities. It was my grandfather's uncle, Dewan Fazle Rabbi, along with Nawab Abdul Latif from another old family of Bengal, who broke from tradition in advising the Muslims of Bengal, including his own family members, to move into the 'modern world' through commitment to an English education. Rabbi himself made the great break from family tradition by embracing English education where he was the first member of the family to acquire a BA degree.

In 1869, Fazle Rabbi, at the age of 21, travelled to England to accompany and superintend the affairs of the last Nawab Nazim

[1] Supreme judge.

of Bengal. He was permitted by the Nawab Nazim to return to Murshidabad in 1874 to take charge of the finances of the Nawab of Murshidabad and around 1881 was eventually appointed Dewan or Chief Minister (CM) of Murshidabad. For his devoted public service, Fazle Rabbi was elevated by the British to the title of Khan Bahadur on the occasion of the Diamond Jubilee of Queen Victoria in 1897.

Fazle Rabbi encouraged his son Khondkar Ali Afzal and nephews to seek English education as a route to government service under the British Raj, which was seen by him as the way forward for the Muslims of Bengal. My grandfather, Khondkar Fazlul Huq, graduated in 1889, and in 1891, was appointed as Deputy Collector in the service of the Bengal government. He eventually officiated thrice as a District Magistrate and was duly awarded the title of Khan Bahadur. In his later life, after retirement, he also served for a while as Dewan to the Nawab of Murshidabad. Significantly, not all members of our family appreciated the move towards English education, and even boycotted my grandfather for departure from tradition. My grandfather and some of his generation encouraged their own sons to seek an English education. Among his three sons, Fazle Akbar and my father, Fazle Sobhan, graduated from Presidency College in Calcutta, while their eldest brother, Fazle Haider, sought higher education in England.

In my father's generation, while the Raj was at its zenith in India, government service remained the primary mission for those seeking higher education. My father's first cousin, K.G. Morshed, the son of my paternal grandmother's sister, who lived in the adjoining village of Salar, was one of the few Bangali Muslims to enter the elite Indian Civil Services (ICS), way back in 1925. My father, however, from his boyhood, wanted to enter the army. According to my grandfather's treatise, my father, after graduation from Presidency College, appeared for the entrance examination and was admitted to the elite Sandhurst military academy in England. At Sandhurst, one of my father's contemporaries was Field Marshal Ayub Khan, who was the first native Commander-in-Chief (C-in-C) of the Pakistan army from where, in 1958, he captured State power and elevated himself to the Presidency.

My father, who could have been the first Bangali Muslim to serve in the highest ranks of the Pakistan army, did not eventually follow the career path of Ayub Khan. My grandfather reports that under the advice of the Chief Secretary of Bengal, my father was recalled from Sandhurst and appointed to the Indian Police Service around 1926, where again, he was one of the first Bangali Muslims to enter this elite service under the imperial Raj. He remained in service till 1946, but on the eve of the independence of India, he chose to retire from service and take his chances in the world of business.

My father's middle brother, Fazle Akbar, also travelled to England and graduated as a barrister from Lincoln's Inn. On his return home, he built up a successful practice at the Calcutta High Court, but then opted for public service through the judiciary and was elevated to a judgeship in the High Court of East Pakistan around 1949. He was appointed to the Pakistan Supreme Court in 1960 and was eventually elevated to the position of Chief Justice of Pakistan in 1968.

Fazlul Huq's eldest son, Fazle Haider, travelled to England in 1920 for higher studies but stayed on for 13 years to engage himself in the world of business. However, he too eventually moved towards public service at the invitation of the Nawab of Bhopal, one of the largest of the princely states of India, who met him in London. The Nawab, who retained great confidence in my uncle, persuaded him to return to India to look after the state's finances, where he was eventually appointed the Finance Minister of Bhopal. At the independence of India, my uncle encouraged the Nawab to diversify his personal finances and, inter alia, invest in establishing Pakistan's first insurance company, the Eastern Federal Union Insurance Company, which was then established under the leadership of Fazle Haider, who was its first Chairman.

Two among three of Fazlul Huq's daughters married public servants. While Fazlul Huq educated his three sons, he did not extend this privilege to his three daughters. Afzala, the oldest of the siblings, married her first cousin, Khondkar Ali Mohsin, a graduate, who also entered public service. Her sister, Sara, married Syed Ghulam Kabir from Faridpur, who was a member of the Bengal Civil Service (BCS). The youngest daughter, Hosnara, was the only member of the family married to a professional, a doctor, Ahmed Hossain from Barisal.

In contrast, the next generation, my own, largely preferred to work as independent professionals. Our parents sent us to the best available English medium schools from where we equipped ourselves to travel abroad for higher education in some of the most renowned universities or to acquire professional qualifications in such areas as law, accountancy and medicine. I studied at Cambridge, while my cousins—Kaiser Morshed, son of K.G. Morshed; Kamal Hossain, son of Ahmed Hossain; and Anwar Akbar, son of Fazle Akbar—and my younger brother Farooq studied at Oxford. Our cousins Sajjad Haider and Rafi Akbar qualified as chartered accountants from London, while Farooq Akbar qualified as a doctor in USA with specialization in gynaecology.

Some of my father's generation, unlike their own parents, opted to educate their daughters. Fazle Akbar's daughter, Shireen, obtained a BA, standing first among all women candidates in East Pakistan, and then earned an MA in English literature from Dhaka University. Ahmedi, the daughter of Dr Ahmed Hossain, attained a BA from Loreto College, Calcutta. This lack of education for women in my father's generation and even among some of my own cousins did not discourage a number of our womenfolk from emerging as strong, intelligent personalities with formidable skills as organizers, managers and leaders. This tradition of strong women extended into my mother's side of the family and has been perpetuated into my son's generation where my nieces are no less formidable than their male cousins.

In my generation, only Kaiser Morshed and my younger brother Farooq opted to join the Foreign Service, where they both eventually attained its highest level, retiring as Foreign Secretaries in the service of Bangladesh. One of our older cousins, Syed Ali Kabir, son of Ghulam Kabir, joined the Central Bank of Pakistan and eventually retired as the Deputy Governor of Bangladesh Bank.

Very few from my generation opted for the world of business. Some of my cousins, for example, Syed Humayun Kabir, brother of Ali Kabir, was the CEO of a multinational—Pfizer—and eventually set up his own company, Renata. Humayun and another cousin, Rokiya Afzal Rahman—the daughter of my grand-uncle, Syed Ali Afzal, who prospered as an entrepreneur in her own right—achieved the distinction of being elected as presidents of the Bangladesh Metropolitan Chamber of Commerce and Industry (MCCI).

Few among the Khondkars opted for an academic life; I was perhaps the only one in either my father's or my own generation to make a living as a university teacher and researcher. In the next generation, Khondkar Habibul Haque, son of my first cousin, Khondkar Rezaul Haque, and Mizanur Rahman, grandson of K.G. Morshed, have committed themselves to teaching careers in universities.

Interestingly, by the time we move to the generation of my sons, Babar and Zafar, the 33rd from the first caliph, virtually all our children (girls and boys) have been educated at some of the best universities in the world. However, not a single one from this generation opted for a career in public service. Most of this 33rd generation of Khondkars, both boys and girls, have become independent professionals, lawyers, chartered accountants, development consultants, doctors, engineers, educationists, film-makers, business executives and media persons.

Few among the family sought entry into the political world. My cousin Kamal Hossain, who eventually established himself as a lawyer of national and global eminence, moved the furthest among us. He joined Bangladesh's principal party, the Awami League (AL), in 1969 and was elected as a member of Bangladesh's Constituent Assembly (CA) in 1970. After the liberation of Bangladesh in 1971, Kamal was invited by Prime Minister (PM) Bangabandhu Sheikh Mujibur Rahman, to take the lead in drafting the constitution of Bangladesh in his capacity as the first Law Minister and then served later as Foreign Minister and Minister for Energy. I too entered the world of politics but largely as a behind-the-scenes player. This led to my involvement in Bangladesh's liberation struggle and brief engagement in the post-liberation government as a member of the Bangladesh Planning Commission in the foundational years from

1972 to 1974. My association with the world of politics provides some of the substantive narrative in my memoir as it tracks the long distance I travelled from my spiritual ancestry and also from my family's engagement with government service.

The Sheikhs of Lucknow

If my point of departure from the traditions of the Khondkar family was significant, it was no less so from the inheritance of my mother's family on her father's side. I have more to say about this side of the family in the next chapter on my days in Calcutta. I know little about the ancestry of my maternal grandfather (*nana*), Sheikh Mustafa Alley, beyond the fact that his was a family who also prided themselves on their spirituality. My grandfather, was a handsome man with good education, sufficient means as well as social standing, to warrant the Nawab of Dhaka, Khwaja Salimullah, marrying off his favourite niece, Almasi Begum, to him.

Whatever may have been my nana's antecedents, from what I personally saw of his side of the family, their pursuit of formal education was of little instrumental value since few, if any, members emerged with a capacity either to enter public service or with the skills to work as professionals. Apart from some desultory and usually unfruitful attempts at private enterprise, this side of the family appeared to have had little access to paid employment or regular sources of income.

The Dhaka Nawab Family

The DNF traditionally carries the denomination of *Khwaja*.[2] However, as a number of families, not just in Bengal but across India, carry this prefix, it will be more convenient to talk of the

[2] The title refers to the holder as Master, Lord.

DNF, which is what they mostly use to identify themselves. The locals of Dhaka also tend to refer to the family as *Nawabbari-er-lok*.[3]

Our immediate links to the DNF originate through my mother, Hashmat Ara Begum, whose mother, Almasi Begum, was the niece of Nawab Salimullah, through her mother, Bilquis Bano, the sister of the Nawab and the daughter of Nawab Ahsanullah. Alamsi Bano, my maternal grandmother (*nani*), had two brothers, Khwaja Nazimuddin and his younger brother Khwaja Shahabuddin. Both brothers were highly solicitous towards Almasi Bano's children because she passed away at a young age giving birth to my mother at their ancestral home, Ahsan Manzil.

It is the maternal ancestry of my mother that provided me with whatever genes I may have inherited to acquire a taste for politics. However, the politics of the DNF is about as remote from my own political beliefs as one can get. The first three Nawabs, Abdul Ghani, Ahsanullah and Salimullah, and also my two grand-uncles, Nazimuddin and Shahabuddin, were political players of some significance, associated with the identity politics that contributed to the mobilization of the Muslims of Bengal. Later members of the DNF were more inclined to treat politics as a family vocation, divorced from any clear set of beliefs beyond a vague adherence to the politics of the Muslim League, the party which led the political mobilization that culminated in the emergence of Pakistan.

The members of the DNF were not always nawabs. The family had its origins in Kashmir from where they brought with them the denomination of Khwaja. Two brothers, Khwaja Abdul Wahab and Khwaja Abdullah, travelled to Dhaka from Kashmir around 1730 in the expectation of furthering their business interests and made their home in Begum Bazar in the heart of what is now the old town of Dhaka. Even today the family graveyard remains located in Begum Bazar where Salma as well as my mother and her siblings lie interred among their ancestors.

The Khwaja's business fortunes prospered greatly to a level where they could afford to buy up a large number of *zamindaris*[4]

[3] Members of the nawab's household.

[4] Landed estates.

across East Bengal from improvident *zamindars*.[5] By the middle of the 19th century, the Khwajas, having established themselves as one of the largest landowners in East Bengal, came to be better known as a family of zamindars rather than for their business antecedents.

When India's first war of independence, known in imperial history as the Indian Mutiny, broke out in 1857, the then head of the family, Khwaja Abdul Ghani, presciently backed the British. When the insurgents were defeated and repressed, the British moved to reward all those foresighted Indian families and tribes who sided with them in their hour of peril. Many of the now leading feudal landowners of Pakistan and India owe their wealth and elevation to such loyalty. The Khwajas too were well rewarded. Khwaja Abdul Ghani was not only knighted by the British but invested with the hereditary title of Nawab around 1878, which was further upgraded to Nawab Bahadur in 1892. A number of other zamindar families of Bengal, both Hindu and Muslim, were similarly rewarded by the British and invested by the Raj with the title of *Nawab* or *Rajah*, but only a few such as the Khwajas had their title made hereditary.

The first three Nawabs, Abdul Ghani, Ahsanullah and Salimullah, demonstrated a strong sense of *noblesse oblige* and invested part of their fortune in various public works such as the establishment of Mitford Hospital, the establishment of the first public waterworks, the first modern system of electricity supply, the establishment of the Ahsanullah School of Engineering and the Salimullah Hall for residence of Muslim students in Dhaka University. Nawab Salimullah had indeed played a pioneering role in the establishment of Dhaka University, where the British had responded to his advocacy, partly in recompense for undoing the partition of Bengal for which the Nawab had been one of the leading advocates.

Most of the other DNF members appeared to be more inclined to emulate the social practices of the Hindu zamindars whose extravagances had contributed to the fortunes of the Khwajas. Unlike many of the Hindu zamindars who sought to educate their sons, rarely their daughters, the DNF did little to ensure a

[5] Landed gentry.

comprehensive English education for their offspring. Some of the family members attended local schools in Dhaka, while a few studied at English medium schools such as St. Paul's in Darjeeling or were sent to Aligarh College, but did not always stay on to obtain a passing out school certificate or to move on to college. Insufficiency of formal education did not discourage erudition or creativity so that some members of the family demonstrated noticeable poetic and musical talents.

The end result of this inadequate formal education or professional skills meant that several generations of the DNF could neither aspire to enter public service nor work as professionals but remained exclusively dependent on rentier incomes from the DNF estate. Lack of gainful work encouraged a life of leisure, extravagance and improvidence for the morrow. The more ambitious among the family opted to invest some of their fortune in politics, mostly in the service of the Muslim League, at the municipal or provincial level. But in the days of the British Raj, politics for the natives, unlike today, did not yield any significant financial return. It was not too surprising that by 1909 the DNF estate was placed by the British government under the Court of Wards, where a British official was appointed to administer the large revenues generated by the state.

Nawab Salimullah was one of the more far-sighted among the DNF, possessed with a longer-term vision for the family and beyond that for the Muslims of Bengal. He was an active advocate for the partition of Bengal enacted in 1905 and was, thus, disillusioned at its undoing by the British under what he believed was the pressure of the Bangali Hindu elite. Salimullah, consequently played a leading role in the founding of the All-India Muslim League which had its inaugural meeting in his ancestral home of Ahsan Manzil on 30 December 1906. He remained active in Muslim identity politics until his death in 1915.

Salimullah believed that some of his family members should be groomed to play a leading role in Bengal politics. He identified as his political heir his nephew Khwaja Nazimuddin and decided to invest in his education in England, first at Dunstable Grammar

School and later at Trinity Hall, Cambridge, my own alma mater. Khwaja Nazimuddin was a person of integrity and enormous decency. More than any other DNF member, he carried forward the political fortunes of the family, initially as a member of the Viceroy of India's Executive Council and later as a cabinet minister in various Muslim League ministries in the Bengal legislature, where he was eventually elevated to the position of CM in 1943. Other members of the family also entered the Bengal assembly or engaged themselves in Dhaka municipal politics but did not attain much recognition.

The fortunes of the family, notwithstanding the discipline on their extravagance imposed through the Court of Wards, had already been exposed to some decline because of demographic pressures. By 1947, there were already around 80 DNF members, listed as *B: proprietors*, who were directly eligible for a share of the estate revenues. The DNF fortunes emerged as one of the principal casualties of the emergence of Pakistan and the Partition of Bengal in 1947, which severely eroded the political influence of the zamindar class that was largely drawn from the upper caste Hindu community. The historic bill abolishing zamindari in East Bengal was consequently enacted in 1952 without any serious challenge. Within East Bengal, the DNF were one of the principal casualties of the Act. With the takeover of the DNF estates, the family descended from a state of affluence to virtual penury as much of their rentier income dried up. By the time I returned to Dhaka in 1957, Ahsan Manzil and its adjacent estates were degenerating into slums. Impoverished family members had been illicitly selling off or renting out parts of the immoveable properties and even disposing off whatever moveable assets they could extract from their ancestral home.

Only a few members, such as Paribano Begum and Khwaja Shahabuddin, chose to invest in the education of their children. Paribano Begum, the sister of Nawab Salimullah and Bilquis Bano, my great-grandmother, ensured quality education for her son, Khwaja Sudderuddin and daughter, Zuleikha Bano who graduated from Calcutta University with a 1st class in Sanskrit and received a gold medal. She later married my father's cousin K.G. Morshed.

Khwaja Shahabuddin also ensured that his four sons and three daughters received the best education. Other DNF members tended to be less provident in educating themselves or their children. With limited education to sustain them, many family members were left with few skills to market.

The final stage in the downward trajectory of the family fortunes was reached after the overwhelming defeat of the Muslim League in the 1954 elections to the East Bengal legislature. Those of the family members who contested the elections in 1954 on a League ticket were defeated, even in their traditional constituencies located around Dhaka. The 1954 elections rang the death knell of the social and political influence of the DNF in East Bengal.

In the 1960s, the then Nawab of Dhaka, Khwaja Hasan Askari, joined the ruling Muslim League party and was appointed a minister in the provincial government by Governor Monem Khan, which provided some visibility to the DNF. But in the 1960s, cabinet ministers in the Monem regime were objects of derision. In the course of demonstrations against the Ayub regime at the end of 1968, Askari's residence in Shahbagh was torched by the anti-government agitators. A cousin of his, Khwaja Khairuddin, who had been active in local Muslim League politics, had rashly decided to contest Sheikh Mujib in the 1970 elections from a constituency in old Dhaka but was comprehensively defeated.

Over the years, the decision of the DNF members to retain their exclusive identity, where they made little attempt to learn Bangla or come close to the native population, alienated them from the very people among whom they had made their home. Their historic intimacy with the increasingly discredited Muslim League deepened this alienation. By the time Bangladesh emerged in 1971, the DNF members were viewed as a breed apart from the Bangalis so that this once dominant family in East Bengal dwindled into obscurity. Their ancestral home, Ahsan Manzil, was reduced to the status of an abandoned ruin until President Ershad, in the 1980s, was persuaded by the then Curator of the National Museum, Dr Enamul Huq, to take it over and restore it to its former glory. It survives today as a museum to educate tourists on the vanished world of the DNF.

The second DNF home in Dilkusha has been erased from the face of the earth. A large part of the estate had been taken over by the East Bengal government after partition in 1947 to serve as the residence of the then Governor and today serves as the residence of the President of Bangladesh. The remainder of the Dilkusha estate remained the residence of various family members until the early 1960s when it was requisitioned by the government for development as the Motijheel Commercial Area. Today, the unaesthetic Dhaka Improvement Trust (DIT) offices and sundry commercial buildings stand over grounds where I once played cricket or the pond where family members swam and fished. The only evidence that Dilkusha was once the home of the DNF is provided by the survival of a small family mosque with an attached graveyard where a few family members such as Lieutenant General Khwaja Wasiuddin, son of Khwaja Shahabuddin, lie at rest.

It has taken at least two generations or longer for the DNF to accommodate themselves to a world that was totally removed from the privileged life enjoyed by their ancestors. After 1971, the DNF divided itself between Bangladesh and Pakistan while many moved beyond South Asia and dispersed themselves across the globe. The present generation has made a new life for themselves and their children as qualified professionals who are no longer dependent on family influence or inherited wealth and have had to prosper in a highly competitive world. What they have retained from their inheritance is a strong sense of family, the exquisite cuisine pioneered by the DNF that sought to blend the rich flavours of Kashmir with the delicate flavour of Bangali cuisine and a hunger to remain connected. This task has been heroically accomplished through the dedicated labours of my uncle, Khwaja Sayeed Shahabuddin—the third son of Khwaja Shahabuddin—who is now 90 years old, the oldest surviving member of the family and a person of enormous decency. He embarked on a labour of love to fashion a unique DNF monthly newsletter that he has sustained for over two decades. The newsletter has now been moved online with its own website, which links what is now an extended, globalized family, spanning several generations.

My Father: A Friend to All

I will conclude this account of my family heritage by looking back at the two principal characters who connected me to their families, my father and my mother. My father was a person of exceptional charm. His interpersonal skills at making friends with people from all spheres of life were legendary. He was the life and soul of any party where his relaxed, good-humoured style made everyone feel comfortable. While my father, in his early life as a police officer, enjoyed an outdoor life playing tennis and riding, in later years, his great love was for cards where he regularly played bridge at the Calcutta Club and was recognized as one of the city's leading players. His skills bypassed me but were inherited by Farooq who, in his time, captained Bangladesh's international bridge team. Farooq honoured our father's memory in 1981 by establishing the Khondkar Fazle Sobhan Trophy, which is awarded every year to the winners of the national bridge championship of Bangladesh.

Within the police service, my father was a highly regarded officer who earned a reputation for being a genuinely non-communal person at a time where officers were being associated with their respective communal loyalties. This non-communal aspect of my father's character was manifest in the multi-communal nature of our social circle where some of the closest friends of our family were Hindus and Sikhs. It will be reassuring to my father's memory that this aspect of his values has been inherited by his sons and now by my two sons Babar and Zafar.

During my father's tenure as Superintendent of Police (SP) in Khulna, he helped to establish a school at Kachua in the subdivision of Bagerhat. The school, Coronation Sobhan Pilot High School, Kachua, was established in 1935 and still bears his name. I retain an inspection report of the school, written by my father in his inimitable handwriting, in my possession, which was preserved over the years by his nephew, Rezaul Haque, who served as a public official for many years in Bagerhat.

My father's social and interpersonal skills extended to helping out all those in his extended family and any others who sought his help, a quality inherited by Farooq. My father's urge to help extended to matchmaking, where he was reported to have arranged the marriages of two of his junior colleagues in the police service, Alamgir Kabir and Musa Ahmed, to Tahera and Bilquis, the daughters of his uncle-in-law, Khwaja Shahabuddin. He was also instrumental in arranging the marriage of his niece, Ahmedi, Kamal Hossain's elder sister, to Yusuf Amanullah Khan, then a bank manager in Narayanganj. I cannot recollect his other successes as a matchmaker, but he did not apply this talent to either of his sons who arranged their own marriages.

For reasons of incompatibility, my parents got divorced in 1944. My father married Shaukat Begum from Calcutta in 1946, but this marriage also ended in a divorce in 1955. In 1957, he married Nayyar Begum, whose family originated from Delhi but was settled in Karachi, and our youngest brother, Naveed, was born to them in 1958. They remained married until my father passed away on 26 August 1962, sailing back to Karachi from London after attending my wedding.

Our parents got divorced when I was nine years old and Farooq was only four. It should also be remembered that from the age of seven until the age of 15—that is, from 1942 to 1950—I spent nine months of the year incarcerated in a boarding school in Darjeeling. After the separation of my parents in 1944, Farooq and I spent all our winter vacations staying with my mother in her father's home at 53 Elliot Road. Thus, in the 27 years of my life, apart from my childhood up to the age of seven, I had little opportunity to spend any extended period of time with my father.

Notwithstanding our limited interaction, I was tremendously fond of my father and was always happy to see him. As I grew to the age of consciousness, whenever we spent time together, he engaged me in discussions about my life and intellectual interests where we tended to have divergent views on a number of issues. I remember his lament about me when I was just 14: "arguments, always arguments." When I was at Cambridge and my intellectual concerns were moving leftwards, we engaged in more cerebral arguments on my political views and on the state of politics in Pakistan. I had hoped to get to know my father more intimately when he finally returned to Dhaka in 1962, but the fates willed otherwise.

My Mother: An Unconventional Life

My father married a person from a very different background to his own with a totally contrary personality and temperament. It was not a match made in heaven but forged, with much affection by her uncle, Khwaja Nazimuddin, who paid special attention to the future of his sister Almasi Begum's children. The children were brought up by their father, Sheikh Mustafa Alley, and their step-mother, Zubeida Begum, who was my grandfather's first cousin. However, Khwaja Nazimuddin felt that his brother-in-law was not well connected enough to arrange a good match for his daughters, so he took on this responsibility on himself.

My mother's eldest sister, Shawkat Ara, was married off at a young age to a cousin, and after giving birth to four sons in quick succession, she too died young. The only son in the family Sheikh Mohomed Alley—Pearay to his family—was educated at St. Xavier's in Calcutta and remained unmarried throughout his life.

Pearay Uncle (1915) was born between his two sisters, Sikander Ara (1914) and my mother (1916), who being the youngest, was known in the family as *nanni*.[6] Arranging marriages then, and perhaps even now, required more attention to family pedigree and the spouse's CV. Little, if any, attention was paid to whether the two personalities would match so that marital outcomes tended to be something of a gamble.

In the family tradition of their times, my mother and her sister Sikander, whom we addressed as Sika aunty, were educated at home through private tutors and remained in strict purdah. Their uncle arranged a double marriage for his two nieces in 1932. Aunty Sikander was married to M. Syeduzzaman, from Boalia village, in Kishoreganj in the district of Mymensingh in East Bengal.

[6] The youngest.

He qualified as the first Muslim chartered accountant in India, but his family was rather traditional and integrated into the culture of rural Bengal. Syeduzzaman was the eldest among his siblings. One of his sisters married Syed Nazrul Islam, also from Kishoreganj, who years later served as Vice President of an independent Bangladesh while their son Ashraful Islam is today a minister and Secretary General of the ruling AL party. The son of one of Syeduzzaman's brothers married the first cousin of the PM of Bangladesh, Sheikh Hasina, from her mother's side of the family. The Zaman family thus had close ties by marriage to Bangladesh's political leadership at the highest level. But neither my uncle nor his surviving daughter, my cousin Qamarara, ever sought any advantage from or even publicized these high-powered relationships.

My father's family, while also originating from a rural background—as we have observed—had a much longer exposure to urban life. Though the Khondkars of Murshidabad spoke Bangla at home, the menfolk—led by Fazle Rabbi—prided themselves on their erudition in Urdu and, in some cases, in Persian as well as Arabic. There was, thus, greater cultural compatibility between my father and mother as well as their families. However, my mother was only 16 when she was married off with her older sister, then 18. Up to her marriage, my mother had little exposure to a world outside her family, spoke little English and tended—as the youngest sibling—to be rather spoilt.

Shortly after their marriage, my father, prior to his departure for England on some course, decided to leave his new bride behind in Loreto Convent, a boarding school in Darjeeling, patronized by girls from the more elite families. My father hoped to expose my mother to the company of girls from English-speaking families so she could emerge better equipped to cope with her responsibilities as the wife of a member of the Indian Police Service, which involved interaction with a largely English-speaking society. This enforced enclosure to a married woman, in a nunnery designed for schoolgirls, was not much appreciated by my mother.

When my father returned from London, my mother spent some years in the districts of Bengal as the wife of a SP, first in Faridpur and then in Khulna. It was not until after I was born in 1935 that my mother could enjoy her first exposure to Calcutta society. She was barely 20 years old when she entered this new world, inhabited by an anglicized elite, where the sahibs occupied its top echelons. My mother took to this world as a fish takes to water and never looked back. She was full of life, learnt to play tennis, rode horses, roller-skate and revel in the active social life of pre-war Calcutta where she was recognized as one of the great beauties of her day.

My mother was barely 27 years old when she got separated from my father. She returned to her father's home at 53 Elliot Road to live in one room, shared with her two sons. While she remained a welcome guest in her former social circle—as a divorcee with moderate means to sustain her past lifestyle—she could never hope to remain the glittering star that had once dazzled Calcutta society. It is to my mother's credit that she demonstrated the courage to restructure her life while caring for her two sons within the limited resources provided by my father and her share of her mother's estate in the DNF.

After Farooq and I left for Lahore in January 1951 to attend Aitchison College, my mother eventually moved to Karachi at the end of 1951 where she lived with her uncle, Khwaja Nazimuddin, the then PM. In 1954, my mother got married to Syed Masood Husain, whose family had moved to Karachi from Delhi in 1947. Masood Husain was the Deputy Director of Navigation in the central government, but then moved to Dhaka as the first Chairman of the East Pakistan Inland Water Transport Authority (EPIWTA). After his tenure as Chairman ended in 1965, he was appointed as the Chief of the Transport Division in the United Nations Economic and Social Commission for Asia and the Pacific (UNESCAP), in Bangkok, where they lived together until his death at the beginning of 1980.

My mother lacked a formal education, but she was intelligent, resourceful as well as independent-minded and was quite capable of looking after herself. She was also a headstrong person from her childhood, with an unbridled temper that could intimidate even her amazonian sisters-in-law and kept her friends as well as family members in mortal fear of crossing her path when she was on the rampage. She believed she inherited her temper from her grandmother, Bilquis Bano. Legend has it that Bilquis Bano was once so displeased with a single dish served at a banquet in her honour, hosted at Ahsan Manzil by her brother, Nawab Salimullah, that she pulled up the handsomely laid out *dasterkhan*,[7] scattering the succulently filled dishes and walked out of the hall.

My mother's fiery temperament persisted throughout her life, but she compensated for this with her charm, her wit and her sense of gaiety, which remained with her until she passed away in Dhaka in 1997 at the age of 81. Her devotion to her two sons was the one unchanging element in her life. Even though our values and approach to life were completely at variance, she bequeathed to me many of her tastes such as for Cadbury's chocolates, ice cream and movies. Whereas her cinema-going capacity acquired legendary proportions, less known was her phobia for spiders, which she also passed on to both her sons. She remains enshrined in my memory for encouraging her sons to be self-reliant and investing the care and love which made her the driving force in ensuring that we were afforded the best possible education. My great regret is that, in her lifetime, I never adequately recognized her contribution to my life or could persuade her that I fully appreciated all that she did for us in our upbringing.

Family by Choice

Salma

I met Salma for the first time in Cambridge in October 1955, when she had just come up to Girton College, Cambridge, to read law after completing her Higher School Certificate (HSC) at Westonbirt, a boarding school in the west of England. I accompanied my friend Dilip Adarkar to Girton to induce Salma to join the Cambridge Majlis society where I had just taken over as President. Dilip knew

[7] A big, ceremonial dining spread.

her from their school days in New Delhi in the years just before the independence of India. In subsequent correspondence with her sister Naz, Salma indicated that she was not too impressed with me. I did eventually improve my standing with her at Cambridge but did not really get to know her until some years later, in Karachi, when our lives came together.

At our initial encounter, all that we knew about Salma was that she was reported to be formidably intelligent and that she commanded an impressive pedigree. Her father, Muhommed Ikaramullah, was Pakistan's High Commissioner in London while her mother Shaista, from the eminent Suhrawardy family was, perhaps, even more formidable a figure. It was only when I came to know Salma better that I could fully appreciate her exquisite wit, exceptional intelligence and her unquenchable love of books; I knew very few people who could match both the extent and variety of her reading.

At our first encounter, Salma, who was all of four feet nine inch in height, could easily have been taken for a schoolgirl. Nor did she demonstrate any capacity or inclination to project her high-powered origins or her great erudition. I subsequently learnt that her extreme modesty was ingrained in her personality which encouraged her to make herself as inconspicuous as possible even when she acquired considerable eminence in her own right over the years—first as a Senior Lecturer in Jurisprudence at Dhaka University and later as one of the founders and architects of one of Bangladesh's premier human rights organizations, Ain-O-Salish Kendro. This reluctance to proclaim her antecedents was bequeathed to our sons, Babar and Zafar, who demonstrated little consciousness of their family history.

Salma's disinclination to proclaim her family identity was in some contrast to her mother's considerable self-awareness of her family's distinctive status. Salma's mother's family, the Suhrawardys, earned their eminence largely through the family's long exposure to education and their scholastic achievements. The Suhrawardys originated from Iraq but had eventually made their home in the district of Midnapur in Paschimbongo. This tradition of education was bequeathed to them by her grandfather, Obaidullah Al-Obaidi Suhrawardy, a great scholar and founder of the Dhaka Alia Madrasah. When he passed away, his wife made considerable sacrifices to ensure that her three sons received the best possible education. Sir Hassan Suhrawardy, Shaista's father, was one of the few Muslims from India at that time to obtain a medical education in England and the second to qualify as a Fellow of the Royal College of Surgeons (FRCS). Hassan was appointed Vice Chancellor (VC) of Calcutta University in the 1930s where he earned a footnote in history by saving the then Governor of Bengal, Sir Stanley Jackson, from assassination by a young girl student at the convocation ceremony of Calcutta University in 1932. Hassan was subsequently knighted by the British.

Sir Hassan's sister, Khujaista Akhtar Banu, who was a distinguished scholar in her own right, married her first cousin, Sir Zahed Suhrawardy, a judge of the Calcutta High Court and was the mother of Hasan Shahed and Hussain Shaheed Suhrawardy, who were both educated at Oxford. Shahed, the older brother, was a literary figure of great distinction. His younger brother, Shaheed, was better known across both India and Pakistan, having served as CM of undivided Bengal, following the 1946 election victory of the Muslim League in Bengal and also later as PM of Pakistan.

Sir Hassan Suhrawardy married into a distinguished family from Dhaka. His wife, Shaher Banu, was the daughter of Nawab Syed Mohommed Azad and Saleha Banu, the daughter of Nawab Abdul Latif. Shaher Banu's elder sister was married to Sher-e-Bangla Fazlul Haq, one of the heroic figures of Bengal politics. Another brother of Shaher Banu, Syud Hussain, was a political activist in the Indian National Congress and a close associate of Pandit Nehru in the struggle for India's independence.

Shaista, known to many as Soghra, had a brother who died young, so she was raised as the only child. Her father, in spite of strong disapproval from her mother's side of the family, ensured that she had the best possible education where she attended and graduated from Loreto College, one of Calcutta's best schools. Shaista eventually acquired a PhD from London University after her marriage, when her husband was posted in London in the late 1930s.

Shaista, who had become involved with the political movement for Pakistan, was elected as one of two women members of Pakistan's first CA. She was the first person recorded in the proceedings of Pakistan's CA, way back in 1948, to point to the growing sense of deprivation then felt by the people of East Bengal who, she argued, felt that they were being treated like a colony. She was at that time also appointed as a member of Pakistan's first delegation to the United Nations (UN) General Assembly in 1948 and was a widely read essayist.

Shaista was married, at the age of 18 to Mohommed Ikramullah, whose family originated in Benares but later settled in Nagpur. Ikramullah and his two brothers, Ahmedullah and Hedayatullah, were educated at Trinity College, Cambridge. Hedayatullah, who qualified as a barrister, was eventually elevated to the Supreme Court of India and subsequently to the position of Chief Justice. After his retirement from the bench, he was elected as Vice President of India.

Ikramullah, after graduating with a degree in history from Cambridge, competed and qualified on merit, rather than through the Muslim quota for the ICS. He made a name for himself in the service and was appointed to serve as Trade Commissioner in London for the Government of India in the mid-1930s. It was here that both Salma (August 1937) and Naz (November 1938) were born. At Partition, Ikramullah was appointed as Pakistan's first Foreign Secretary. He held this position until 1953 when he was transferred as Pakistan's High Commissioner to Canada.

Salma and I remained married for 43 years and were blessed with three sons, Taimur (1963), Babar (1967) and Zafar (1970). Her compassion, courage, honesty and loyalty sustained me through the most critical phases of our life where she faced up to various political hazards that destabilized our family life. Later, when we were confronted with the devastating, unbearable loss of Taimur, the eldest of our three sons, who passed away at the age of 18, Salma's presence beside me was indispensable to our survival through this crisis in our lives. Salma's capacity for caring played a critical role in ensuring that our sons, Babar and Zafar, would continue to remain at the centre of our concerns and affection so they could get on with their lives.

Our two sons have amply compensated us by what they have done with their lives, through their character, innate intelligence, educational attainments and determination to move ahead on their own merit rather than draw on their family inheritance. Babar initially did a BA at the University of Massachusetts, Amherst and then won a scholarship to study for his M.Phil. in Development Studies at Cambridge University, where he performed with sufficient distinction to be awarded a further scholarship to work for his PhD. He eventually opted for a career in the UN system where he has continued to demonstrate his worth and creativity. Babar is blessed with natural leadership skills, which under different circumstances, would have made him the heir to the political legacy of his three ancestors who lie interred in the National Mausoleum at Dhaka.

Zafar, in turn, inherited his parents love for books and his mother's felicity as a writer, so much so that his first preference was to study English literature. He was awarded a scholarship to Pomona College in California, where he earned a BA in literature and then worked as a teaching assistant at the University of British Columbia in Vancouver while studying for his MA. Zafar eventually moved away from a career in literature to win a full scholarship to study law at the Pepperdine University School of Law in Malibu, California. After receiving his law degree, he qualified for the New York Bar while working for a top law firm in New York, Debevoise & Plimpton. However, he chose to forego a lucrative career in corporate law and returned to Dhaka to work in journalism where, in a few years, he established himself as a bold and widely read columnist at the *Daily Star* before moving on to take up the enormous challenge of setting up and now editing a new English-language daily, the *Dhaka Tribune*. Babar married Aparna Basnayet from Nepal, and Zafar married Farzana Ahmed from Faridpur. Babar's son, Sahel, and daughter, Samana, and Zafar's son, Shamel, have now joined the ranks of the 34th generation of Khondkars.

Rounaq

I first met Rounaq in August 1970, at a conference in Rochester University in upstate New York. She was then a postdoctrate scholar at Columbia University working to transform her prophetic thesis into a seminal work, *Pakistan: Failure in National Integration*, which was published in 1972 by Columbia University Press. Rounaq had been an outstanding student since her earliest school days till her MA in Political Science at Dhaka University. On the strength of her academic results at Dhaka University, she won a state scholarship to Harvard where, at the age of 26, she was the first Bangladeshi woman to be awarded a PhD and also to teach there. Her thesis and the extraordinary timing of its publication at the break-up of Pakistan in 1971 ensured immortality for her and her work which has, ever since, been studied around the world by students of South Asian affairs.

Rounaq, who was unknown to me in her days at Dhaka University, came across as an attractive, lively, young lady with a sharp intelligence and without inhibitions about speaking her mind during our first encounter. On my way back to Dhaka, I spent a pleasant day with her walking around New York where we consumed ice cream at Greenwich Village, which for me always serves as a strong bonding experience.

Rounaq had been offered several academic positions in the USA but chose to return to Dhaka at the end of 1970 as a Reader in the Department of Political Science at Dhaka University. She was appointed as the Chair of the Department in 1973 and then elevated to a full Professorship in 1977. She moved abroad in the 1980s to work in the UN system, first in Kuala Lumpur and then in Geneva, but eventually settled down to life as an academic at Columbia University, New York in 1990.

Rounaq's academic achievements and extensive publications (on politics, women's rights and health care) did not diminish her joie de vivre, which she demonstrated at our first encounter when we consumed ice cream together. Over the years, we became good friends as we shared many common interests, arguing about politics, reading and commenting on each other's writings, as well as enjoying movies and good food. She was also a good family friend and shared with Salma common concerns about women's rights. On her visits to New York, Salma usually stayed with Rounaq, who greatly appreciated her sense of humour. When Salma unexpectedly left us one night in the last days of 2003 and the days ahead for me appeared desolate, it was Rounaq who restored a sense of purpose to my life. Through her warmth and companionship, she invested me with the courage to face the future with her by my side. Her intelligence and integrity have served as a source of strength in troubled times. Her capacity to relate to people and spread radiance wherever she is remains a life-giving resource not just for me but for all around her.

Rounaq's family is from Noakhali. This family—as in the case of the Khondkars and Salma's family—attached a high value to education. Rounaq's father, Ahmadullah, who passed away in 1971 at the age of 57, was the first graduate from his village. He was encouraged by his father, who was a schoolteacher, to pursue higher education. He studied at Calcutta University and subsequently entered the BCS. He was an independent-minded public servant and faced many 'penalty' postings in his career in Pakistan for not bending to the political whims of the ruling Muslim League. He encouraged all of his six children to establish themselves as independent professionals rather than seek careers in government service so that they would not have to abase themselves by signing a letter as 'your most obedient servant'. He was ahead of his time in his desire to prioritize the higher education of his daughters over their early marriage. He also insisted on his children being educated in Bangla medium schools and completing their MA at Dhaka University before they went abroad for higher studies so that they would remain well grounded in Bangali culture. Rounaq can, even today, recognize most of the well-known *Rabindra Sangeets* when they are sung on TV and periodically educates me on the Indian classical myths and Bangla literature to which she was introduced by her parents during her formative years.

All six children were good students and won scholarships for postgraduate study in such well-known US universities as Chicago,

Harvard, Berkley, Iowa, Boston and Indiana from where three of them received PhDs. They all worked as professionals, as university professors, engineers, bankers and in international organizations. Rounaq's mother, Razia Begum, also from Noakhali, came from a zamindar family, which, as in my own family, followed the customs of the time and did not send their daughters to schools. But after her marriage, she was encouraged by her husband to study and read voraciously. She eventually wrote two volumes of very readable memoirs of some literary merit when she was in her 80s.

Six Degrees of Separation

Looking back at my extended family, it is noticeable how ostensibly disconnected families can be linked together. In some cases, a shared social ethos brings some families together. Thus, the Khondkars remained connected to the DNF and even the Suhrawardy family to a point where my father sent a proposal of marriage, albeit infructuous, for Shaista before he married my mother. My father and his cousin K.G. Morshed both married into the DNF where the family ties of the Khondkars to the DNF, as much as their service credentials, encouraged the relationship.

The DNF was, both socially and politically, particularly close to Salma's family. In recognition of this intimacy, Salma's mother invited my grand-uncle, Khwaja Nazimuddin, to write the foreword to her memoirs, *From Purdah to Parliament* (1963). In his foreword, my grand-uncle managed to capture the proximity of their family relationships. He wrote:

> I consider it a privilege to write the foreword to the book of Begum Shaista Ikramullah. Very close relations have existed between our two families for the last four generations. The grandfather of Begum Ikramullah, Maulana Obaidullah Al-Obaidi Suhrawardy, who was the Principal of the Madrassa Alia and one of the great scholars of Dacca, was a personal friend of my grandfather, Nawab Sir Ahsanullah. Her maternal grandfather, Nawab Syud Mohammed was also a great friend of my family... Sir Hassan Suhrawardy, father of Begum Ikramullah, materially helped me in the start of my public

> career... Begum Ikramullah, in spite of the official position of her husband, was a comrade in the struggle for the achievement of Pakistan... I remember the author as a young girl in school who was allowed to appear before me at her father's house because of the relationship between the families and because of her extreme youth. I have thus really seen her coming out from Purdah to parliament.

When I courted Salma, she had little idea of the history of our family relationships. In similar vein, I had no more idea about any linkage between my family and that of Rounaq's than she had. As it transpired, well before I met Rounaq, her older sister Roushan, had married my Dhaka University colleague, Muzaffer Ahmed, whose mother's brother Musa Ahmed, was married to my mother's first cousin, Bilquis Shahabuddin. Years later, Rounaq's brother Kabir married Yasmin, the youngest daughter of the industrialist A.K. Khan, whose eldest son Zahiruddin—who was at school with me at St. Paul's and Aitchison—married my relation, Asma Afzal, daughter of my grand-uncle Khondkar Ali Afzal.

My marriage to Salma established a connection by marriage—through her youngest sister, Sarvath—to the Hashemite Royal Family of Jordan, who were the direct descendants of Prophet Muhammad (peace be on him), who was married to the daughter of Hazrat Abu Bakr Siddiq. Babar's marriage to Aparna connected us by marriage to the former ruling family in Nepal, the Ranas.

These intricate family networks, which were woven around my life, ultimately did not greatly influence the person I became or the life I lived. This owed much more to my own choices, originating from my beliefs and eventually to the two women, who I chose as individuals rather than as members of a family, as my life partners. The subsequent story of my life will elaborate on this journey I made from my family inheritance to a life shaped through my own choices.

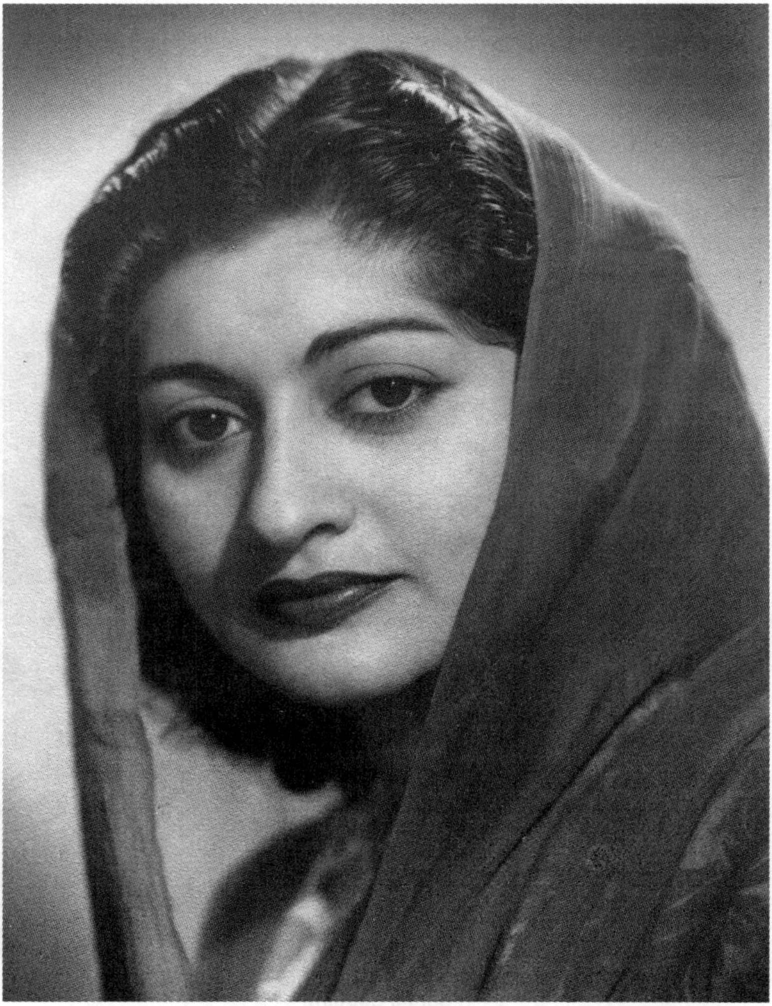

My mother, Hashmat Ara Begum, Calcutta, 1949

Salma Sobhan

Rounaq Jahan, at our garden in Dhaka 2005

My paternal grandfather and members of Khondkar family

Front (L–R) K.F. Haider, K.M. Ali Afzal, Khondkar Fazle Huq
(my paternal grandfather A.R. Siddiqui, K.G. Morshed
Back (L–R) Khawja Sudderuddin, Ahmed Hossan, K.F. Sobhan (my father), Unknown,
K.F. Akbar

My maternal grandfather, Shaikh Mustafa Alley, 1912

My father, K.F. Sobhan, on joining the Indian Police Service, 1925

My sons, 1974

(L–R) Babar, age 7; Taimur, age 11; Zafar, age 4

2

Growing Up in Calcutta

Childhood Memories

A Child of the Raj

My childhood memories do not emanate clearly beyond my fourth birthday. Before that I have vague recollections of being introduced to the world of education through my induction into the kindergarten of Loreto House in Middleton Row, Calcutta, a Catholic school for the daughters of the elite of Calcutta. Apparently, boys were accepted only in a state of innocence that was deemed to have ended as they graduated from kindergarten.

My own career in Loreto, or what I dimly recollect of it, appears to have been short and rather traumatic. At the age of three, I was taken there one morning by my mother, informed with only the vaguest of ideas of what school was all about. This did not include being abandoned by my mother so that when she left me with my class teacher—an Anglo-Indian lady, I naturally sought to accompany her back to our home. When I was detained by my teacher from this normal pursuit, I proceeded to bite the hapless educationist on the wrist. This was a skill in which I had already established some artistry and had perfected the technique of neatly sinking my small teeth into the upper side of the wrist, thereby leaving perfectly formed tooth marks that resembled a circular watch. My art had been well practised on sundry nannies and had not gone unappreciated by my household domestics who used to say, in the vernacular, that I had adorned the victim with a watch. My artistry was less appreciated in Loreto, so that at the age of three, I joined a distinguished heritage of those who had been persecuted for their art by being detained in a small room adjacent to the classroom. This martyrdom, at so young an age for the cause of both art and liberty could, no doubt, account for the origin of the resentment of authority that permeated my adult life. I do not recollect whether a more mutually tolerant relationship was established with my teachers at Loreto House so that those halcyon days, passed in a nunnery, remain erased from my memory.

What I do retain as my first memories are on life at 113 Upper Circular Road, the official residence of the Deputy Commissioner (DC) (North), of the Calcutta Metropolitan Police. In my memory, this was a capacious territory that housed what seemed to be a large residence as well as buildings, which went to make up the offices of the DC. A more recent glance at the compound, on a visit to that area in my adult life, suggested a much smaller compound. However, then it was an area for exploration with space for play and adventure.

I have fond memories of the principal staff members of my father. These included two Bihari constables, Jumma Khan and Mardan, as well as the driver, Rafiq. Jumma Khan, I remember, as a big strapping, handsome fellow whom we all presumed to be a Pathan. He remained loyal to my father's memory long after my father left service. On a visit to Calcutta in early 1957, on my way to Dhaka after my return from Cambridge, I was staying with my maternal grandfather—whom we addressed as Papa—in his home at 53 Elliot Road when, somehow, Jumma Khan materialized. He was posted as a sub-inspector at a thana in Wellesley Square and seemed to have, over the years, kept in touch with Papa. When he heard that Baba—as he used to affectionately address me at 113 Circular Road, had returned to Calcutta—he came to see me as a grown man. He had greyed a bit but still walked ramrod straight, and appeared no less handsome and noble than in my childhood memories.

Life at Upper Circular Road was somewhat removed from our family circles, who lived largely in South Calcutta. But I recollect games of imagination and daring, played with my numerous cousins, on its premises. There is a historic family photograph, taken on the occasion of my fourth birthday, in which I stand in the front row, a round-faced, rather solemn-looking, boy. Around me are youthful facsimiles of many relations who have stayed close to me in later life, including a thinner rather demonic-looking facsimile of Ali Kabir, my first cousin, his younger brother Humayun and their three sisters. Others in the photograph include the greatest friends of my youth, Qamruzzaman known as Qamru to his family, the only son of my mother's second sister Sikander. Qamru's sister, Qamarara, was captured in the photo as a baby, in the arms of her Burmese *ayah*,[1] Daisy. I was flanked by Khwaja Saifuddin, technically my maternal uncle, the youngest son of my grand-uncle Khwaja Nazimuddin. Saif was another of my close companions with a ready eye for mischief and adventure that transformed itself into an exceptional capacity for excelling in whatever sport he pursued.

I have fond memories of growing up in Calcutta as the son of the DC of Police, a post held in great esteem by Calcutta society during the Raj. My earliest memories were of being saluted by constables on duty at every traffic intersection in the city, as my father's red Adler car, a small but distinctive car of German make, was a well-recognized landmark on the streets of Calcutta. In the years immediately after my father left the police, I experienced a strange unrequited feeling, when passing by unrecognized and unsaluted by constables on duty throughout Calcutta.

North Calcutta was and remains a crowded mess, far removed from what was then the open opulence of South Calcutta. Every time we passed through the smoke-infested, crowded sectors of Entally and Sealdah station, on the way home, my mother would roll up the window glasses of the car. When we got home, she used to make me disinfect my nostrils and throat with hot-water gargles. We lived next to an old, decrepit movie theatre, Chaya, which showed mostly Hindi movies but occasionally had second-run English movies. I vaguely remember seeing such classics there such as *Tarzan Finds a Son*, starring Johnny Weissmuller with his

[1] Housemaid or children's nurse.

famous jungle call, and *The Mummy's Hand*, a more terrifying horror classic starring Boris Karloff. I have remained addicted to horror movies ever since and must have seen most of the classics where Karloff plays the Frankenstein monster, Lon Chaney terrorizes us as the Wolfman and Bela Lugosi bares his fangs as Count Dracula and intones in a dubiously continental accent, "I haf com to trink your blood."

I retain less sinister memories of Christmas parties in the Fire Brigade station in Free School Street, where the children of police officials were greeted by a large Santa Claus, who I presume was an Anglo-Indian sergeant of police. Treats in Calcutta included outings for ice cream at Magnolias on Park Street, visits on Sundays to the botanical gardens on the Hooghly, the Victoria Memorial in the heart of Calcutta's green spaces, Alipore Zoo and the lakes in South Calcutta.

On our visit to the lakes in South Calcutta, we had access to the palatial Bedi Bhavan, a rather baroque structure in which marble had been used quite lavishly. This was home to one of our family's closest friends, the Bedis, a prosperous family of Sikh businessmen whose father, Laddha Singh, had established the family fortunes in Calcutta. The sons of Laddha Singh, Maluk, Anup and Iqbal, became the closest friends of my father and his brother Fazle Akbar, with whom they had studied at college and subsequently with the Sobhan family.

In the 1940s, we stayed with the Bedis in their homes in Nagpur, Poona and Darjeeling, where we were treated as family. Over the years, with the emergence of Pakistan and then Bangladesh, these ties became frayed. By a strange irony, our relationship with the Bedis was renewed in, of all places, Kodaikanal School in South India, where I encountered a second-generation Bedi, in the person of Narinder Singh—the son of Iqbal Singh Bedi—the youngest of the three Bedi brothers. Narinder was putting in a stint as a teacher in Kodaikanal School where my son Babar spent two years studying for his International Baccalaureate (IB) degree. In Babar's moment of travail at the school, the Bedis stood loyally by him, as had an earlier generation stood by my parents in their moments of need. I was touched by the element of continuity in our family relationship that had managed to span the generations from Narinder's grandfather, Laddha Singh, to my son Babar, who had never even heard of the Bedis or knew of our life in Calcutta.

We eventually moved away from North Calcutta, first to Loudon Street, off Park Street, when my father was appointed DC (South). By this time, I had moved on to boarding school at St. Paul's in Darjeeling and was taken there by my father in March 1942. We moved to Belvedere Road in Alipore in 1943 when my father was appointed to head the Port Commissioners, who oversaw the security of Calcutta's ports.

Air Raids Over Calcutta

I remember accompanying my mother on a visit to Bogra to stay in the *Nawab Bari* of Altaf Ali Chowdhury, the father of Bogra Mohammad Ali, former PM of Pakistan. As we were setting out for Bogra from Sealdah station, I think on New Year's Eve, 1942, the Japanese chose to launch their first bombing raid on Calcutta. We were told that Sealdah station was a target and were advised to shelter under a table in the station waiting room. The Japanese bombed Calcutta again in early 1943. On that occasion, I was watching a morning movie at the Lighthouse Cinema with my mother. A news flash came on the screen that Calcutta was being bombed and that patrons at the cinema could stay at their own risk. My mother was not one to be deterred from watching a good movie to its conclusion merely by a few Japanese bombs. So we stayed till the end and then drove back home with the sound of sirens and possibly bombs falling on Calcutta port, echoing in the distance. This was possible only because my father's car was known to the police; all other cars were taken off the road during such air raids.

This was a period when Calcutta was obsessed with the fear of Japanese bombs and an eventual invasion. Many families packed off their women and children up country to Punjab and Uttar Pradesh or to their village homes in Bengal. All houses in Calcutta dug trenches in their gardens and packed them with sandbags for shelter during air raids. Sundry unemployed citizens were recruited as air-raid wardens who roamed the streets after dark blowing their air-raid whistles in a self-important tone, ensuring that all lights were shaded. Even my uncle Saheb Alam, my mother's first cousin, was inducted as an air-raid warden and used to patrol Elliot Road wearing a helmet.

Calcutta eventually survived the Japanese threat, which did not get beyond Burma. However, their takeover of Burma led to a big exodus of Bangalis who were very active in the professional and business life of Burma. This included the Zaman family who were residents of Rangoon, where my uncle Syeduzzaman had, after his marriage, established his practice as a chartered accountant. One day, around 1940 or so, we found the Zaman family—as refugees from the Japanese invasion—on our doorstep.

A Place of Enchantment

My most vivid recollections of my youth remain backed up at 53 Elliot Road, which also became home for Farooq and me when my mother came to live there after her divorce from my father in 1944. This home will always stay in my childhood memory as a place of enchantment, bewitched by the tales of its magical powers, narrated to me by my Papa's second wife, Zubeida Begum, whom we called Jani. Papa was known to all as Abban Mian, distinguished from his younger brother Sheikh Irtiza Ali, known as Babban Mian.

A landmark at the crossroads of Royd Street and Elliot Road, 53 Elliot Road was recognized by its high double-panelled green gate topped with sharp spikes. The house was modelled after a plantation in the Southern states of the USA. It had tall columns, holding up the rather spacious verandah at the front of the house, fronted by palm fronds which were planted in profusion around the house. The building was in the shape of a large box with a capacious living room at its centre. The compound was skirted with a variety of fauna that grew in rich profusion. At the front, there were a string of outhouses which, in better days, housed numerous servants, hangers-on who included a resident Maulvi Sahib and a garage for my grandfather's private phaeton.

My own early recollections of 53 Elliot Road were of a rather rundown but still majestic establishment where the broad cracks in the verandah, opened up by some epic earthquake which had rocked Calcutta years ago, still remained unrepaired. Many of the outhouses had become repositories of household scrap, accumulated over generations, whilst the well-kept lawn in the back of the house had become a derelict jungle where, as Jani assured me, even wild beasts had been seen.

The old Maulvi Sahib had stayed on and gave me my first instructions in Quranic lore and Urdu, as he had done for my mother and her siblings. I remember the Maulvi as a largish white-bearded, handsome figure of a man who resembled a rooster both in his stride and aspect, as seen in Terrytoon's cartoon films. I had reason to be impressed by his mystical powers. One of his statutory household obligations had, from time immemorial, been to slaughter the chickens consumed at the family dining table. I had grown quite attached to one such fowl, and when the said fowl was, in the fullness of its time, executed by the Maulvi Sahib, in my rage and grief, I went and kicked this venerable sage. As I fled from the outhouse kitchen, appalled at the enormity of my misdeed, a passing crow saliently defecated on my head. This pinpointed aerial reprobation was invested by Jani with the properties of an act of divine retribution, invoked by the holy powers of the Maulvi Sahib. I cravenly apologized to him and never again questioned either his divinity or his role as high executioner for our dinner table. One winter, I came home on vacation from my boarding school in Darjeeling to find that he had passed on to higher office and his old room had become one more scrap-ridden room in the crumbling outhouses of 53 Elliot Road.

It was this process of genteel decay that invested 53 Elliot Road with its magical properties. At the centre of the house lay the forbidden *gol kamra*.[2] None of us were permitted to enter there. The gol

[2] A living room.

kamra housed Papa's lifetime collection of Chinese porcelain. He had built up this collection over the years on the basis of knowledge accumulated from books on porcelain, which lay in serried rows, wrapped in brown paper covers, on his bookshelves purchased from Lazarus and Company, Calcutta's premier furniture makers. He had used his book knowledge to visit auctions in Calcutta, over many years, where the genteel bric-a-brac, bequeathed to less caring relations by the wealthier families of Calcutta, was passed on to the numerous auction chambers, which used to be the staple of Calcutta life. It was rumoured that Calcutta's flee-ridden Chinatown was also a favourite haunt of Papa in his search for precious Chinese porcelain.

Whatever may have been the source and cost of Papa's purchases, his china collection was the joy of his life, held far more dear to him than the fate of any member of his family. Each piece was lovingly preserved, documented and personally dusted by him. This fabulous china collection was locked away in the gol kamra, encased in magnificent, dark mahogany showcases and tables acquired from Lazarus. No one was allowed to touch this precious china but Papa himself. The room was kept shuttered most of the time, opened only for a few hours during the day to let in the sun and dusted periodically under his direct supervision. As Papa grew older, it seemed that the room was dusted less frequently so that my distant impression, viewed from the fastness of the verandah, when the doors were opened, was of a dust-covered room, full of cobwebs, guarded by the busts of what appeared to be two blind Roman senators. According to Jani's tales of enchantment, the room was inhabited by djinns, a tale I was only too inclined to believe. I do not recollect how old I was before I accumulated the courage to actually set foot in the gol kamra and eventually wander around examining its treasures, concealed under thick layers of dust. It appears that Papa could afford less time to personally clean the china or supervise the dusting of the room. By the time of his death, the room looked rather like one of the closed chambers in Miss Havisham's gothic house in Dicken's *Great Expectations*.

When Papa died in January 1957, his treasured china collection was inherited by his surviving children, my aunt Sikander, my uncle

Pearay and my mother. When the house was sold, the precious china and Lazarus furniture were carefully packed and then shipped in the river barges of Pak Bay and company, which then regularly trafficked between Calcutta and Guwahati in Assam, through the rivers of East Pakistan. The cargo from Elliot Road was consigned to Narayanganj, where it was collected by me and trucked with care, fear and trepidation to be stored in my garage at Kamal Court, on New Bailey Road, where I was then a resident. The goal was to then dispatch the china with Uncle Pearay, to Karachi and thence to London, to be sold for a fortune, at Sotheby's or Christie's.

To test the market, Uncle Pearay flew to London, with some selected porcelain treasures and other antique bric-a-brac, which were expected to yield a handsome reward that would pay for his travel and stay at Claridges and cover the cost of packing and shipping the rest of the china for auction in London. Much to the distress of the family and torture to the soul of Papa, the experts at Sotheby's advised Uncle Pearay that the china pieces were not original Ming and Tang porcelain but cleverly replicated fakes, manufactured with great skill in China and Hong Kong, sometime in the late 19th century. The pieces were worth some money but certainly not the millions of pounds, which had tantalized the imagination of my grandfather and briefly aroused expectations of great wealth accruing to his offspring.

What remains of Papa's famous china collection is what accrued to my mother and Sikander *khala*.[3] My mother's collection was divided between Farooq and me so that relations, friends and guests to our homes can still admire the remnants of Abban Mian's famed china collection, housed in what is left of the Lazarus furniture we inherited. Qamarara has also retained her china heirlooms, which are on display in her Gulshan apartment. Papa's china pieces still retain their lustre, even if they may not be originals and attract the admiration of those with an eye for beautiful things.

53 Elliot Road was covered by a rather splendid terrace that was used only by Papa for his morning yoga exercises. The young were, on special occasions, permitted closely supervised access to

[3] Aunt.

the terrace, usually to watch kite-flying contests held in the neighbourhood. Presumably in order to discourage access to the terrace, Jani worked her magic on all its approaches. The first access to the terrace was through Papa's bathroom, a dark, dank place, infested with large spiders, which were quite enough to keep me away. There was no running water in the house. The principal source of water was an ancient tube well in the compound and twice daily visits by the *bhisti*[4] who filled the iron water tanks and tubs located in the four bathrooms of the houses. Jani encouraged me to believe that the water tank in Papa's bathroom housed a small crocodile. This seemed, even at that young and credulous age, to be somewhat improbable without exposing my grandparents to excessive daily hazard for the loss of life and limb. But I was a lot older before I could pick up the courage to expose this story to empirical verification. More plausible to my heightened imagination was her story that the staircase leading from the bathroom to the terrace was haunted. In some remote past when my mother and her sisters were young, Sika aunty had ventured alone up the staircase to the terrace and was terrorized by the appearance of a burning hen which inhabited a storeroom halfway up the stairwell. The prospect of being set upon by pyromaniacal poultry kept me from solo ventures up the stairwell. Attempts to test the veracity of this story with Sika Aunty were greeted by a sphinx-like smile and remained a secret which she took to her grave.

Elliot Road was very much the domain of my grandfather who ran the house and his family with all the discipline of military barracks. His daily life followed an inflexible routine, which, in my memory, he maintained through his life, until he was confined to his bed prior to his death. The day began at sunrise, with his *fajr*[5] prayers which he performed on the terrace, to be followed by yoga exercises. Clad in a green silk loincloth, he religiously performed these exercises till the last days of his life when he was too ill to ascend to the terrace. His commitment to yoga left him with the slim physique of a young man even when he must have been in his

[4] Suppliers of water.

[5] Dawn.

60s and invested him with an iron self-discipline, that appeared to govern virtually every aspect of his life—bound by inflexible codes of behaviour and rigidity—and inconceivable to a generation such as ours.

After his morning yoga and breakfast, Papa read *The Statesman* sitting in the verandah in one of those cane easy chairs, with long armrests, which appear to be an integral part of our colonial inheritance. From there he addressed various household matters such as instructing the gardener or even receiving visitors. He then took his bath, and later in the morning, clad in his achkan and Aligarh pyjamas, he went out to the market returning before lunch with the best fruits and vegetables, and delicious sweets from Dorans, located in Wellesley Square. I have still to eat the equal of the *peras* and *lowz*[6] of Doran. On a recent trip to Kolkata, I passed by Dorans, which still survives but in a rather decrepit state.

At night after dinner, Papa sat down with his hookah in a chair in the dining room and worked on the crosswords of *The Illustrated Weekly of India*, the get-a-word of the daily *Morning News*, and his daily accounts. Much of his time, in between these fixed routines, was spent, clad in his silk pyjama coat and silk lungi, on the prayer mat, reading his *wazifa*,[7] from where he kept a vigilant eye on the functioning of the household. Once on the prayer mat, he took a vow of silence. But this did not preclude him from visiting his outrage, through clenched teeth, on some perceived misdemeanour by any member of the household.

Papa's iron codes of life did not include the discipline of supporting his lifestyle through paid employment. His finances largely depended on income from property. This mostly came from revenue from the share of his first wife, Almasi Begum, in the extensive zamindari of the DNF in East Bengal. Papa, himself, appeared to have title to some mysteriously derived property of his own, located in Akyab, in the Arakan region in Upper Burma, which yielded a modest income. As the income from the Nawab Estate contracted under the pressures of inflation and family demography, while

[6] Indian sweets.

[7] Koranic prayers.

the income from Akyab also ceased to flow after Burma was fully occupied by the Japanese in 1944, the family finances went into a gradual decline. This erosion in the family fortunes sharply accelerated, after the partition of India and the eventual abolition of zamindari in East Bengal, when the payments from Almasi Begum's estates virtually ceased.

The decline in living standards became visible in the progressive deterioration in the maintenance of 53 Elliot Road, the decline in the number of servants, the fewer purchases made by Papa on his visits to the market and the steady erosion in the quantity of food put on the table. Jani, however, maintained the quality of the food at least when I was there. Her *tehari*,[8] *kata masala*,[9] tomato and *chukundur gosht*[10] and *shami* kebabs[11] were to die for and have, at least for me, never since been replicated even on tables of the highest quality. But then perhaps this was also part of the happy memories of my youth. Notwithstanding his declining fortunes, Papa lived out his life to the end, without any break in his iron schedule or codes of conduct and merely imposed a greater austerity on himself and the conduct of his household.

Throughout his life Papa supported his brother Babban Mian, Jani's mother, who had title and income to a property in Ezra Street which supplemented the household income, and Saheb Alam, the only son of Babban Mian. All three of them occupied one room at the back of the house, where they slept on separate wooden *khats*.[12] Babban Mian was a gentle man, totally suppressed by his brother, who did little in his life except eat, sleep and nurse his asthma. Sahib Alam, his son, maintained the family tradition of shunning work but was splendid company with his good humour, street wisdom and choice phrases. His presence in this rather sombre household was always a ray of sunshine, and days spent in his company,

[8] A kind of biryani that is usually vegetarian in Indian and Pakistani homes.

[9] A beef delicacy. The recipe uses whole spices rather than powdered spices.

[10] A beetroot curry made with mutton.

[11] A popular local variety of kebab in the Indian subcontinent.

[12] A bed with wooden slats.

playing cards and listening to his idle gossip, left one with a sense of repleteness.

Elliot Road always served as a place of passage to some of our bizarre relatives who all shared a disbelief in the value of earning a livelihood. All such families, who live off property, have a retinue of poorer relations, with little or no income-generating assets or work skills. Such relations tend to drop by at mealtimes for a free lunch or occasionally expect to be invited to stay a few days. In return, they tend to be available to perform sundry services such as paying household bills or making occasional market visits for the family.

An exception to the general retinue of unemployed family members who dropped into Elliot Road was Sheikh Waris Ali or Neazoo Mian, Papa's cousin. In my childhood memory, he was an impressive figure of a man who always appeared, impeccably attired in a white linen suit, wearing a khaki solar topee. He had an impressive moustache waxed at the ends and was always chewing paan, so that his perpetually red lips took some of the edge of his appearance as a character from a Max Sennett movie. As the years moved on and his fortunes declined, his white linen suits appeared to look shabbier and frayed at the ends and came to hang loosely on his increasingly emaciated frame, stricken by what seems to be the family malady of asthma. In his prime however, Neazoo Mian was a gentleman of some substance derived—according to family folklore—from trapping wild animals in the Sunderban forests that he sold to the famous Carl Hagenbeck Zoo in Hamburg.

Legend has it that some of the animals trapped by Neazoo Mian, which included fierce Royal Bengal tigers, prior to their dispatch to Hamburg, used to be kept in storage in one of the outer garages of 53 Elliot Road. Their roars used to terrify the neighbourhood and visitors so that tradesmen entered our green gates with the greatest trepidation. Jani used to excite my imagination with tales of two such tigers named Duke and York which, as cubs, used to have the run of the inner household where I used to play with them as one does with a house cat. One such apocryphal memory narrates of an occasion where Papa was visited by one of the several *hazoors*[13]

[13] A title of reverence.

who used to be a regular visitor at Elliot Road, Chote Hazoor of Lucknow, who was held in great veneration by the family. The hapless Hazoor, quite unaware of the four-legged denizens which had the run of the house, sat on a sofa whose cushions concealed the sleeping presence of the tiger cub, Duke. The cub's resultant loud roar of anguish made the Hazoor jump an undignified six inches into the air shouting "*wallah, khatam ho gain*" (Dear God, my life is over).

Now, 53 Elliot Road is now a distant memory. I have passed by there several times, first with Salma, then, more recently in February 2014, with Rounaq, to introduce them to a vital landmark in my life. But little remains to be shown that may evoke my past. After the house was sold off by the end of 1957, it changed hands several times and is now transformed into a shabby multistoreyed building which bears no resemblance to its origins. Nor do Elliot Road or the adjacent Royd Street ring any bells in my memory. My old kindergarten no longer survives, nor does the bookshop where I bought my first Captain Marvel comic, nor even the chemists, Sen and Law, which stood at the intersection of Royd and Wellesley Street and was a regular port of call for toiletries and potions. The landscapes of my childhood and youth, thus, remain barely recognizable, and 53 Elliot Road can only be resurrected by an effort of memory which happily, still remains vivid.

O' Calcutta

Roaming the Streets of Calcutta

In my more mature, schoolgoing years, Calcutta took on a new aspect as I came to discover its pleasures for myself without any dependence on my parents. In this phase of my life, my stays in Calcutta coincided with St. Paul's long winter vacations, which extended from the last week of November to the first week of March. Looking back over the years, this was part of the treasured memories of my growing up, particularly after I became street-smart. This moment could be identified from the time my mother gave me the freedom to wander around the streets of Calcutta or travel by tram, unescorted. This would be around the time I came down from Darjeeling for the 1945–46 holidays after graduating from junior school at the age of 10 years and nine months. This golden age lasted until I passed through senior school at St. Paul's, completed my Senior Cambridge exams in December 1950 and took off for Aitchison College, Lahore, in Pakistan in January 1951. I revelled in my freedom to roam the streets of Calcutta in winter, overcast by the distinctive, environmentally hazardous wood smoke released by thousands of charcoal-burning stoves, which provided heat and light to the street community of Calcutta's proletariat, wrapped in winter shawls, puffing at their *biris* and exchanging the news of the day.

For me, the core of my freedom was to be able to go to movies alone. In the early years, until I reached my teens, this did not extend beyond the 2:30 matinee show. Armed with a 15-anna ticket, booked in advance, I left 53 Elliot Road after lunch, around 2:00 p.m. The Calcutta Tramways Company's (CTC), sleek white trams, had a stop on Royd Street directly opposite 53 Elliot Road. A two-anna ticket got me to ride first class, which meant sitting on padded seats rather than the wooden seats in the second class. At that time of day, I could easily find a seat and watch the scenery go by as the tram sped down Royd street, turned right on Wellesley Street, went past Dorans—our favourite sweet shop on the left opposite Wellesley Square—down to Dharmatala Street where it turned left, heading past Chowringhee Street, down Esplanade to Dalhousie Square.

My 15-minute ride concluded in Dharmatala, opposite Wachel Mollah's, the store of choice for middle-class Bangalis. Once off the tram, I walked south to Cinema land, located around the New Market. I would first pass the flee-ridden, non-air-conditioned Regal Cinema that occasionally attracted my custom to watch old runs of B-films such as *Jungle Jim* with Johnny Weissmuller or *Cobra Woman* starring the exotic Maria Montez. Due east, on Corporation Street, was the Elite Cinema which, after its renovation around 1946, did first runs of Hollywood movies. Close to the Elite was another new movie house, the Society, just behind the New Market and immediately adjacent to the famous kebab shop, Nizams.

My favourite cinema hall was of course the Lighthouse, which, along with its neighbour, the older, more baroque New Empire, was owned by Humayun Theaters, though the Metro Cinema on Chowringhee, a no less palatial retreat, also had its appeal. The Lighthouse was Calcutta's movie heartland for me. I would walk down from Dharmatala up to the side entrance of the New Market. The Lighthouse and New Empire were located in a small square connecting the New Market to Chowringhee. The first part of the Lighthouse scene that assailed me was its delicious air-conditioning where the cold air generated its own special aroma. Similarly, the sound of the brassy Lighthouse signature tune, which would win no place on the hit charts, yet after 60 years still remains in my memory. In those days, its ushers were well dressed, usually Anglo-Indians. The cinema premises were immaculately maintained, and even a reserved 15-anna seat in the rear stalls downstairs was a luxury. When I came with my mother, which was often, we sat upstairs in the Rs. 1 to 11 anna seats in the rear circle, which was, for me, the epitome of luxury. The movies at the Lighthouse were all first-run shows—Olivier's *Hamlet*, Bob Hope's *The Paleface*, Cecil B. DeMille's, epic, *The Unconquered* with Gary Cooper and Paulette Goddard.

When I was on my own, arriving with time to spare, I would make a preparatory dash into the New Market or, as a variation, come through the New Market entrance just beyond the Regal Cinema and opposite Nizams. This part of the market housed the confectionery shops. My preference was for Nahoums, which made excellent vanilla and chocolate fudge. Equipped with a stock of Nahoum's fudge, a most satisfactory afternoon went by at the Lighthouse, watching the stars of the 1940s and 1950s such as Gary Cooper and Errol Flynn playing the dashing hero in movies that I now gather are regarded as classics. The MGM (Metro–Goldwyn–Mayer) movies were usually screened at the Metro, another luxury retreat, where you could expect to see Esther Williams, June Allyson or Red Skelton. I remember seeing the first-run MGM version of *The Three Musketeers* at the Metro, starring Gene Kelly, playing D'Artagnan in a highly athletic mode, Lana Turner, as a breathtakingly beautiful Milady, with Vincent Price playing an appropriately sinister Richelieu.

The matinee usually finished between 5 p.m. and 5.30 p.m. There were further runs at 6:00 p.m. and 9:00 p.m. We rarely went to a 9:00 p.m. show. A 6:00 p.m. show was often favoured by my mother though never as much as the matinee. When I was with my mother, at the end of the movie a special treat meant tea at Ferrazinis, which was located on Lindsay Street, at the back of the New Empire. The taste of Ferazzini's mouth-watering collection of pastries and chicken patties still linger on the palette after all these years.

Not infrequently, a Ferazzini tea was followed by a luxurious shopping spree in the New Market. In the age of the supermarket, department stores and now shopping malls, the Calcutta New Market remains provincial by comparison. In the days of my youth, however, our New Market seemed to me to be a veritable Aladdin's cave, carrying everything under the sun. I remember its fruit and vegetable stalls at the northern entrance, leading east into toy and shoe shops and ending up in the confectionery section where pastry shops competed for space with stalls marketing the delicious guava cheese and the famous Bandel smoked cheeses. At the heart of the New Market, around its *chowrasta*,[14] were the cloth and ready-made garment shops with the Bengali owners shouting "*Ashun*, Begum sahib."[15] My mother, an epic shopper in her time, was a well-known figure about the market, including among the coolies, armed with their wicker baskets, who attached themselves to a shopper and then accompanied them around picking up their particular purchases.

When I was on my own, I pursued my own rituals. It was just reaching dusk when the movie was rounded off with Gary Cooper riding off into the sunset. The end of such a replete afternoon was somewhat of an anticlimax and thus needed to be turned into an

[14] Four crossroads.
[15] 'Ashun' meaning 'come' in Bengali.

event in itself. This was no problem for me as the route home was itself a journey full of adventure.

My first stop was always the New Market bookshops, located around the entrance leading in from the Lighthouse. This area offered a collection of about 10–12 small bookshops, which were neither Blackwells nor even W.H. Smiths. But for a 10–12-year-old, these shops were a treasure trove. They stocked all the best comics from England and the USA. How they managed to keep their collections updated remains a mystery to me, but I could always expect to find, perhaps, a fortnight out-of-date issues of *Beano*, *Dandy*, *Film Fun*, *Radio Fun* and *Knockout*, which I read avidly until about the age of 10. By then I had graduated to more serious comics such as the unillustrated *Champion*, *Wizard*, *Adventure* and Hotspur.

These bookshops also stocked the more colourfully illustrated American comics of that period, where I grew up on a diet of Batman, Superman, Captain Marvel, Spy Smasher, Wonder Woman and the more elevated classic comics that provided pictorial renderings of all the literary classics ranging from the novels of Dickens to those of Tolstoy. If, at an early age, I appeared to be rather well read, it owes largely to these illustrated introductions to the classics. My American comic collection, accumulated between 1943 and 1950, which I left behind in 53 Elliot Road when I set out for Lahore in January 1957, would today be a collector's treasure in New York worth, I am told, many thousands of dollars.

The New Market bookshops were also well stocked with some of my favourite books. My then none too erudite tastes favoured Richmal Crompton's William books, Edgar Rice Burroughs' books on Tarzan, Sapper's Bulldog Drummond books and, when I had entered my teens, P.G. Wodehouse, who remains a source of pleasure even today. The Bangali shopkeepers, with whom I established a certain intimacy over the years, managed to produce what I sought the moment I entered their shop.

Equipped with my latest finds, I set off home with a lightsome step. It would by now be dark. Moving out of the Market, I crossed the long car park for shoppers which traversed Lindsay Street, went across to the Globe Cinema, opposite the New Market.

The Globe was a less favoured place compared to the Lighthouse but provided B-film entertainment of a higher order than the Regal or the Tiger Cinema, located on Chowringhee, just round the corner from Lindsay Street. The Globe usually did a run of old films, but their specialty was their Sunday or holiday morning shows at 10.30 a.m. where they screened some enjoyable second runs of Abbott and Costello films or a selection of cartoons.

Moving past the Globe, down Lindsay Street, I headed into Free School Street's dark and fairly sinister ambience. This was a famous street in Calcutta, which was home to Calcutta's Fire Brigade which, in my early years, used to host a Christmas party for children of the officer class. Further down was the Armenian College. The dank environs of Free School Street housed a number of second-hand bookshops lit either by oil lamps or a single low-wattage bulb. These were owned by Biharis, who again became part of my extended circle. A good browse could yield older editions of comics which had eluded my attention, particularly as I spent nine months in Darjeeling.

The walk down Free School Street extended up to Ripon Street or Royd Street, which were, along with Elliot Road, known as the heartland of Calcutta's Anglo-Indian community, who shared space with Muslims and some of Calcutta's Jewish and Armenian population. Royd Street was more favoured by me as it went past 53 Elliot Road. I walked down this well-appointed street; crossed Wellesley, where the chemist, Sen and Law, was located; and continued down Royd Street, which housed yet another well-stocked comic shop, of somewhat better aspect than the Free School Street shops. The final run home took me past Little Flower School, just opposite Elliot Road, where I had briefly attended their kindergarten, and I finally arrived before the large green gates of 53 Elliot Road. Such was a day in the life of Rehman Sobhan in the winter months of the 1940s.

Outings with my mother were more elaborate affairs. As she was the inspiration for my movie mania, we went in for some epic excursions. On a Sunday or a public holiday, we would take a taxi to the Globe Cinema to see a morning show of Abbott and Costello or Laurel and Hardy movies. This was followed by the luxury of a Firpo's lunch, where, for Rs 3 and 8 annas, we could have a set lunch of tomato soup, fried *bhetki*[16] with finely sliced potato chips and vanilla ice cream topped with hot chocolate sauce. I have roamed the world, eaten at the best places, but 50 years on, I know of no place that could match each of the three items on the menu of Firpos.

From 1946 onwards, I was introduced to the world of lawn tennis by my mother who enjoyed the sport as well as the social scene associated with the All-India Lawn Tennis Championships in Calcutta, which was convened every year at the end of December, culminating in the finals on New Year's Day. During the tennis season, we invariably ended up in the Calcutta South Club at Woodside Park to see Ghaus Mohammad, Man Mohan, Sumant Misra, Dilip Bose and other giants of Indian tennis test themselves against quite eminent international visitors. Each year, some globally ranked players such as the Czech, Jaroslav Drobny, or the Swedes, Lennart Bergelin and Sven Davidson, played at the South Club. Occasionally, glamorous stars, such as the American, Gussie Moran, famous for her frilled panties, turned up. This ritual visit to the South Club continued every year until I left Calcutta in early 1951.

In my last winter in Calcutta, my class friend Rajinder Malhotra persuaded me to compete in the junior section of the 1950 championship on the sensible grounds that we would, as competitors, then be provided with complimentary passes for the whole tournament. I availed of his advice and was drawn against a 14-year-old youth from Madras, Ramanathan Krishnan, then participating in his first tournament at an all-India level. Malhotra advised me, with little evidence, that Krishnan would be a pushover for me. We were both somewhat surprised when he defeated me 6–0, 6–0, but were more comforted when he defeated everyone else in tournament by the same score, to end up as junior champion of India. Krishnan rose to be India's number one and captain of their Davis Cup team. I tantalize my sons with the thought that I launched Krishnan on his tennis career since, had I defeated him, he would have retired

[16] A popular fish among Bengali people.

to Madras a demoralized boy, who would probably have ended up as a bank clerk rather than a tennis champion!

On such weekends, when we were not watching tennis, my mother took me to a 3:00 p.m. show at the Lighthouse. As an alternative to Firpos, we usually went across to Nizams for a lip-smacking round of *khiri* kebabs.[17] This was rather down market from Firpos but a no less pleasurable repast. The matinee at the Lighthouse was followed by tea at Ferazzinis, often rounded off with a 6:00 p.m. show in the environs, at the New Empire or Metro.

On such days, sated beyond imagination, we staggered home, with me firmly believing that I had discovered my ultimate taste of the good life. Three and a half months of such a life, every winter, not only prepared me for the nine months of austerity at St. Paul's but taught me that one did not need to be enormously wealthy to really enjoy oneself in Calcutta. I learnt to take my pleasures as they come and my youth yielded more than I could have expected. I am grateful to my mother, who raised us, as a single parent in straitened circumstances. But never did I feel want, even when I visited the more well-appointed homes of friends such as my classmate at St. Paul's, Monu Palchaudhuri.

I did have a year of semi-luxury in the winter of 1948–49 when my mother was in Bombay and my father was, exceptional for him, living in Calcutta, in Karnani Estate on Lower Circular Road with his second wife, Shawkat Begum. I negotiated a weekly pocket money from my father of Rs 15, which he rashly challenged me to save on the promise that he would double whatever I saved at the end of the week. All it took was a week of old-style austerity, riding trams, going to the 15 annas' seats and I never looked back. That winter, I rode taxis everywhere, went to dress circle seats at Rs 1–11 and could treat myself to Nizams and Ferrazinis. At the age of 13 years and nine months, I could even go, on my own, to a midnight show on Christmas Eve at the Lighthouse (dress circle) to see Bob Hope and Jane Russell in a first showing of *The Paleface*. This event was negotiated by me, with much skill, with my father

[17] 'khiri' means cow's udder.

who was quite liberal but rightly apprehended adverse comment from his family. My aunts deemed my adventure to be a bit over the top and duly registered their disapproval, but it was greeted with admiration and envy among my cousins.

Apart from my set piece outings, another centre of my social life was Park Street. This was a morning place—10 minutes' walk from Elliot Road, reached by turning left rather than right, when I reached Free School Street. During the day, my target was usually the Oxford Bookshop, which also carried a lending library. It was the best bookshop in Calcutta and a good place to browse. The street located one of the famous tea shops of Calcutta, then known as Flurys and Trincas, which later split into two establishments. This was another place of the standard of Ferazzini and Firpos. Flurys, at least, has survived to this day, though it is not nearly as classy as it used to be.

Located at the end of Park Street, was one of Calcutta's three department stores, Hall and Anderson. The other such stores, patronized by Europeans and the Indian elite, were the Army and Navy Store and Whiteways and Laidlaw. We frequented Whiteways because they were the designated stockist for kitting out Paulites. Such stores usually carried a larger stock of imported goods and were mostly served by Anglo-Indian English-speaking salesgirls. Prices thus tended to be higher than elsewhere. Expeditions to Whiteways were usually followed by a visit to the Metro Cinema, which was next door, so that outings for school shopping usually carried the bonus of a matinee movie.

Another area of pleasure was my visit to the Eden Gardens. Every winter, a touring cricket team came through Calcutta around the end of December. In the winter of 1948, I managed to see the West Indies play India in a Test match; the three Ws, Everton Weekes, Clyde Walcott and Frank Worrell, were just beginning to take the cricket world by storm. Worrell was not on the team, but Weekes mercilessly thrashed the rather mediocre Indian bowling and completed a then record-breaking fifth consecutive Test century at the Eden Garden's Test match. Among the Indian bowlers, only Vinoo Mankad's left-arm spin bowling demonstrated any merit. However, India's batting line-up which, even without Vijay Merchant—then retired—included Mushtaq Ali, Vijay Hazare, Rusi Modi and Lala Amarnath was somewhat more distinguished than its bowling. But apart from Mushtaq's rather dashing batting at the Garden, with his famous leg sweeps, the rest of the batting was rather dour and runs were accumulated so slowly that most matches ended in a draw.

In later years, I ventured to the Calcutta maidan to see some club hockey where, occasionally, India's Olympians, such as R.S. Gentle, Jansen, Claudius, Keshav Dutt, K.D. Singh Babu and Gurbux Singh, were on view. I unfortunately could never see the famous football clubs of Calcutta in action as, during the football season, I was up in Darjeeling. It was not until 1971, during my working visit to Calcutta in July, that I was taken by friends to see Mohun Bagan play East Bengal.

On some winter vacations, we travelled outside Calcutta, on family outings to Madhupur, a rural retreat in Bihar. The place where we stayed had no electricity and was lit at night by Petromax lanterns. Nor did it have modern toilet facilities. I did not appreciate such inconveniences as I was missing out on some good movies in Calcutta. In the winter of 1946, we went off on a visit to the Zamans in Madras, where my uncle had been posted. I remember a green city with open spaces, outings to the seaside and the ruins of Mahabalipuram.

In the winter of 1948–49, we went off for a spell at the seaside, to Gopalpur-on-Sea. The resort, on the coast of Orissa, was a favoured watering place for Calcutta's middle class. It had only one classy hotel, the Palm Beach, but was then full of comfortable seaside boarding houses, excellently run by Anglo-Indian ladies. It was not very crowded in winter and offered clean beaches, though the waves at that time of the year were quite high. I learnt to swim in these rather turbulent waters.

Much of my pleasures in the winter in Calcutta were solo affairs or en famille. However, I did have a few ports of call in Calcutta, which included Monu Palchaudhuri's home at 64 Lake Place or to my cousin Kamal Hossain's residence on Amir Ali Avenue or Qamruzzaman's apartment in Park Circus, when his parents moved to Calcutta in 1947–48. These comrades were occasionally pressurized by me to join some of my movie expeditions or safaris to Eden Gardens to watch a Test Match. I also made occasional visits to Kaiser Morshed at his home in Auckland Place, but there was no scope for persuading him to join us as his father, my uncle K.G. Morshed, discouraged such frivolities as outings to the cinema, unless he could organize it himself. This usually meant an annual visit to the movies where the entire family of four children and their parents were packed into the family's small Mercedes car and taken to see a family-friendly matinee at the Metro.

Revisiting Calcutta

Calcutta remains one of my most favoured cities. Though it's overcrowded streets, crumbling buildings and refuse-ridden streets would not inspire such confidence in any but those who have lived in and loved its unique atmosphere. I returned to Calcutta as an adult from 1957 to 1965, when I visited it almost three to four times a year to disentangle the complex property affairs bequeathed to us by the passing of my mother's father and the far more intractable affairs of my father. I then saw Calcutta, without the sheen of the Raj, from a more mature perspective. I could then taste some of its rather limited high life, centred around Park Street, eat chicken Ala Kiev at Mocambo and dance the cha-cha to the dulcet strains of Pam Crane, an Anglo-Indian crooner with dyed blonde hair. We could even enjoy the famous Firpo's authentic lunch, now priced at Rs 7 and 8 annas, for a while just before it closed down at the end of the 1960s. But Calcutta's tea rooms were just that much less mouth-watering, Nizam's a bit grubbier and health threatening, the Lighthouse more rundown, its films not quite as current.

At this later stage, social and intellectual life in Calcutta was, for me, fuller. I stayed initially with Dipankar Ghosh at his family mansion on 137 Lansdowne Road, where we led a carefree bachelor's existence, though Dipankar worked hard during the day as the junior of the eminent barrister Subimal Roy Chowdhury. Other friends from St. Paul's, such as Monu Palchaudhuri, Peter Prasad and Arjun Pramar, were part of our social circle and helped to liven up my social life. Oxbridge friends such as Amal Bose, who was with me at Trinity Hall and later worked for Tatas in Calcutta, and Kajol Basu, who was at Oxford and later taught English at Presidency College and was an excellent dining companion, provided ports of call. But, above all, the home of my cousin Sarwar and her husband—my closest friend—Jamilur Rahman Khan, at Adela House in Ballygunge Park Road, made my later Calcutta visits enjoyable in their own special way.

In 1957, Amartya Sen had just returned from Cambridge as the founding Chair of the Department of Economics, at Jadavpur University, where he was—at the age of 24—reported to be the youngest professor at any Indian university. He lived with his parents on Ironside Road in Ballygunge and sported a brand-new car in which he took me out to attend occasional *addas*[18] at the home of Ranajit Guha, a famous historian with strong left-wing views who pioneered the historiography of subaltern studies. Ranajit lived in the South Calcutta and was a guru to young progressives where he and his Polish wife, Martha, hosted addas for the likes of young academics such as Amartya.

After the Indo-Pakistan war in 1965, all links with Calcutta were cut off until I returned in July 1971 as a freedom fighter and envoy of the first government of Bangladesh which was located at 12 Theatre Road. I have since returned periodically to Calcutta, but never for long and somehow cannot relive the romance that sustained my relations with Calcutta. Something was missing, which perhaps I will not find again. All I can now look forward to is Calcutta's never-ending capacity for high-class adda among numerous friends but that is part of a different experience.

[18] A place where people gather for conversations.

3

Darjeeling: School Days in the Shadows of Kanchenjunga

My rather idyllic nostalgia for Calcutta is perhaps not disconnected from its juxtaposition to the nine years I spent at St. Paul's School, Jalapahar, Darjeeling. For young boys who were monastically incarcerated for nine months on a hilltop in Jalapahar, overshadowed by the awesome presence of Mount Kanchenjunga, three months of parole in Calcutta was elevated to the dimensions of a vacation in London or Paris. Unlike boarding schools in England or indeed in Pakistan, where I subsequently spent two years, where the school year is punctuated by a long summer and shorter winter and spring holidays, borders in the Darjeeling schools were sentenced to nine months of uninterrupted hard labour. While this did not condemn us to bread and water, it exposed us to what for active school boys was prolonged malnutrition and deprivation from the creature comforts of home and metropolitan life. For nine months, over nine years, from the age of seven when I entered St. Paul's in March 1942 in Junior 1 to my departure in November 1950, after I appeared for my Senior Cambridge exams, I felt underfed. The three winter months we spent on vacation in Calcutta or elsewhere were given over, wherever opportunity presented itself, to unrestrained gluttony that embarrassed my mother to no end.

At St. Paul's we were, in fact, fed five meals a day. This began with *chhota haazri*[1] at 7:00 am, where we were given two salted biscuits and a cup of unsweetened tea. Breakfast was followed

[1] A little breakfast taken at dawn, usually tea and biscuits, served in households and barracks.

by a half hour of physical exercises, compulsory morning chapel and a first period of class. Breakfast involved a plate of oatmeal porridge without sugar, which has inculcated me with a lifelong abhorrence to porridge, followed by a main dish which only occasionally included an egg, two slices of white bread, with a pat of butter, and more unsweetened tea. Morning class from 9:30 a.m. to 1:00 p.m. concluded with lunch, which involved a watery soup, a meat dish, usually of a tasteless composition, and a pudding. Tea at 4:30 p.m., after afternoon games, was on the same lines as *chhota haazri*, followed on three days in the week, by afternoon classes and then supper, on the same lines as lunch. The day concluded with an hour of prep involving academic tasks set by our teachers and then bed with lights out by 9:00 p.m. On three days in the week, Tuesday, Thursday and Saturday, we had no classes after games, which served as a half holiday.

Sunday was a full day of holiday where meal schedules were maintained but included an additional chapel service in the evening. Senior boys at the level of Forms 4–6 (the Senior Cambridge class) were permitted to go into town on Saturday afternoon and Sunday. Boys who had relations or friends living in Darjeeling, or who had parents visiting Darjeeling, could go out of school to spend the weekend with them, beginning from after lunch on Saturday and returning in time for chapel at 6:00 p.m. on Sunday. For this overnight parole, we needed an exeat obtained from the dormitory matron on the basis of a written letter from our prospective overnight host.

This detailed protocol of a week in St. Paul's is presented to expose the reader to the discipline of life in a well-regarded boarding school in the India of my youth. I am not sure if this routine has changed much over the past half century, but perhaps the inmates are better fed than we were. Hard work in class; PT in the morning and compulsory games, six days in the week; the monotony of the routine; and the special scent of the air on a Himalayan hilltop made the strictly rationed portions of our five meals totally inadequate to our needs. The poor quality of the cuisine, for those with more sensitive palates or allergies to such health-giving items as cabbage, carrots or cauliflower, further sharpened the edges of our hunger.

All boys were given a derisory amount of pocket money; I think it was 6 annas a week in junior school, and 9 annas in senior school, which perhaps was raised to Re 1 by the time I left the school. This meagre wage was used to supplement our normal diet with visits to the 'tuck shop' run by a Muslim, who was known by the unfortunate appellation of Blackie, who ran a general store in the Jalapahar market. He came down to the school every day to operate a small shop in the junior school in the morning and a more well-provisioned shop, from 2:00 p.m. to 5:00 p.m., in the senior school.

Our pocket money did not buy us much, but prices then were also affordable, to a point, for indigent schoolboys. While our pocket money was added to the school bills paid out by our parents, its strict ceiling was designed to impose a form of economic democracy among the boys whose parents had varying levels of income. This discipline was, to some extent, undermined by the provision of 'private money', where parents could authorize the school to pay an additional sum, I forget the ceiling here, to their more fortunate wards. This private money was necessary, particularly for senior boys, if we wished to eat a meal in the few available restaurants in town such as the Park or see a movie either at the more upmarket Capitol in the centre of town or even at the more flee-ridden Rink Cinema further down the hill. Obviously, some boys with very rich parents had access to rather more funds than were permissible, under school rules, and could thus treat their friends to big meals on weekend trips into town.

The boys were housed in dormitories where 50–100 infrequently bathed boys slept side by side. The junior school dormitory (Junior 1–4, usually for the age group 7–10) was separately located at a lower level, between the school chapel and the quadrangle, which was the heart of the school. The quad was circumvented by three dormitories, Cotton Hall (Forms 1–3), the smaller Lyon Hall (Form IV) and the Senior Dormitory (Forms V–VI). The dormitories were located above classrooms or the school offices (in Lyon Hall). The school Headmaster or Rector, as he was titled, lived with his family in a house, just below the quad, and also provided lodgings to a selected handful of boys, whose parents were willing to pay for the privilege of closer supervision under the tutelage of the Rector's wife and a slightly better diet and other creature comforts for their wards. Such denizens of what was known as the Rectory were held in some contempt by the rest of the school and regarded as sissies.

Our beds usually had a red top blanket with three further under blankets so that each dormitory was recognizable by its serried row of red-covered beds. Four blankets were usually adequate except in the first two weeks of March, after we returned from our long vacation on the plains. At that point, the bitterness of the Himalayan winter assaulted us and even four woollen blankets seemed quite inadequate. As part of the austerity regime, while our sleeping outfits were usually made of light wool, we were, under pain of chastisement, not permitted to wear vests or socks in bed.

In the morning, these large numbers of incontinent youths had to compete for limited toilet space and wash their faces in cold water, which was an added misery in those March months. We were rationed two baths a week. When our turn on the roster came up, the dorm bearers poured two buckets of hot water into a small tin tub, which was the standard bath ration. Each boy had a locker, where their weekly clothes were to be stored. This was traded in every week to be washed and replaced by a freshly laundered set of clothes. Our clothes were all purchased from two designated department stores in Calcutta, Whiteways and Laidlaw or Hall and Anderson. For senior boys, this involved a school uniform of grey flannel suits to be worn during the week, a blue serge suit to be worn on Sunday and a blue school blazer. We had to wear the colours of the house for our tie, worn during the week, and the school colours of red and blue for the school tie worn on Sunday. The junior boys wore grey shorts and jerseys adorned by their house ties, but also wore blue Sunday suits, but with short pants on Sunday.

Life in a school such as St. Paul's was not for the sensitive. The boarding school tradition, established by the British Raj in India, was modelled on the English public school culture of muscular Christianity, immortalized in the novel *Tom Brown's School Days*, based on Rugby school under its Olympian headmaster, Thomas Arnold, whose persona and values have been brilliantly captured by Lytton Strachey in *Eminent Victorians*.

The British hoped to inculcate the same values of the so-called empire builders who went out to rule India and Africa into the offspring of these expatriates. It was deemed uneconomical and inefficient for the British, whether as bureaucrats, soldiers or merchants, to send their wards to England for their schooling. Both the Anglican and Catholic churches were encouraged to set up schools, many of which were located in the cooler climes of hill stations across India, such as Darjeeling, Simla, Mussoorie, Nainital and Ootacamund, to recreate a reasonable facsimile of the English boarding school. Eventually, it was decided that such schools would also provide openings to the children of the Indian elite who would be infused with British and Christian values to equip them to serve as junior bureaucrats and mercantile assistants to serve the British Empire. Such children were taught little of life in India or its culture and tradition but were educated in the faith, values and traditions of our rulers.

When I arrived in St. Paul's in March 1942, just after my seventh birthday, Indians could not have accounted for more than 20 per cent of the school's population. The school rolls, of around 200 boys, was mostly made up of children of British expatriates and the upper echelons of the Anglo-Indian community, along with a small component of Armenians who had established themselves in business in Bengal during the 19th century. As most of the school community were Christians, the practice of compulsory chapel was readily accepted. Those of other faiths, who were mostly Hindus, Muslims or a small group of Jews, were compelled to accept the Christian ethos of the school for the privilege of being admitted to such an elite establishment. This was particularly challenging to the small community of Muslims in school. When I entered St. Paul's, I was the only Muslim in the junior school, while in the senior school, there were perhaps another seven boys made up of my three uncles, Shahid Shahabuddin, Fayyaz Alam and Reshad Nasrullah and four others. In later years, more Muslims came in, but in my nine years in St. Paul's, there were never more than a dozen of us there at one time.

Well before I entered St. Paul's, I was tantalized by the prospect of going there. I dimly remember the envy I felt for my two uncles Sayeed (he left St. Paul's at the end of 1938) and Shahid Shahabuddin, when they came to meet my mother, who was then holidaying with me in Darjeeling, dressed in their St. Paul's school uniform. The possible cruelty of sending a seven-year-old boy away from his home, to spend nine months located far away in a boarding school, never entered my head. I do not know if this thought bothered my mother, who was the prime mover behind sending me to St. Paul's, or my father, who had to pay the fees. As he was a member of the Indian Police Service, he could indeed afford to do so as could most of the parents who sent their children to boarding school.

Most of the parents whose sons were at St. Paul's came from various fractions of the business or mercantile class, though some such as my father were also in government service. It was, thus, not surprising that the primary mission of St. Paul's seemed to be to educate their charges to serve in the mercantile community, which was then the dominant presence in Bengal. The St. Paul's graduates usually aspired to be recruited as 'covenanted assistants' by such mercantile companies as ICI, Birds, Gladstone Wylie, James Finlay, Williamson Magor and other such symbols of empire. In later years, the Indian business families, then establishing themselves to take over the business sector once the British left India, began sending their sons to St. Paul's. Interestingly, few of the Indians from the ICS, or other elite services, sent their children to St. Paul's, preferring the day schools of Calcutta, such as St. Xavier's or La Martiniere, for educating their children.

Within the ethos of such boarding schools, the sportsman or 'jock' was more valued than the scholar. It was the muscular, well-built young men who went on to become school captain or captains of the four houses, named after former empire builders such as Clive, Hastings, Havelock and Lawrence. These leaders usually represented the school or even captained the cricket, football or hockey team or won their colours in boxing, athletics or gymnastics.

Armenians figured prominently in the lists of school heroes. These athletic young men, whose forebears migrated from Armenia to dominate the indigo and jute trade in Bengal, produced the sportsmen who came to dominate St. Paul's. When I arrived in

1942, the school captain then was an Armenian named John Martin. He was the school heavyweight boxing and long-distance running champion as well as the centre forward of the football team. Six years later, his younger brother, Leon Martin, also went on to become school captain, a star sportsman and eventually light heavyweight boxing champion of Burma. Both brothers lived their later lives, well into their eighties, in California, which is probably home to more Armenians than Armenia. One of my best friends, John Lazarus, was an Armenian from Dhaka, whose father set up Lazarus and Company, one of the biggest jute trading firms in East Bengal. Lazarus entered St. Paul's with me in 1942, in Junior 1, and stayed on until the end of 1948 when he left for England with his father.

I managed to fit quite comfortably into the boarding school ethos, though this may not have been so evident when I was taken up to school by my father in March 1942. I remember we went up by train and then drove up to the school from Siliguri. I cannot recollect whether I wept in the solitude of my bed on the first few nights away from home, but I soon settled into my life with my new mates. Apart from Lazarus, I became close friends with David Clark, a Scot from Aberdeen, and John Talbot, whose family came from Chesterfield in Yorkshire. Clark did well in his studies as well as in athletics and eventually broke the junior school record for the 100 and 220 yards in 1945. However, with the end of the Second World War, he joined the large exodus of expatriates who left St. Paul's for 'home' in UK or Europe. Talbot stayed on until around 1947 before he went home to Chesterfield. Apart from me, our class included two other Indians.

Our class teacher was Miss Nora Magry, who that year married one of the senior school teachers, Malcolm Elloy. Both were—I suspect—Anglo-Indians, but Malcolm Elloy, who had a BA in geography from Selwyn College, Cambridge, had acquired a very British accent. Nora Magry was a warm person who did much to make my introduction to boarding school more congenial. Her sister was married to the junior school headmaster B.O. Jansen; both were very pleasant. I subsequently met both the Jansens and the Elloys at an old Paulites reunion, I think in Brighton, around

1968 when I was spending time at the London School of Economics (LSE). Both couples were settled in Brighton and we greeted each other with much warmth and nostalgia. The matron of the junior dormitory was Miss Collet. I remember her as a largish lady with cotton wool white hair. This gave her a rather motherly air, which was another factor in my settling into boarding life without too many qualms.

The Rector of St. Paul's when I entered the school was Leslie John Goddard, known by all in the school as Pa. I remember him as a thin, bald-headed man. He had earned an MA degree at Trinity Hall, Cambridge, which I subsequently attended. He went on to become Senior Master, at St. Lawrence College, Ramsgate—an English public school—prior to his coming out to St. Paul's School as its Rector. Goddard took over as Rector at St. Paul's in 1934, when he was just 34 years old, and served the school for three decades until he retired around 1964. After his retirement, he bought a house in Penn—a village in Buckinghamshire—which he appropriately named Jalapahar.

As with all long-serving schoolmasters, Goddard spoke with a patrician air where his words were delivered as obiter dicta to generations of impressionable young students. He spoke with a characteristic nasal twang that was much imitated behind his back by us students as was his famous 'butterfly' signature. Indeed, my own signature originates from long practice in copying Pa's butterfly. In later years, in St. Paul's, I developed an amicable relationship with Pa. He had a tradition of inviting senior boys to come down to his study at the Rectory once a week after prep. We could use this time to browse in his library and listen to the radio. I was particularly attracted to his enormous collection of books on cricket, a game in which Goddard believed he had some expertise not only from the armchair but also on the cricket field. He used to play in various matches for and against the school team until he was in his 50s. His medium-slow swing bowling was quite effective, while he could protect his wicket with a practised dead bat.

I remember sitting in his library one night listening on his radio to a commentary of the Football Association Challenge Cup (more commonly known as FA Cup) final in 1948 between Manchester

United and Wolverhampton Wanderers, which was won, 4–2, by United. I have since that night in 1948 been a lifelong supporter of Manchester United. We also listened into the Test matches with Goddard. I remember, in particular, hearing commentaries on the 1948 Test series in England between Australia and England, which was Bradman's final Test series, and rooting aggressively for Australia, much to Goddard's irritation.

Goddard obviously had an eye on me, and in my last year, we would chat and argue about a variety of subjects apart from cricket. In that year, he used to teach us divinity, in which I excelled. He had in my last year at school—in1950—invited me to become house captain of Hastings House, which I declined to accept because it meant I had to leave Clive House, where I had built up deep loyalties since I entered senior school in 1946. Goddard was very impressed at my willingness to sacrifice a house captaincy out of loyalty to my old house and made me vice captain of Clive as well as vice captain of the school hockey team. He told me then that he had been invited in 1948 by Khwaja Nazimuddin, the CM of East Bengal, to move to Dhaka to set up the equivalent of St. Paul's in East Bengal. Goddard had been excited by the offer but declined out of loyalty to St. Paul's and, I suspect, out of a sense of uncertainty about the feasibility of the project.

In later years, I had an opportunity to meet Goddard again after his retirement and visited him at Jalapahar in Bucks several times in 1967 and 1968. I again visited him on a number of occasions at Bucks when we were living in Oxford in the late 1970s, which must have been just before he passed away. In between, Goddard had managed to take notice of an article I had written in *The Guardian*, in 1971, on Bangladesh's liberation struggle. Goddard had, in response, written a letter to *The Guardian*, endorsing my views. Mark Arnold Forster, at *The Guardian*, forwarded this letter to me, which encouraged me to call Pa on the phone and thank him for what for me, his former pupil, was seen as the award of an 'A' mark for a good essay.

I have run ahead of my narrative of St. Paul's from where I left off after my arrival there in 1942. It did not take me long to settle down and readily embrace the culture of public school life.

This encouraged me to be good at games and to admire those more accomplished at this than myself. In junior school, I played all the games with great enthusiasm but without much distinction, except in the field of boxing. In my first two years, I had shown some promise in the lower weight classes but lost on my first entry into the junior school boxing finals in 1943. I made up for this in 1944, winning my weight in the final against my good friend Arun Sen. Our bout obviously attracted the attention of the school boxing coach, so that Sen and I were invited to perform again in the senior school boxing finals. I managed to defeat Sen again and was than selected to box for St. Paul's in the inter-school tournament against another boarding school, St. Thomas from Calcutta. St. Thomas was populated largely by Anglo-Indians who were particularly skilled at boxing, and I was defeated by a diminutive youth by the name of Macquire. I feel I was unfairly judged the loser in that fight, and the defeat still rankles after all these years.

My boxing successes were sustained into senior school, where I won my weight every year from 1947 to 1950. In 1947, I defeated Sen again, but my greatest accomplishment was in 1949, when I fought against a Sindhi, K.M. Assomul, who was then at 18, four years older than me. Assomul was no boxer but a hard puncher and thus no one gave me much of a chance against him. I remember studying his style from his preliminary bouts and decided to box him close in with body punches, in order to escape his wild swings that could have done me serious damage. I emerged victorious and became something of a hero among my classmates and in Clive House. In my final year, I was awarded school colours but never boxed again after I left St. Paul's. As I had a tendency to gain weight, this was a wise decision. My group photos show me to be of slim, athletic proportions while I was at Jalapahar, where my weight never exceeded 8 stone.

In junior school, I was better known for my academic accomplishments and for being articulate. We had three term exams in the school year, where I usually tended to be in the first three to four positions. In 1943, I was awarded the second prize for my class, but my year of glory was in Junior IV, my last year in junior school, when I stood first throughout the year. As a result of this performance, I was given a double promotion and entered senior school in 1946, at the age of 11, in Form 2. This meant that I sat for my Senior Cambridge exams at the age of 15, a year earlier than the norm of 16. I also parted company with those of my junior school classmates who had stayed on to enter senior school in Form 1.

By the time I left junior school in 1945, I was a recognized personality not only for my academic achievements but also for my quality of engaging with the class teachers. This may have contributed to my appointment, in my last year in junior school, as a prefect and vice captain of Cable House. I read more than most of my classmates though not with any great erudition. My favourite reads were the William books by Richmal Crompton. She wrote about William Brown, a perennial 11-year-old, who lived in a typical English village and with his gang of 'outlaws', Douglas, Henry and Ginger, who were perpetually up to some mischief. The scenes of English village life, which provided a back drop to the stories, have remained in my imagination as have the characters in the stories.

The public school culture, even for those below the age of 11, elevated the tough guy into a position of leadership. In my time, the junior school godfather was an Armenian by the mafia-like name of Charlie Mendoza. In my first three years, he was the terror of the junior school and presided over a gang of good sportsmen. As in all such group cultures, the less well-endowed tend to either suck up to the tough guy or keep out of their way. I occupied a place somewhere in between and was thus not unduly distressed when one day, in 1944, we learnt that Mendoza, then in Junior IV, had been expelled from school, for bullying. Apparently, some boys had complained once too often about Mendoza's intimidations. I remember Mendoza well. He was not very big, and no one ever tested how tough he really was. But he had a George Raft–like gangster's air about him, spoke with a quiet, menacing air and walked around school wearing thick crepe-soled shoes.

In the four years up to 1945 that I was in junior school, the British Raj was at its zenith and the colonial ethos of the school as well as its student composition remained largely unchanged. The world was still at war and expatriates in India had little choice but to stay on here rather than return home. Indians were still a minority of the school intake. The school personalities, personified in the house prefects and leading sportsmen, were mostly non-Indians. The first Indian to captain the school was Paul Raschid. In 1944, Raschid was initially appointed school vice captain and captain of Havelock House. He was an excellent sportsman, particularly as a boxer, where he was not only captain of the school team but moved on to earn a blue in boxing, when he was up at Selwyn College, Cambridge, between 1945 and 1948 and eventually represented Pakistan in the London Olympic Games in 1948.

Apart from Raschid and Stan Naidu from South India, no other Indian served as a house captain between 1942 and 1947, though some had excelled on the sports field. My uncle Shahed Shahabuddin, who had played in the school hockey team as a left-winger since 1942, was appointed captain of the team in 1944. Significantly, Reshad Nasrullah also played left wing for the school hockey team in 1946 and won his colours, as did I in 1950, also playing at left wing!

In contrast to the sports field, the few Indians who attended senior school performed much better academically, being well represented among the First Divisions in the Senior Cambridge exam and also managing to win a number of competitive special prizes in particular academic subjects.

I am especially indebted to my uncle Shahed because of his sporting distinction. He also won colours in boxing and football, where he had the distinction of scoring a spectacular equalizing goal from the left wing, against our deadly rival, St. Joseph's, a school at the lower end of Darjeeling, who we contemptuously called Spajjies. In that historic match in 1944, St Joseph's led one-nil and defended their lead largely though the brilliance of a goalkeeper by the name of Rosambeau, who wore a light blue jersey. Uncle Shahed's last-minute goal, salvaging the school's reputation, greatly enhanced my standing in the junior school.

My other uncle Fayyaz Alam, who tended to be overweight, gained his own immortality in the sports arena but at a rather heavy cost to his person. In my very first year at school, 1942, I witnessed Fayyaz being battered into a bloody pulp in the school boxing finals by Mac Chaytor, one of St. Paul's heroic Armenians and among its best pugilists. Fayyaz demonstrated exceptional courage and remained standing, thereby winning the Best Losers Cup, a dubious but deserved distinction. Fayyaz subsequently preceded me to study at Trinity Hall, Cambridge, but sensibly chose to play cricket there rather than re-enter the boxing ring.

I used to visit Shahed every Sunday, where my plaintive cry, "where is my cousin Shahabuddin," became well known around the senior school. Shahed, occasionally aided by Fayyaz who was his classmate, fed me well at the tuck shop and occasionally took me into town, where we were entitled to spend the weekend at the home of a family friend, the Jabbars, who rented a house, Chevremont, down the hill from St. Paul's. The Jabbars were a Calcutta-based family whose son Sayeed was a day scholar at St. Joseph's and his older sister, Bella, was also a day student at the local girl's school, St. Michael's. They were looked after by a governess, Farukh Begum, who was from the DNF. This meant that our weekly outings to Chevremont exposed us to culinary excellence, where we could stuff ourselves to compensate for our nutritional deficiencies at school.

One of the great treats of going into town for the holidays was to visit the Darjeeling Gymkhana Club, at least when my father, who was a club member, came up to Darjeeling to visit me. The Gymkhana had a splendid roller skating rink where my mother had learnt to skate. I also managed to acquire some proficiency in the rink. After a strenuous workout on our wheels, we could order up the most delicious potato finger chips I have ever tasted. Having enjoyed the Gymkhana in all its glory, I was deeply distressed when I revisited it with Rounaq in 2006, to have dinner, with my class friend Mohan Jethvani, who stayed on in Darjeeling to run the family haberdashery on the mall, Lekhraj and Sons. The Gymkhana was a dark and dusty mausoleum, bereft of its skating rink and of its delicious cuisine.

Trips into town, whether based in Chevremont or in residence with my father or mother when they came up to Darjeeling, or even during day trips on weekends when we were in senior school, meant we had to wear our school blazer and cap and carry an umbrella that earned Paulites the retaliatory sobriquet *Chatawallas* from the Spajjies. Wearing our badge of office, we would usually go to a movie and/or have a meal at the inexpensive Park Restaurant that served a hybrid Asian cuisine of uncertain provenance. Movies shown at the better-endowed Capitol, located in the centre of town, were more up to date. I remember seeing the fabulous version of *Great Expectations*, directed by David Lean, and still remember the tears shed by my friend Lazarus, when Estella was transformed from the delicious young Jean Simmons into the mature Valerie Hobson. The less salubrious Rink Cinema, located below the Capitol, near the town bazaar, was much favoured by my cousin Qamru and me to see horror films such as the *House of Frankenstein* or the *House of Dracula*, in black-and-white print of rather low quality.

When in town, if funds permitted, we would hire a horse and gallop up to school. I remember the thrill of racing Lazarus up the St. Paul school drive, riding scrawny ponies with names such as Ginger boy, with the Nepalese groom running behind us on foot. Other pleasures included standing on the mall to ogle the girls from St. Michaels, which was a sister school to St. Paul's, or from the more well-known Loreto Convent, which was the sister school of St. Joseph's because of their shared Jesuit ancestry. Sisterhood in the old days meant an annual school dance between the senior boys and girls of the two schools. Regrettably, by the time we were senior enough to be exposed to the annual dance, St. Michaels had closed down.

When my father or mother occasionally came up to Darjeeling during the one-week Whitsun or Puja holidays, Farooq and I would stay with them at the home of one of their friends or at the luxurious Everest Hotel, where we could invite our friends for a four-course lunch in their high-end restaurant, serviced by liveried waiters. Other extravagances encouraged by such parental visits included tea at the more upmarket Plivas on the *chowrasta*, which served delicious pastries.

The year 1945 was a watershed year for St. Paul's. I remember the excitement, when we heard first of the Nazi surrender in Europe and then of the Japanese surrender, which signalled the end of World War II. Many old Paulites had already enlisted in the war after leaving school, and some had even become war heroes and martyrs. If I recollect, a school holiday was declared first to commemorate Victory in Europe Day in May when Germany surrendered and then, in September, to celebrate the end of the war when Japan surrendered after the second atom bomb was dropped on Nagasaki.

Such extracurricular holidays were always appreciated but none more than the occasional sunshine holiday. This special event was unique to Darjeeling, which, during the monsoon season from April to September, was exposed to continuous rain. Globally, Darjeeling was, indeed, second only to Cherrapunji, in its volume of rainfall. This meant playing football every day during the monsoons amidst heavy downpours. Very rarely during the monsoons, we would wake up to see bright sunshine and Kanchenjunga staring down at us in all its magnificence. On such an occasion, the school captain would ceremonially walk to the Rectory with the boys waiting in the quadrangle with bated breath, to formally request the Rector for a sunshine holiday. When he emerged flashing a thumbs up sign, a roar of joy would erupt as we prepared for a glorious day of leisure, possibly a specially arranged school picnic to Senchal Lake, the source of Darjeeling's water supply, or a visit into town, or simply lazing around the school.

Sunshine holidays were, unfortunately, a rarity in Darjeeling. A more deadly hazard was the arrival of a cyclone and the consequent landslides that precipitated on the hillsides. We were exposed to such a natural disaster in my last year, 1950, which set off landslides of such a magnitude that the main road from Siliguri to Darjeeling was blocked in several places, thereby cutting the town off from its main supply routes. The road from Darjeeling town to our school in Jalapahar was also blocked, which interrupted the supply of foodstuffs for several weeks. This compelled the school to live off its accumulated stocks that exposed all of us to food rationing through provision of two meals a day. For those two weeks, the boys in the fifth and sixth forms were given time off from some classes to go down the hill and participate in clearing a path through the mudslide that was blocking access to the school. My exposure to life as a day labourer was an adventure but became less so as blisters appeared on our hands and the exertions from our efforts remained nutritionally undercompensated.

With the end of the war, and the more relevant yet unexpected triumph of the Labour Party, led by Clement Atlee, in the post-war general elections in Britain, the prospect of an end of the British Raj emerged as a real possibility. When we returned to school in March 1946, we found that a large number of our friends were no longer there to greet us. David Clark and many others in classes above and below us had left India with their parents, to go back 'home' wherever that may be. Many who chose to go home never saw Blighty (a slang for England among the Anglo-Indian community), as they were born and brought up in India but felt insecure at what an independent India might mean for the Anglo-Indian community. Many of those who stayed behind, left by the end of 1947, just after the end of British rule in India. The changed composition of the school was visible with the diminishing quotient of non-Indians whose numbers fell to below 50 per cent in 1946 and below 20 per cent by 1949. By the time I left St. Paul's, the non-Indians were below 10 per cent.

The exodus of non-Indians created spaces on the sports field that could be filled by the less gifted though equally enthusiastic sportsmen such as myself. In junior school, apart from boxing, I was adequate in games but never made it into the school team. My reputation had been established in the classroom. However, in senior school, I had to once again establish myself as I was now in a class above my age group due to my double promotion. Happily, I did reasonably well, right from the outset and was placed in the first five in my first term. (The school year was divided into three terms, each of three months' duration, and we faced exams at the end of each term.) I never looked back throughout my stay in senior school and ensconced myself in the top three to four positions in my class throughout my remaining years in senior school.

In senior school, I once again established a reputation for being articulate, with a willingness to argue with the teachers, being fairly well-read, and appropriately won the Karan Mazumdar General Knowledge Prize in 1950. The school had a practice of awarding these special prizes through essay competitions in various subjects that were competed for by the brighter fifth and sixth formers. Regrettably, I did not win all the prizes I had aspired to, though I received honourable mentions in most of the prize competitions that included English essay, history, divinity, geography and Latin—I had no capacity to compete in maths or science. In my year, the top student and winner of the most prizes was my lifelong friend Monu Palchaudhuri, who was smart and well read but eventually chose to commit himself to his family's business enterprises in tea and engineering.

In senior school, I took advantage of the exodus of many of the non-Indians and gained more recognition as a sportsman, particularly after 1947. Apart from my proficiency in boxing, I had acquired an unexpected talent for long-distance running. In 1946, in my first year in senior school, at the age of 11, I had come in fourth in the Junior Marathon, open to boys in the senior school below the age of 14, which covered a three-and-a-half-mile course run on hillside roads around the school. Next year, I had a fair chance of winning the Junior Marathon, but failed to do so as my belt broke and I had to run nearly half the distance holding up my shorts but managed to cross the finishing line in third place. In 1948, I went on to win the Junior Marathon as well as the Victor Ludorum, awarded to the best athlete in the age group 12–13. In 1949, in my first year of the competition in the Senior Marathon course, much to everyone's surprise, including my own, I came in first, which was the only time that a boy who had just graduated from the junior to the senior course had ever done so. I once again came in first in 1950 when I also won my second Victor Ludorum cup for the best athlete in the age group 14–15, winning, in addition to the Senior Marathon, the long jump, low hurdles, 440 yards, 880 yards and coming in second in the mile race.

I was awarded colours in athletics and also in boxing, football and hockey, where I was the vice captain of the school team. I even played for the St. Paul's cricket team but without much distinction, except as a fielder. I was, thus regarded as an all-rounder who not only achieved some distinction in sports but was recognized as a person of academic merit who also commanded debating skills and even demonstrated a modest ability as a thespian. I played the role of Thomas Mowbray, in the school performance of *Richard II*, which was also our text for the Senior Cambridge. This was an ideal role as I appeared only in the first scene where I entered on the stage from among the audience bellowing "my name is Thomas Mowbray" and was then exiled by Richard II at the end of the first scene, so I could relax and take my place in the audience. The school chronicle recognized my performance by regretting my early exit from the stage!

My days in St. Paul's ended in November 1950, though the icing on the farewell cake was tasted by me when I learnt that I was one of the six members of my class of 17 who had passed the Senior Cambridge exam with a First Division. Our class was obviously of some academic merit since, at least in my senior school years, from 1946 to 1950, no other class had managed to graduate more than two members with First Divisions.

I look back on my days in St. Paul's with much nostalgia. I moved there at the age of seven, as the second smallest boy in the school and emerged—I believe—a man even at the age of 15. I had learnt to be self-reliant and acquired much of my self-assurance at St. Paul's. I played a custodial role to my younger brother Farooq, who was placed in the junior school by my mother in 1947 at the tender age of six and left with me in 1950 to go to Aitchison. In consequence, Farooq never went beyond junior school at St. Paul's, where he performed well academically and won several class prizes.

Just as I used to once visit my uncles in senior school, I, in turn, was visited by Farooq every Sunday, who expected to be entertained by me. Younger brother care also involved escorting Farooq from Calcutta to Darjeeling and back every year. When we travelled to school by train, the school party went from Sealdah station, travelling through what was then East Bengal, over the Hardinge Bridge through stations such as Ishurdi and Santahar to Siliguri. From there we boarded the famous 'toy train' that chugged up the hill to deliver us, with a stop for lunch in Kurseong to Darjeeling in the afternoon. On this long journey up and around the hills, Farooq was a serious liability as he was prone to travel sickness.

When I revisited St. Paul's in 1980 for the first time since my departure in 1950, I took my sons Babar and Zafar with me to see how they felt about going to boarding school. It was a damp, bleak day and the boys took one look at the place and gave it a thumbs down. Salma would, in any case, not even consider the possibility of sending her boys to boarding school at that age but eventually relented and let them leave home after their 'O' levels. In the mid-1980s, Babar went to Kodaikanal in the hills of South India, to an American-run co-educational school, which was then much favoured by Bangladeshis. Two years later, Zafar also went to boarding school in the American missionary establishment—Woodstock—in Mussoorie in the hills of North India. Both my sons, being highly extrovert and exceptionally talented in sports, fitted into boarding school life no less comfortably than did their father. Indeed, in Kodaikanal, Babar earned some distinction by being elected as president of the school student council and leading a minor insurrection against the authorities. However, the co-educational lifestyle in American co-ed schools tends to be a good deal more relaxed than anything we experienced at St. Paul's. I doubt if either would have survived the austerity and more severe disciplinary demands of my old school.

In 2006, I returned to St. Paul's with Rounaq. We had taken a short vacation in Darjeeling and stayed at the Windamere Hotel on the Mall, just below the Gymkhana Club. The Windermere, still run by the Ladenlaw family, is one of the few surviving institutions that has managed to preserve the graces of the 'old' Darjeeling and even serves scones to guests at teatime. As I was no longer capable of walking 1,000 feet up the hill to Jalapahar, we took a taxi that delivered us at the edge of the school playground where I had spent much time. We were invited by the Rector, an Indian Christian, to have tea in the Rectory. He not only showed us the new structures but also took us on a visit to the chapel, which was much as I remembered it, where I attended daily services for nine years. I had in my last year, as a school prefect, occasionally read the lessons from the Bible. Nine years of compulsory attendance at the chapel taught me a great deal about Christianity without converting me into a Christian. We were told by our host, the Rector, that in the year 2006, six decades after India's independence, attendance at the chapel for all students at St. Paul's is still compulsory, though perhaps 95 per cent of the students are non-Christian. Such an obligation is written in as a precondition for admission and is readily accepted by Indian and indeed Bangladeshi parents who at that time had 43 of their children enrolled at St. Paul's for the privilege of going to this elite school. I doubt if any of these boys will be Christianized by their chapel attendance anymore than I was.

This culture of muscular Christianity, which treats religious observance and compulsory games as a form of discipline needed for character building, has been bequeathed by the Raj through institutions such as St. Paul's, to the ruling elite of the postcolonial subcontinent. This culture, which believes that character as defined by the willingness to 'play the game' rather than achieve mere academic excellence, was deemed to be more relevant to the process of nation building. This inherited culture of sporting supremacy from a British ruling class, drawn from their not very gifted aristocracy and landed gentry, remained at sharp variance with the Indian tradition of earning scholastic distinction.

Indian students who could not afford the fees to go to the anglicized boarding schools usually opted for day schools, which encouraged a belief in all work and little play. Its students felt compelled to swot, studying late into the night, to gain positions in the matriculation and intermediate exams run by the Indian education boards rather than the Cambridge-designed exams. It was these boys—such as Amartya Sen—who went on to score first classes in their BA exams from Presidency College and then often moved abroad for promoting their academic career or for appearing in the ICS or later the exams for the Indian Administrative Service (IAS). Hardly anyone from St. Paul's competed and qualified for the IAS. I can only remember S.V.S. Juneja and Lalit Parija, who earned first classes in their Senior Cambridge exams in 1946, competing for and entering the IAS. Parija, however, was also a gifted cricketer at St. Paul's and eventually went on to captain Orissa, his home state, in the Ranji Trophy tournament, where he once scored a double century.

Very few Paulites chose an academic career and I was perhaps the only one of my generation, or indeed among students who graduated from St. Paul's between 1946 and 1950, who chose to become a university teacher. Most Paulites chose careers in British-owned mercantile companies, and later in the Indian corporate sector or entered their family business. Entry into such careers did not depend on academic excellence but on family connections or inheritance, which was also what the British public school system was all about.

This emphasis on training young boys to become young men who will integrate with a particular class in the prevailing social order inevitably tended to delink the students at such schools as St. Paul's from what was going on in the broader world around us. This was particularly true for the students who had to spend nine months of the year physically disconnected from the world, encapsulated in their mountain retreats. During my tenure at Jalapahar, a global war was fought and came to its conclusion, thereby drastically changing the nature of the world order. Within India, the country moved through a maelstrom of blood and tears towards independence and the partition of a subcontinent.

While we celebrated the end of the Second World War with holidays and feasting in St. Paul's, at the age of 10, I had little idea of what this meant for the world or even India. The defeat of Churchill's Tory party in the general election of 1945 was greeted at the level of our teachers with much surprise, as his larger-than-life image with cigar in one hand and his famous 'V' for victory proclaimed by the other, had left us with an image of his invincibility. We knew or indeed cared little for the social upheavals across Europe precipitated by the war that culminated in the massive victory of the Labour Party.

While our abysmal ignorance of the politics of post-war Europe may be understandable, our innocence of events in our own country was less so. We knew something about the ongoing freedom struggle led by a dhoti-clad gentleman named Gandhi, but many of us understood little about why we should want him to replace a regime that had enabled us to live a good life in Calcutta and study peacefully in schools such as St. Paul's with a subject class who could not speak correct English. This view was corrected for us around 1950—three years after Independence—by Goddard, who once observed in class that the best rendition of the English language he had ever heard was by Nehru. Once India became independent, the school teachers were happy to extol their loyalty to the Congress raj and to speak highly of its leaders. We even entertained a visit by India's Governor-General, C. Rajagopalachari, who the less reverential boys referred to as 'ruggerballcharlie'.

The final passage to Independence, through the bloodletting of the Partition riots and closer to home, in the great Calcutta killing of 1946, when Hindus and Muslims indiscriminately slaughtered each other, occurred when we were cut off from the world in Darjeeling. I was then in Form II in senior school and cannot recollect if these terrible events registered in my consciousness or that of my classmates'.

I was one of the few in my class who went daily to the school library—then located next to the Rector's office in Lyon Hall—to read *The Statesman* from Calcutta. But I invariably turned to the sports page at the back of the paper to find out the latest cricket scores registered by the Indian cricket team that was touring England in the summer of 1946. This was the last integrated team and was led by Iftikhar Ali Khan and the Nawab of Pataudi, the father of the better-known Nawab, Mansoor Ali Khan, who also led India in the 1960s.

These sporting distractions discouraged me from turning to the front page of *The Statesman* where I could have read about the riots in Calcutta, Bihar, Noakhali and eventually the horrors in the Punjab. My wilful ignorance was not disturbed by my cousin Qamruzzaman, then in Form 3, or anyone else in my or his class. I do not recollect if the last of my Paulite uncles, K.M. Reshad, then in his final year at St. Paul's, drew my attention to these events. Reshad was one of the few Paulites who was politically conscious as his father, Khwaja Nasrullah, was the chief whip of the Muslim League Parliamentary Party in the then Bengal legislature, where Suhrawardy was the CM. Reshad, who was academically not too smart but played excellent hockey, was teased by his classmates in the sixth form for his ardent Muslim League views and was tauntingly christened *panwallah*,[2] a profession that was, for some reason,

[2] Betel leaf seller.

associated with Muslims. Reshad surprised everyone by winning the Tower History Prize, where competitioners were expected to write an essay on the Minto–Morley reforms, which were seen as the first steps initiated by the British to promote self-rule in India. Since Reshad's credentials as a scholar of history were not widely recognized, it was popularly believed by his classmates that the essay was written for him in Calcutta by one of his father's political secretaries and sent on to Reshad to pass off as his own. I have never tested the veracity of this story, but Reshad always regarded his winning the History Prize as the high-water mark of his not-very- distinguished academic career.

My ignorance of the traumas of Partition was compounded by my dim appreciation of the subsequent partition of India, the emergence of Pakistan and its implications for not just the subcontinent but for me and my family. In 1947, when India was partitioned, I never fully realized that one day I would have to choose between leaving my home in Calcutta and moving to another country. Until 1950, we could still freely travel between India and Pakistan. I had evidence of this when early in 1948, I travelled to Dhaka in the newly emerged State of Pakistan with my mother and Farooq to spend a month staying with my *nana*,[3] Khwaja Nazimuddin, who was then the CM of the province of East Bengal. I remember we boarded the train at Sealdah station and travelled overnight to Goalundo Ghat on the west bank of the Padma, from where the steamer took us to Narayanganj. Indeed after 1947, our school train which carried us from Sealdah station in Calcutta to Siliguri, passed through East Bengal without hindrance. When I finally emplaned with Farooq for Lahore from Delhi, in January 1951, we could make this journey without need for travel documents. The concept of two countries, thus, did not fully register into my consciousness until I actually stayed for two years in Pakistan.

This level of ignorance on the part of a boy, who was intellectually one of the lights of the school, is a measure of my own political illiteracy at that time. But it also tells you something of the cocoon-like existence we led at St. Paul's, where neither our

[3] Maternal grandfather.

teachers, or our education system or our socialization among ourselves exposed us to the political and social realities around us. While I may look back today on my state of innocence with some anxiety, at that stage in my life, ignorance was bliss and my carefree life at Jalapahar rolled along undisturbed by the passage of events in the wide world around us.

This idyllic, if insulated, existence on a hilltop in the shadow of Kanchenjunga came to an end in November 1950. I remember those last days well. The end of the school year, after the final school exams in mid-November, was always a particularly delicious moment in our school life. The monsoons had ended, the cold mountain air was particularly crisp in the winter sunshine and we could see Kanchenjunga almost every day. Three and a half months of vacation lay ahead of us. The school year ended with a carol service in the chapel the day before we went down from school. I loved the carol service—which began with the school choir, made up of boys with some vocal skills—moving in procession into the chapel as the whole school sang the carol "Once in Royal David's City." Other carols such as "God Rest Ye Merry Gentlemen," "Silent Night, Holy Night" and "O Little Town of Bethlehem" have always remained in my memory, but my particular favourites were "The Holly and the Ivy" and "O Come, All Ye Faithful."

At the end of the carol service, we walked up the hill in an exceedingly mellow mood to the school dining hall where the whole school had assembled for a farewell supper. This offered us a special and more filling fare, with amusing speeches and much jollity. In my last year, I was invited to give a farewell speech on behalf of the students. I forget what I said, but it was quite amusing if not memorable.

The next morning, the first batch of students walked down to the Darjeeling railway station to board the 'toy' train down the hill to Siliguri, from where we boarded the train to Calcutta. Usually, the whole train was reserved for the school, so we traditionally prepared a colourful decoration that was placed at the front of the train. The next morning, we were received by our parents in Calcutta. From then on, days of feasting and festivity lay ahead of us until we again boarded the train for Siliguri next March.

In my last year, the Senior Cambridge class stayed behind at school to appear for our final exams, which were usually held after the rest of the school had dispersed for their vacations. In that last week of November 1950, it was strange to find just 17 of us occupying the senior dormitory, left behind in an empty school. The Cambridge exams usually extended over two weeks. At the end of the first week, we had two days off, so our class travelled down to St. Joseph's to play our counterparts there in football. If I recollect, we held them to a draw. The end of the exams brought my life in St. Paul's to a close. When I walked down the hill at the end of November, it was a brisk, cold day, but the sun was shining, lighting up Kanchenjunga in all its magnificence. As I bade farewell to nine years of my life in the shadows of Kanchenjunga, I did not realize that another 30 years would pass by before I returned to Jalapahar, to another world, in another age.

4

Lahore: Coming of Age among the Chiefs

I arrived in Lahore with Farooq, my younger brother, in January 1951. After completing my nine years of schooling at St. Paul's School, Darjeeling, with my appearance for the Senior Cambridge exams in November 1950, my mother was keen for me to prepare for the Cambridge HSC exam. As this was not on offer at St. Paul's, my mother decided to send Farooq and me to Aitchison College in Lahore. She had heard that Aitchison was a good school of the same standard as St. Paul's from Bhupinder Singh Bedi, the oldest son of our family friend Maluk Singh Bedi. Bhupinder had, in fact, been the school captain of Aitchison in 1947 and managed to finish his schooling there just before the partition of Punjab made Sikhs in Lahore into an endangered minority. Bhupinder had joined the Indian army when, on a visit to Calcutta, he had met my mother and extolled the qualities of Aitchison to her.

Bhupinder's views added strength to the praises of Aitchison, which had been constantly retailed to me for the last two years at St. Paul's by my classmate Amar Singh who had, with his two brothers, also been at Aitchison up to 1947. Amar and his brother had migrated to St. Paul's in 1948. Due to my profound political illiteracy, I kept asking Amar (known as Ambie) why he chose to leave such an enviable school as Aitchison and move to St. Paul's, to which Ambie used to darkly reply, "I was not keen to have my throat cut." Shamefully ignorant as I was then about the horrific communal genocide that had taken place on both sides of the border of a partitioned Punjab, I did not fully appreciate the meaning of Ambie's fateful message.

Bhupinder's encomiums to Aitchison were reinforced by the fact that the family of my mother's older sister, Sikander (Sika Aunty), had migrated to Pakistan with her family in 1949. As the Zamans were in residence at Lahore, my mother felt that we would be well looked after. My mother, at that moment, had decided to stay on in India and thus left me and Farooq to find our own way to our new home in Pakistan. She took both of us part of the way from Calcutta to Delhi. In our short stay in Delhi, we were privileged to have a front row seat at India's first Republic Day parade on 26 January 1951 where Dr Rajendra Prasad, the first President of the Republic, and Pandit Jawaharlal Nehru, the PM, took the salute from the march past. Our presence at this historic event owed to the courtesy of a friend of our family—Wing Commander Chamman Mehta—who was one of the organizers of the Republic Day events.

Farooq and I departed for Pakistan shortly after the Republic Day. Our mother put us on a flight to Lahore, having sent a message to the Zamans to receive us. In those days, one needed neither visas nor passports to cross these newly drawn national boundaries, so the notion that I had now crossed into another country did not fully register in my consciousness.

My mother's message to the Zamans did not get through. When Farooq and I landed at the Lahore airport, which at that time was not much more than an open field with a single, sparsely furnished structure serving as a terminal, we found no welcoming family to receive us. Here was I, not yet 16, with a 10-year-old brother in tow, arriving for the first time in a new country as a complete stranger and being left to fend for myself in this alien landscape. My survival skills had obviously been well developed during my nine years of coping with life, far from home, stranded on a hilltop in Darjeeling. I took my chances and boarded the airport bus that ferried passengers from the airport terminal to Faletti's Hotel in the centre of Lahore. At Faletti's, which was then Lahore's sole first-class hotel, I was advised that Empress Road—where the Zamans lived—was close by, so I hailed a tonga, and then, along with Farooq and our piles of luggage, set out to search for our family refuge. Sikander Aunty was quite stunned to see us ride into her compound on a tonga. Thus began my introduction to life in Pakistan.

The Zamans had a comfortable, single-storeyed house, at 45 Empress Road, which was adjacent to the rear entrance of the Governor's residence. I became quite familiar with this house over the next two years where I used to spend every weekend enjoying the splendid hospitality and cuisine of the Zaman household. Qamruzzaman, known to all of us as Qamru—their son and my first cousin—had attended St. Paul's with me from 1945 to 1948. His family moved to Lahore in early 1949 where he had already spent a year at Aitchison as a day boy. He had not done too well in his first-year exams in the HSC and had to repeat a year so that we both attended the first-year HSC class together, even though Qamru was two years older than me. His younger sister, Qamarara, who was then 13 years old, was a student at Queen Mary's, which was a school favoured by the daughters of Punjab's elite, in the same way Aitchison was home to their sons.

Qamru was not just my first cousin but my closest friend. We had been close from our childhood days. Qamru had a creative mind and considerable inventive skills that he invested in devising table games and literary compositions. He could have made a living as a designer for some board game manufacturer or as a playwright but did neither. Qamru and I shared many things in common, including a sense of humour, a love of horror movies and sports, though, unlike me, Qamru's interest in sports was more academic and innovative, rather than registered on the sports field. In his later life, having quite inappropriately been compelled by his father to follow his profession into chartered accountancy, he failed his exams and, on returning home, never quite found his niche in life. His descent into schizophrenia was a tragic and unnecessary waste of a life, which, if otherwise directed, could have registered some quite positive accomplishments.

As arrangements had already been made for our admission to Aitchison, a few days after our arrival in Lahore, my aunt and Qamru took us over to Aitchison, where Farooq was installed in Leslie Jones (LJ) House, which housed the entrants to the senior school. I was then taken to Kelly House, which was to be my place of residence for the next two years.

Compared to St. Paul's, Aitchison College represented quite a different world. St. Paul's—an elite school that largely catered to the needs of the educated middle class of eastern India—was designed to produce the workforce for the colonial business and administrative establishments. Its ambience was spartan and designed to instil toughness in their wards.

In contrast to St. Paul's, Aitchison was one of what came to be known as chief's colleges, which also included Mayo College, Ajmer, and other such colleges in Northern India. These colleges were set up by the Raj, to quote the famous writer K.L. Gauba, "to transform barbarian princelings into English gentlemen." The target groups were indeed the offspring of the feudal elite of this region with a fair sprinkling of Rajahs and Nawabs at the apex. In the initial years, these colleges, opulently laid out on spacious grounds, permitted their wards to bring their own retinue of servants as well as their horse and carriage. These cultural extravagances of the feudal order were tempered by a rather superficial imposition of the ethos of the English public school system overseen, initially, by headmasters and teachers imported from Britain. These headmasters discovered the tensions inherent in this attempt to marry India's feudal values to the Calvinist inheritance of the English public school system.

In the motherland, such displays of self-indulgence had been deemed to be inappropriate to the needs of English gentlemen, who were sent to Eton and Harrow to shed some of their lordly ways, though not necessarily to learn much about democratic values. Thus, after some years of living as barbarian princelings, the students of Aitchison were gradually pushed by such headmasters as Kelly and Barry towards a somewhat more disciplined lifestyle, sans servants, horse-and-buggy, though equestrians could bring their own horses for use in the riding school. By the time I reached Aitchison in 1951, its lifestyle was still quite opulent by the standards of St. Paul's, but this reflected the largely feudal background of its student population rather than the culture of the school itself.

My first initiation to Aitchison College was in the person of Mr Pinson, a somewhat desiccated Frenchman who rather improbably taught us English literature at the HSC level. He was not one of those teachers who seek to connect with the boys through a shared enthusiasm for games and girls. Pinson obviously ranked a 'C' in any popularity contest and ruled us with the sharpness of his tongue and a somewhat pedantic adherence to school rules.

I entered Aitchison at the Cambridge HSC level where my classmates were in their final years of school and 16-plus in age. They thought of themselves as men rather than boys, and many sported well-trimmed moustaches (in St. Paul's, moustaches were impermissible unless you were of the Sikh persuasion) and wore quite elegant clothes as one of our privileges in the HSC was to be spared the compulsion of school uniforms.

On my first day in college, Pinson entrusted me to the good offices of Shawkat Hayat, a young man from Multan, then appearing in his matric exams. Shawkat, being both dark of skin and modest of manner, was difficult to associate with the common or garden upper-class Punjabi who tended to be lighter skinned and loud. While I did not have much in common with Shawkat, we became good friends, played hockey together and, if I recollect correctly, even won the Kelly House table tennis doubles championship together. Shawkat introduced me to my room and my Man Friday, Sagheer, a rather dour rustic from Multan, whose rural Punjabi dialect was initially quite incomprehensible to me so that Shawkat had, among other tasks, to serve as my interpreter with Sagheer.

I was led by this duo to my quite extravagantly commodious suite of rooms, available to HSC students. This paints a somewhat misleading picture of feudal opulence for these rather sparsely accommodated rooms—a rather capacious but bare bedroom-cum-living room, a small dressing room and a bathroom without toilet or running water, which was serviced daily by Sagheer in the form of buckets of water. This, fortunately, included hot water to get one through Lahore's rather sharp winter. For those who could afford it and brought in furnishings from home, the three rooms, sans running water, could indeed be made to look quite elegant. For someone who had, for the last nine years, shared living space with a hundred malodorous bodies in the dormitories of St. Paul's and in our winter holidays lived three to a room at 53 Elliot Road with my mother and Farooq, my rather spartan chambers at Kelly

House were the penthouse at the Ritz. Regrettably, my taste in furnishings did not go beyond some rather inelegant, inexpensive curtains purchased in Anarkali Bazaar and coloured cut-outs from *Photoplay* of Esther Williams and Rita Hayworth, to decorate my bare walls. But I loved it all and luxuriated in the solitary splendour of my chambers.

The second of my acquaintances at Kelly House was none other than Abdul Aziz Khan—known to all as Abdaal, who was the college prefect or head boy of Aitchison as also of Kelly House. After all those years and the division of a country, I continue to remember Abdaal as my friend and remember our two years together at Aitchison with a particular affection. Abdaal was, for a young man not yet out of high school, an impressive figure of a man. He was over six feet in height and handsome in a rather central Asian sort of way. This, no doubt, was inherited from his Yusufzai forebears, settled in Hoti, Mardan, in the North-West Frontier Province (NWFP), where Abdaal's chacha was the local Nawab. Abdaal had a firm tread that could be heard 50 yards down the corridors of Kelly House. As the house prefect, his resounding strides down the corridors, keeping a watchful eye on any misdemeanours in Kelly House, inspired fear and awe among the younger inmates. Abdaal was undoubtedly the most elegantly dressed student in Aitchison or perhaps anywhere. He claimed he only wore clothes tailored at Rankens or Pitmans of Lahore, which for Pakistan had the distinction of a suit from Savile Row. Needless to say, when Abdaal went up to Cambridge in the autumn of 1953, he ordered his clothes from Anderson & Sheppard of Savile Row and his shoes from Lobbs of Pall Mall.

For all his elegance, Abdaal was a great raconteur with quite incredible bits of arcane knowledge at his command, culled from a carefully chosen, if limited, range of literature and his quite fertile imagination. His great literary favourites were Stanley Lane-Poole's *History of India* and H.C. Armstrong's biography of Kemal Atatürk, *Grey Wolf*. I can, after more than half a century later, still remember Abdaal quoting in his stentorian voice, Babar's memoir, as reported by Lane-Poole, "I put my feet in the stirrups of resolution and took in my hands the reins of hope as I set out to do battle with the tyrant Ibrahim Lodhi," or something to that effect.

Abdaal's favourite reference from Armstrong was about Bald Ali, the 'hanging judge', who apparently put down a quite large number of Turks following a failed rebellion against Atatürk. Abdaal's pièce de résistance was when Atatürk received the news that his closest friend, once his comrade in the deposition of the Sultan, had been hanged—Abdaal liked to spin out the story—Atatürk is supposed to have merely shaken the ash off his cigarette. I was so impressed by the tale that one of the first things I did when I arrived in England in the spring of 1953 was to search the second-hand bookshops for a copy of the *Grey Wolf.* I cannot remember if Abdaal's thrilling narrative about Bald Ali was validated, but my early, rather authoritarian, views must have originated from the *Grey Wolf.* Abdaal narrated these stories with a rather wistful air as he saw himself playing the role—if not of Atatürk then perhaps of Bald Ali—in putting Pakistan to rights. Abdaal passed on to me his rather prejudiced and highly scatological views of the incumbent Muslim League government, then headed by Liaquat Ali Khan, whom he held in particularly low esteem.

Through Abdaal and Shawkat, I came to know more of the rather colourful ensemble of Kelly House who have since passed into oblivion. Some, such as Irshad Abdul Qadir, Aziz Sarfraz, Usman Aminuddin and Haroun-er-Rashid, were up at Cambridge during my time there. Irshad and Aziz were great friends with strong literary and artistic interests. While Aziz was an excellent sportsman, Irshad disdained any such physical activity. Usman distinguished himself in school as the long-distance running champion.

Another of my HSC colleagues was Abdul Khaleque, a Chinioti from the Amin family. The Amins were among the top 22 business families of Pakistan. Khaleque had been a close friend of my cousin Kaiser Morshed at St Xavier's School in Calcutta, where he was known as Ibn-e-Adam and brought with him all the academic conceits of that establishment along with a rather low opinion of the intellectual qualities of his new colleagues in Aitchison. He again, was quite as unlike the standard Punjabi as I was unrepresentative of the popularly held idea of a Bengali. Khaleque used to wear a wicker cap of the sort favoured in the East Bengal countryside and occasionally played the *basree*[1]—quite unmelodiously. Both these affectations perpetuated his popular but quite inaccurate image of being one of those arty Bengali types.

Kelly House had a fair sprinkling of the Punjabi landed classes who I came to know mostly on the playing fields. We had a Tiwana in the person of Anwar Tiwana, who was, in my first year, the school's long-distance running champion. As I had enjoyed such a reputation in St. Paul's, he saw me as a potential rival. But I never did seek to enter into the sort of training regime that could effectively pose a challenge to him, and in the cross-country race, which was run a month after I arrived at Aitchison, I came in fourth behind Tiwana. I might have been third or even second, if I had not missed a turning at the end of the race. Indeed, I missed coming in second the next year behind Usman Amin, the winner, by again missing a crucial signpost and running an extra quarter of a mile that relegated me to fourth place. Punjab thus triumphed over Bengal in the long distances, thanks to my incompetence as a sign reader!

My HSC colleagues outside Kelly House came from a similar elitist background. One of my immediate contemporaries in the HSC class, Malik Muzzafer Khan, then resident in Godley House, was the eldest son and heir apparent of the Nawab of Kalabagh, the then Governor of Punjab. The Nawab was an epic figure renowned for his fierce, well-polished moustache and exquisitely starched turban as well as his ruthless temperament that extended over his family, his feudal domain in Kalabagh and eventually through his iron rule over Punjab, as the sword arm of Ayub Khan. His son and my classmate, 'Muz'—as he was then known to us—was the silent type, not very bright or even good at games and hence rather diffident. He eventually became the Nawab when, ironically, his father was assassinated over an intra-family matter by his youngest son. Muzzafer was elected in the 1960s as Member of Parliament (MP) from Kalabagh, but was himself, like his father, also assassinated.

[1] Flute.

I became particularly friendly with Shahid Hosein and Riaz Mahmood, who were both a year senior to me and completed their HSC at the end of 1951, both graduating from Aitchison with outstanding results in the HSC. Shahid and Riaz were intelligent, articulate and witty, which provided opportunities for a conversation that moved beyond sports and girls, though such subjects were not necessarily excluded from our exchanges. Shahid and Riaz eventually joined me in Cambridge in our freshman year. Both of them remained my lifelong friends. Riaz tragically passed away in 2009 after a protracted struggle with cancer.

Aitchison College was laid out on a vast expanse of grounds along the Mall Road. Most of its structures, made up of brownstone, were dispersed across the estate. The Assembly Hall was a rather baroque pastiche of colonial and Islamic architecture that housed the offices of the principal and the school administration. The Assembly Hall was so named because every morning the school assembled there in their uniforms and blue turbans for a prayer and singing of the national anthem. Abdaal would occasionally read the prayer in his sonorous voice and on one occasion introduced, as a prayer, the famous invocation of Tagore from *Gitanjali*, "when the head is held high," which was a great favourite of his and was, I think, the school prayer at Doon School, where Abdaal studied prior to the Partition, before coming to Aitchison. In the State of Pakistan, this prayer was somewhat off-centre but was, at least in those days, still acceptable. I cannot imagine Tagore's immortal lines being read at an Aitchison College assembly today.

The school was structured around houses in the tradition of the British public schools. There was a junior school for boys in Classes 1–4. On graduation to senior school, the boys in Classes 1 and 2 were segregated into LJ House. Once they were promoted to Class 3 (known as M-1), the boys moved from LJ House into separate residences in Godley House and Kelly House (mine) and stayed on in residence until they left school after the HSC. This meant that each of these two senior Houses had a resident population of boys ranging from the ages of 13 to about 18. The Houses were the centre of social life because its residents lived and ate together and were under the discipline of the housemaster, assisted by house prefects drawn from the senior boys.

A significant section of the school, perhaps a third, were day students who went home every day after classes, returning only for games in the late afternoon. These boys usually had families with homes in Lahore and commuted to school every day. The day boys in senior school were assembled in Jubilee House. They constituted a living link between the resident students and city life in Lahore so that, unlike in St Paul's, Aitchisonians did not feel cut off from the mainstream of life in the country. However, as Aitchisonians largely came from the landed elite of Pakistan, they were a distinct group who were by virtue of class, cut off from the common folk.

Resident students were given leave to go off and stay with their relations over the weekend, so that from Saturday afternoon to Sunday evening, the school took on a rather empty look. I used to move to 45 Empress Road to spend the weekends at the Zaman household. As HSC boys, we also enjoyed the privilege of going out on any evening as long as we were back before 10:00 p.m. We often rode off on our bicycles to the Mall Road, where a number of cinemas showing western films were located on or around this central artery of Lahore.

Academic classes were held in a separate building, during the morning from around 8:00 a.m. to 1:00 p.m. Afternoons were reserved for siesta, which was a great luxury for me as no such facility had been on offer for me at St. Paul's. I mostly spent this time catching up with my reading, and particularly remember reading Margaret Mitchell's thousand-page epic *Gone with the Wind*, during those hot summer afternoons, lying in bed in my room in Kelly House, consuming a kilo of delicious fresh grapes.

We surfaced from our siesta around 4:00 p.m. for games, which included, depending on the season, hockey, cricket, athletics, swimming and tennis. Aitchison had the luxury of half a dozen playgrounds of which two were used for the school teams. The hockey ground, the Jaffer Memorial, was reputed to be the best-kept hockey pitch in Pakistan, at least in the days before synthetic pitches replaced grass. It was named after Mohammed Jaffer, an alumnus of the school who represented India, playing on the left wing in the 1936 Berlin Olympics. The ground was used for the trials for the selection of the Pakistan hockey team for the 1952 Olympics in Helsinki.

As a member of the Aitchison College hockey team, I played regularly on this ground and remember the luxury of its velvety sheen compared to the rather bumpy pitches of St. Paul's, where we had played all our games. Playing hockey in summer, even in the late afternoon, was no easy task as the temperature was in the 40s. At the end of the match, we felt as if we had been in a hot shower. Mercifully, the groundsman served us with buckets of *shikanjbeen*,[2] which, after a hard game, tasted like elixir.

After hockey, during summer, we went off to the swimming pool. The general students then showered, donned *salwar kameez*[3] and went for prayers in the school mosque. This was compulsory for the school, but optional for the HSC-level students. I rarely exercised this option so that my free time began after our swim. After their prayers, the boys went for dinner to the House dining room. However, all resident HSC students again had the luxury of a special dining room situated in our neighbouring Godley House. Here we were served somewhat better-quality food, usually measured by the occasional serving of 'English' dishes. However, the pleasure lay in a leisurely meal at the end of the school day, with friends of one's own age, where conversations ranged far and wide, from girls to politics.

Aitchison was never reputed for its academic standards. In my HSC class, no one had graduated from the Senior Cambridge class with a First Division. In contrast, at St. Paul's, six of our classmates, including myself, had first classes. Abdul Khaleque, who had like me, come into the HSC class from outside—from St Xavier's, Calcutta, which prided itself on its outstanding academic results—also had a first. Khaleque, who was in the science group of the HSC class, became my competitor for top academic honours in our class. To Khaleque's surprise, I went on to win the Churchill House Medal which went to the Aitchisonian who had the best

[2] Iced lemon juice.
[3] A type of suit worn by Panjabis with long shirt and loose trousers.

results in the final HSC exam. This achievement has earned me immortality in Aitchison, as the Assembly Hall has a number of plaques of winners of various prizes that includes a plaque for the Churchill House Medal.

At the HSC level, we were taught history by the Principal, G.M. Gwynn, who was an excellent teacher, with a degree from Oxford. While his classes were quite stimulating, they were something of a physical ordeal, particularly in the Lahore summer where Gwynn came to class, always wearing a Harris tweed coat. He did not approve of the use of fan but would, sportingly, toss a coin to determine whether it should be switched on or off. Since he frequently won the toss, we attended his classes with some trepidation and ended it, bathed in perspiration. The classroom climate notwithstanding, Gwynn equipped me with a good grounding in English history, covering the reigns of the Tudors and Stuarts. I also did a special history paper with him on the Age of Discovery, where I learnt a great deal about Pizarro, Cortés, Vasco da Gama and Magellan.

We were taught literature by our Kelly Housemaster, Monsieur Pinson, who was a painstaking if unexciting teacher. In his rather dry, unsmiling manner, he inducted me to the pleasures of Chaucer (*The Knights Tale*) Spenser (*The Faerie Queene*, Book 2), Shakespeare (*King Lear*, *Othello* and *Merchant of Venice*), the Lake Poets and Jane Austen (*Mansfield Park*). Pinson must have done his job well as my knowledge of these texts and some of the literary debates related to them still survives, if somewhat faintly, in my mind after all these years. Pinson used to run a small literary study circle for senior boys where we discussed books and poetry. I remember doing a reading of *Pickwick Papers* to the group that I could only complete with some difficulty due to my being convulsed with laughter at the antics of the 'fat boy'. Another plus point for Pinson.

Our teacher of economics and government—a Punjabi by the name of Aslam—was not on the permanent staff of Aitchison, and also taught at a local college. He taught us economics out of Sen and Das, a staple introductory course in the 'subcontinent', while for government, we were instructed from a textbook on government written by Ogg. Aslam's grasp of economics was as shaky as his grasp on English and he used to arouse much amusement in his class by his reference to Hugh Dalton—the famed Chancellor of the Exchequer in the first Labour Government of Clement Attlee—as 'Huff' Dalton. We were cruel enough to regularly ask the hapless Aslam questions about Public Finance, where Dalton's work was the standard text, to elicit a reference to 'Huff' Dalton.

One of the innovative features of extracurricular life at Aitchison was the institution of the Council of State, a sort of mock parliament for students. Two senior boys, as heads of their respective 'political parties', contested for elections with the senior school boys of Aitchison constituting the electoral college. In my second year, I contested this election, with the backing of my HSC colleagues, against Khaled Amir, also in Kelly House, who was backed by the students of the C-2, the Senior Cambridge class. It was an unequal contest because Khaled had been at Aitchison from junior school and had the campaign support of the numerically larger cohort of C-2 boys. In contrast, I had been at Aitchison for just a year and campaigned with the backup of the HSC class whose much smaller numbers could not be compensated by the oratory of Abdul Aziz Khan or the muscular support of Malek Muzzafer Khan. In spite of our superior eloquence on the hustings, I lost the election by a good margin.

With the Principal, Mr Gwynn as the Speaker, Khaled went on to become PM, while I was the Leader of the Opposition in the Council of State. This, as it transpired, was far and away the best position on the Council. The HSC team, drawing on their superior knowledge of economics culled from our casual readings of Sen and Das and on politics from Ogg, ran rings around Khaled and his team. Questions on how they would handle the 'fiscal deficit' left Khaled tongue-tied and reduced Asad Hayat, his campaign manager, to tears of frustration as he accused me of being an intellectual snob, which I was heartless enough to take as a compliment. It was good fun while it lasted and inculcated in me a lifelong appreciation of the advantages of the freedom enjoyed by those in the Opposition.

In those days, most boarding schools, built on the English public school tradition, tended to elevate sporting prowess over studies or other extracurricular activities, as a measure of achievement. In this, Aitchison was no different from St. Paul's. The top sportsman of our time in Aitchison was Perveze Hussain, who excelled in athletics and had he persisted, could have gone on to represent Pakistan in the Olympics. Perveze was tall and handsome, looking rather like Rock Hudson but having quite different tastes. His success with the ladies was quite legendary and appeared to have remained with him long after Aitchison. We became extremely good friends and remained so until his untimely and sudden death (due to cancer) in 2008.

Apart from Perveze, Aitchison produced a number of sportsman of distinction, the most eminent of whom has been the cricketer Majid Jahangir Khan and his nephew Imran Khan. In his memoir, Imran has observed that he learnt his cricket from his uncles Humayun and Javed Zaman, who were both my contemporaries, albeit some classes junior to me. At Aitchison, I played in the school hockey team with Humayun, where he played full back with outstanding ability. Even though Humayun was a cricketer of distinction, we assumed he would eventually represent Pakistan in hockey. Humayun and Sajjad Haider, who played inside right, were exceptionally good players and could hold their own, even playing at the school level, against Olympic-level players such as Latifur Rahman, and Neaz Khan, who played against the Aitchison College team, for their local club.

Many of the Aitchisonians came from the top landed families of West Pakistan so that their feudal fiefdoms provided them with safe constituencies. It was thus, not surprising that in later years, they entered political life as part of a family tradition. In Pakistan, elective office has and continues to be heavily influenced by where you stand in the feudal hierarchy. In the pecking order of Pakistani society and politics, being an Aitchisonian was equivalent to being from Harrow or Eton in relation to Tory politics in Britain. The Noons and Tiwanas expect to be elected from Sargodha, the Legharis from Dera Ghazi Khan and the Gilanis from Multan. It is not surprising that a plethora of Aitchisonians have ended up in high office in Pakistan. The highest of these has been Farooq Leghari, a contemporary of my younger brother Farooq in Aitchison, Oxford and, finally in the Civil Service Academy, who moved on to join the Pakistan Peoples Party (PPP). He was eventually elevated to serve as the President of Pakistan, during the second premiership of Benazir Bhutto, but ended up deposing her from office.

Apart from Farooq Leghari, other Aitchisonians who have made it into politics include the Baluch tribal chiefs, Balak Sher Mazari and his younger brother Sherbaz Mazari, who was the college prefect in 1950. Sherbaz has written one of the best political memoirs I have ever read that projects an extraordinarily insightful analysis of the Zulfikar Bhutto regime and its aftermath. Their contemporary at Aitchison was Khair Baksh Mari, another tribal chief from Baluchistan, who was elected as an MP and eventually led a tribal insurgency against the Pakistan State. Khair Baksh, a handsome man, in his Aitchison days was given the honorific of Robert Taylor, the Hollywood box-office star.

Another Aitchisonian two years junior to me, Hamid Raza Gilani, who was a member of the Ayub Khan-sponsored 'Convention' Muslim League, was elected to Parliament from Multan in the 1962 and 1964 elections. His nephew Yousaf Raza Gilani was elevated by President Asif Zardari to the position of PM of Pakistan. Shah Mahmood Qureshi, also from a leading family in Multan, with extensive family associations with Aitchison, was the Foreign Minister in Gilani's cabinet. Shah Mahmood's brother-in-law, my friend Ifi Bokhari, and his brother Zulfi were also politically active. Another brother-in-law of the Bokharis, Fakhr Imam, was elected Speaker of the Parliament during the time of President Zia-ul-Haq. When Fakhr Imam was the Speaker of the Parliament, as many as 40 Aitchisonians were sitting in Parliament and reportedly came together to influence the election of the then PM. A more colourful political player from Aitchison was my close friend Arif Iftikhar, the son of Mian Iftikharuddin—also an Aitchisonian—who published

Pakistan's leading English daily, *Pakistan Times*. Arif was a member of the left-leaning National Awami Party (NAP) and represented it in the 1964 Parliament during the Ayub regime.

Apart from Parliament, a number of Aitchisonians, such as Lieutenant General Alamdar Masood (who was the goalkeeper of the college hockey team in 1950) and Lieutenant General Ali Kuli Khan, have commanded high positions in the army and were, respectively, competitors for the position of Chief of Staff, with Pervez Musharraf. Others have distinguished themselves as businessmen (the Saigol brothers, Abdul Khaleque of the Amin Group, Asif of Hyesons) and even as journalists (Najam Sethi).

In my days at Aitchison, feudal society in Pakistan was at its apogee so that the ambience at Aitchison was one where its alumni expected to rule this society for ever. East Bengal was viewed as a remote colony in the same way as the students of Eton must have viewed the Indian empire. Bengal was seen as being inhabited by short, dark people, who spoke strange tongues. I remember my first exchange in the HSC dining room where, by way of conversation, one of my Punjabi colleagues remarked to me, "Why do you Bengalis breed like rabbits?" My even more provocative retort on the sexual tendencies of the Pathans and Punjabis ensured that my HSC classmates never again made snide remarks about Bangalis, at least in my presence.

It was not as if I was a hard-core Bangali nationalist at that time. I had until then only spent one month of my life in East Bengal and my emotional ties with Dhaka were rather nebulous. I recollect that when the Bengali Language Movement was taking place in 1952, I took little cognizance of this in Lahore. I remember having a conversation with my uncle Syeduzzaman and asking, rather naively, how was it possible for a country to have more than one national language. He sapiently educated me on the subject and informed me that Switzerland was a bilingual State with French and German as their national language, as was Canada, where both French and English were the national language.

There were relatively few Bangalis in Aitchison when I was there. Apart from Qamru, two other Bangalis in the HSC were

Munirul Islam from Dhaka, who was my direct contemporary but resident in Godley House, and Haroun-er Rashid, who came up a year later. I have lost touch with Munir after Aitchison but have kept closer contact with Haroun, who followed in my tracks by winning the Churchill House Medal in 1953 and then went on to do the Geography Tripos at Emmanuel College, Cambridge, graduating a year after me. Haroun and I remained good friends over the years, where he was particularly supportive in 1971, when I was campaigning in Washington on behalf of the Bangladesh Government to stop aid to Pakistan.

Another Bangali who made a mark in Aitchison was Zaheeruddin Khan, the son of A.K. Khan, the leading Bangali industrialist of that time. He was quite a few years junior to me and had initially been at St. Paul's, where he was a contemporary of Farooq's. He preceded me to Lahore and, during his tenure, distinguished himself as a long-distance runner and as a horseman, skilled in the sport of tent-pegging. These skills may seem rather difficult to digest for those in Dhaka who remember Zaheer's rather commodious dimensions, in his mature years as a business leader and eventually as a cabinet minister in the 1990s. But then how many would also imagine that I too was once a sportsman of some merit in my school days!

The world of Aitchison College in which I came of age cannot be divorced from the wider world of Pakistan, in which such elite establishments could prosper. Lahore in the 1951–52 period was a city still dominated by its feudal elite, though some from this class had graduated into the bureaucracy and were an integral part of the ruling elite made up of landlords, the armed forces and the nascent business elite. In the early 1950s, the feudalists of Pakistan still regarded the business elite with some disdain, though they were now sharing the space at Aitchison with Chinioti families such as the Saigols and the Amins.

The elite world of Lahore was centred around the elegant suburbs of Gulberg and the Canal Bank, extending into the even more opulent estates off the Mall Road, such as the residence of Mian Iftikharuddin at 21 Aikman Road. In those days, Lahore's traffic was light because relatively few families owned cars, so that the bicycle and tonga were the favoured means of transport, even for the middle class. The Mall was the centre of commercial life with a few well-known departmental stores and cinemas, which in those days when Bangladesh's jute exports were booming, could sustain a fair traffic of imported consumer goods. Anarkali was still a shopper's paradise, which catered to a multi-class customer base.

At Aitchison, our encounters with the general population of Lahore were limited to our commercial needs. Somewhere in 1952, the HSC class went out on a tour of parts of the NWFP. The tour started with an adventure. Our party was bundled into two multi-berthed first-class compartment. Just as the train was about to depart, an officious-looking rotund man, backed by some flunkeys, tried to muscle into our reserved compartment. Abdaal, aided by some of us, would have nothing of this and rather unceremoniously evicted him from our compartment. Lo and behold, at the first stop out of Lahore, Gujranwala, this same gentleman, backed by several policemen, turned up to have us arrested. It turned out that we had insulted the Additional District Magistrate (ADM) of Gujranwala, who in those days held life-and-death powers over citizens within his local domain. A combination of apologies from the master-in-charge of our party, Mr Akram, the school bursar, and his retailing of the fact that one of our fellow travellers, Malik Muzzafer Khan, happened to be the eldest son of the then Governor of Punjab, the feared Nawab of Kalabagh, saved us from an uncomfortable night in the local *hajjat*.[4] In Punjab of those days, in remote district towns such as Gujranwala, even a lowly ADM, in his own domain, could give anyone a hard time, before the forces of law or feudalism could come into play.

Our first stop in that safari was Abdaal's hometown of Mardan in the district of Charsadda, in the NWFP, where we were hosted by his eldest brother, Abdul Rahman Khan, known to us as dada. Abdul Rahman had, against all convention, married an Indian Christian. At their home, dada plied us with meals of astonishing variety, quantity and quality, which could only be digested by young men in their teens. We were then encouraged to work some

[4] Jail.

of this out of our system by visiting the nearby ancient Buddhist ruins at Takht Bahi.

From Mardan, we moved on to Malakand and then to Swat. These were tribal-dominated areas with their own rulers. The Wāli of Swat ruled this picturesque rural area with the landscape, if not the facilities of Switzerland, as an absolute monarch. Road traffic was disciplined, the people exceptionally courteous and, reportedly, crime rates were low. That this idyllic retreat would today spawn a fundamentalist uprising that could close girls' schools, drive women off the roads and fields and bring the culture of the Wahabis to this tolerant land seems, looking back to the 1950s, to be inconceivable. Apparently, whatever may be the undemocratic features of feudalism, an enlightened ruler can make all the difference.

During my first year at Aitchison, Qamru and I decided to visit Karachi and wrote to our *nana* Khwaja Nazimuddin, who was then resident in Karachi as the Governor-General of Pakistan. Our *nana* immediately invited both of us to come and spend a part of our summer holidays as his guests in the Governor-General's house. This exposed me to what passed for high life in those days. The Governor-General's house—by contemporary standards of ruling-class opulence—was quite modest, but to someone like me, whose view of life was rather more low-key, this exposed me to a life of some grandeur.

The Governor-General's house, located opposite the Sind Club, was spread out and surrounded by spacious lawns. Saifuddin, the younger son of my nana, who was the same age as me and a friend since childhood, then lived with his parents and studied privately. He was our companion and guide. He took me riding every morning with the Governor-General's bodyguards. This meant mounting those large whalers, twice the size of the ponies I had ridden in Darjeeling. I managed to get accustomed to this elevation in scale and became reasonably competent in managing these large, but highly disciplined creatures. The grounds had their own swimming pool and tennis courts that we patronized, but not too regularly as it was then midsummer. More time was spent playing table tennis in the verandah of the residence with Saifuddin and three of Pakistan's top paddlers, who had become good friends of Saif.

Karachi itself was still a *mufassil*[5] town with two main streets, Elphinstone and Victoria, with what passed for quality shops and cinemas showing foreign films. The new residential areas such as the Pakistan Employees Cooperative Housing Society (PECHS) on Drigh Road were just coming up, but the town in 1951, was not very different from what had been left behind by the British. What had changed was the demographics of the city on account of the big influx of refugees from India and the elevation of the city from a sleepy provincial capital into the capital of Pakistan.

I managed to see a bit more of Karachi after both my parents moved there. In those days, my father was floating between Calcutta and Dhaka in his new incarnation as a businessman. When Liaquat Ali Khan was assassinated in Rawalpindi in October 1951, the Muslim League, for quite devious reasons, decided to invite Khwaja Nazimuddin to step down from the position of Governor-General to assume the mantle of PM of Pakistan. This move was possibly part of a conspiracy being hatched by Ghulam Mohammed, the then Finance Minister; Col Iskandar Mirza, the then Secretary of the Interior; and General Ayub Khan, the Army Chief, to eventually capture power and overthrow the parliamentary system. Under the cover of propitiating the Bangalis, they hoped to keep Khwaja Nazimuddin as a pliant PM, while Ghulam Mohammed was elevated to the position of Governor-General, who retained considerable power under the 1935 Government of India Act inherited from the British Raj. As it transpired, Nazimuddin turned out to be less pliant than they expected. Eventually, in April 1953, Ghulam Mohammed used his powers as Governor-General under the Government of India Act, to dismiss Nazimuddin, even though he had just received a vote of confidence in the Parliament. Another Bangali, Mohammed Ali of Bogra, the then Ambassador to the USA, was summoned home to play the role of the Bangali stooge for this evolving conspiracy against democracy.

I do not intend to explore the historical circumstances surrounding my grand-uncle's political demise but to merely reflect on this

[5] District town.

from my perspective as a young man who was a bystander to significant historical events. When Khwaja Nazimuddin took over as PM, he invited my father to come over from Dhaka and become his Political Secretary. As my father had had no previous exposure to politics, it is not clear why Khwaja Nazimuddin entrusted him with this sensitive position. Possibly, he trusted my father and respected him for his good sense, even though he was no longer married to my nana's favourite niece, my mother. My father, thus, came over to Karachi and took up his position as Political Secretary to the PM, which he held until the dismissal of Khwaja Nazimuddin, following which he too was removed from his position. Around November 1951, my father arrived in Karachi, accompanied by his wife Shawkat Begum, and took up residence at 204 E.I. Lines.

Sometime early in 1952, my mother had decided to leave India and come over to Pakistan. As she had no home to go to, Khwaja Nazimuddin invited her to stay with him in the PM's residence in Karachi. My mother remained his house guest there for over a year throughout his remaining tenure as PM. During the summer holidays of 1952, I turned up in Karachi to visit my mother and joined her as a guest in the PM's residence, where I spent part of my summer.

The Zamans had also moved residence from Lahore to Karachi when my uncle was appointed as the Chief Accountant of the newly established Pakistan Industrial Development Corporation (PIDC). The PIDC—a public sector agency—pioneered the industrialization process in Pakistan, where industries were largely non-existent and its business community consisted largely of traders who had immigrated from India to Pakistan after the partition of the country.

Early in 1952, Saifuddin, who had not done too well in his exams through dependence on private coaching, had been sent off to join me and Qamru at Aitchison College. Saif entered the final-year matriculation class in 1952 and took up residence in Kelly House. At Aitchison, he demonstrated enormous sporting potential, representing the school in cricket, hockey, athletics, and became the school tennis champion. Having him at Kelly House was a special bonus for me. Qamru had also moved into Kelly House, as a resident, once his family moved to Karachi so that our family now commanded a significant presence in the House.

I spent part of the summer holidays of 1952 sharing my mother's room in the PM's house. I thus had the unique privilege of spending one summer in the residence of the Governor-General of Pakistan and another in the residence of the PM. Life in the PM's house was more like a family picnic, given that it had so many family members, at one time or another, in residence or visiting. The PM and my father, who both tended to work late, would usually drop in to join the family gatherings after 9:00 p.m. or 10:00 p.m. I remember participating in a family football match on the front lawn of the PM's house, where the younger ladies of the family were enthusiastic participants.

In the later part of our summer holidays, my mother, Saif and I travelled to the hill station of Nathiagali to stay with my grand-uncle Khwaja Shahabuddin, younger brother of Khwaja Nazimuddin, who had been a cabinet minister during the premiership of Liaquat Ali Khan but had later been appointed Governor of the NWFP. The Governor had access to a summer residence in this picturesque hill station, a thousand feet above the more popular resort of Murree. Both Saif and I were expected to put in some hard work for our forthcoming matric and HSC exams, which we did with due diligence. This, however, gave us time to play tennis every afternoon in the courts of the residence and enjoy the splendid cuisine provided under the guidance of my *nani*,[6] Begum Farhat Shahabuddin.

I remember, every evening, the two brothers, Nazimuddin and Shahabuddin, would hold long conversations over the phone in Bangla! This was designed to thwart the intelligence services of the army, who presumably tapped both their phones, to ensure that no Bengali political conspiracies were underway. It would be typical of the then Punjabi-dominated army not to have any Bengali-speaking agents to monitor the phones so that the evasive action of the two brothers may have served its purpose. Khwaja Nazimuddin indeed

[6] Maternal grandmother.

relied greatly on the political advice of his younger brother, who was generally more astute in such matters and far less trusting of his fellow politicians, than his brother.

All said and done, Nathiagali provided us with a splendid vacation. We also visited Murree and then, via a frightening downhill drive to Abbottabad, visited Farooq, my brother, then at Burn Hall School in Abbottabad. After spending a year at Aitchison, where he had kept indifferent health, my mother moved Farooq to the cooler climes of Abbottabad, where he stayed on until he completed his Senior Cambridge at the end of 1957.

The last few months of 1952 were spent back in Aitchison preparing for my final exams, which went rather well for me as I obtained the best results in the HSC from the school, which earned me the Churchill House Medal. By December of 1952, my life among the chiefs drew to its close. I cannot recollect any agonizing regrets or tearful farewells during my departure from Lahore, where I had spent a full and congenial two years, but I was glad to be moving on. I eventually reconnected with quite a few of my Aitchison contemporaries in Cambridge and remained in touch with some of them well after that, up to the emergence of Bangladesh. When I revisited Aitchison in the 1990s, after a passage of two decades, I felt no special excitement or nostalgia. I was happy to meet some of my Aitchisonian friends, now in their autumnal years, and to note that the passion and violence that permeated our abandonment of a shared sovereignty had not eroded the personal relationships I had forged with them in the days of our youth. This was somewhat unexpected as our paths had moved in quite different directions.

My involvement with the Bangali nationalist movement had taken some of my Aitchisonian friends by surprise, as I did not appear to them to be a rabid nationalist in my Lahore days and even at Cambridge. One of my HSC contemporaries invited me to a party at his home in Karachi, around 1969, just after I had returned from London and, semi-seriously, after imbibing a few hard drinks, charged me as to why I was so anti-Punjabi as he did not recollect that at Aitchison I had been at all victimized by my classmates. This was true enough, because at a personal level, I got on exceeding well with them and continued to do so even when I was chastising the excesses of the West Pakistani ruling class in my writings and speeches.

As the school year ended, I again travelled back by train with Saifuddin to Karachi. In winter, this was a much more pleasant journey than in the heat of midsummer. Once there, I moved in with my father at their official E.I. Lines residence, whence I had ample leisure to contemplate my post-school future. I spent part of this time learning to drive in a new De Soto car acquired by my father but still seemed to have surplus time on my hands. I remember accompanying my father to a New Year's Eve party at the Karachi Gymkhana Club ushering in 1953, where he ran into Huseyn Shaheed Suhrawardy, who was then leading the political opposition to the Muslim League government headed by Khwaja Nazimuddin. My father, rather optimistically, invoked his friendship from Calcutta days, with Shaheed Saheb and suggested that the New Year might serve to bring him politically closer to Khwaja Nazimuddin. As Shaheed Saheb was then building up the AL as a major opposition party, he must have greeted this sentiment with some scepticism. However, as it transpired, bigger forces were then conspiring to topple the whole edifice of democratic politics in which both Suhrawardy and Nazimuddin became casualties.

During that winter of 1952–53, my father, as the PM's Political Secretary, was engaged with providing inputs to the raging debate within the Basic Principles Committee (BPC) established by the CA to frame the Pakistani constitution. Key issues related to the wisdom of setting up an Ulema Council to ensure that no legislation was passed that would be repugnant to the tenets of the Holy Quran. An even more politically explosive debate addressed the issue of provincial autonomy and whether seats in the national parliament would be distributed among the provinces on the basis of population, which would have favoured East Bengal's demographic majority, or on the basis of parity in seats between East and West Pakistan, favoured by West Wing leaders. I remember my father borrowing my HSC textbook by Ogg on constitutional government to seek guidance in the matter. I was not greatly impressed by his choice of references. My own awareness and engagement with such political dramas being staged in Karachi, where my grand-uncle and father were at centre stage, remained shallow. This reflects that even at the age of 17, living in close proximity to major political events of the time, my political consciousness remained decidedly underdeveloped.

During this fallow moment in my life, my father advised me to seek guidance from Akhter Morshed—the eldest son of my uncle K.G. Morshed—who had just returned from London, where he had spent some years seeking to qualify as an actuarist. As I was unsure about what I wanted to do if I went abroad, Akhter provided me with some useful practical advice along with a few valuable lessons on the art of Latin American dancing where, during his London days, he had acquired some proficiency at the Coconut Grove, presided over by a Latino bandleader, Edmundo Ros. These skills were passed on to Saif and me in periodic jam sessions convened in the apartment of our mutual cousin Ayesha Shahabuddin, who lived at Ilaco House, an apartment block on Victoria Road, with her husband Sayeed, the third son of Khwaja Shahabuddin. Ayesha, who was one of the most lively, engaging and indeed beautiful woman I have ever known in the image of Sophia Loren, helped to brighten up our evenings in Karachi through these *hulla gollas*,[7] as she termed them.

Ever since our Ilaco House days, the beat of the bongo drums still stirs banked fires within me. Happily, whenever opportunity presented itself—which regrettably has become increasingly infrequent—Salma and now Rounaq have been enthusiastic partners in testing our moves to the rhythms of the Rumba and Cha-Cha. Our well-wishers would be surprised, perhaps even alarmed, to learn that even today Rounaq and I episodically visit the Sounds of Brazil, a club in downtown New York to practise our skills at the Samba.

[7] Noisy fun happening.

5

London: Imagined Realities

Sailing the High Seas

While I awaited my HSC results in Karachi learning to dance the Samba and Rhumba, I appeared to have no clear idea of what to make of my life. I had a vague idea that I wanted to go abroad but was obviously less committed to the goal of higher education than one would have expected from a person of my intelligence and academic achievements. My father deduced from my ambiguity on the issue of my future that all I wanted was to have an opportunity to spend some time abroad. He therefore suggested that I go to England for six to nine months to learn about the leather business and then return to Dhaka.

My father took the pragmatic view that a nine-month stay in London would get the 'craze for foreign' out of my system and could also be put to good use by enabling me to learn something about the leather business. My father had, after his retirement from the police service, acquired a 51 per cent interest in Dhaka Tanneries, the very first modern tannery to be set up in East Pakistan. Since my father, rather optimistically, thought he would spend a long time in Karachi as a Political Secretary, he hoped I would look after his interests in Dhaka Tanneries and could be better equipped for this task by a spell in London learning about the leather trade. To this end, he negotiated with a well-known leather trading company located in Bermondsey, London, B.B. Voss and Sons, to take me on as an unpaid apprentice. For reasons which to this day I cannot explain to myself, I uncomplainingly went along with this rather dismal prospect for my future.

I eventually set sail for London, on the Polish steamship MV Batory which, along with two of the Anchor Line vessels and the Lloyd Triestino Line of Genoa, provided maritime passenger services from Karachi to the UK and Europe. I remember being seen off for England by a large contingent of family members around mid-February 1953. I was accommodated in a four-berth cabin in the second class, which meant we were located in the lower decks of the boat. This was my first trip abroad as well as my first long-distance sea voyage, so it was something of an adventure for me. One could eat one's fill; play games, which included my winning the Batory's table tennis singles championship; and attend dances in the evening, though female dance partners were in short supply. I was joined at Bombay by two friends from St. Paul's, also travelling to the UK, which added to the congeniality of the voyage. One of my travelling companions on the Batory was the Bangali journalist S.M. Ali, then en route to London to learn the finer points of journalism. I became good friends with Ali in my initial years in Dhaka, where he had already established himself as a well-known journalist.

The voyage passed uneventfully with stops at Bombay, Aden, Suez and Gibraltar. We eventually docked at Southampton on the morning of 6 March 1953, the day after Stalin's death, which was made apparent to us when we noted the *Batory*'s flag flying at half mast. Thus began another and more decisive chapter in my life that opened in London but reached its summation in my life-changing three years at Cambridge.

Frognal and Football

After clearing immigration and customs at Southampton, passengers boarded the boat train to Waterloo station in South London, where we arrived at around 7:00 p.m. I was met by an official from the Pakistan High Commission, Mr Wali Mohommed, courtesy of my being the son of the Political Secretary of the PM. His presence was much appreciated as London on a cold, damp, March evening looked most unpromising.

Wali Mohommed took me by taxi to 30 Frognal, a four-storeyed boarding house, just off the Finchley Road at Hampstead NW 3. This was to be my home for the next seven months until I departed for Cambridge, which was then not on my cards. I was greeted at Frognal by a muscular, jolly, Irish landlady who, along with Wali Mohommed, kindly helped me to transfer four rather heavy suitcases to my room in the attic on the top floor. Two of these back-bending cases contained supplies of tinned Anchor butter, Kraft cheese, packets of refined sugar, bags of basmati rice and sundry other provisions. Pakistanis, then benefiting from an import surge, made possible due to a global boom in the price for our jute and cotton exports, believed that Britain was a land of austerity where sugar and all dairy products were rationed. My mother's apprehensions about my dietary constraints proved to be outdated as such rationing had largely been eliminated by the Tory government of Winston Churchill that had recently assumed office.

My first exposure to life in an English boarding house, a staple of British life, was not unpleasant. My room was spacious with its own washbasin. The central heating revolution was far from universal in those days so that my room was served by a coin-operated gas heater, which during the winter, required a regular supply of coins. Fortunately, in March, winter was in retreat so that I needed to feed the heater for only a few nights of my stay at Frognal. My weekly rent at 30 Frognal was a modest 4 guineas (one guinea was 21 shillings) that included breakfast and supper, a wholesome meal of rather indifferent quality.

The next morning, Saturday, I met my fellow tenants, distributed over four floors, which included three elderly ladies who were long-term boarders, an Irish gentleman by the name of Murphy, a Sri Lankan with whom I shared a table and a Ghanaian gentleman reportedly engaged in a relationship of some intimacy with the landlady. I immediately established amicable relations with the menfolk and eventually became friendly with the senior tenants.

In conversation with Murphy at breakfast, I informed him of my long-time interest in British football and my ambition to attend a football match. Murphy immediately offered to escort me to a

First Division League match of Chelsea at Stamford Bridge. Thus, within less than 24 hours of my arrival in London, I travelled by bus to Stamford Bridge, was helped by Murphy to pay 2 shillings and 6 pence at the turnstiles and at 2.30 p.m. was watching my first football match. The match did not linger in my memory as Chelsea was then languishing somewhere in the middle of the league table.

In the next few months, on my own initiative, I attended matches of Tottenham Hotspur at White Hart Lane, Arsenal at Highbury and travelled for an hour by bus to South East London, in the company of Sudarshan Sur, to the grounds of Charlton Athletic to see my favourite team, Manchester United, in action. Within my first three months, I even managed to travel to Wembley Stadium and purchased a black-market ticket at the cost of £1 to see England play Scotland. I remember that match because England's forward line included its legendary wingers Stanley Matthews and Tom Finney, renowned for their exceptional dribbling skills, the goal-hungry Tommy Lawton as centre forward and Frank Swift, an outstanding goalkeeper. My colleagues at work at B.B. Vos, were deeply impressed by my entrepreneurial skills in the service of soccer.

On that first evening in London when I exited Stamford Bridge, I was left on my own devices to navigate my way to Piccadilly Circus by the underground. Murphy had provided me with further guidance on this excellent medium of transport for travelling across London and had equipped me with a most user-friendly map of the underground. Once I was introduced to this extraordinarily serviceable means of travel, I never looked back and virtually from my first day, found that I could travel almost anywhere in London without losing my way.

The visit to Piccadilly was more in the nature of an adventure by a young man whose literary exposure had educated him to believe that this elegant street was the centre of the universe. I then had neither the resources nor the courage to taste its reportedly splendid cuisine or nightlife and merely gorged myself traversing the bright lights of Piccadilly and Leicester Square, gazing at the opulently decorated shop windows and exploring the first-run movies on offer, where I learnt that tickets at 5 shillings cost double of what was on offer in the neighbourhood cinema houses.

My first meal was out at Lyons Corner House as supper on Saturday night at 30 Frognal was traditionally substituted by lunch. I did not stay out late as I was still road-testing my skills on the underground, where I discovered that Finchley Road, my local station, was only a 9-pence ride from Piccadilly Circus on the Bakerloo line.

On my second day in London, which was a Sunday, I called up my uncle Khwaja Mohiuddin—the eldest son of Khwaja Nazimuddin—who had recently moved to London with his beautiful wife, Shireen, to work for Thomas de la Rue, the world's leading printer of currency notes. The Mohiuddin's lived in an apartment near Sloane Square, in South West London. When I enquired from the doorman at Mohiuddin's apartment as to the floor of his flat, I was advised to follow the smell of the curry. Apparently, Mohiuddin's cuisine had earned him instant recognition, courtesy of the culinary skills of his cook who had been trained by the DNF and could serve up most of the family delicacies. After being splendidly fed, Mohiuddin and Shireen drove me around parts of London and briefed me about survival strategies in the big city.

On Monday morning, I established connection with the local branch of Lloyds Bank at the corner of Frognal and Finchley Road, where my father was to remit £40 to me every month. I had frugally committed myself to withdraw £8 every Saturday, from which I met my rental obligations and used the balance on various miscellaneous expenditures that I faithfully recorded in account books, which I have preserved to this day. My ancient accounts reveal that in 1953, a Mars bar cost 6 pence and a big plate of fish and chips cost 2 shillings and 6 pence.

Bermondsey Days

After establishing my solvency, I set out to visit the office of B.B. Voss and Sons located in Bermondsey in South East London, the heartland of London's leather business. This involved a longish ride to London Bridge station, from where I descended down a stairwell to the leather district in Bermondsey. At the entrance to the street, there was a derelict bombed-out site of which there were quite a few disfiguring various parts of London. The area was bleak and radiated decay that did not encourage any casual strolls in the neighbourhood.

B.B. Voss and Sons was a long-established firm, one of several, which specialized in import of various forms of leather, mostly from India. My father had come to know its founder, B.B. Voss, who he hoped to interest in importing the products of Dhaka Tanneries. My father believed that a few months of unpaid apprenticeship with Voss would provide me with a good exposure of the trade while building up connections with a potential customer.

In the five to six months I spent at B.B. Voss, I did not learn much about the trade. I was mostly deployed as a ledger clerk helping out a friendly Scottish lady to enter the arrival and invoice records of consignments of leather coming into the warehouses of B.B. Voss from India. I was periodically invited to visit the warehouse next door, where the newly arrived consignments were stored in order to witness the sorting and grading of the consignments. This exercise was supposed to educate me on the varieties of product and quality of the imported leather. I did learn something of the business but did not get the impression that B.B. Voss were particularly interested in enhancing my expertise in this area. I was advised that if I aspired to learn about the fine points of the leather industry, I should enrol as a student at the Leathersellers' Technical College down the road from the office of B.B. Voss. I did visit the college, but it failed to enthuse me sufficiently to invest two years of my life in deepening my knowledge of the leather business.

As the days passed by, I commuted every morning from Finchley Road to London Bridge as did thousands of office-goers who however could live with this soul-deadening routine in the knowledge that this provided them with a weekly pay packet on Friday evening. Few such wage earners or their bosses felt any compulsion to work over the weekend where the two-day holiday was recognized as an inflexible part of the British way of life.

Sporting Summer

As a non-wage-earning prisoner of this work culture, I gradually came to recognize the pointlessness of my days in the insalubrious surroundings of Bermondsey. When the cricket season commenced at the beginning of May, I began to take a day off to watch the Australian touring team whenever they had a fixture in London. From my St. Paul's days, I had become a great lover of cricket, largely as a spectator sport, though I was a mediocre player. I had enhanced my knowledge of the game through regular access to the library of L.J. Goddard at St. Paul's and had attended occasional Test matches at the Eden Gardens in Calcutta and subsequently at the Lawrence Gardens in Lahore, when Pakistan entertained the Marylebone Cricket Club (MCC). When I took up residence in Frognal, I regularly visited the Hampstead Public Library, where I further enhanced my knowledge of the game, particularly after I discovered the inspirational, almost poetical cricket writings of Neville Cardus. For a reader of such cricket literature, Lord's—located at St. John's Wood just two stations away from Finchley Road—was a place of pilgrimage.

The touring Australian team, captained by Lindsay Hassett, was not quite up to the level of the invincible and possibly best ever team of 1948 captained by Don Bradman, on what was his last tour. However, many of the heroes of the 1948 tour such as Morris, Miller, Lindwall, Harvey and Tallon were still in their prime so that the series promised to be particularly exciting. When the touring team took on Middlesex, whose home was at Lord's, I took off several days from 'work' to watch Miller and Lindwall bowl at Denis Compton and Bill Edrich, the star batsmen for Middlesex and England.

In June, when the Second Test commenced at Lord's, I took four days off from B.B. Voss (Saturday was a holiday) to watch the full Test. This required queuing up at the entrance to Lord's from around 9:00 a.m. to secure entry through the turnstiles at a cost of 5 shillings, for a day's cricket that extended from 11:00 a.m. to 6:00 p.m. I remember that in this particular match, Miller and Lindwall almost bowled Australia to victory but were frustrated by a heroic stand involving Watson and Trevor Bailey, an all-rounder with a capacity to defend his wicket for long hours. England, led by Len Hutton—its first ever captain drawn from the professional ranks—won the series with a final victory at the Oval in South London, to which, as a strong supporter of Australia, I was an unhappy spectator.

Apart from my cricket watching, I had also taken time off at the end of June to travel to Wimbledon in South West London to watch the All-England Lawn Tennis Championships, the premier event in world tennis that lasted for a fortnight. Here, as at Lord's, if you queued, possibly from around 9:00 a.m., you had a good chance of getting in through the turnstiles, for a payment of 5 shillings that entitled you to standing room on the Centre and adjacent No. 1 Court. To witness the semi-finals and finals, one needed to queue up from the night before, which I deemed over and above my love for the game.

A most pleasant feature of the visits to Wimbledon was the opportunity, during the early rounds, to wander around, consume their famous strawberries and cream while watching matches on the outside courts. On my first visit, I remember watching my South Club nemesis, Ramanathan Krishnan, then only 16 years old, take a set off Mervyn Rose of Australia, then ranked fifth in the world.

The prospect of seeing many of the world's leading players in action was enormously tantalizing, so I took almost 10 days off from work, which persuaded my supervisor at B.B. Voss to conclude—what was already apparent to me—that there was little mutual benefit to be derived from my persisting with the charade that I was learning much about the leather trade in Bermondsey. My visits to London Bridge tended to become more infrequent and were effectively discontinued by the beginning of September, when I came to recognize that I should either return home or attempt to revisit my interrupted quest for higher education.

In Search of William Brown

Apart from my desultory efforts to apprentice in the leather trade and indulge my youthful enthusiasm for spectator sports, I gradually enhanced my acquaintance with a country that had for over a decade been a part of my literary imagination from the days I began reading *Film Fun*, *Beano* and *Dandy* comics around the age of seven. Much of that literary England, whether drawn from the world of Desperate Dan or Lord Snooty, or the more visible world of rural England embedded in my mind from Richmal Crompton's William books or the leisured upper-class world of Bertie Wooster and Lord Emsworth in the P.G. Wodehouse novels, was set in a more tranquil pre-war England. The England of 1953 bore only a passing resemblance to that bygone world. The London of the 1950s, apart from the bright lights of Piccadilly, Leicester Square and Oxford Street, was a dingy grey, still pockmarked with empty spaces devastated by the German Luftwaffe during their Blitz of London. A few new buildings were visible, but the ones that remained, including those that resonated with history, looked as if they needed refurbishment. In the fading winter months of March, this London tended to dampen my spirits. The arrival of spring and the Australian cricket team restored some of my enthusiasm for this land of my imagination where watching spring flowers bloom in Hyde Park and Regent's Park lifted my spirits.

A bus ride to the village of Uckfield in the undulating Sussex downs—to spend the day with my Aitchison College headmaster J.M. Gwynn—on a mellow summer's day in May, gave me my first exposure to the glories of the English countryside. Uckfield was much as I had imagined William Brown's village would be, but I was unsure if a brown gentleman from Pakistan could have fitted into this world.

During the languorous summer months, my stepmother, Shaukat Begum, then visiting London, managed to obtain passes for witnessing the coronation of Queen Elizabeth II and invited me to accompany her. Our passes entitled us to sit in stands erected outside Westminster Abbey, from where we were able to view the passage of the royal procession as it moved towards the Abbey. This was not quite the same thing as sitting in the Abbey as an eyewitness to the actual coronation ceremony, but it provided us with a sense of vicarious participation in a rare historic ritual.

My more exciting discoveries of life in London related to the world of theatre. In those days, an investment of 5 shillings could buy you a seat in the stalls of a matinee show in a theatre on Shaftesbury Avenue. My early ventures to the theatre included seeing David Tomlinson and Joan Collins star in *The Little Hut* and Peter Ustinov's great performance in *The Love of Four Colonels.* I subsequently discovered the Lyric Theatre in Hammersmith, where I witnessed a series of epic performances by Donald Wolfit of *King Lear*, *Othello*, *Macbeth* and Shylock in *The Merchant of Venice*, which remain embedded in my memory. Wolfit whetted my appetite for Shakespearean theatre of quality where I eventually saw Olivier and Vivien Leigh perform *Macbeth* at Stratford-upon-Avon and John Gielgud perform *King Lear*.

The Camel's Eye

Over the months, sundry friends and relations turned up in London with whom I whiled away some weekends. As the days went by, I found myself increasingly underemployed with time to reflect more deeply on the somewhat pointless nature of my existence. When Kamal passed through London around the end of August, en route to study for his BA at Notre Dame University in Indiana, USA, he stirred me from my soporific existence by encouraging me to aim higher than Bermondsey. Kamal had stood first in the intermediate exam in Dhaka, so his college, Notre Dame, ensured that he received a full scholarship to their parent university in the USA, from where he graduated with a degree in Economics within two years, at the age of 18. He then won a scholarship to do his MA in Economics at Michigan University but eventually opted to move to Queen's College, Oxford, to study for his BA (Hons) in jurisprudence.

Day trips to Cambridge and Oxford, where I met friends already up at the University, had further diverted my thoughts towards reviving my educational aspirations, but I was still undecided on any decisive course of action. I had not been encouraged in my endeavours after a conversation with the then Pakistan High Commissioner in London, Mirza Hasan Ispahani, the father of my St. Paul's colleague Isky Ispahani. I met him at the Pakistan Independence Day reception on 14 August, where he responded to my queries about admission to Cambridge by observing "Young man, it is easier for a camel to pass through a needle's eye than for you to get into Cambridge." My urge to restore some purpose to my life eventually set me off on my life-changing journey that began at Cambridge University. But this safari was no less the product of chance than my initial voyage to England.

6

Cambridge: The Transformative Years

Changing My Destiny

The redirection of my destiny was set on a Sunday afternoon in October 1953 in front of a red postbox just down the road from 30 Frognal. I stood poised before that red box, a letter in hand, addressed to the Master of Trinity Hall, Cambridge. It was a letter written by my grand-uncle Khwaja Nazimuddin, requesting the Master to consider the candidacy of his grand-nephew for admission to Trinity Hall, to read for the Economics Tripos at Cambridge. There was nothing exceptional about such a letter since Oxbridge academic culture, in those days, attached much value to the old school tie as a serviceable measure of whether a person was suitable for admission to their ancient colleges. It helped if you were academically qualified, but this was not an essential case. One only had to see the procession of brain-dead public school grandees parading around Cambridge outside the Pitt Club on Trinity Street in their bow ties, tweed jackets and cavalry twills, to appreciate that your family tree could comfortably compensate for the Third Division in the Cambridge School Certificate exam.

That I should indeed have been banking on a letter from Khwaja Nazimuddin was hardly flattering to my intellectual self-esteem. As it turned out, I had indeed managed a 'first' in the Cambridge School Certificate exam at St. Pauls and won the Churchill House Medal at Aitchison College for the best Cambridge HSC result in the college. My academic qualifications were thus, rather above the average for many undergraduates then in residence at Cambridge so that, on merit, one should not have been invoking family connections to get into Trinity Hall in the way that most Pakistanis of that generation tended to get into Oxbridge.

Beginning my academic career with an act of nepotism owed, in some measure, to my father's misperception of my career choices. The fact that my presence that Sunday afternoon in October, before the red postbox, happened to be one day before the new academic session at Cambridge for 1953–54 was about to begin, was part of the problem. I, in fact, had this letter from my grand-uncle in my possession, for the last several months, as a sort of capital asset.

Khwaja Nazimuddin had, as we have noted, studied at Trinity Hall before World War I. My grand-uncle may not have done much, when at Cambridge, to immortalize himself, but he did go on to become both a member of the Viceroy's Executive Council and the CM of Bengal in undivided British India, which according to the values of Oxbridge, were not inconsiderable achievements. He had, for his loyal services to the Raj, also been knighted and used to be known as 'Sir Nazim'. He renounced the title at the orders of his leader Qaid-e-Azam, Muhammad Ali Jinnah, who was at that stage of the Pakistan movement, keen to demonstrate his displeasure at the actions of the Raj. However, 'Sir' stays with you all your life, however publicly you may renounce it, so my father and other loyal friends of my grand-uncle continued to address him as 'Sir Nazim' until the end of his days.

The high office held by my grand-uncle must have helped my uncle Fayyaz Alam to get into Trinity Hall just after the World War II. Fayyaz too was no academic genius, but he had, like me, been to St. Paul's, whose rector, L.J. Goddard, was also an alumnus of Trinity Hall. But I imagine it was his uncle's (Khwaja Nazimuddin) links with Trinity Hall and his position as CM of East Bengal that saw Fayyaz into Trinity Hall.

As Fayyaz went to Cambridge, Khwaja Nazimuddin had in fact graduated to become Governor-General of Pakistan at the death of Jinnah in 1948 and had then stepped down to become PM of Pakistan at the assassination of Liaquat Ali Khan in October 1952. It was when he was PM that Trinity Hall finally decided to honour Khwaja Nazimuddin by electing him as an honorary fellow.

However, when he wrote that historic letter on my behalf to the Master of Trinity Hall, he was an ex-PM, having some months before been unceremoniously evicted from office.

Khwaja Nazimuddin while being a defunct PM was still a living Fellow of Trinity Hall. My suspicion is that a letter written by him as an ex-PM, rather than as a sitting PM, probably carried more weight with the Master of Trinity Hall. To have denied a request from a person, an alumnus elected as Fellow when being PM, would have been bad form, now that he was no longer holding high office. It is this particular sense of fair play that was perhaps one of the most endearing features of ancien régime British values. However, as I stood before the Frognal postbox, I was less confident about the relevance of those old values of sportsmanship and merely felt ridiculous.

I have already observed that my cousin Kamal Hossain had momentarily revived my nostalgia for higher education. However, it was not until my other cousin Kaiser Morshed arrived in London at the beginning of October 1953, en route to read law at St. John's College, Oxford, that my banked fires for university education were fully ignited. Kaiser's father, my uncle K.G. Morshed, and his daughter Mariam (Minta) had, some months earlier, moved into 43 Maresfield Gardens, just round the corner from my digs at Frognal. Kaiser was spending a few days with his father, storing up on woollen long johns, his father's staple for survival in the English winter. I was, thus, spending all my time with Kaiser, who managed to disturb my self-imposed acceptance of a life without higher education.

If there is any one person whom I must attribute my commitment to an academic life, of all people I have known, I must really register my debt to Kaiser. I have always rated Kaiser, along with Amartya Sen, as one of the finest minds I have known. In our Calcutta days, Kaiser's intelligence, his erudition, his capacity to make things of the mind exciting left me in some awe of him. At St. Paul's, while I was one of the academic stars, I did not think of myself as an intellectual. Kaiser was, for me, an exotic creature whose outstanding academic results at St. Xavier's were always an incitement to superior intellectual effort, while his much wider erudition, even if he was two years older than me, inculcated a yearning in me for things of the mind.

It was Kaiser, who in a few days, revived my suppressed hunger for further education by not only exciting me about the prospects of being an undergraduate at Cambridge but challenged me to question the narrow limits that had been imposed upon my own future. It was at Kaiser's instigation that I wrote a letter to the Master of Trinity Hall seeking a place at Cambridge. I padded the missive with some quite futile excuse for applying so late but enclosed Khwaja Nazimuddin's letter as about the only safeguard against the letter not ending up in the wastepaper basket of the Master. However, I had yet to post this letter. At Frognal that afternoon, I remember telling Kaiser and Minta that I felt like a horse's arse sending such a letter to the Master of Trinity Hall a day before the new academic year commenced. I recollect Kaiser, looking manic, saying "put it in, you have done crazier things" and Minta, offering her million-dollar smile, saying "what have you to lose." So in it went and two days later I had a letter in reply from the Master, inviting me to come up to Cambridge and call on him at Trinity Hall.

I remember travelling up to Cambridge on a day return ticket, in a rather life-and-death frame of mind, thinking that I would be put through an incredibly challenging interview. The Master met me in his lodge along with the senior tutor C.W. Crawley. The meeting was rather cryptic. If I remember, as I entered the Master's study, without too many preliminaries, I was told by him that they had decided to admit me into Trinity Hall for the commencing academic year. However, given the lateness of the hour, I had to live in outside 'digs' rather than in college. As I moved to leave, the Master enquired politely after the health of my grand-uncle. This, I suspect, was to let me know why I found myself a first-year student at Trinity Hall in the autumn of 1953. That debt to my grand-uncle remains unredeemable because it changed the course of my life.

As I travelled back to London in a rather dazed frame of mind, I began to think of more mundane issues such as what my father would say and, more to the point, would he pay my bills at Cambridge. In those days, incredible as it may seem today, a full year at Cambridge University, including tuition and college fees along with all other costs of spending a year in Cambridge, came to £630. The rupee was then worth around Rs 5 to the pound sterling, so that a year at Cambridge cost around Rs 3,150. This was equivalent to a month's salary of a senior Pakistani civil servant and hardly a crippling claim on middle-class finances, even in those days. By way of comparison, a year at Cambridge today comes to around five times the annual wage of a secretary to the Government of Bangladesh. However, I had no knowledge of my father's financial status or indeed his reaction to my postponing my commitment to Dhaka Tanneries.

I sought the advice of my stepmother, Shaukat Begum, who was then visiting London. She, may her soul rest in peace, gave me some wise advice, "Never have any regrets in life, go to Cambridge if this is what you want to do." She promised to intercede with my father who uncomplainingly accepted my decision.

Introduction to Trinity Hall

Thus, it came to pass, that I bade farewell to B.B. Voss and arrived as a first-year Tripos student at Cambridge, two days after the commencement of academic year 1953–54. I was hardly friendless at Cambridge, which was replete with my Aitchisonian friends. But, my first mentor at Cambridge was Amal Bose, introduced to me by C.W. Crawley. Amal was into his third and final year, reading Economics but readily assumed a mentoring role in educating me on life at Cambridge. I remained friends with Amal for the next 38 years until he died of cancer in Washington D.C., where he had settled after he retired from a career at the World Bank. Amal had somehow managed to attain middle age at birth and tended to take life seriously. This meant always wearing a tie, always carrying an umbrella and never laughing out loud. But he remained a good friend, loyal, sympathetic and a repository of sensible advice, with whom everyone felt safe. In a society that favoured flamboyance, Amal's low-key approach to life would have normally kept him in the corner. But he managed to keep himself publicly engaged and ended up as President of the Cambridge Majlis, whence he brought me in as a Committee member, thereby launching me into public life at Cambridge.

Apart from Amal, I cannot say I made too many lifelong friends at Trinity Hall. Though this list included Ramzan Ali Sardar, who came up to the Hall the same year I did, from the Mathematics Faculty at Dhaka University where he was already a teacher. Ramzan was rather older than the average undergraduate and so felt a bit of an outsider at Cambridge. He spent some of his time at Cambridge with two other teachers from Dhaka University, who were closer to him in age. One of these was Shahabuddin, who was studying for the Law Tripos, and went on to become Dean of the Law Faculty at Dhaka University at the time that Salma was a Senior Lecturer in the faculty. The other senior contemporary was Habibur Rahman, who ended up as Professor of Mathematics at Rajshahi University. Habib was eventually brutally murdered by the Pakistan army at Rajshahi in 1971. I would occasionally drop in on Ramzan in his rooms at Trinity Hall and thereby catch up on events in Dhaka about which I then knew little. Ramzan went on to become a Wrangler, the title given to those who earn a 'first' in the Maths Tripos at Cambridge. He returned to Dhaka University in triumph and spent his life there, eventually retiring as a Professor in the Mathematics Department.

I made some Sri Lankan friends at Trinity Hall; Sunita Jayawickrame came up the same year as I did to read Economics. We both played table tennis for Trinity Hall, a rather stronger bond than our economics. Sunita spent most of his professional life as the Secretary General of the Chamber of Commerce in Colombo. Sunita and I attended a weekly tutorial with Peter Bauer at Caius College, where we were joined by Nestor Pierakos, a vocally anti-communist Greek, from a wealthy family then settled in Alexandria, Egypt. Apart from Sunita, I came to know Ranji Salgado, who also read economics and ended up at the International Monetary Fund (IMF) via the Central Bank of Sri Lanka. Finally, there was Ranjan Amarasinghe, who got a first in the Law Tripos and seemed to hold great promise as a future Chief Justice of Sri Lanka but settled for becoming Legal Counsel at the World Bank.

Another friend, courtesy of Amal, was Austin Arnold, whose father had served in the British High Commission in Pakistan. Austin was then going through a Moral Re-armament (MRA) phase, which provided for rather sterile arguments over coffee, resisting Austin's futile efforts to convert me to MRA. Austin ended up with the International Trade Centre in Geneva, where we met periodically in Dhaka, Bangkok and Geneva on our mutual travels.

Trinity Hall was a small, boutique college, located in the shadow of the more famous Trinity College. The Hall had traditionally, been reputed as a college for turning out lawyers and divinity scholars, where economists received short shrift. Since the college then had no economist as one of its resident fellows, anyone who read for the Economics Tripos had to be farmed out to other colleges for supervision. In my first term, I was accordingly tutored by P.T. Bauer, a Fellow of Caius College, who Amartya Sen regards as the finest development economist then teaching at Cambridge. These credentials were less apparent to me in our first encounter when my ideas on both economics and politics were unformed. My encounter with Bauer was short as, in the next term, the Trinity Hall nomads were assigned to a younger economist, Malcolm Fisher, and later to Mike Farrell, an econometrician. This cavalier treatment by the Economics Faculty towards my education as an economist was rather frustrating. Therefore, in my final year, I decided to take the law into my own hands and requested Joan Robinson to be my tutor, which she agreed. This enterprising act by me was accepted without demur by both Trinity Hall and the University Economics Faculty.

I cannot say that a great deal of my Cambridge life centred around my college or that it inspired any enduring loyalties from me. About the only distinguished contemporary I remember was Nicholas Tomalin, who became President of the Union when I was at Cambridge and went on to earn fame as an intrepid journalist with *The Sunday Times*. I never knew him at the Hall and only met him once in 1971 when he covered the Liberation War in Bangladesh with great passion. He became, if I recollect, a fatal casualty of the war in Lebanon initiated by the Israeli invasion in 1981. Other friends I made in the Hall were on the hockey field where I played for the college without too much distinction. One of these was Maharaj Kumar Jai Singh, younger brother of the Maharajah of Jaipur, who used to play alongside me in the Trinity Hall hockey team. He was a jolly fellow, not too interested in academic pursuits and ended up transforming Jaipur's stately palaces into five-star tourist resorts.

The Hall was not particularly renowned for its intellectual life and has, to my knowledge, contributed few scholars of distinction. Trinity Hall did however bring in the distinguished constitutional lawyer Sir Ivor Jennings to succeed Mr William Dean—the same who brought me into Trinity Hall, as Master. As Jennings had advised Pakistan on its constitution making, I used this as an occasion to meet him and invite him to address the Cambridge Majlis during the tenure of my presidency in the Michaelmas term, in 1955.

I lived only a year, my second, in college in first-floor rooms off the main quad of Trinity Hall. It was a longish way from the toilet that made life rather uncomfortable in winter. I never did develop the courage or skill to use the porcelain basin placed strategically under my bed, by Benny, our staircase attendant, known as a 'scout', to address emergencies on a winter's night. I preferred to commute to the toilets in the common bathrooms several staircases away. When I visit the Hall, which I do from time to time over the last 40 years, I do so without much nostalgia. I, thus, did not make too strong an effort to get Babar in there when he was admitted to Cambridge on a scholarship, to do his MPhil. This did, however, disturb my sense of continuity since Babar would have been the fourth generation from our family to go up to Trinity Hall in the footsteps of Khwaja Nazimuddin.

Old Friends in a New Town

Outside of the Hall, life at Cambridge was eventful and exciting. I already had a community of friends from Aitchison and at least one Paulite, my Rajput friend Arjun Pramar, who was supposed to study medicine at John's but ended up reading philosophy. Samiran Nundy, who had an outstanding academic record at St. Paul's, came up as a first-year undergraduate, during my last year, to read medicine, but beyond mentoring him, rather inadequately, on his arrival, I did not have much to do with him. Samiran has since gone on to become a distinguished surgeon in New Delhi, specializing in gastroenterology and is much sought after by the media as a commentator on medical issues.

Cambridge was more heavily populated with Aitchisonians with whom I kept in rather closer contact, as I had more recently studied with them in Lahore. At that time, Aitchisonians at Cambridge included Abdul Aziz Khan (Abdaal to his friends), who moved from Kelly House to Trinity College just next to Trinity Hall; Aziz Sarfraz, who was at Downing; Irshad Abdul Qadir, who was at Emmanuel and a year ahead of me; Shahid Hossain at Sidney Sussex and Riaz Mahmud at Fitzwilliam, both of whom read economics.

Riaz and Shahid were the two Aitchisonians who were initially closest to me, have since remained my closest friends. For financial reasons, as they then claimed, both left Cambridge after their first year. Shahid left to work for Lever Brothers in Karachi and Riaz to join Pakistan Tobacco. This was sad for me as we had become inseparable during our first year. Shahid had rooms at Sidney Sussex College, but Riaz was stuck in a non-residential college, Fitzwilliam. Leaving Cambridge after just a year was tragic for them as they were both ideal Cambridge material.

Shahid had a really agile and creative mind, and we could chat together for hours on end. Riaz had a more robust attitude to life, radiating warmth and integrity. His recent passing due to cancer was especially painful for me. Shahid has carried the hurt of his withdrawal from Cambridge through his life. His wife, Yasmeen, made up for this. She was Salma's contemporary in Cambridge, where she read English and once confided to Salma that her countrymen appeared to be a poor lot if regarded as prospective matrimonial material. Little did either of them know with whom they would eventually share their lives.

Abdaal was no less close to me, but he decided to try his luck with the Pitt Club set into which he moved with great facility and graduated his wardrobe from Ranken's in Lahore to Anderson & Sheppard of Savile Row. With his impeccably tailored clothes, good looks, polished accent and inexhaustible fund of stories about the Raj, he rapidly made it to the Pitt Club without ever having been to Eton! I dropped in on him from time to time in his digs off Trinity Lane and, except for the hazard of running into one of his Pitt Club gang, enjoyed a good gossip about Pakistan.

Abdaal moved on to join the Pakistan Foreign Service (PFS) in the same batch as my cousin Kaiser, a career for which he was eminently suitable. I met him for the last time when I was visiting Kuala Lumpur, where he was into his final posting as Pakistan's High Commissioner, and found that the passage years had not disturbed the warmth of our friendship. Unfortunately, he was in poor health and appeared deeply unhappy with the course of his private life. He passed away shortly after his retirement and return to Islamabad.

The Aitchisonian and Cantabrian with whom I have eventually retained the longest association was Syed Iftikhar Ali Bokhari, Ifi to his friends. Ifi's claim to fame at Aitchison was his skill as a cricketer that earned him the captaincy of the college cricket team. We all believed he would be Aitchison's first Test cricketer since the senior Nawab of Pataudi, who had captained the Aitchison team before going on to captain the Oxford University team. Ifi was an opening bat in the Geoff Boycott mould, dour yet elegant and a prolific run-getter. Regrettably, and quite unfairly, as many of us believed, Ifi failed to get his cricket blue at Cambridge, even though he did turn out several times for the University. He played regularly for the second team of the University, the Cambridge Crusaders, where his high scores earned him an invitation to play for Cambridgeshire, whence he topped the Minor Counties batting averages.

Ifi read engineering at Caius College, though he subsequently did not pursue this as a profession. At Aitchison, we had known each other rather casually, but up at Cambridge, we became good friends. He was a generous, affectionate person, and quite well informed, in a non-partisan way, about Pakistani politics, a subject over which we had long chats over coffee. In later years, when visiting Lahore from Dhaka, when I did not stay with Arif Iftikhar, I often stayed with Ifi in his family home at Wazir Ali Road, just off the Mall Road. Even when I stayed elsewhere, I unfailingly met Ifi on my visits to Lahore, and he soon became my main source of knowledge on Punjab politics. Several of my pieces in *Forum*—"Journey to the Heartland"—for example, were derived from Ifi's intimate knowledge of the Byzantine intrigues that made up the politics of Punjab's feudal rulers.

In my days as the bane of the Pakistani ruling classes, when I would descend, in Lahore, to participate in some seminar or the other, Ifi was often my host, chauffer and cheerleader at the particular seminar. He reminded me of this when I met him after a lapse of 22 years, during a visit to Lahore in November 1993 to attend the third South Asian Dialogue. He was unchanged in appearance and personality, and the warmth of his greeting, even though he had greyed, retired from playing cricket and had served as a Senator in Pakistan's Parliament, was undiminished. In subsequent visits to Lahore, I have continued to enjoy his hospitality and depend on him to reconnect me with an aging cohort of my Aitchisonian contemporaries.

Remembering Arif

In October 1955, Arif Iftikhar turned up at John's to read economics. I had known Arif at Aitchison, where he was a year junior to me, but I then only knew him as the cousin of Shahid Hosein. Even in his Aitchison days, Arif was a rather flamboyant figure. His father,

Mian Iftikharuddin, a zamindar from Baghbanpura in Kasur, was one of the richest men in Lahore and lived in a magnificent house at 21 Aikman Road, a short distance from Aitchison. Mian Sahib owned the famous *Pakistan Times*, a paper with a left orientation, which was, far and away, Pakistan's best daily newspaper. He sat in the Parliament, as one of two members of the Azad Pakistan Party, founded by him with Sardar Shawkat Hayat, another rich landlord from Wah, the son of Sir Sikander Hayat. Mian Sahib was known as the 'red' landlord. The contradiction between his radical views and his lavish lifestyle was one of the staple jokes of Pakistani politics. For all his contradictions, Mian Sahib was a genuine supporter of a progressive, secular Pakistan and invested a good part of his fortune in backing such causes.

Arif inherited his father's political views but was not taken very seriously at Aitchison. When he turned up at Cambridge, I met him again, more as Shahid's cousin, than as a new light on the radical front. I had by then begun to move to the left in my thinking, more under the persuasion of the weekly *New Statesman* as edited by Kingsley Martin and reading Nehru's autobiography and his book *The Discovery of India*, than by reading *Das Kapital* or the *Daily Worker*. Nehru's life story had resonated with me for its narrative of how a person from his elite background evolved into a committed political activist, motivated by a mission to transform Indian society.

Arif took up residence at St. John's College. His bookshelves were stocked with hard-core Communist literature from Lawrence & Wishart and the less scholarly works of the Foreign Languages Publishing House in Moscow, eulogizing Stalin and talking of the 'great conspiracy against Russia'. Arif's knowledge of Communist history or Marxist theory was rather sketchy. But he read his red hagiography with great diligence, as I observed from his underlining in red ink of his books, with passages of special import marked 'IMP' or 'V. IMP', which I remember with clarity and some sadness at the memory of what eventually happened to Arif.

Arif at Cambridge, however, became his own legend. He held his radical views with great passion and argued it with extraordinary fluency as well as wit. It was no surprise that his flamboyant style went down rather well at the Cambridge Union, where he established himself as an outstanding debater and eventually rose to become Vice President. Unfortunately, he was defeated in the contest for the Presidency of the Union, when the Cambridge Tories closed ranks to keep him out.

In my time, Arif's habit of rising in time for lunch, which he ate at either the Kohinoor, Taj or Bombay, all in the vicinity of John's, was again part of his legend. Rising when he did, obviously did not leave much scope for attending lectures, writing tutorial essays or preparing for exams so that academically Arif barely kept his head above water and remained on the margins of being sent down. His unpunctuality was as famous as his casual approach to hospitality. Having invited my cousins Kamal Hossain and Kaiser Morshed, who were both students at Oxford, to visit him in Cambridge, he took off for Pakistan. One apocryphal story has it that he invited someone to lunch at the Kohinoor, told him to wait at the entrance of John's while he crossed the road to buy cigarettes and then caught a taxi to Heathrow for a flight to Pakistan.

Whatever be his eccentricities, Arif was, in Cambridge, one of my closest friends. Our politics bound us together, though I did not share his rather unquestioning faith in the infallibility of the Soviet Union, which always made him taunt me about my *New Statesman*-ish version of socialism. I can never forget Arif's soulful reference to some significant moment in Soviet history or current event where he would hold me and say in a voice loaded with emotion *Yeh toh barih cheese hai,*[1] and once when I insensitively snorted derisively at his burst of emotion, he actually wept at what he felt was my cynical attitude to life.

After returning home from Cambridge, much was expected from Arif. Tragically, the untimely death of his father appeared to have a more lasting impact on Arif than we imagined. When Field Marshal Ayub Khan seized the *Pakistan Times* in 1959 under a martial law diktat, Mian Iftikharuddin was traumatized and suffered several

[1] This is really a big thing.

heart attacks before he died in 1962, a broken man. Arif never rose to Mian Sahib's stature and, without his father's stabilizing influence, remained a shooting star. Unlike his father, Arif never could handle both his great wealth and his radical politics. His self-indulgent lifestyle, which at Cambridge was accepted as an affectation, annoyed party colleagues who were called to meetings at 21 Aikman Road or his suite at the Hotel InterContinental when he came to Dhaka, to attend meetings of the NAP then led by Maulana Bhashani, and were then kept waiting for two to three hours while Arif slept late and breakfasted at leisure.

Arif peaked politically as a member of the second Ayub parliament where, with his eloquent command of the English language, he established himself as a match for Zulfikar Ali Bhutto, who tended to fancy himself as the Demosthenes of the House. Arif remained with the pro-Peking NAP, which was a depleting political force in both wings of Pakistan, and he eventually lost in his family constituency of Kasur to a PPP candidate in the 1970 election. He subsequently joined the PPP after the 1970 elections but had obviously missed his opportunity with Zulfikar Bhutto. He died prematurely in the mid-1980s, a person with an unfulfilled promise who had the potential to become a political figure of some consequence.

I visited 21 Aikman Road in November 1993, after a gap of some 22 years. It looked deserted and a bit shabby. In the dining room, which once hosted magnificent parties, I found Begum Iftikharuddin sitting alone. She had aged, had been injured from a fall but appeared more injured in her soul. The menfolk closest to her had departed this world, leaving her to live out her life alone in Aikman Road. Her mind was now unsteady, and she seemed to remember me rather episodically, associated with recollections of better days when I used to engage in passionate political arguments with Mian Sahib or Arif in their famous library or at the dining table at Aikman Road, with Begum Sahiba observing us with a bemused smile. I fled away from the ghosts that haunted the house and was seized by an ineffable sadness at the vanished glories, hopes and vision for the future, which lay entombed within its once magnificent portals.

Pakistanis at Cambridge

Apart from Arif, I cannot claim to have been particularly close to the other Pakistanis at Cambridge but kept up a hearty camaraderie with them, mostly through the Pakistan Society, where I was a member without aspiration to high office. At that time, there was some natural law of institutions at work that ensured that the Cambridge Majlis and the Pakistan Society rarely flourished together. This, to a point, also applied to the Indian society as well, though less so. I am not sure why this was, but this law of nature has persisted to this day and no doubt has something to do with the time and energy the South Asians at Cambridge were willing to invest in local concerns. In my day, the Majlis was the society of choice for the South Asians and the Pakistan, and Indian society served as lesser orders of preference. This raised occasional questions about our patriotism, but we liked to think of ourselves as statesmen who created a community of South Asians that still persists over the space of five decades. However, my Majlis preoccupations did not prevent me from maintaining a presence with the community of Pakistanis at Cambridge.

Among the non-Aitchisonian Pakistanis, I became good friends with Shaharyar Mohammad Khan, the grandson of the Nawab of Bhopal. Our family had, through Uncle Haider, had long connections with Bhopal from whom we learnt to call Shaharyar, *Mian*.[2] Shaharyar was one of the most lovable human beings I have known, full of decency, loyalty and warmth. Shaharyar joined the PFS, where he was a batchmate of Abdaal's and my cousin Kaiser. He had an outstanding diplomatic career and retired as Foreign Secretary of Pakistan.

Perhaps the most distinguished Pakistani at Cambridge in my time was Professor Abdus Salam who, after obtaining a first class in physics, had been elected a Fellow of St. John's College. In those days, he both taught and engaged in research that would ultimately

[2] A family name and title of nobility used by Muslims in the Indian subcontinent.

earn him a Nobel Prize. However, as a faculty member, he remained a somewhat remote figure to us undergraduates but was usually available to attend functions of the Pakistan Society, where he demonstrated an endearing modesty in his interactions with us.

Another of my contemporaries at Cambridge was Nasir Zahed, a law student attached to Fitzwilliam Hall. My chief recollection of Nasir was playing him in an intercollegiate table tennis match—I forget who won. Nasir, however, went on to establish a successful law practice in Karachi. He was eventually elevated to the bench where he became Chief Justice of the Sind High Court, where his integrity and independent views were widely recognized but may have also precluded his advancement to the Supreme Court. Javed Iqbal—the son of the Pakistani poet laureate Mohommed Iqbal—was also up at Cambridge doing his PhD, but I did not see much of him. He too was elevated to the judiciary in Pakistan and served as the Chief Justice of Panjab.

The Pakistani undergraduate with more proximity to my interests, who did make his mark in later life, at both home and globally, was Mahbub ul Haq. Mahbub came up to Cambridge in 1953 at the same time as myself and Amartya and was Sen's direct contemporary in the MA Prelim Tripos for Economics. Mahbub had also obtained a first-class at Government College, Lahore, in the BA honours exams and was expected to do well at Cambridge. Mahbub was a student at King's College, where he was tutored by Nicky Kaldor and Harry Johnson. I remember him as a rather shy, quiet young man, very soft-spoken and not inclined towards extracurricular involvements with us at the Majlis, as was the case with Amartya. He went on to do his PhD at Yale and then returned to Karachi in 1957, where he joined the Pakistan Planning Commission as an Assistant Chief Economist. Later when Mahbub's worked at the Planning Commission, we became political adversaries while retaining a congenial social relationship.

The other Pakistani who registered his presence at Cambridge, in a rather different context, was Mujeebur Rahman, who set out to make a name for himself in the Cambridge Union. Mujeeb's best efforts to be elected to high office in the Union never moved beyond his being elected to the Committee. Once Mujeeb peaked at the Union, he made his final bid for public recognition by getting himself elected as President of the Pakistan Society in his, if I remember, penultimate term at Cambridge. His presidency was rather undistinguished beyond his rather lame efforts to defend the positions of the then Pakistan government, possibly as a prelude to his seeking a career in the Civil Service. His rather pathetic attempts to defend the regime occasioned amusement in Arif and me, who were known to be less than complimentary about the Ghulam Muhammad–Iskander Mirza regime that had Pakistan under its grip and was setting the stage for the advent of military rule under Ayub Khan.

The Bandung Connection

Mujeeb's self-serving attempts to defend the official position surfaced during his presidency of the Pakistan Society when he rashly decided to invite the Iraqi Ambassador in London, who I remember was named Hasan Askari, to speak on the Baghdad Pact where Pakistan, along with Iraq and Turkey, was a member. This was the era of the Eisenhower's presidency in the USA, where his Foreign Secretary, John Foster Dulles, had earned notoriety for his attempts at dragooning aid-dependent Third World countries into military pacts against the USSR and China. Pakistan had the distinction of joining two such pacts, the Baghdad Pact in the Middle East and the South East Asia Treaty Organization (SEATO).

Among the Pakistani community at Cambridge, Arif and I were known to be vocal critics of the Pacts. In order to fend off any embarrassing interventions by us at Ambassador Askari's meeting, Mujeeb invited us to lunch, where he disarmingly suggested that, as a great personal favour to him (Mujeeb), we should refrain from asking Askari any embarrassing questions. This rather unexpected entreaty from Mujeeb was treated by us as a big joke. When Mujeeb recognized that he would get no change out of us, he proceeded to warn us that he had no alternative but to inform the Pakistan High Commission of our unpatriotic behaviour. This transformation in the tenor of our conversation, we thought rather unbecoming of a smooth character such as Mujeeb. We proceeded to tell him that he should feel free to report our 'unpatriotic' response to the Pakistan High Commission and also to the Foreign Minister and PM of Pakistan but we would continue to speak our mind. I doubt that Mujeeb ever reported us to anyone, but the episode did provide us with some amusing theatrical opportunities.

As it transpired, Askari's defence of the Baghdad Pact turned out to be rather feeble. While Arif and I did needle him rather politely, Askari was given a much harder time by our friends from the Arab Society, led by my friend Syed Zulficar, an Egyptian, the then President of the Arab Society, who gave him a real roasting.

Zulficar, along with Abu Myanja (a Ugandan) and I, had earlier come together, as the respective presidents of the Arab Society, the Africa Society and the Majlis, to form the Bandung Society. This was the first attempt to form a pan-Third World grouping in Cambridge and was inspired by the recently concluded Afro-Asian Conference convened at Bandung, Indonesia, where the likes of Chou En-lai, Nehru, Soekarno, Nasser and Nkrumah had come together for the first time in a gesture of Afro-Asian solidarity. This institutional initiative had enabled me to interact more closely with the Arabs and, to a lesser extent, the Africans in Cambridge.

The Arabs at Cambridge were a mixed group, which included the son of the President of Syria, Hasan Quwatli; the son of the Secretary General of the Arab League, an Egyptian, Abdel Malek Hassouna; and even Hisham Chalabi, from Iraq, the uncle of the notorious Ahmed Chalabi of Iraq invasion fame, along with sundry upper-class Sudanese. Most of the politically conscious Arabs were strongly anti-Pact, which explains the hard time given to Ambassador Askari.

I do not know what become of my Afro-Asian contemporaries, but I did meet up again with Syed Zulficar in Geneva when he was working with the Aga Khan Architectural Awards Foundation. I also discovered that Abu Myanja went on to become a minister in pre-Idi Amin Uganda, acquired a number of wives and sired many children. Today, I suspect, there is little, if any, interaction among the Afro-Asian community in Oxford or Cambridge, where interactions tend to be much more parochialized within their national or regional bodies.

Friends for Life

Outside of my Aitchisonian connections, I came to know Dipanker Ghosh, 'D' to his friends, who became and remained one of my very closest friends until he passed away in the 1990s. I think I first met him in Shahid's rooms at Sidney Sussex. Dipankar came up to Cambridge from La Martiniere in Calcutta with quite dazzling results in the HSC, an air of brash self-confidence and a really bright mind. He was reading law, though his father, Dwarkanath Ghosh, was one of India's best-known first-generation economists who had preceded D to Magdalene in the 1920s and, as a student of Keynes, had taken a first in the Economics Tripos. Dipankar was, however, no swat and settled down to enjoy life to the full, played and partied with the best of them and ended up with a first in the Law Tripos. We soon became inseparable, particularly after Shahid and Riaz left Cambridge.

Our group was later joined in 1954 by Dilip Adarkar, an Engineering Tripos student whose father had also been at Cambridge and was a well-known economist. Dilip was smart, outgoing and excellent for bringing people together. Had he not opted to become an engineer, he would have been an excellent diplomat. Ironically, he married Chitra Joshi, who was one of the first women to qualify for the Indian Foreign Service (IFS). However, in those darker ages, any woman in the IFS had to either pledge herself to spinsterhood or was compelled to resign if she chose to get married. Thus, Dilip's only venture into diplomacy was to end the service career of a promising diplomat. Dilip, who had a successful career with the Douglas Aircraft Corporation, where he even managed to sell some DC-10s to Bangladesh Biman, continues to live with Chitra in Los Angeles, and both have remained lifelong friends with me and my family.

Amartya Sen was another member of our inner circle. He came up to Cambridge the same year as I but did not enter our circle until our second year. During his first year, I remember Amartya, wearing a green coat and golfing cap, cycling up the Magdalene hill to his digs along the Girton Road. We knew each other casually and occasionally exchanged greetings as we pedalled our lonely paths. Amartya, at this stage of his life, projected the persona of a rather retiring Presidency College product of whom little was known beyond the fact that he had a first class first in Economics from Presidency. Later, Sen mythology reported that when, at this first interview at Trinity with his tutor, the well-known Marxist economist Maurice Dobb, he was asked if he had read Samuelson whose book on Introduction to Economics was a staple for all first-year Economics Tripos students, the precocious young Bengali replied, "Do you mean Introduction or Foundations (Samuelson's rather more advanced book)." Amartya advised me, more recently, that his initial anonymity at Cambridge owed to a sense of shyness, which to those who came to know him later, may appear rather unimaginable.

It was not until the end of our first year, when we read on the noticeboard announcing the exam results that Amartya Sen had scored a first in the prelims of the Economics Tripos, that we began to take notice of him. In that same year, Mahbubul Huq scored a 2–1, thus establishing his presence at Cambridge. Mahbub, Amartya and Sam Brittain, who earned fame as an economic journalist with the *Financial Times*, went on to earn firsts in the final year of the Economics Tripos, in the summer of 1955. In that same year, Amartya also won the Adam Smith Prize and the Wrenbury Scholarship to do graduate studies at Trinity. However, we all had to await Amartya's prelim results to realize that a new star had emerged in Cambridge. We immediately brought him into the Majlis, and I embarked on another of my lifelong friendships.

When I look back at Cambridge and some of the more enduring friendships I made there, which continued over the years, I can only remember that phase of my life with unalloyed pleasure. Apart from the two to three weeks of pre-tripos tensions every year, those were halcyon days, walking down Trinity Street; having long arguments over coffee at the Copper Kettle; intense debates with Arif, Amartya, Dipanker and Dilip at the Taj Mahal or Kohinoor or in one of our college rooms at Trinity Hall, or John's or Trinity or Magdalene; or simply sitting on the river bank at Cambridge in summer, watching the Cam flow by with its stream of punters. Another great pleasure of mine was to wander round the bookshops, Heffers, Bowes & Bowes, or the second-hand bookstalls in the Central Square at Cambridge. This used to be a post-lunch hobby of mine where I built the foundations of my library.

This was a period when life was full, when I flowered intellectually, enlivened by the lectures of Noel Annan or Nikki Kaldor; provoked by Joan Robinson in my tutorials with her; in the unending dialectical exchanges with Amartya, Dipanker, Mahbubul Huq, Jagdish Bhagwati or Lal Jayawardena, when we had the leisure to exercise our expanding minds. I studied and played hard, learnt about politics through the Majlis, or at the evening meetings of the Union or at Cambridge's numerous political societies where we listened to the best brains of British society and occasionally crossed swords with them. Arif and I, in my last year, joined the Cambridge University Conservative Association (CUCA) in order to attend their meeting where we could heckle Tory speakers, who never quite figured out why these two brown men were asking them embarrassing questions, from left field, at a CUCA meeting.

The Cambridge Majlis as a Political Incubator

My own, more direct engagement with public and political life in Cambridge derived from my involvement in the Cambridge Majlis. This ancient society originated in the late 19th century as a forum for students from the Indian subcontinent, then made up of India and Ceylon, where they could both socialize and engage in political discussion. The Majlis had, among its distinguished alumni, Pandit Jawaharlal Nehru and other prospective leaders of South Asia. In my years in Cambridge, we were privileged to host Pandit Nehru during his visit to Cambridge in 1955 as part of an official visit to the UK. I was then the Treasurer of the Majlis when Shyam Sarda, an engineering student, was the President and Dipanker was the General Secretary. At that meeting, Nehru addressed the Majlis in what he presumed was its native language but turned out to be polished *badshahi*[3] Urdu, which proved to be quite incomprehensible to a Bengali speaker such as Amartya who needed to have the speech translated for him by a Pakistani—Iran Ispahani—herself a former President of the Majlis.

I still retain a group photograph of that historic event with Arif Iftikhar and Lal Jayawardena of Sri Lanka, both Committee members of the Majlis, Dipanker and I standing side by side in the second row. Of these four comrades, drawn from four countries of South Asia, I am the only survivor. Though my own presence in the ensemble is open to challenge, as I was, in 1971, decapitated in the photo when the Pakistan army came to my house on 27 March to take me into custody. Not finding me at home, they extracted my head from the group photo to use as a way of identification for those jawans sent out to search for me. Some hapless young man, with a moustache and a full head of hair, was probably picked up on the pictorial evidence provided by my decapitated head.

Dipanker Ghosh succeeded Shyam Sarda as President of the Majlis in the summer term of 1955, and I took over as Secretary. In the Michaelmas term of 1955—the first term for 1955–56—our last year in Cambridge, I took over as President of the Majlis with Dilip Adarkar as Secretary and Amartya Sen as Treasurer. My presidency of the Majlis was quite eventful. Apart from hosting Sir Ivor Jennings to speak on Pakistan's constitution, we entertained the renowned statistician P.C. Mahalanobis, the then Deputy Chairman of the Indian Planning Commission, who talked about the Mahalanobis model that was giving shape to India's Second Five-Year Plan then under formulation. We further entertained two of our radical mentors, Kingsley Martin, Editor of the *New Statesman*, and Rajani Palme Dutt, a leading figure of the microscopic Communist Party of Great Britain.

[3] Royal.

One of the highlights of my presidency was a seminar we organized on the then infant discipline of development economics. We invited Professor Thomas Balogh of Balliol College, Oxford, along with Joan Robinson and Peter Bauer from the Cambridge faculty, to speak at the seminar. Bauer however, declined to share a platform with his fellow Hungarian on the grounds that he regarded Balogh as a politician and not an economist. More likely, he disliked Balogh's left-wing views and his sharp tongue.

Prior to the meeting, the Majlis Committee entertained Joan Robinson and Balogh to an Indian meal at the Kohinoor Restaurant, where he was at his provocative best. He had just returned from a trip to Bangkok and caustically remarked that the Thai's were a non-serious people who would never amount to much. I wonder if he would share the same opinion if he were alive today to revisit Bangkok. Balogh ended up as Lord Balogh and, along with Nicky Kaldor, also elevated to a peerage, was one of the key economic advisers of the Labour Party during the tenure of Harold Wilson as PM.

During my term as President of the Majlis, we sought to engage with other political clubs. We organized a debate with the Cambridge University Conservative Club on the theme 'This House rejects SEATO', in which Amartya joined Arif and me in taking on the Tories, represented by Ralph Parsons and Harvey Stockwin. As I recollect, we scored over the Tories, pointing out the counterproductive nature of the Dullesian strategy of corralling undemocratic States across South and South East Asia, in the post-Dien Bien Phu era, into military pacts such as SEATO where Pakistan, along with Philippines, Vietnam and Thailand, was a member. Ironically, Harvey Stockwin graduated from being a working-class Tory to becoming a radical journalist who made his career in South East Asia, questioning the very policies he defended in his debate with us at Cambridge.

One of the concluding events of my tenure as President of the Majlis was the annual joint programme with the Oxford Majlis, this time in Oxford. My cousin Kamal Hossain was then the President of the Oxford Majlis and Barun De, later to emerge as an eminent historian, was the General Secretary. We had decided to organize a debate on the evening of our visit, preceded by a hockey match during the day. The Oxford team was captained by my former Kelly House colleague at Aitchison, K.D. Noon, who played for the University second team. To rise to the challenge, I persuaded Shaharyar Mohammad Khan, who played hockey for his college, Corpus Christie; Swaranjit Singh, then at Christ's, who won a cricket blue for Cambridge but also played hockey; and Bill Singh, a burly Punjabi, to accompany us to Oxford. The three piled into Bill Singh's sports car to travel to Oxford. When they arrived there and climbed out of the car, looking large and ferocious, the sight of them so alarmed Barun that he promptly cancelled the match, much to K.D. Noon's chagrin. We, however, persisted with the less muscular debate on the theme 'This House fears China', where the motion was defended by Kamal, our cousin Kaiser Morshed and me. In the debate, we were challenged by Amartya Sen, Arif Iftikhar and Sadiq al-Mahdi, head of the Mahdi clan in Sudan, the victors over General Gordon, who at a later stage in his life was elected its PM. None of us three cousins actually feared China, but we gave our formidable opponents a run for their money even if we failed to carry the motion.

Shaping a Political Identity

My political perspectives were given shape largely at Cambridge. When I entered the university in 1953, I cannot claim to have had any clearly formed views, though I have pointed out that I had been much impressed by the left-leaning nationalism of Nehru's writings. I had broadened my reading to include the less doctrinaire writings of progressives such as R.H. Tawney, whose moral outrage against social injustice impressed me.

In retrospect, I cannot immediately identify any particular person in Cambridge who influenced my views. By the time Arif Iftikhar arrived in Cambridge, for the academic year 1954–55, my move to the left had already begun, largely through reading the *New Statesman*, a left-oriented but non-doctrinaire weekly, or through attendance at the meetings of the Cambridge University Labour Club or the Socialist Society, where radical speakers introduced me to a view of politics that thus far I had had little exposure.

The Cambridge Union was another forum that contributed to my political education in a more non-denominational mode. The Union, which met every Tuesday evening during term time, provided the best opportunity for listening to some of the most eminent speakers in the land who were not necessarily politicians. While the Union was a social club, where I still remain a life member today, along with its counterpart, the Oxford Union, it was Britain's premier debating society, second only to the Houses of Parliament. The Union has been a nursery for the oratorical skills and political ambitions of many a British and not a few ex-colonial politicians, including in its alumni of presidents, some British PMs such as Rab Butler and political leaders such as Pieter Keuneman of Sri Lanka and Mohan Kumaramangalam of India. Not surprisingly, those who made it to the top echelons of the Union, as president or vice president, were not just good debaters but flamboyant personalities, which served them well in future life, though not necessarily as PMs.

Quite a few other Union personalities entered politics. One of our close friends Tam Dalyell, who read Economics at King's College, then a president of CUCA, was elected Vice President of the Union but failed to make it to the Presidency. In our company, Tam moved leftwards ending up as a Labour MP from his home constituency in Linlithgow, Scotland, which re-elected him for many years until he retired recently as the grand old man of the House of Commons. He was one of few critics of Mrs Thatcher's war on the Falklands and later was one of Tony Blair's most vocal critics over the Iraq War.

The Cambridge Union debates addressed serious topics, but the tone needed to be light-hearted, argued extempore, with style, wit and the gift of quick repartee, as the principal currency in use rather than through heavy-handed, fact-laden information delivered from prepared notes. The first debate of the academic year invariably argued that 'This House has no confidence in Her

Majesty's Government', which usually pitted a cabinet minister against a senior Opposition leader who discussed, with wit as well as insight, the key issues of British politics. However, non-political topics also attracted discussion where philosophers and theatre personalities were invited.

Among many speakers who spoke at the Union, I remember being particularly impressed by Richard Crossman, later a cabinet minister in the Labour government under Harold Wilson, who was speaking against a motion in the Union that supported Britain's joining the then first moves to form a European Community. Sir Robert Boothby, a Tory MP, had spoken brilliantly in favour of European unity so that Crossman's riposte, arguing that a West European–centred Union that excluded a socialist Eastern Europe would be counterproductive, was both devastating and persuasive. Another speaker invited to address the Union, who greatly impressed me, was Cheddi Jagan, who had been deposed by the British as PM of British Guiana, which was then ruled by the British Colonial Office. Jagan, a man of the left, and his even more brilliant colleague, Forbes Burnham, both roasted the British government much to the chagrin of the Tory members of the audience. Arif Iftikhar first established his presence at the Union by speaking eloquently in defence of Jagan in the face of a hostile House.

Listening to progressive ideas, eloquently presented by some of the finest academic and political minds, whether at the Union, the political clubs or in the classroom, inevitably influenced my world view. I entered Cambridge a largely apolitical person inclined to view the world from the lenses of the Western-educated elite with a tendency to accept the demonization of the socialist world. Exposure to ideas from such speakers, reading literature from the left and the fertilization of my ideas in discussions in our own circle educated me to assume a more left-nationalist anti-colonial perspective that encouraged me to question the world as I knew it. Visits to Collets Bookshop on Charing Cross Road in London kept me well stocked on left-wing literature published by Lawrence & Wishart as also by the more propagandistic publishing houses such as People's Publishing House. Alas, Collets has been out of business for many years.

In consequence of these changes in my political perception, I had become a strong supporter of the Viet Minh, led by Ho Chi Minh, in their struggle against French colonialism. I vividly remember my sense of exhilaration at the fall of Dien Bien Phu that marked the end of French rule in Indo-China. I was also strongly incensed at France's colonial occupation of Algeria and supportive of the Algerian war of liberation, where I made common cause with my friends in the Arab Society.

I needed to know more about economics before I could begin to give shape to a more articulate support for socialistic solutions to the problems of the Third World and Pakistan in particular. In this context, my exposure to the ideas of Amartya, from the beginning of our close association at the outset of the academic year 1954–55, was particularly important. Amartya arrived at Cambridge in 1953, with his left-wing views already strongly shaped by his years at Presidency College, Kolkata, which was dominated by the communists who percolated their radical ideas in the coffee shops on College Street. Amartya was never a hard-line believer in the credo of the communists, which in those days demonstrated an unswerving faith in the infallibility of Joseph Stalin and Mao Tse-tung. He was exceedingly well read in the classical texts of Marxism without again surrendering his free will to be critical of Marx. In our encounters and arguments with the hard-core Party faithful at Cambridge—such as Alan Brown, the Secretary of the Cambridge Communist Association; his comrade, Ruth Loshak; and the more erudite, though less doctrinaire, graduate students such as Pierangelo Garegnani, an Italian, and Charles Feinstein, from South Africa—Amartya and I broadly shared their global critique of the unjust nature of bourgeois society and the pervasive evils of imperialism. However, we were more willing to question the rigid orthodoxies of the Communist world view. After the revelations by Khrushchev, at the 14th Congress of the Soviet Communist Party after the death of Stalin, this blinkered view of the USSR was exposed to much questioning by many left-oriented people.

Those of us who had occupied a position on the left of the political spectrum were moved by the prevailing injustices of our respective societies and particularly the global order that was heavily dominated not just by the West, led then by the USA, but their world view which dominated the print media across the world. Among my teachers, Joan Robinson had a left-wing orientation, but of them only Maurice Dobb was a practising Marxist. The dominant influence in the Economics Faculty at Cambridge was largely Keynesian, though a few economists of the neo-liberal school were also on the faculty. However, in those days, when Keynesian ideas were part of the mainstream of economic policy, even in Conservative regimes, no one thought of these economists as left-oriented, and even Joan Robinson was viewed as a left-leaning Keynesian.

Exposure in tutorials and lectures from Joan and my more frequent exchanges with Amartya educated me on the theoretical weaknesses of a market-dominated approach to economic problems and provided me with some exposure to the empirical literature exposing the limits of the capitalist system. Amartya, in particular, was always a rich source of arcane information, drawn from both history and contemporary evidence, of the weaknesses as well as injustices of capitalism. We of course drew on the politically partisan but quite informative writings of Rajani Palme Dutt, on the depredations of colonial rule, to reinforce our capacity to engage in debate with the Conservatives.

While my concerns were global, I had also begun to give some shape to my thinking on the direction of politics in Pakistan. Arif and I were deeply critical of the emerging assault on democracy in Pakistan associated with the cabal of Ghulam Muhammad, Iskander Mirza and Field Marshal Ayub Khan. We rejoiced over the rout of the Muslim League by the Jukta Front[4] led by H.S. Suhrawardy, Fazlul Haq and Maulana Bhashani, in the provincial elections in East Pakistan in 1954. We were appalled by the subsequent dismissal of the Jukta Front government, led by Fazlul Haq, under Section 92-A of the Constitution, followed by the appointment of Iskander Mirza as the Governor of East Pakistan.

The subsequent dissolution of the CA in 1955, which had included the defeated and discredited Muslim League, ushered in a

[4] United Front.

so-called cabinet of talents in Pakistan, which did not inspire much faith in the restoration of representative government. I remember Mirza Hasan Ispahani, who had until recently been Pakistan's High Commissioner in London, and now a member of this new cabinet, turning up at Cambridge to speak on the subject at the Pakistan Society. We argued with him on the direction of democracy in Pakistan and the need to restore an elected government to office in Dhaka. I had by then became more conscious of the deprivations of the Bangalis by a Punjabi, bureaucratic and army-dominated central government, but my views were still in a formative phase. Interestingly, it was Mian Iftikharuddin, during encounters with him at the Blue Boar Hotel in Cambridge or at his favoured country retreat at Selsdon Park, who first exposed me to the need for a more provincially devolved system of government in Pakistan that ensured much greater autonomy for East Pakistan.

When I reflect back on my growing political consciousness, influenced by my three years in Cambridge, it is evident that this shaped my perspective towards both my future goals and also my decision to build a life in Dhaka. I had come to recognize that my ideological leanings needed a political home where they could be meaningfully expressed within a specific national and social context. I reckoned that the world view towards which I was inclined resonated more strongly among the Bangalis who were exposed to both political and social injustice. It was this perception of my emerging political identity that encouraged me to identify my future with a country which was yet to be born. My judgments were, at that stage, made largely on a priori grounds but turned out to be validated by my own responses to the passage of events that shaped the future of my prospective homeland.

Intellectual Influences

I am not sure what Cambridge itself did for my intellectual development. The system encouraged creative enquiry, where to be able to sound original was more important than to be learned.

This inspired creativity, extravagance of expression and a tendency to be gratuitously provocative in argument. While I perhaps carried enough of these qualities around with me when I entered Cambridge, the system itself ensured that these qualities would come to full flower. Whether in Noel Annan's tutorials on my special paper on Politics, sitting in his rooms in King's, discussing Karl Popper or Marx, or in Joan Robinson's living room at 62 Grange Road, during my weekly tutorials with her, or in animated exchanges with Amartya or Dipankar, one felt obliged to say something out of the ordinary. Egos were thus nourished and deflated with equal facility. This capacity to challenge received wisdom, pomposity or authority established by virtue of age became part of my persona and put me into argumentative discourse with my elders if not my betters throughout my life.

As part of my education, I presume I also learnt something about economics. In the Economics Tripos of that period, one could get by without a rigorous command of maths. I doubt if I could survive the Tripos of today without investing rather more of my energies in understanding mathematical techniques. In those days, Joan Robinson was developing her work on Capital Theory, through her lectures. This eventually appeared in her volume on *The Accumulation of Capital.* Nicky Kaldor taught us microeconomics in his lectures on value and distribution. I learnt a good deal about the economic history of the USSR from Maurice Dobb and that of the USA from Frank Thistlethwaite, that I took as a special paper. I drew upon both these courses to begin my career as a teacher at Dhaka University, in my lectures to first-year honours students in the Economics Department, on the economic history of the USA and USSR.

Other classes that stayed in my mind were those by Harry Johnson, Dennis Robertson, Austen Robinson and Piero Sraffa. Among the younger teachers who went on to greater fame, R.C.O. Matthews appealed to us. However, far and away, the most enthralling of our teachers was Noel Annan, who taught us our special paper on Politics. Annan eventually became Provost of King's and earned other academic distinctions, becoming a member of the British Academy and eventually a Lord. In our days, one simply remembered the brilliance of Annan's language and the provocation of his thoughts. I still have his notes with me and leaf through the faded pages with a sense of wonderment at his erudition and inspirational capacities.

Outside of the economics faculty, academic luminaries of our day whom we heard about with some awe and sat in on their talks at one or the other Society were E.M. Forster, F.R. Leavis and scientists such as J.D. Bernal and Joseph Needham, among others. In those days, such academics, however eminent, were much more accessible to students as they spent most of their time in college where trips outside Cambridge were something of an event. Today's academics at Oxbridge and anywhere else are fully globalized, jetting around the world, and can only be accessed in their studies through appointments made weeks in advance.

By today's standards, Cambridge was, thus, a rather inward-looking traditional and elitist institution, where to merely reply, with just a touch of casualness, when asked where I was studying, "actually, I am up at Cambridge," gave one a sense of perhaps underserved distinction. Today, those words somehow do not seem to carry the same weight or implication of arrogance they once did. My son Babar has done his MPhil and later studied for his PhD at Cambridge but does not, for a moment, believe himself to be among the privileged academic elite.

Glorious Days

Beyond the shaping of my intellectual views, I will always remember the sheer pleasure of life that Cambridge offered us. I look back with a sense of repleteness on our non-academic life, whether in term time or during the vacations, when I used to move into rooms at Trinity Street with whichever of our friends stayed back at Cambridge. I enjoyed those periods of leisure, with no classes or tutorials to attend, when we could indulge ourselves without guilt, walk over to the Rex Cinema to see old movie favourites or just hang out in the long summer evenings where, if there was no party to go to, I ended up at the Kohinoor arguing over *chicken dhansak*[5] until midnight with Arif, Dipanker Ghosh, Amartya and Dilip Adarkar.

I did not of course spend all my vacation time in Cambridge. One of our favoured outings, just after the summer vacations, which began at the end of May, was to hire cars and set out to attend a Shakespeare play at Stratford-upon-Avon. Usually, one car was driven by Peter Rogers—historian at Fitzwilliam—and another by Arif, who were the only two among us with driving licences. Our entourage included Dipanker, Dilip, Suresh Pai, Arif, Peter and me. I remember one such excursion to see Laurence Olivier and Vivien Leigh perform in *Macbeth* and on another occasion we saw John Gielgud and Peggy Ashcroft in *King Lear*. For reasons of economy, we did not spend the night at Stratford but drove back to Cambridge through the night. This was a somewhat hazardous proposition as there was some risk that our respective chauffeurs may fall asleep at the wheel.

Other outings from Cambridge were mostly to London, where I would spend a few days with some of my Aitchisonian friends and also my cousin Qamruzzaman, who was studying Chartered Accountancy. In the four-month summer vacations, stays in London tended to be longer and used for visits to the theatre or watching some major sporting event such as tennis at Wimbledon or cricket at Lord's. I recollect visits to Wimbledon with Shahid Hossain in the summer of 1954, to watch the early rounds from a standing-only enclosure surrounding the Centre Court, for which we had to queue from 9:00 am. That summer, along with Shahid and Riaz, we also spent a rain-interrupted day at Lord's watching Pakistan play England in the Second Test, where Hanif played one of his usual defensive match-saving innings. On other occasions, Kaiser Morshed was press-ganged to accompany me to Wimbledon and, on one memorable outing, to watch the world table tennis championships at Wembley.

[5] A delicious and popular Parsi dish.

A Cobbler in Ischl

On the occasion of my first summer vacation in 1954, I travelled to Bad Ischl in Austria, to spend a month apprenticing as a prospective cobbler. My father had not given up hope that I would remain committed to the leather business even if I had spent time at Cambridge. During one of his European visits, he had visited the remote resort town of Bad Ischl, the birthplace of the composer Franz Lehár, to visit Schuhfabrik Panzl, a boutique shoe manufacturing establishment that produced quality shoes. How exactly he connected with this remote establishment remains a mystery to me, but he persuaded its owner, Herr Panzl, to take me on as an unpaid apprentice to learn how shoes were made. I, thus, set out on my first European trip around July 1954, travelling by train, first to Brussels, where I spent a few days walking all over the city seeing the sights and then moved onward to Frankfurt, where I spent a few more days. Frankfurt in 1954 was still a war-devastated city, with bombed-out spaces and a general air of desolation. The postwar miracle initiated by Chancellor Adenauer and his Economics Minister, Ludwig Erhard, was only just beginning to yield its harvest, which could be seen in some modern new constructions, interspersed among the bombed-out sites.

From Frankfurt, I travelled via Munich to Salzburg and then by a smaller train to Bad Ischl, a small, rather sleepy town, which apart from its famed son, had also hosted the summer retreat of one of the Austro-Hungarian Emperors, possibly Franz Joseph. Schuhfabrik Panzl was one of the few industries in the area. It was a family-owned and managed enterprise set up by Herr Panzl and managed with the assistance of his son Matt, who was in his late twenties. I was warmly received by the family who were not entirely sure what to do with me. Communication was the most serious problem because the senior Panzls spoke no English while Matt's skills were rudimentary. My principal interlocutor with the family was their daughter, Lisl, an attractive young lady who was, alas for me, betrothed to a young man from the area.

I was initially accommodated in a small hotel in the centre of Ischl. While I had occasional meals at the Panzls, I mostly had to fend for myself drawing on an economy budget, further constrained by language. With my rudimentary skills in German, acquired through a teach-yourself-German handbook, I could limit myself to items on the menu that involved *kalb* (calf) or *hunn* (chicken) and had to preface all others selections with the cautionary, *ohne shweinfleisch* (without pig's meat). My diet thus, tended to be rather restricted, punctuated with the occasional luxury of a wiener schnitzel, which was a regional speciality.

My working days at Schuhfabrik Panzl were educational if not particularly helpful in transforming me into Bangladesh's first shoe entrepreneur ahead of Bata and Apex. At the end of my month's stay in Bad Ischl, I cannot claim to have emerged as a qualified shoemaker. I did, however, immensely enjoy my holiday in Ischl and learnt enough German to essay a few conversational gambits even today. My memory of the holiday was sufficiently evocative for me to revisit St. Wolfgang with Salma, Taimur and Babar around March 1969, when we were travelling back to Dhaka at the end of our stay in London. I took them on a sentimental journey to Bad Ischl to have tea with Matt Panzl. He was by then a middle-aged man with greying hair, who had taken over the running of the Schuhfabrik Panzl from his father and remembered our carefree excursions in his green Lancia car with nostalgia. Many years later when Rounaq and I were holidaying in Salzburg, we visited St. Wolfgang but did not get to Ischl, so I do not know if Schuhfabrik Panzl has survived the competition from shoes made by Apex in Bangladesh.

European Adventures

In the autumn of 1955, at the end of the summer holidays, Dilip, Amartya, Suresh Pai, an engineering student, and I decided to hitchhike our way across Scandinavia. This was a low-cost mode of travel though not necessarily costless. Dilip was the entrepreneur of the adventure and planned out the logistics of our trip. We were advised that accessing a lift was a piece of cake and that good-quality youth hostels across the region would ensure economical living. We accordingly set out from Cambridge in late September 1955 and hitchhiked, without too much trouble, to Newcastle with a stop en route at Darlington. At Newcastle, we took the ferry to Bergen in Norway. Bergen, which had once been a major seaport and centre of the Hanseatic League, was somewhat reduced in its glory. It was then a modest-sized town largely known for its fishing industry. Their youth hostel was perched upon a hill overlooking the town that required a rather taxing climb, particularly as we were carrying all our belongings in rucksacks strapped on our back.

Ironically, this first trip to Bergen in 1955 was to evolve into a lifelong relationship, courtesy of my dear friend Just Faaland, who headed the development wing of the venerable Chr. Michelsen Institute (CMI) in Bergen. Since 1975, I have visited CMI and Bergen quite frequently and once stayed there for six weeks in the autumn of 1976, where Muzzafer Ahmed and I wrote a 600-page epic, *Public Enterprise in an Intermediate Regime*.

Hitchhiking beyond Bergen to Oslo was more problematic because of the intervening mountainous terrain, so we took the train and went on to spend three days in Oslo. From Oslo we set out, full of hope, to hitchhike to Stockholm. In order to facilitate travel and not intimidate potential hosts with the prospect of giving four brown men of as-yet-unproven antecedents a long ride, we divided ourselves with Dilip and Suresh as one pair and Amartya and I as another duo. Amartya and I easily managed to get some drivers to take us from Oslo across the Swedish border. Just when things were going well, the truck driver told us he was now branching off the highway, to take a small country road to his farm, so the two of us were debouched in the middle of the Swedish countryside some miles outside of a small town named Flensburg. We spent many hours waiting for the next ride. Traffic in that area was light and those that went by seemed disinclined to give a ride to two foreigners standing in the middle of nowhere. South Asians in rural Sweden, in those pre-migrant days, appeared as exotic to the Swedes as Martians.

After an interminable wait, with dusk setting in, we managed to get a lift up to the rail station at Flensburg. At that point, Amartya and I made the fateful decision that Sweden was going to be inhospitable to South Asian hitchhikers and we had better try our fortunes in Denmark. We accordingly took a train south from Flensburg to Gothenburg and then another train onward to Copenhagen. I pointed this out to a big audience in the auditorium of the National Museum in Dhaka, when we were honouring Amartya on the award of the Nobel Prize in Economics in 1999. Amartya had travelled directly from Stockholm to Dhaka after receiving his award so that we in Bangladesh were privileged to greet him even before his countrymen in India. On that occasion, Amartya dedicated a part of his Nobel Prize earnings to setting up the Pratichi Trust (Bangladesh) and invited me to become its Chair. I reminded Amartya and the audience, on that occasion, that the first time Amartya set out for Stockholm way back in 1955, he did not reach his destination. He had finally managed to get to Stockholm after a lifetime, this time without the inconvenience of having to hitchhike there. I have, myself, visited Stockholm at a less elevated level than Amartya but reached there perhaps more easily than in 1955.

Whilst Amartya and I chickened out of trying our fortunes in Sweden, Dilip and Suresh reached Stockholm without any such setbacks, spent several days there and then comfortably hitchhiked to Copenhagen, where we met up at a rather commodious and well-provisioned youth hostel there. Amartya and I spent close to a week in Copenhagen, a stay that was much facilitated by Amartya locating a Bangali friend, Ajay Mahalanobis, several years his senior, who had been a student at Santiniketan. Copenhagen was a very friendly and engaging city and fully compensated us for our Swedish misadventure.

We set out in a similar twosome, to hitchhike from Copenhagen to Hamburg. Again fortune did not smile on Amartya and me. Instead of landing at Hamburg, we spent the night in a farmer's loft in the Danish countryside, halfway between Copenhagen and the Danish–German border. The farmer's wife fed us on soup, cheese and bread, which assuaged our hunger pangs and restored our faith in Scandinavian hospitality. The next morning, we set out for Hamburg but found ourselves landed in the middle of a forest. To ease our chances of a ride, Amartya and I decided to split up. Much to my chagrin, Amartya could get a ride to Hamburg at least an hour before I did. I, at that stage, decided that the black beard that I had cultivated was a no-no for the more rustic Scandinavians. However, a truck driver eventually offered me hospitality and delivered me to Hamburg, where the four of us once again came together at the local youth hostel.

My memories of Hamburg are not sharp, beyond a ritual visit by us to the infamous Reeperbahn. At Hamburg, I decided to part company from my fellow travellers as I needed to get back somewhat earlier to Cambridge, to prepare the programme for my imminent Presidency of the Cambridge Majlis, during the Michaelmas term of 1955–56. While the other three hitchhiked back to England, I took a train to Rotterdam and spent a half day touring the city that had been virtually rebuilt after being devastated by the Luftwaffe and now appeared to be the most modern city in Europe, architecturally. From Rotterdam, I took the ferry across the Channel and travelled by train all the way back to Cambridge. I obviously rate 'C'—as a hitchhiker.

During the Christmas holidays at the end of 1955, Kamal and I decided to take a holiday in Paris. We stayed in a rather seedy hotel near one of the main train stations and performed the traditional rituals for young men in Paris, visits to the famed museums, long strolls along the Champs-Élysées, Montmartre, Montparnasse and through the Latin Quarter, with excursions to taste the nightlife of Place Pigalle. We even managed to entertain ourselves in the early hours of the morning at the vegetable market in Les Halles, which served an incomparable onion soup along with fresh hot rolls just out of the oven. During our stay, I shamelessly exploited Kamal's inflexible aversion to alcohol by pointing out that the piece of pastry he had chosen for his coffee break was laced with sinful alcohol. This greatly enhanced my share of the delicious French pastry we consumed. Nemesis has since settled accounts with me for this exploitation of Kamal's piety as I can today only consume such pastries with some caution.

Academic Fulfilment

I look back on my last summer at Cambridge with both satisfaction and sadness. The summer began with a sense of accomplishment when I read on the noticeboard outside the Senate that I graduated with a 2–1 or Second Class, First Division. This was no great distinction, but in 1956 not more than a half-dozen Pakistanis had done as well academically, in the years past. In my year, we had a record seven firsts in the Economics Tripos, which included my friends Lal Jayawardena and Jagdish Bhagwati, Walter Eltis, Richard Jolly, George Cyriax (who attended my first tutorial with Peter Bauer), Mike Nicholson and Neil Laing. Among these Jagdish followed Amartya in winning the Adam Smith Prize. All of these seven attained some distinction in later life. Jagdish, who has a chair at Columbia University, is one of the leading international trade economists; Richard Jolly was Director of the Institute of Development Studies (IDS) at Sussex and then Deputy Director General of UNICEF; Lal was the first Director of the World Institute of Development Economic Research (WIDER) in Helsinki; George Cyriax made a name for himself as an eminent financial journalist with *The Economist*; and Walter Eltis taught economics at Oxford.

In the year before we graduated, Amartya had been the star of the economics faculty, pursued by Mahbubul Huq, the first Pakistani to take a first in the Economics Tripos, and Sam Brittan, one of the leading economic journalists of his generation. The year after me, Manmohan Singh earned the lone first in the Eeconomics Tripos and also won the Adam Smith Prize. Manmohan, who came up to John's in our final year, was an exceedingly shy, reticent person who then betrayed no indication that he would serve as PM of India for over a decade.

Ours was something of a golden age in the Economics Tripos, and I did not feel too diminished by not leaving with a first, an aspiration I never really entertained. Thus, a 2–1 remained the summit of my academic ambitions at Cambridge and gave me an inflated sense of academic self-esteem that set me off in pursuit of an academic career. With rooms in Trinity Street, Amartya, Dipanker, Dilip, and for a while, Arif to keep me company, my last glorious summer went by too fast.

Behind the Curtain

The summer culminated in an adventure behind the Iron Curtain to Prague to attend, at the instigation of Arif, an International Youth Congress. On that trip, if I remember correctly, Nooru Gupta, who moved on to serve as Attorney General of West Bengal and a luminary of the Communist Party of India (Marxist)–CPI (M), along with a bunch of other Bangali lefties, were also in the South Asian delegation from England. We travelled by rail via Nuremberg and entered a drab-looking Prague. Arif, inevitably, did the equivalent of a *sijda*[6] as we crossed the border, and wiped away tears of emotion at his first visit to a part of the holy land of socialism. We were lodged in student dormitories of rather spartan aspect and offered adequate if not very palatable fare. My own rather agnostic views, which Arif attributed to my habit of reading the *New Statesman* and admiration of Richard Crossman, did not suggest that I had seen the future.

While we were still in a frame of mind to look for the successes of a socialist revolution, Czechoslovakia in 1956 was far from a golden country. However, its drabness was at that time not too distinctive—compared to Britain, West Germany, France and Austria, already visited by me—as it became in later years once the post-war recovery of Europe had fructified. The rather pedantic and dogmatic young commissars who accompanied us around and parroted the standard eulogies of socialism even managed to irritate Arif.

At Prague, we fell in with a bunch of Americans, one of whom went by the name of Bob Lucas. Lucas had arrived in Prague in his own car in which he took us off on various illicit, unescorted

[6] Lying in prostrate position for prayer.

explorations where Lucas sought to discover the darker aspects of socialism. This took us in search of a military airfield, where I am not sure what Lucas hoped to discover, except some ancient USSR MIGs. However, in the Czechoslovakia of that era, such excursions, particularly if concluded in the company of Americans, whom Arif firmly believed to be Central Intelligence Agency (CIA) agents, carried the prospects of incarceration in the dungeons of the *Narodnyy Komissariat Vnutrennikh Del* (NKVD), exposed to the *Darkness at Noon* experience we had read with disbelief in Koestler's denunciation of communism. The adventure, thus, carried its frisson of excitement. Fortunately, we returned, uninterrogated, to Prague having seen no more than a few guards goose-stepping around a barbed wire fence that may well have been a secret Soviet airbase.

The Youth Congress at Prague brought a large number of left-oriented young men and women of the world together to ventilate their national as well as global grievances. While the gathering was possibly underwritten by the budgets of the Soviet and Czech governments, not all those present were party faithful. Some like Lucas had either come along for the adventure of a trip behind the so-called Iron Curtain or may even have done so at the behest of a Western intelligence agency. But most of those who had made the effort largely shared a left-wing perspective of the world. This may have been inspired by a strong desire to bring about some form of socialism in their respective countries. But the most common denominator was a strong hostility to a Western-dominated world order and particularly the USA, with its Dullesian view of world affairs. The African students at Prague, for example, mostly came from countries which at that time, were largely under colonial domination. The Algerian War of resistance against France was at its height and French colonialism, which had suffered a humiliating defeat in Vietnam at the hands of the Viet Minh, was particularly excoriated by highly articulate French-speaking Arabs and Africans. The Arabs in particular, were a very visible and vocal presence, ranging from strong nationalists under the hypnotic sway of Gamal Abdel Nasser who was the hero of the hour because of his nationalization of the Suez Canal, to those of more radical persuasions.

Apart from the French, the British because of their aggressive moves to recapture the Suez Canal from Nasser, and of course Israelis—for what was then perceived as the usurpation of Palestinian lands—were seen as villains. Yasser Arafat who was then the president of the Palestine Youth Federation—and had not yet acquired his permanent two-day facial stubble—was one of the stars of the Congress and led the move to mobilize us youth to challenge the imminent invasion of Egypt by the British, French and Israelis to recapture the Suez Canal. The USA, because of the Eisenhower doctrine, ostensibly designed to contain Soviet influence in the Arab world through the cordon sanitaire of the Baghdad Pact, was seen as the emerging global leader of Western imperialism, a view strongly propagated by the organizers of the Congress.

Given the dialectic of the Cold War, the USSR and its Socialist allies in Europe and China were seen as natural allies of the South. While most of us may have had some reservations about the workings of a one-party State and were hardly impressed by the grim and repressive environment that prevailed in Prague, the more hardcore believers still perceived the Eastern Bloc as part of a worker's paradise. It should be kept in mind that our Congress was held just a few months before the Hungarian uprising in November 1956, which was crushed by Soviet tanks. This event never shook the faith of Arif, though many of the Hungarian youth who were visible in the Congress probably took part in the uprising. But such was the anti-imperialist climate of the gathering in Prague that none of us could scent the deep anger that boiled beneath the surface in Eastern Europe and culminated first in the Hungarian uprising, in the Prague spring of 1968 and eventually in the destruction of socialism in Eastern Europe a quarter of a century later.

My Prague adventure over, I returned to London with Arif, via Cologne, which was still devastated by the allied bombing of this historic city. I had already visited Frankfurt in 1954 on my way to Bad Ischl and Hamburg at the end of our hitchhiking safari in Scandinavia in the autumn of 1955. So I finished my Cambridge years, an accomplished European traveller having also visited Brussels in 1954, Rotterdam in 1955 and Paris during the Christmas of 1955 in the company of Kamal.

Returning to an Undiscovered Homeland

I booked a passage to sail home in October 1953, on the Polish ship, Batory. The night before I sailed for Karachi from Southampton, my three cousins Kaiser, Kamal and Sajjad Haider, who was qualifying as a chartered accountant in London, entertained me to dinner at the Angus Steakhouse on Leicester Square, London. It was an enjoyable farewell, full of plans for the future, though the meal was less satisfactory. As was my bad habit, I complained of this to the management and, aided by the advocacy of Kamal and Kaiser, managed to extract a rebate on the bill from the Angus management.

The evening ended in an all-night effort by Kamal and me to dissuade Kaiser from sitting for the exam to qualify for the CSP. Our efforts were unfruitful. Kaiser appeared for and stood first in the exam, thereby condemning himself to a career in the Foreign Service rather than as a distinguished academic, which I believe was his true calling.

The next day, I travelled from Waterloo station to Southampton to sail for Karachi. On this voyage, I travelled in first class but, on account of the low fare, was relegated to the smallest cabin in the lowest passenger deck. I had already been a passenger on the *Batory* on my travel from Karachi to Southampton in 1953, where I had emerged as the undisputed table tennis champion of the voyage. This time I lost out in the final, but not before I had defeated Khushwant Singh in the semi-finals. As I had just read his novel *Train to Pakistan*, this victory gave me no small sense of achievement. Khushwantji once saw me sitting on the deck reading Sardar Panikkar's *Asia and Western Dominance* and told me that Panikkar had invented most of these mythological Indian military victories reported in the book so I should not take the book too seriously! I have often wondered about this arcane bit of historiography but remember my encounter with the great Khushwant Singh largely in terms of table tennis.

On board, I met Amena Zaheer, who had been up at Oxford with Kamal and Kaiser and had studied English literature, which she hoped to teach at Miranda House, in New Delhi. I was quite entranced with Amena's wry, self-deprecatory humour, her capacity for understatement and the sensitivity of her spirit. I spent long hours with her, looking out over the expanse of the Indian Ocean, with the stars above us, thinking of her as a prospective soulmate—a view that must have been entirely unilateral as my own rather brash persona and political obsessions were hardly to her taste. Our paths never crossed again. She now lives with her husband in Pune. I learnt this from a nephew of hers who works for the World Bank and is married to a niece of Rounaq's sister-in-law. Another six degrees of separation!

As we approached Karachi, I experienced both tension and excitement at the prospect of constructing my future in a homeland that had never been my home. At the age of 21, I was not unduly worried by the unchartered terrain which lay ahead of me. At that stage, I felt that life's possibilities were infinite and that I was prepared to cross rivers and ascend mountains to realize my aspirations, however unfocused they may have been.

7

Dhaka: Life and Times

Homeward Bound

Return to Karachi

I arrived in Karachi in October 1956, on the eve of the Anglo-French-Israeli invasion of Egypt to capture the Suez Canal. As with much of Pakistan, I was deeply incensed by the invasion, though I did not join the demonstrations that culminated in the burning of the British Council offices in Karachi and Dhaka. I was particularly angered by the ambiguous position of the Pakistan government, which even though it condemned the invasion, played a rather dubious role prior to the invasion in trying to mediate on behalf of the West, a move that greatly irritated the Arabs. The *Batory* had sailed through the Suez Canal where the armed garrisons of the none-too-impressive Egyptian army were visible to all of us. The best the Egyptians could do to resist the invasion was to sink a large number of their own ships in the Canal and block it to traffic for the best part of a year. Fortunately for me, this act would wait until I was safely in Karachi.

However, at that time there was little scope for such political activism as I had to resolve my own future. In Karachi, I stayed with my mother and stepfather at their residence at E.I. Lines, contemplating my future course of action. My father's urge for me to return to Dhaka had diminished as he had come to an arrangement with his business partners to lease out Dhaka Tanneries to them while he returned to public service.

At that time, Shaheed Suhrawardy had taken over as PM of Pakistan, as head of a coalition government, where the AL was a minority partner. As part of his policy to place qualified Bangalis, who had hitherto been largely ignored by the central government, in responsible positions, my father was invited by Shaheed Sahib to become Chairman of the Karachi Improvement Trust (KIT), later transformed into the Karachi Development Authority (KDA). My father was now better positioned to walk away from his business affairs in Dhaka and took up residence in Karachi at the end of 1956. He occupied this position for two years after which he was appointed as Pakistan's Commissioner to what was then British East Africa and moved off to Nairobi, just after martial law was imposed by Ayub Khan in October 1958. For all his business entanglements, my father's first preference remained to return to his true vocation as a public servant.

My father's distancing himself from the affairs of Dhaka Tanneries meant that he was now more inclined to see me settled in a steady job. Options ranged from the CSP to the Planning Commission and the inevitable cushion for the sons of the elite, a job with a multinational company. I had never really entertained the idea of becoming a CSP, which was incompatible with my yet notional ambitions of being part of the politics of the then East Pakistan. As far as I was concerned, I wanted to return to Dhaka and take my chances there. My father, now that Dhaka Tanneries was no longer his main concern, pushed me to try my chances with a multinational and lined up some appointments for me. To appease him, I proceeded to meet the burra sahibs of several companies, such as Imperial Chemical Industries (ICI) and Glaxo, and, if memory holds good, even had a job offer from one of them.

Before I landed in Karachi, I already had a job offer in my pocket. Professor Wise, Chair of the Economics Department, had, even before I left Cambridge, offered me my first job, as a Reader in Economics, at Peshawar University, at the then handsome salary of

Rs 800 per month, on the strength of reading about my 2–1 in the tripos in the lists published in the *London Times*. I had been greatly flattered at this, my first job offer, but had declined it as politely as I could because I had committed myself to return to Dhaka. Thus, with job offers from both the academic world and the multinationals, I did not feel unduly perturbed at my prospects for earning a livelihood. When my father arrived in Karachi around December 1956 to take up his position as Chairman, KIT, I told him that I was going back to Dhaka as I saw my home and future there rather than in West Pakistan. He did not think this was a wise move but did not attempt to dissuade me from my decision.

Between my disembarkation from the *Batory* around mid-October and my departure from Karachi to Lahore in early January, I lived the life of a gentleman at large in Karachi, basking in the transient glory of being a Cambridge-returned. My re-entry to Pakistani society was greatly facilitated by the presence in Karachi of Shahid Hossain and Riaz Mahmood. Since their premature withdrawal from Cambridge, Shahid was a young sahib with Lever Brothers and Riaz with Pakistan Tobacco. They shared a flat in PECHS, enjoying the status of eligible bachelors at large and exposed me to what social life was on offer in the Karachi of the 1950s. This was not much to excite the imagination. It was still the era of chaperoned dating where only the most advanced girls went out with boys but did so in pairs, rarely alone. The highlight of Riaz and Shahid's social life was thus an opportunity to take the Akhund sisters, Rasheeda and Hameeda, to the movies and possibly to dinner. Life was, however, pleasant enough with social encounters and some occasional mixed parties, courtesy of ex-Aitchisonians or ex-Cantabrians, to enliven a rather uneventful social scene.

At that time, Karachi had still not moved much beyond the mofussil town from which I had sailed to England in March 1953. 'New' Clifton had emerged from the sands overlooking the Indian Ocean, and I used to spend quite a bit of time there at Qamar Court, 111 Clifton, where my uncle Haider and his family were in residence, just opposite Kashana, at 117 Clifton, which was Salma's home. Salma, however, was still at Cambridge and her parents were then occupying the residence of the Pakistan High Commissioner in London at Avenue Road in Swiss Cottage. The newly built Al-Murtaza, the family residence of the Bhuttos, was a little further down the road.

The other new development was at PECHS, which, in 1953, had been little more than a desert scrubland but was now a whole new residential area. The heart of Karachi was still located around Elphinstone Street and Victoria Road, which constituted what passed as a shopping centre for the fashionable. This was the era of import substituting industrialization, built around a heavily protected economy so that the shops of Pakistan's capital had few things to buy and those mostly of local origin. The business centre in Macleod Road was still a rather run-down affair, located in pre-independence residential structures. The Metropole Hotel was the acme of luxury living in Karachi with two other rather seedy hotels, the Palace and Beach Luxury, catering to a non-existent tourist industry.

For a prospective political leader, my political education was not pursued with undue energy even though I was in the capital city. This was the era of the Suhrawardy ministry, and strange names to West Pakistani ears, such as Sheikh Mujibur Rahman, Abul Mansur Ahmed and Zaheeruddin, were hitting the headlines of the *Dawn* and *Civil and Military Gazette*, the principal English dailies serving Karachi.

Notwithstanding these political developments in Karachi, I managed, perhaps a few days before the Suez War, to attend a Test match in Karachi where Pakistan was playing the Australian cricket team that was on its way back home from a rather miserable tour of England where Jim Laker had taken 19 of their wickets in one of the Tests. At the Karachi Test, the team, led by Ian Johnson, was handsomely defeated by Pakistan. Fazal Mahmood, whose swing bowling on a matting wicket was virtually unplayable, destroyed the Aussies whose batting line-up included Neil Harvey, Colin McDonald, Ian Craig and an aging Keith Miller. I met old friends at the Test who appeared as oblivious as I was to the impending Suez War.

En Route to Dhaka

Once my father turned up in Karachi at the end of December to take up his assignment at the KIT, I decided to set out for Dhaka to begin my new life. I took the bold decision to travel to Dhaka overland rather than by air. It transpired that a close businessman friend of my father was sending a new car for his Lahore office, so my father suggested I take a ride in the car and get to see the West Pakistan countryside. Shortly after the New Year, I embarked for Lahore, a journey that then took two days by road. The road was quite serviceable and the countryside in the winter sunshine looked tranquil. I remember, en route, through both rural Sind and Punjab, noticing that the police stations tended to be more in evidence and better maintained than the local schools.

On our first day on the road, we passed through Sind, and the princely states of Khairpur and Bahawalpur. At Khairpur, as we passed through the small town of Gambat, I remembered that my Aitchison friend Fakir Aizazuddin's family owned a textile mill there. I took a chance and decided to visit the factory, where I greatly surprised Aizaz by popping in to say hello. As few people visited him at Gambat for social purposes, to see me of all people totally bowled him over. He fed us well and pressed me to stay a few days with him, since life there, for a highly social animal like him, was unbearably irksome. I declined this offer as we had to press on and eventually spent an uncomfortable night at a government rest house, I think in Multan, managing to reach Lahore the next evening.

In Lahore, I stayed with Riaz Mahmood's father, Mir Hasan Mahmood, at his house in Gulberg. Mr Mahmood, a member of the Punjab Civil Services (PCS), lived alone and was a generous host with a dry sense of humour. He was an excellent bridge player and taught Riaz, who eventually captained the Pakistan team, to play bridge. Riaz, in turn, claims to have taught his nephew, Ali Mahmud, who became a world-class bridge player, the finer points of the game. While in Lahore, I caught up with a few of my

Aitchison friends such as Imtiaz Nazir, but others such as Arif and Ifi Bokhari were still at Cambridge.

At Lahore, I took the even more adventurous decision of travelling to Dhaka via a train journey through India. It is hard to imagine, given the fractured land transport systems across South Asia today, that I could buy a ticket in Lahore to travel by rail to Calcutta. My initial rail journey took me from Lahore Cantonment station to Delhi via Amritsar. At Delhi, I transferred to the Howrah Mail, which delivered me two days later to Howrah station in Kolkata. It was a delightful journey where we could savour the various local cuisines at stations along the way. As it was winter, I could travel comfortably in a shared second-class four-berth compartment. These were non-corridor trains, but waiters visited each compartment at key stations to offer us the local fare or meals from the restaurant car.

At Kolkata, I stayed with my grandfather, Sheikh Mustafa Ali, in his house at 53 Elliot Road. My childhood home appeared even more run-down than when I left it in January 1951 to attend Aitchison College in Lahore, reflecting the more straitened circumstances of my grandfather. When I had left Calcutta six years ago, Papa was still in excellent shape. His lifelong commitment to yoga had invested him with the physique of a young man. I now found him emaciated and bedridden, a sorry sight for such a handsome and fit figure of a man. He was, however, alert enough to point out to me the need to improve my spelling and handwriting, which were not obviously up to his standards in the letter I had written to him from Karachi, alerting him to my pending visit to Calcutta. Little did I realize, as I said goodbye to Papa, that this would be the last time I would see him. He passed away within two weeks of my leaving Calcutta.

Jani, my grandmother, prepared some of my favourite dishes, which had remained on my palate throughout my Cambridge days. These included *tehari* to die for, *kata masala*, *chukundur gosht* and her incomparable *shami* kebabs. Beyond meeting a few relations who had remained in Calcutta, I visited some of my old haunts, which included seeing a film at the Lighthouse, having lunch at Firpos and feasting on *khiri* kebab rolls at Nizams.

I did not prolong my stay in Calcutta as I was in some haste to finally reach Dhaka. Travelling from Calcutta to Dhaka by train and boat was still feasible, but I decided to make the hour-long journey by air on Orient Airways, a private airline owned by the Ispahanis, which flew Second World War vintage Dakotas.

A Stranger in Dhaka

Early Exposures

I arrived in Dhaka, my prospective home and the capital of my eventual homeland, Bangladesh, on the morning of 3 January 1957, to begin yet another phase in my life. Dhaka has remained my home ever since and will hopefully be the place where I will be laid to rest when my time comes. I had, before January 1957, spent only a month of my 22 years of life in Dhaka in what was then East Pakistan, in February 1948, when I accompanied my mother and brother, Farooq, to spend a month as the guest of my nana, Khwaja Nazimuddin, the then CM of East Bengal. We had stayed in the CM's residence at Burdwan House on Mymensingh Road. After the electoral massacre of the Muslim League by the Jukta Front in the historic 1954 elections to the provincial legislature, Burdwan House was transformed into the Bangla Academy. The core residence remains intact today, so I still recognize the bedroom on the first floor that I shared with my mother and Farooq during my stay there. It overlooked the entrance and the pond, both of which are also still intact. I remember the pond with nostalgia as I ran races around its perimeter with Khwaja Saifuddin, the younger son of Khwaja Nazimuddin, who was of my age, which was 12. Saif usually won the races.

I have a very limited recollection of the Dhaka of 1948 where my exposure was limited to the area between Mymensingh Road and Dilkusha Gardens in Motijheel, one of the ancestral estates of the DNF. The estate abutted the open fields of Paltan Maidan that served as cricket or football grounds. I remember watching a cricket match there between Mohammedan Sporting Club, then strongly patronized by the Nawab family, and Dhaka Wanderers. Various family members were quite skilled in sports and represented the Mohammedans in cricket, football and hockey. A makeshift movie theatre, Britannia Talkies, located in a tin-roofed structure in one part on the maidan screened English-language movies using rather decrepit prints. Beyond Dilkusha, occasional visits were made by me to Ahsan Manzil, in Islampur, the residence of the Nawab of Dhaka, which was then occupied by various members of the family, some of whom also lived in a number of buildings around Ahsan Manzil.

Other ports of call were the Dhaka Club, which Saif and I usually visited in order to use their new swimming pool, walking there from Burdwan House, across the Race Course. A short bicycle ride took us as far north as Paribagh and Baitul Aman located on Mymensingh Road. There was no Eskaton, no Tejgaon and no Dhanmondi at that time so that most of these areas were then just open fields.

By the time I returned to Dhaka in January 1957, it had begun to resemble a city rather than a mofussil town. However, it should be kept in mind that even at liberation in December 1971, Dhaka's population did not exceed a million, and in 1957, it was perhaps below half a million. At that time, Eskaton Gardens and New Eskaton had come up as new housing developments while Dhanmondi had been developed up to Road No. 7. I was a regular visitor, in those early years in Dhaka, to the residence of Alijoon and Khaleel Ispahani on Road No. 4 in Dhanmondi, which still appeared to be the back of beyond. I still recollect the spectacle of a former CM from the Krishak Sramik Party (KSP), Abul Hossain Sarker, sitting on the porch of his modest one-story house at the entrance of Road No. 4, clad in a *ganji*[1] and lungi. In those days, a sojourn as a minister did not transform you into a millionaire. A plot of land in Dhanmondi appeared to be the summit of their material aspirations. The New Market had been developed and

[1] A cotton vest.

was the main shopping centre along with Jinnah Avenue, now Bangabandhu Avenue.

In Search of a Home

Once in Dhaka, my more immediate concerns were of a rather mundane nature such as finding a place to live and connecting with the social scene where I was, outside of my family, a complete stranger. This process took rather longer than I had expected. It took me a year to find a permanent home in the ground-floor apartment of Kamal Court, 7 New Bailey Road, owned by my *phupi*,[2] the mother of Kamal Hossain. On my arrival in Dhaka at the beginning of January 1957, I had been temporarily accommodated by my uncle Justice Fazle Akbar, my father's middle brother, who was a judge of the Dhaka High Court, in his residence at 29 Minto Road. This residence, with its spacious grounds, was, in later years, assigned as the residence of the Leader of the Opposition in Parliament. In the early 1990s, I recollected visiting Sheikh Hasina, the President of the AL who was then in residence at Minto Road, and recognizing another old haunt where I had spent some happy days.

My uncle was a generous and affectionate host who was happy to educate me on life in Dhaka, as to its politics, our law courts and the state of Dhaka University. However, it took me another year and four changes of residence before I settled down to enjoying the life of a bachelor at large in Dhaka.

My brother, Farooq, who had come to Dhaka after appearing for his Senior Cambridge exams at Burn Hall, Abbottabad, and was now studying for his Intermediate Arts exams at Notre Dame College, shared a room with me and took on the housekeeping responsibilities. We, in turn, shared the apartment with Manzoor Hayat Noon, the son of a former PM of Pakistan, Feroz Khan Noon. Manzoor had been a year junior to me at Aitchison and was up

[2] Paternal aunt.

at Oxford during the years I was at Cambridge. Even though the Noons were one of Punjab's most prominent landowning families, Manzoor had opted for a professional career and had taken up a position with Burmah–Shell in Dhaka. We had secured the services of a Dhaka family cook, Lalli, which ensured that I enjoyed a daily standard of cuisine that I have never been able to attain for the next 55 years of my life. We entertained regularly and our dinner invitations were greatly appreciated.

In my bachelor years at Kamal Court, I improved my mobility by investing Rs 2,500 in a second-hand Škoda car. This investment gave value for money. This became painfully apparent when a front wheel became detached from the car while I was driving to Dhaka University. This, my first car, was eventually put out of its misery when, in my absence from Dhaka, Farooq, to test his non-existent driving skills, took the Škoda for a joyride and turned turtle. The demise of my Škoda encouraged me to move upmarket when I had the good fortune to be able to book one of the first of a batch of Austin Minis being imported to East Pakistan by Dienfa Motors. This could then be purchased for a mere Rs 8,500 and enormously enhanced my sense of well-being and mobility.

My immediate social circle, which at that stage consisted of a few family members, was limited. I was introduced by my uncle Fazle Akbar to Alijoon Ispahani, with whom I immediately established a special friendship that has been sustained to this day. Alijoon and his younger brother, Khaleel, were nephews of Mirza Ahmed Ispahani, known to all as burra sahib, the doyen of the East Pakistan business community. Alijoon was an enormously decent, generous person without any pretentions as to his family's elite status. We used to regularly visit the Gulistan and Naz cinema theatres on Jinnah Avenue to view mostly second-run English movies.

My uncle and Alijoon had put me up for membership to the Dhaka Club, where I was elected a member at the end of 1957. Membership opened up opportunities to swim, play squash and socialize. Otherwise, I simply hung out at Alijoon's bachelor pad on Road No. 4, Dhanmondi. It was easy to slide into this laid-back, irresponsible lifestyle that remained largely untouched by the then chaotic world of Bangali politics.

In Quest of a Profession

My father had expected me to devote some time to his business affairs. However, looking after these interests was hardly likely to be my primary mission on returning to Dhaka. Within a few weeks of my arrival in Dhaka, I read in the papers that the Pakistan Planning Commission was interviewing prospective candidates for positions in the organization. As work in the Planning Commission approximated to my aspirations for influencing public policy, I decided to turn up for the interview. My only tension was that if I was offered a position this would involve my moving to Karachi, the then national capital and seat of the Planning Commission. This could have been counterproductive to my political ambitions that were tied to my presence in Dhaka.

The interviews at the Dhaka Circuit House were being conducted by S.A.F.M.A. Sobhan, no relation, a CSP officer who was one of the few Bangalis to hold a Secretary-level position at the Planning Department of the Provincial administration. He was assisted by two foreign advisors, an Englishman by the name of Philip Chantler and an American by the name of Fred Shorter, who subsequently spent the best part of his career at the Population Council in New York. Sobhan was immediately tantalized by my name, and when he learnt that I was the son of K.F. Sobhan, who he knew well as did most senior bureaucrats at that time, he immediately assumed an avuncular air and was prepared to select me for a position in the Planning Commission. However, when I confessed to my dilemma over seeking such a position but wanting to make my future in Dhaka, Sobhan suggested that there were professional opportunities available in the East Pakistan Planning Board where I could reconcile my immediate career interests with my longer-term aspirations.

Sobhan invited me to visit him at the Provincial Secretariat, at Eden Building in Topkhana Road, which I did in the next few days. He advised me to meet the members of the East Pakistan Planning Board who were reputed teachers at Dhaka University and presided over the planning process. The Board had been recently elevated in status and recast after the AL were sworn into office in the Provincial government. It was at the same time that H.S. Suhrawardy took over as PM of Pakistan towards the end of 1956.

The assumption of office by the AL at the Provincial level had exposed the party to the realities of power in East Pakistan. They soon discovered that the elected government occupied office largely for ornamental reasons while the business of government remained within the exclusive domain of the non-Bangali Secretaries, the highest tier of the Civil Service, who ran the Provincial administration. These Secretaries, who at this stage were mostly members of the CSP or the Audits and Accounts Service, had largely been recruited into the elite services during the British Raj that enhanced their sense of self-worth. They tended to believe that elected politicians were unqualified to formulate policy which required experience and technical skills beyond the capacity of people who could not speak correct English. Under this dispensation, the Provincial government functioned as an extension of the central government while the patronage of the State was channelled to a non-Bangali business elite connected to them through a shared social universe that largely excluded Bangalis.

To challenge this technocratic supremacy of the bureaucrats, the then CM, Ataur Rahman, sought to bring in some expertise of his own from Dhaka University through a strengthened Planning Board that was better equipped to advise the government on economic issues. Professor M.N. Huda, Chair of the Economics Department; Professor A.F.A. Hussain, Chair of the Commerce Faculty; and Mr Abdur Razzaq, a teacher in the Department of Political Science, were brought in as members of the East Pakistan Planning Board. Razzaq had been a contemporary of the then CM, Ataur Rahman, at Dhaka University in the mid-1930s and remained his close confidant. Razzaq was held in high esteem not just within the AL but by other opposition parties and had counselled some of them, in years past, on constitutional matters. When I entered the office of the Planning Board, I expected to see a hive of activity with an array of experts, led by senior economists, preparing weighty papers.

What passed for the Planning Board turned out to be less elevated in status and practice than I had presumed. At the entrance to their office was a small anteroom with two desks. One was occupied by a cherubic, fair young man with a gnomic aspect. He immediately intercepted me, introduced himself as Dr Mosharaff Hossain, Deputy Chief Economist of the Planning Board. The other gentleman, a dark, dour balding man, tending to overweight, was introduced as Mr Monwar Hossain, Assistant Chief Economist, a statistician by training. I was asked by Mosharaff, in impeccable English, not only about my business there but also about my educational antecedents and possibly even my family history. When he learnt that I had an economics degree from Cambridge, he became far more congenial. He observed that he had recently returned with a PhD from the London School of Economics (LSE) where he had been a student of Alan Peacock—distinguished for his work in public finance—and had earlier earned an MA in economics at Manchester University where he was a student of Arthur Lewis, later a Nobel laureate. As I had occasion to read the works of both these eminent scholars, I was much impressed and felt I could entrust my career aspirations into Mosharaff's hands.

From this very first encounter, Mosharaff decided to assume the mantle of my godfather in Dhaka, taking me for an innocent, de-cultured expatriate who would be eaten alive for breakfast by the wily Bangalis who I would encounter along the way. Outside of office hours, he introduced me to his Finnish wife, Inari, who looked disconcertingly young but was, with great fortitude, coping with life in this alien land living with Mosharaff's family at Lal Chand Mukim Lane, off Nawabpur Road, where she had already acclimatized herself to living in a joint family in a house with an outdoor toilet. Never once did Inari complain of her life in Dhaka and embraced me as warmly as Mosharaff, looking on me as an English-speaking partner in a social milieu where everyone conversed in Bangla. Mosharaff and Inari remained among my closest friends over the next 55 years where our lives periodically intersected.

On that fateful encounter, after further enquires had established that I was not a plant of the intelligence agencies but a well-intentioned fool who suffered from the illusion that he could be of some public service, Mosharaff took me to see those formidable professors who had once been his teachers at Dhaka University. At that first encounter, the only inhabitant of a large room furnished with three desks was a rather dark, thin gentleman clad in khadi kurta and pyjama who had his legs stretched across a desk devoid of any papers and was reading a weighty volume, which on closer inspection, turned out to be Gibbon's *The History of the Decline and Fall of the Roman Empire.* The relevance of this literary material to the tasks of planning the economy of East Pakistan was not immediately apparent to me unless it was being studied as a metaphor for the future of the Pakistan State.

Razzaq, who was addressed by Mosharaff as 'Sir', an appellation all of us have since used, soon became a mentor and intimate friend to me and my family. While Sir's academic publications were sparse, his erudition was legendary and underwritten by one of the finest private libraries in Dhaka. He was possessed of a genuinely creative mind that traversed disciplines and inspired a generation.

None of these great qualities were apparent to me in our first encounter. Sir was not too impressed by me or my educational antecedents, particularly after he ascertained my complete unfamiliarity with Bangla. Fortunately, Professor Huda soon appeared and was more sympathetic to my aspirations but pointed out that all recruitment was done by the Planning Department that involved various bureaucratic procedures of Byzantine proportions. This included a written application for the post that was passed on to the Joint Secretary of the department, an ex-police officer by the name of Shamsul Alam, and his subordinate, Shamsur Rahman, known as 'Johnson' on account of his formidable erudition, a younger brother of the then CM, Ataur Rahman.

Over the next nine months, I made periodic visits to the offices of Shamsul Alam and mostly Shamsur Rahman with no prospect of employment in sight. On these visits to the Eden Building, more time was spent in convivial conversations over coffee and *singharas*[3] with Mosharaff and Monwar, where I eventually learnt that these

[3] A seasonal fruit; its English name is water caltrop.

two gentlemen and their three teachers constituted virtually the entire professional capacity of the Planning Board. As Sir pointed out, there was little that the Board's professional services could contribute to transcend the realities of power in the Pakistan State where the CSPs ruled the Secretariat and were accountable not to their political ministers but their administrative superiors in the central government.

On the imposition of martial law across Pakistan in October 1958, the elected governments at the Centre and Provinces were dismissed. As a result, what was recognized as de facto power exercised by bureaucrats was now formally appropriated by the CSPs in a regime headed by the Governor, who was appointed by the Chief Martial Law Administrator (CMLA), Field Marshal Ayub Khan. The three teachers promptly relinquished their positions with the Board. Huda and Hussain returned to Dhaka University, but Razzaq moved abroad on a year's sabbatical at Harvard University, arranged by some of his friends at the Harvard Advisory Group (HAG) who were much impressed by his understanding of the political economy of Pakistan.

First Exposures to the World of Politics

Initial Explorations

When I arrived in Dhaka at the beginning of 1957, the AL had recently ascended to provincial office in East Pakistan. It is not my intention to retail the various intrigues in Karachi and Dhaka that culminated in the AL assuming office in the Centre and in Dhaka. While the Suhrawardy government's minority status at the Centre ensured a rather precarious life, the AL presence in the Provincial parliament was more secure but by no means unshakeable as they depended on the coalition support of some smaller parties. However, at the time that I arrived in Dhaka, there was an element of excitement in the air at the ascendance of the AL, as a party with a strong democratic mandate, who could use it to redress some of the injustices that had hitherto characterized the functioning of the Pakistan State over its first decade.

The provincial CM, Ataur Rahman Khan, was a much respected political figure. Bangabandhu Sheikh Mujibur Rahman, the then General Secretary of the Provincial AL, who was regarded by the Dhaka elite as something of a firebrand, was appointed Minister for Commerce, Labour and Industries (CLI). The AL leadership were an unknown quantity to the real rulers of East Pakistan, the senior bureaucrats and business elite, almost exclusively non-Bengalis, who were inclined to exchange off-colour jokes among themselves about the linguistic infelicities and gauche table manners of these Bangali upstarts who had suddenly been elevated to power.

I had my own personal encounter with this new leadership, courtesy of my nana, Khwaja Nazimuddin, when he moved back to Dhaka. In spite of over three decades in high office as a member of the Viceroy of India's Executive Council, CM of undivided Bengal, CM of East Bengal, Governor-General and then PM of Pakistan, he did not own his own home, even in Dhaka. When he returned to Dhaka after a decade's absence in Karachi, he had to avail of the invitation of his brother, Khwaja Shahabuddin, to occupy his house, Baitul Aman, at Mymensingh Road. His financial circumstances may be compared with the sharp escalation in the fortunes of our contemporary politicians for whom politics has largely become an instrument for material gain.

I was at that time in temporary residence in Baitul Aman with Khwaja Saifuddin. At that time, around June 1957, my nana hosted an intimate dinner for Ataur Rahman, and Bangabandhu. As my nana had returned to his ancestral home in Dhaka after a long absence and was associated with the Muslim League, the long-standing rival of the AL, the dinner was in the nature of a political bridge-building exercise. Such was the civilized nature of political life in those days that these two AL leaders readily accepted the invitation, arrived formally attired in white sherwanis, were exceptionally respectful to my nana and receptive to any assistance he required to settle his affairs in Dhaka. They were, in turn, fed a meal of exceptional splendour, which would have done honour to a Visiting Head of State. As a bystander of this event, I had my first introduction to these two leaders who were politely impressed by my educational attainments and aspirations to be of public service but took no special cognizance of me.

On my arrival in Dhaka, I had exchanged regular letters with Kamal, who was still at Queen's College, Oxford, where he completed his BA in the summer of 1957 and his Bachelor of Civil Law (BCL) in the summer of 1959. Kamal regularly berated me for my irresponsibility in not involving myself in some form of political activism. Agitated by Kamal's epistles, I attempted to touch base with the world of politics but found that my ignorance of Bangla, as also the remoteness of the Dhaka Club from this world, provided few points of entry. Here, fortunately, my growing friendship with Mosharaff served as a serviceable introduction to a more engaged group of middle-class Bangalis who tended to engage in discussions on the iniquities and inequities of the Pakistan State.

During the dinner hosted by my nana for Ataur Rahman and Bangabandhu, they had informed him that a crucial meeting of the Council of the AL was to take place in the next few days, where Maulana Bhasani, Co-founder and President of the Provincial AL, was about to challenge the national President of the party, H.S. Suhrawardy, then the PM of Pakistan, for his failure to realize the degree of autonomy demanded for East Pakistan in the 21-point manifesto of the 1954 Jukta Front. A further and no less explosive critique of the Suhrawardy government, related to its continuing adherence to the pro-Western Baghdad Pact and SEATO, would also be presented at the Council that promised to be polarized between the right and the left wings of the party. These criticisms had already been ventilated at a recent meeting of the AL Council convened by Bhashani at Kagmari.

I had learnt from the dinner conversation between my nana and the AL leaders that the AL Council meeting was being convened at a big hall off Armanitola Maidan. I had begun visiting Armanitola regularly because the offices of Dhaka Tanneries were located next to the Maidan. On the day of the AL Council meeting, it was, thus, easy for me to stroll across and infiltrate myself into the audience.

In these rather casually secured gatherings, it was easy to walk in and hear some of the speakers hold forth with great passion and fluency.

At the meeting, Bhashani and his followers argued strongly to keep the AL-led government loyal to the 21-point demand for both full autonomy and an independent foreign policy. However, Bangabandhu, who was not only General Secretary of the Provincial AL but effectively controlled the organization, persuaded the Council, many of whom were possibly sympathetic to the Maulana's concerns, to stay loyal to Suhrawardy and his policies. Bangabandhu himself was far from sympathetic with the positions of Suhrawardy, who he invariably addressed as Boss, that sufficient autonomy had been invested on East Pakistan during the tenure of his regime. Bangabandhu had, from his days as a student activist in Calcutta, emerged as a dedicated disciple of Suhrawardy, and remained unflinching in his loyalty to his Boss throughout his lifetime. In consequence of his defeat at two consecutive AL council sessions, Bhashani subsequently resigned from the AL, along with a number of progressive elements in the party.

Discovering the Left

The defeat of Bhashani at the AL Council meeting, which I had witnessed, provided me with further opportunities to pursue my rather casual study of East Pakistan politics. Around the beginning of July 1957, some weeks after the Council meeting, I had a strange call from someone who claimed to know me from Cambridge, one Harvey Stockwin. The Stockwin I knew at Cambridge had been a loyal member of the CUCA. I have already reported on my encounter with Stockwin at Cambridge, on the occasion of the debate between the Cambridge Majlis and CUCA, where Harvey had argued fiercely against the motion rejecting SEATO.

This same Harvey Stockwin had now materialized in Dhaka as a first step towards building a career in front-line journalism. Notwithstanding our political differences, I had maintained perfectly amicable social relations with Harvey at Cambridge, so he did not feel too embarrassed to request me to provide him with bed and board while he was in Dhaka as he had begun his journey with a rather meagre budget. Regrettably, though perhaps fortunately for me, I had no home of my own to offer as I was then a guest at Baitul Aman. All I could do was to take Harvey along to the Press Club on Topkhana Road and persuade its secretary to offer him one of the few guest rooms available to itinerant journalists. The Press Club then consisted of a modest two-storeyed building with rather basic residential facilities and culinary options, but it did offer these services at a cost that Harvey could afford. Though these were normally available for only short stays, Harvey spent close to two months at the Press Club.

At that time, Bhashani had already quit the AL with his followers. He was now actively engaged in establishing an all-Pakistan party of the left drawing in left-wing members of the AL along with other left parties such as the Communist Party. They expected to join hands with a variety of regional-based and left parties in West Pakistan with a more progressive and secular orientation. This included the famous Khudai Khidmatgars known as Red Shirts, of the NWFP and Baluchistan, led by Khan Abdul Ghaffar Khan, the revered Frontier Gandhi; the leader of Sindhi nationalism, G.M. Syed; and a number of leftists from Punjab, such as Mian Iftikharuddin and Mian Mahmud Ali Kasuri, one of the leading lawyers of Lahore. This configuration of historic political figures, along with a large body of their followers, was flying into Dhaka to attend a convention at the Roopmahal Cinema in Sadarghat, to launch this new party. All Dhaka was buzzing with the exciting prospect of such historic figures sitting on the same platform.

The meeting at Roopmahal was to be convened for 25–26 July 1957. Harvey demanded that I take him there to be an eyewitness to this episode of anti-imperialist history. I duly turned up on the first day of the event, 25 July, in the late morning, at the Roopmahal, with Harvey and his camera in tow. Our first exposure to the event was to come across a picket, established some distance from the event. This not very numerous gathering was controlled by A.R. Yusuf, a founder of the National Students Federation (NSF), a gaunt, sinister-looking man who was reputed to be close to the

Muslim League and also patronized by the intelligences agencies. While Yusuf was clearly the mastermind of the event, the gathering, at least when we were present, was being harangued with considerable eloquence by a young man by the name of Mahbubur Rahman, whose repeated slogan, *Bhashani goonda*,[4] *Bharat-er-dalal*,[5] has remained embedded in my memory over the next half a century. These memories invoked a sense of irony in me when the Maulana, after the emergence of an independent Bangladesh, in the final years of his political life, graduated into an anti-Indian phase, expressed through his paper, *Haq Kotha*, where he castigated the AL regime, led by Bangabandhu, for its subservience to India.

While Mahbub continued his harangue, Yusuf appeared quite willing to educate us on the 'Indian-sponsored' antecedents of the meeting underway at the Roopmahal. During the course of our discussions with Yusuf and some other demonstrators, it became apparent that the gathering was not exclusively an NSF affair and had considerable representation from the East Pakistan Students League (EPSL), the student wing of the AL, even though their erstwhile president, Maulana Bhashani, was hosting the meeting at Roopmahal.

So far the demonstration, conducted at a safe distance from the Roopmahal behind a police cordon, had been noisy and rhetorically offensive but not violent. This modus vivendi threatened to take an uglier turn when a taxi turned up when we were there, carrying Mian Iftikharuddin, president of the miniscule Azad Pakistan Party based in Lahore that was part of the conclave assembled at the Roopmahal. Mian Sahib must have been rather taken aback when his passage to the Roopmahal Cinema was blocked by this small but aggressive mob who, identifying him as a participant of the Roopmahal gathering, began striking the roof of his taxi with lathis. Mian Sahib was a smallish man but no coward. He, therefore, rashly opted to step out of the taxi and reason with the mob. As always, he was dressed in his favourite uniform, tight pyjamas made from the finest cotton and an immaculately tailored sherwani. Before any

[4] Hoodlum.
[5] Agent of India.

such conversation could take place or I could step forward to warn Mian Sahib, a lathi descended on his knee. This, if anything, further aroused Mian Sahib's combative instincts, but his taxi driver, who was possessed of more sense, dragged him back into the car and drove off as fast as he could to the Shahbag Hotel where Mian Sahib was in residence.

This adventure had its own amusing aftermath. That evening, I dropped into the Shahbag to enquire after the health of my friend's father. I found Mian Sahib lying in bed nursing a swollen knee. Mian Sahib had, in consequence of his injury, been compelled to opt out of the remaining events of the day at Roopmahal. At this stage, who should materialize at his room unannounced but Bangabandhu. They knew each other well since the early 1950s. Until the present political developments, Mian Sahib and his party had been strong advocates of the 21-point programme of the Jukta Front and were perceived as a strong ally of the democratic movement in East Pakistan.

Bangabandhu's opening gesture was to proclaim "Mian Sahib, you are my guest in Dhaka who would dare to do this to you." As Mian Sahib's injury may possibly have been inflicted by a Student's League hoodlum, this piece of theatre was much appreciated by Mian Sahib who winked at me. Politics in those days appeared to observe some decencies so that Bangabandhu had himself turned up at the Shahbag to mend fences with his opponent. I explained my personal ties with Mian Sahib to Bangabandhu who had immediately recognized me from our dinner encounter at Baitul Aman and wondered at my rather eclectic political relationships, traversing from the right to the left.

After the exit of Mian Iftikharuddin from Sadarghat, Harvey and I had managed to negotiate our way through A.R. Yusuf's mobs to explore the atmospherics of the gathering at Roopmahal. The immediate outcome of the gathering was a decision that all the component parties present at the Roopmahal would subsume their political identities in a single party, the NAP, committed to full autonomy for Pakistan's five provinces, an independent foreign policy and a secular polity. At the meeting, we learnt that a public meeting at Paltan Maidan was scheduled for the 26 July at the conclusion of the conclave and was to be addressed by the same leaders.

Harvey, who had sensed that there may be some excitement in the offing at Paltan Maidan, insisted that I escort him there. When we arrived there in the afternoon of the 26 July, the meeting was already in progress with this assembly of emminent leaders from all over Pakistan sitting on the podium. I sensed that the crowds assembling outside Paltan Maidan, as also in the rear of the gathering inside, could not all be regarded as sympathizers of the event and suggested that we locate ourselves at a position with clear exit points. But Harvey merely scoffed at my caution and insisted I take him to the front of the crowd sitting on the ground from where he clicked away on his Brownie camera at the leaders on the dais as well as the crowd behind him.

As the meeting proceeded, hostile murmurs, escalating into shouts and slogans from the crowd behind us, gathered momentum. It was not long before the first volley of brickbats directed at the leaders on the podium sailed over our heads and progressively grew in volume. I suggested we make for the exit, but Harvey would have nothing of this and positioned himself at the front of the gathering so he could photograph these acts of political violence. As the volley of stones increased and started landing with regularity on the podium, one such stone narrowly missed Harvey's head. At this point, I physically dragged him away from the front line so we could position ourselves at a safer vantage point behind rather than in front of the crowd. From there, we observed the stone throwing was now assuming an intensity that threatened the lives of the leaders. At this stage, it was decided to abandon the meeting and the leaders moved in a procession along the south side of the maidan, towards the exit opening onto Jinnah (Bangabandhu) Avenue. As they moved towards the exit, the stone throwing continued. I recollect vividly the spectacle of some of the heftier Pathan and Baluch workers forming a cordon to protect their leaders and leaping into the air to intercept the stones that threatened them.

The emergence of the NAP did not have any significant impact on West Pakistan politics, though it did strengthen the movement for provincial autonomy. In Bangladesh, the NAP at its creation was a significant force led by one of East Pakistan's most prominent and respected leaders, Maulana Bhashani. The NAP became a home to all the left-wing political formations as also to the influential left-wing intelligentsia of East Pakistan. The East Pakistan Student's Union (EPSU) was the student wing of the party where it attracted the brighter and more committed students. Unfortunately for the cause of the left, the NAP in East Pakistan let itself be used as a political instrument by anti-democratic forces out to destabilize and discredit the democratic process. The end result of such intrigues, where the NAP played its part, was the declaration of martial law by Ayub Khan in October 1958.

8

Dhaka: Adventures in the Private Sector

The Pioneering Entrepreneur

The first phase of my life in Dhaka coincided with my rather brief engagement with what passed for the private sector in the then East Pakistan. It will indeed come as something of a surprise to my well-wishers in the business community when they learn that I was one of the earliest of the Muslim Bangali participants in the private sector of East Pakistan. This somewhat unexpected feature of my formative years owes entirely to my father who must assume the distinction of being one of the first Bangali Muslim industrialists in the new East Pakistan.

When my father retired from the Imperial Police Service in 1947, he demonstrated a remarkably good eye for entrepreneurial ventures. As far back as 1953, he had moved to set up the first modern tannery in East Bengal if not in all Pakistan. East Bengal goat skins or *kid* were already well known in the world export market so that the conversion of this skin into semi-processed and finished leather was a potentially sound business venture. At that time, only a few Bangali Muslims such as A.K. Khan were active in business. Indeed, when Dhaka Tanneries was set up by my father, in partnership with the late Rai Bahadur R.P. Shaha and two experienced leather technologists from Czechoslovakia, this promised to be one of the first industrial investments in East Bengal after partition.

Somewhere in the early 1950s, the Czechs and R.P. Shaha sold out their share to K.B. Shamsuddahar, a retired colleague of my father in the Police Service. Dhaka Tanneries then moved to construct its own factory in Hazaribagh in Dhaka that was being developed as an industrial estate for tanneries. When I returned from England in January 1957, Dhaka Tanneries was the biggest tannery in East Pakistan and was, in addition to their own establishment in Hazaribagh, managing under lease, a modern tannery set up by the government to provide practical exposure to the trainees of the East Pakistan Institute of Leather Technology in Hazaribagh. Dhaka Tanneries in 1957 employed about 500 workers, had three experienced Chinese tanners aided by two Bangalis from Noakhali, to run the factories.

Taking account of these inspired business moves of my father, one would reckon that our family should have today been enjoying a tycoon-class lifestyle. Unfortunately, this was not to be. My father never lived to enjoy the fruits of his entrepreneurial genius. He really hated having to cheat, lie and debase himself before officials, nor could be spread money around to open all doors for himself. He thought his personality and his extraordinary connections with all the top people of India and Pakistan would be enough to get all his ventures to yield the most lavish fruits. But at the end of the day, it was his less scrupulous business associates who enjoyed these fruits.

Adventures in the Leather Business

By the time I arrived in Dhaka in January 1957, two months before my 22nd birthday, my father was in residence in Karachi, running the KIT. He bequeathed custodial authority of his 51 per cent share in Dhaka Tanneries to me along with a sheaf of instructions of what I should do to look after his interests. In fact, I had very little to do in running Dhaka Tanneries as my father had leased control over his share of the tanneries to Captain Nurruddahar, the eldest son of K.B. Shamsuddahar, and to Mohammed Amin, a Chinioti leather merchant whose family had for several generations engaged in the leather business in Calcutta and now traded in leather and hides in East Pakistan. I was permitted to exercise a watching brief over my father's interests in Dhaka Tanneries, though my precise responsibilities were never made clear to me or the extent of my veto power over the actions of Dahar and Amin.

The head office of Dhaka Tanneries was located at Hasina House, Armanitola. Hasina House was an old zamindar house, known to most people in the neighbourhood as Rai House, which had been bought by Shamsuddahar from its original owners. With this house, he also inherited the Ananda Moyee Girls School that used to share the ground floor of Rai House with Dhaka Tanneries. The upper floor served as the residence of the Dahar's joint family. My exposure to the leather trade in Dhaka thus began in the dark and cavernous durbar hall of a Hindu zamindar.

The Dhaka Tanneries factory was located in Hazaribagh, which in those days was approached through Pilkhana, beyond the New Market and the cantonment of the East Pakistan Rifles (EPR), through winding lanes that landed you in the malodorous tannery colony. My first visits there were akin to a sinner's first exposure to hell. The smell of rotting hides, chemicals and the effluent of the tanneries that flowed through open drains all over Hazaribagh used to haunt me at night and still lingers, after all these years, in my memory if not in my nostrils. It was surmised by Amin that a person of my presumed refined sensibilities, just back from England, would never return to Hazaribagh for a second visit and would remain content to while away my afternoons at Hasina House. In fact, I continued to visit Hazaribagh quite regularly to at least provide myself with a nodding acquaintance of the leather business even if I was to be given little opportunity to be directly involved in its actual management.

It took me some time to learn something of the business dynamics of the tannery sector. It eventually became clearer to me that a profitable part of the leather business originated not just from the tanning of skins and the sale of leather but in the sale of imported chemicals and dyestuffs. In the 1950s and 1960s, Pakistan was one of the most protected and regulated economies in the world. Every industry and trader ran their business on import licences the size of which determined the size of their fortune. The rupee was massively overvalued and the system of import licensing provided such permit holders with opportunities to reap sizeable rents. These rents were extracted from the scarcity premiums derived from a regime of fixed exchange rates in a foreign exchange-constrained economy.

Dhaka Tanneries' substantive business was derived from the export to West Pakistan of a large part of the sole and upper leather made in the factory from cow hides, which provided it with quite a lucrative income. I used to see these unsightly, evil-smelling hides being transformed into leather and became quite fascinated by the conversion process to the point where I adjusted my senses to the unpleasant environment of Hazaribagh.

The Bakrid festival was traditionally the big event of the tannery industry as a large part of their hide purchases were made following the *qurbani*.[1] The tanners descended on the hide market at Postagola to make their purchases immediately after the mass slaughter of animals. In my first year at Dhaka Tanneries, Amin, perhaps as a further rite of passage, invited me to accompany him to Postagola to witness these horrific transactions for purchasing freshly extracted hides and skins. I did not repeat the experience and do not recommend it for those with weak stomachs and sensitive nostrils.

At Hasina House, my command of English made me a useful person to handle office correspondence. These assets became more serviceable when Dhaka Tanneries moved into the export market after the introduction of the Export Bonus Scheme in 1960. This scheme, established by the martial law regime of Ayub Khan, was designed to use the premium on scarce foreign exchange to incentivize exports. Exporters were permitted to retain part of their export earnings and to sell these at a premium, in the open market, to prospective importers. The premium served as a form of export subsidy to all exporters, at a period when the rupee was heavily overvalued. The Export Bonus Scheme was extraordinarily successful in stimulating Pakistan's export of jute goods, textiles and leather, mostly in its semi-processed form, known as 'wet blue'.

[1] Festival of sacrifice.

The ready access to bonus vouchers however reduced the rents from sale of import licences, as all importers could meet their needs for foreign exchange by buying bonus vouchers on the open market. Dhaka Tanneries, along with other better-equipped tanneries, were thereby encouraged to switch from manufacturing exclusively for the domestic market towards the export of processed hides. From 1958 onward, I found myself in the more satisfactory role of promoting exports from Dhaka Tanneries to the UK, Italy, Hong Kong, Singapore and other parts of the globe. My skills as a correspondent were, thus, put to good use in securing export orders where I could claim some modest successes.

The world of private business in the late 1950s seemed largely to depend on keeping the Directorate of Commerce and Industries, the office of the Controller of Imports and Exports and the customs officials at the ports in good humour. In those days, such officials enjoyed the status of minor royalty in the eyes of the business community. The Secretary for CLI in the Eden Building was regarded as a higher deity. Petty officials at all levels also had to be propitiated.

I remember an occasion when Ghulam Ahmed Madani, then the Chairman of the DIT, was persuaded to visit Hazaribagh to do something about its environmentally hazardous state. The state of Hazaribagh, which was an industrial estate developed by the government, was the responsibility of the DIT for its sewerage, maintenance and construction of an effluent disposal unit. When Madani visited Hazaribagh, which he promptly categorized as *Jahannam*[2] Colony, he arrived as a visiting potentate in whose presence the largely Chinioti owners of the tanneries were hesitant to speak at all. I was roped in to practise my Cambridge English on Madani and managed to get back at his observation that Hazaribagh was *Jahannam* by reminding him that it was the job of the DIT to make it into a more saintly habitation. He treated this insolence with a scowl that terrified all because Madani was undoubtedly one of the ugliest people I have met, resembling the goddess Kali, who could easily have served as a presiding deity in the *Jahannam* of Hazaribagh. It says something of the state of governance in the

[2] An Islamic concept of 'Hell'.

then Pakistan and in an independent Bangladesh that the environmentally deadly pollutions of Hazaribagh still remain unaddressed, 58 years after my nostrils were first assaulted.

Lessons on the Political Economy of the Private Sector

Exposure to the business world in that period sowed in me the seeds of my commitment to a self-governed East Pakistan. To see these non-Bangali bureaucrats lording over petty businessmen was a humiliating experience. Witnessing the ways in which businessmen had to bow and scrape, to lie and cheat, persuaded me both on the need for a relocation of power to local hands and also on the need for a stronger State sector to compensate for the weaknesses of the indigenous business community. I should have also been better sensitized about the virtues of import liberalization, deregulation, exchange rate competitiveness and the need to get bureaucrats off the backs of the private sector.

In the 1950s, the private sector in East Pakistan was a largely non-Bangali show dominated by the traditional business communities of Punjabi Chiniotis, Memons, Bohras and members of the Aga Khan community, all mostly drawn from western India. The outliers were the Ispahanis who had migrated from Iran to Calcutta in the 19th century and had established themselves as major figures in the business community in competition with the Marwaris. At the time of Partition, much of the jute trade in East Bengal was controlled by the Marwaris. Some Bengali Hindus had established textile mills in Narayanganj, while R.P. Shaha had established a pioneering presence in the inland water transport sector.

When Pakistan emerged in 1947, these mostly trading communities, such as the Adamjees, Bawanis and Amins, had moved from Calcutta to Dhaka, but, except for the Ispahanis whose businesses remained exclusively located in East Pakistan, the other communities diversified their investments into West Pakistan that remained their home and business base. These migrant business houses eventually displaced the more vulnerable Hindu business houses to the point where they came to dominate the jute business, general trade and eventually the emerging industrial sector built around jute manufactures, textiles, leather and a few other sectors. The Adamjee Jute Mills, established by the Adamjees with strong backing from the State-owned PIDC, was reportedly, the largest jute mill in the world.

Bangalis were barely visible in the business sector. A.K. Khan, a government official who had married into a prosperous trading family that had made its fortune in Burma, was the only Bangali business house to make it into the ranks of the 22 families who came to dominate Pakistan's private sector. When the AL briefly held power in the provincial government of East Pakistan, they were hard put to locate Bangali business houses to patronize.

It was not until the early 1960s that the Ayub regime, in order to build up its local support base in East Pakistan, began to use State resources, first through development finance institutions such as the Industrial Development Bank of Pakistan (IDBP) and then through equity support provided by the East Pakistan Industrial Development Corporation (EPIDC), to underwrite the emergence of a Bangali industrial bourgeoisie. What passed for a Bangali first-generation private sector, located mostly in the jute and textile industry and in a few banks and insurance companies, was a by-product of this State-sponsored entrepreneurship in the 1960s. In the growth of this new class, the role of the Bangali CSP officers, once they attained more senior positions in the Provincial Secretariat, should be recognized along with the contribution of the Bangali Managing Director of IDBP, Mahbub Raschid, in the 1960s.

In the early days, most aspirant Bangali businessmen, who operated in the shadow of their non-Bangali counterparts, remained strong backers of the AL. They hoped that when the AL came to power, it would extend sufficient patronage to empower them to compete with the non-Bangalis. In spite of the State patronage extended under the Ayub regime in the 1960s, at the liberation of Bangladesh, the new Bangali bourgeoisie accounted for a mere

3 per cent of the industrial assets located in Bangladesh. The bulk of the private assets were owned by the non-Bangalis who abandoned them prior to liberation and fled away to West Pakistan.

Trade Diplomacy in South East Asia

I was given some direct exposure to this business world dominated by non-Bangalis when I was invited to join a business delegation being sent abroad in mid-1959 by the newly incumbent Ayub regime to explore business prospects in East and South East Asia. As most of the representatives in the delegation originated in West Pakistan, the government perceived that a token East Pakistani presence would be appropriate. At that time, one of the East Pakistan–based industries that was deemed to have export potential was tanneries. As Dhaka Tanneries was at that point the largest enterprise in the tannery sector, we were invited to participate in the delegation. Nuruddahar was unwilling to join the mission so I was nominated for this, with Dhaka Tanneries covering the costs of my travel. To elevate my status in this delegation, I was—then aged 24—elevated to the position of President of the All Pakistan Tanners Association! While the delegation, which included a scion of the Dawood family, Siddique Dawood, then the largest business house in Pakistan, all travelled first class, I faced the embarrassment of accompanying them from the economy class, which reflected the extent to which Dhaka Tanneries were willing to invest in my mission.

Our five-member delegation included a Punjabi manufacturer of hospital equipment, the President of the Sports Goods Manufacturers Association and the President of the Hosiery Goods Manufacturers Association. This did not indicate that a particularly strong or diversified manufacturing base prevailed in Pakistan at that time.

Our delegation was led by a Joint Secretary from the Ministry of Commerce, a CSP officer from West Pakistan. I discovered that in those days, even a Joint Secretary of the central government of

Pakistan enjoyed plenipotentiary status. In his presence, our businessmen and even ambassadors tended to genuflect themselves. Such was the sense of self-exhalation enjoyed by this official that, as I recollect, when we reached Tokyo, he kept a number of senior executives from such Japanese corporate giants as Mitsui and Mitsubishi, which could even then have afforded to buy up the entire economy of Pakistan, waiting for an hour before he languidly made his appearance at a scheduled meeting with our delegation.

For me the journey to regions east was a great adventure. None of the members were aware of my youth. As I looked older than my 24 years and spoke with the confidence of a more senior person, I was accepted as an equal. My relatively superior command of English and willingness to do some homework on the economies of the countries visited by the delegation soon elevated me to the position of lead spokesman for the group, in spite of my rather modest standing as a business person. Since I was also unwilling to recognize the hallowed status of a Joint Secretary and spoke English more fluently than our team leader, he treated me with more respect than he showed to other members of the delegation who came to resent his superior airs.

At our first stop in Rangoon, we entered through the newly built airport, then more modern than anything on offer in Pakistan and stayed at the historic Strand Hotel, one of those classic colonial relics. At that stage, business in Burma was still heavily dominated by Indians and Pakistanis, while the Burmese entrepreneurs included a strong representation of women. Rangoon, then, was a thriving city compared to the rather faded city I revisited in 1999 in the last days of the stifling military regime.

From Rangoon we travelled to Bangkok, which in 1959 was not much more developed than Dhaka and less so compared to Karachi. There were only a few major hotels on offer. We stayed in the Asia Hotel, close to the Grand Palace, around which most of the government offices were also located. The city was then still a rather laid-back town full of greenery, criss-crossed by canals. In our meetings with the Thai delegations, I managed to impress them with my presumed insightful knowledge of Thai politics, culled from my readings of *Time* magazine and the *New Statesman*.

One Thai official observed that he knew nothing at all about Pakistan so how could I know so much about Thailand!

From Bangkok we went on to Malaysia, which had only recently been granted independence by the British. Kuala Lumpur still retained its largely colonial character with virtually no industrial base of any consequence. Its prosperity originated in exports of its rubber plantations and tin mines. Our next stop, Singapore, appeared to us to be a continuation along the trajectory of the British Raj. We stayed in the then unreconstructed historic Raffles Hotel. Singapore was then still under British rule and was little more than an entrepôt town where Somerset Maugham would have felt comfortable sipping a gin and tonic on the verandah of the Raffles Hotel.

While we were there, an election campaign was underway to establish who would govern Singapore following the imminent end of British rule. The then dominant political figure in Singapore, who had already been brought into the government, Marshall, was expected to head the postcolonial regime. He was being challenged in the election by a fiery, young, Cambridge-educated lawyer by the name of Lee Kuan Yew who headed a party that was deemed by our Singapore business associates to be too far left to be able to win the elections. Some days after we left Singapore, we were much surprised to read in the papers that the leftist party had comprehensively won the elections and that its leader had been elected PM. The rest, as they stay, is history. Singapore, as with other South East Asian countries we visited, was a decade away from emerging as an Asian tiger. It was then a trading hub dominated by British business houses, but we noticed that Chinese and Indian business houses were already emerging to challenge them.

From Singapore we moved further south to Indonesia, then ruled by its charismatic founding father, President Soekarno. In spite of its natural wealth, which had enriched its Dutch colonial masters, the economy appeared less developed than that of Pakistan and appeared to be poorly governed. We stayed in one of the top hotels in Jakarta, but its electricity and water supply tended to be irregular. Soekarno became a strong supporter of Pakistan in the era of Ayub where Bhutto, as Foreign Minister, was his special friend due, in part, to some shared non-political proclivities.

We moved on from Jakarta to Saigon, then the capital of what was South Vietnam. An incipient revolt, spearheaded by the Việt Cộng, was ongoing in the countryside of South Vietnam when we arrived in Saigon. This, in practice meant, we could not travel outside Saigon and had to promote our exports exclusively within the capital city. The insurgency, which grew in intensity from the beginning of the 1960s, culminating in an outright victory by the Communists and the unification of Vietnam in 1975, had not yet penetrated Saigon.

In 1959, Saigon was still a largely French colonial outpost, though the US presence was now more visible. We stayed in an old colonial hotel, the Caravelle. Much of the surrounding architecture had been built and occupied by the French. The French language was still favoured by the Vietnamese elite, though some English was now also spoken so that they could communicate with the US army, bureaucrats and a small community of American business personnel, now increasingly visible. A number of restaurants still served quality French cuisine. In the few days we were there, we read snippets of news about some insurgent action in the countryside, but my attempts to persuade our hosts to take me out on an excursion outside Saigon were politely discouraged. I do not recollect if much export business was secured in Saigon.

Our next stop in Manila was no more fruitful. The city was run-down, and movement outside the Manila Hotel, where we stayed, was discouraged for security reasons. I was fortunate to locate a Cambridge contemporary of mine, Joe Romero, whose father came from one of Manila's elite families and had served as Ambassador to the USA. Joe took me around town and entertained me at his club where I learnt something about the economy and politics of the Philippines from him. Business outcomes remained unpromising as the Philippines economy was neither developed nor prospering. The US influence over the country's business and politics was strong and invoked considerable, if subdued, anti-Americanism.

From Manila we flew on to Tokyo, where we stayed in the classic Imperial Hotel designed by Frank Lloyd Wright. Japan was, as yet, someway from reaching its global eminence as a major economic power, but its rapid growth was visible where the opulence of parts of Tokyo impressed us. Visits to some leading department stores in the Ginza area indicated a level of luxury that appeared to surpass what I had seen on Oxford Street in London. The city itself had just begun its vertical growth, but in those days, much of Tokyo still retained its traditional-style houses with paper-built inner walls and tatami mat–covered floors.

Exposure to the top corporate elite of Tokyo was less productive than it might have been, given the rather casual approach of our delegation leader. However, Pakistan was already heavily engaged with Japan, which had not only invested in some large projects such as the Fenchuganj Fertilizer Factory and the Chittagong Steel Mills but also was one of the biggest importers of cotton yarn from Pakistan. Siddique Dawood, as a member of Pakistan's largest textile manufacturing conglomerate, was much in demand. I managed to locate some export opportunities for Pakistan's leather industry in Japan.

Our final stop was Hong Kong. We were received by Abdur Rab, a Bangali, who served as a trade commissioner for Pakistan and was, far and away, the most efficient and dynamic trade representative we had so far encountered in our travels. He was well connected to the local business community and ensured that we actively engaged with them. Hong Kong was then a British-ruled trading outpost, still a long way from the end of the Empire. British taipans such as Jardine Matheson still dominated the economy, mostly operating out of the island of Hong Kong where we stayed in the Gloucester Hotel. Dhaka Tanneries had already opened up some exports to Hong Kong, thanks to the efficiency of Rab, who had already corresponded with us about business opportunities in Hong Kong so I was kept quite gainfully employed during my stay.

Hong Kong was yet to initiate its explosive growth as a manufacturer and exporter of labour-intensive manufacturing goods so that much of the goods in the market were imported duty-free, which had earned it recognition as a shopper's paradise. I was advised to move to the mainland part of Hong Kong on Kowloon, which was then accessed from Hong Kong by a highly efficient ferry service. Kowloon was largely a Chinese-dominated enclave that resembled parts of North Calcutta and was as overcrowded but better maintained, with opportunities for low-cost purchases as well as access to some excellent Chinese cuisine.

As I returned home, I appreciated that my travels in Asia provided an excellent exposure to a world I knew little about or expected to visit. In Pakistan, our attention was always directed to the West, which was associated with the good life. Our visit to Japan had opened my eyes to the emerging potential of an Asian country. Pakistan, in 1959, had developed a larger, more diversified manufacturing base than any South East Asian country we had visited where the export of primary products was still their dominant economic activity. The explosive growth of labour-intensive manufacturing exports, first in the Republic of Korea (ROK) and Taiwan, then in the Association of Southeast Asian Nations (ASEAN) region, was still to come. None in our delegation, or indeed anyone else in Pakistan or even South East Asia, could have imagined the subsequent transformation in the economic fortunes of these outposts of the empire.

9

Dhaka University: Teaching Economics and Learning to Be a Teacher

Dhaka University: The Beginnings

Introduction to Dhaka University

Since my arrival in Dhaka, I had been preoccupied with educating myself about the leather business, making occasional visits to the Eden Building, punctuated by excursions to Calcutta to deal with the property affairs of my parents and even the occasional touristic adventure in the world of politics. Such an eclectic pattern of life did not lend itself to the construction of a more purposeful professional career. As I pondered my future, providence extended its hand to me through the thoughtful intervention of Professor M.N. Huda.

During his tenure as a member of the Planning Board, Huda had taken note of my growing frustration over my futile safaris to the Secretariat in search of a letter of appointment to the Planning Board. Around September 1957, he suggested that recruitments were about to be made for teachers in the Department of Economics and that I should consider applying for the position of a Senior Lecturer as I had a degree, with a good result, from Cambridge University. He wisely advised me that if I sought a career in government service, it may be more sensible for career mobility for me to compete for and join the CSP. But if I aspired to retain my independence as a professional and leave open opportunities for engaging with the political process, then a position at Dhaka University provided more options.

I was at that stage still set on joining the Planning Board but had recognized that a position at Dhaka University provided greater flexibility for me to combine my teaching obligations with my entrepreneurial engagements and also to attend to other family responsibilities. Huda's guidance was thus extremely valuable in persuading me to put in an application for the position of Senior Lecturer, where I was duly selected. I look back on Huda's career guidance with deep appreciation because my association with Dhaka University turned out to have a defining influence in shaping my future.

My teaching career at the Economics Department of Dhaka University began in October 1957 and effectively continued until 26 March 1971. I remained affiliated to the University up to 1977 when I eventually wrote a letter from Oxford to Professor M.N. Huda, then still the Chair of the Economics Department, tendering my formal resignation from the position of Professor at the Department. Between 1971 and 1977, I had participated in the Liberation War, served as a member of the Planning Commission (January 1972–September 1974) and briefly returned to the Economics Department for a few weeks before I took over from Mosharaff Hossain as Chairman, Bangladesh Institute of Development Studies (BIDS). During this period, I had been dismissed as a teacher of Dhaka University in 1971 as I was proclaimed an enemy of the State by the martial law regime, then headed by General Tikka Khan. I was reinstated at the University, along with other dismissed teachers, after Liberation but remained on official leave, initially during my tenure at the Planning Commission, subsequently at BIDS and after 1975 at Queen Elizabeth House (QEH), Oxford. It was at Oxford that I took the fateful decision to end my teaching career and commit myself to development research at BIDS.

My 14 years at Dhaka University served as the definitive years of my life. Cambridge had played a transformative role in shaping my intellectual views and investing it with a radical ideological perspective. However, it was at Dhaka University that I forged a political identity that continues to define me and what I stand for, even today.

Professor Huda, while a member of the Planning Board, continued to invest time in discharging some of his duties as Chair of the Economics Department. He was thus present at the faculty to induct the new teachers into the Department. When I went in to meet Huda in his office in the Arts Building in October 1957, I had no idea that Dhaka University would play such a significant role in my life. At that stage, I still retained aspirations for working on policy issues at the Planning Board and had been assured by Huda that he would provide such opportunities for me as he retained his presence as a member of the Planning Board while still chairing the Economics Department. It was not until the declaration of martial law a year later, when Huda, Razzaq and A.F.A. Hussain ended their involvement with the Board, that I looked on my association with Dhaka University as a more enduring relationship.

At that time, Dhaka University still retained some of the academic lustre that had once earned it recognition as the Oxford of the East. This title may have somewhat overstated its distinction, but from its foundation in the 1920s to the emergence of Pakistan in 1947, a large number of distinguished scholars had populated its various faculties. At the partition of India and Bengal in 1947, many of those eminent scholars, apprehensive of their future in a State that chose to define its identity by its majority religion, departed reluctantly to continue their careers in India. The residual population of Muslim teachers, leavened by a few remaining Hindu faculty members such as Professor Aiyar, who continued for some years after partition as Chair of the Economics Department, were not without scholastic distinction but could hardly fill the void created by their departing colleagues. In the aftermath of this exodus, Dhaka University still retained some scholars of distinction such as Professor Habibullah of Islamic History; Professor Ahmad Hasan Dani, a famous archaeologist; and Qazi Motahar Hussain, a statistician of some recognition.

The Economics Department was one of the casualties of the exodus. Professor M.N. Huda, who had attained academic distinction as a student having won the Kali Narayan Scholarship for the most outstanding result across the University in the MA/MSc examinations and later acquired a PhD at Cornell University, took over the chair from Professor Aiyar when he eventually departed for India. Huda lent some weight to the Department but did not, in his tenure, expend much time on research and publication. His skills lay in building his department and in later years in policymaking. He served as a member of Pakistan's Planning Commission, later as provincial Finance Minister during the tenure of Monem Khan, the Governor of East Pakistan, and finally as Finance Minister during the regime of General Ziaur Rahman, in the period 1977–81.

Colleagues and Comrades

Huda was an enormously decent human being who attempted to make the best of his limited resources at the Department. His principal colleague and contemporary, from his student days at Dhaka University, was Dr Mazharul Haq—a tall, handsome man with the profile of a Roman emperor. Haq was also Provost of Fazlul Huq Hall. Though only a Reader, he was a well-known personality in the University. He had a doctorate from London University and taught a paper on the history of economic thought but appeared to have little time for research.

The academic star of the department was undoubtedly Nurul Islam. He had an outstanding academic record where he obtained a first-class first in the BA honours and MA exams for economics at Dhaka University. On the basis of his record, he was awarded a state scholarship to do his PhD at Harvard, where he again distinguished himself as one of the top students of his class and his thesis on foreign investment was eventually published. Nurul was, on his return from Harvard in 1955, elevated to a Readership in the Economics Department. At the Department, he taught economic theory and was one of the few senior teachers who was not only familiar with the latest developments in economics but applied himself to serious academic research.

When I met Nurul, we immediately established an accord. I observed that he felt somewhat alienated from his senior colleagues who, he felt, knew little of contemporary economics or had any interest in research. He rightly believed that he too should be elevated to a Professorship on the basis of his academic credentials. In those days, most departments had vacancies for only a single professor so that people of talent, such as Nurul, languished as Readers. A second chair was not created for Nurul until 1960. He eventually took over as Chair of the department in 1962 after Huda and then Mazharul Haq left for Karachi as members of the Tariff Commission. Nurul held his position as Chairman for only a few years until he too departed for Karachi in 1965 to take over as the first native Director of the prestigious Pakistan Institute of Development Economics (PIDE).

Nurul Islam was instrumental in building on the work of his American predecessors, Gus Ranis, Henry Bruton and Mark Leiserson, in transforming PIDE into one of the premier development research institutions in the world. He had brought in a number of young Bangali economists from Dhaka University who worked with him to address a variety of issues that related to the disparate incidence of Pakistan's development process on East Pakistan. PIDE worked on a variety of other aspect of Pakistan's development policy where it served as a source of high-quality research as well as policy advice.

Professor Huda had managed to recruit a number of bright young economists, with excellent academic results, as Junior Lecturers who accompanied me into the Economics Department in October 1957. This group included Anisur Rahman, who had a first-class first in his MA, Maqsood Ali, who had similar credentials, Muzzafer Ahmed, Mohiuddin Ahmed and Mahfuzul Haq. These new recruits not only became my colleagues but we remained friends for the rest of our lives.

Among all my colleagues, the only one who stayed true to his vocation was Muzaffer Ahmed, who remained a teacher for most of his life, until he passed away in 2012. Muzaffer received his PhD from Chicago University, where he met and then married Rounaq's elder sister, Roushan Jahan, who was also a graduate student of English literature at this university. Muzaffer spent some years away from Dhaka University and then joined me in our foundational years at the Bangladesh Planning Commission from 1972 to 1975, where he worked closely with me. Muzaffer eventually returned to the Economics Department in 1975 and then took on the challenge of heading the Institute of Business Administration that he built into one of the outstanding faculties of Dhaka University.

Anisur Rahman, who obtained his PhD from Harvard, was perhaps the most academically gifted of my other colleagues. He had strong theoretical skills, backed by a progressive and creative consciousness that eventually distanced him from traditional economics. Anis accompanied us into the Planning Commission but, after 1975, left the University to spend the best part of his professional life with the International Labour Office (ILO) in Geneva. He returned to Dhaka after his retirement where he attempted to operationalize his ideas on participatory research. But in these later years, his substantive commitment was devoted towards deepening his understanding of *Rabindra Sangeet* where he also acquired some recognition for his writings on Tagore.

My first introduction to the Economics Department was at the office of Professor Huda. The Economics Department then consisted of two cavernous rooms at the end of the corridor of the first floor of the Arts Faculty, which was located in the south wing of the Dhaka Medical College. One room served as Huda's office, while the second room hosted the Department's Secretary and was also used as a meeting place for teachers. We were ably ministered to by Kanu, the Department Assistant, who became an institution in his own right as the longest serving member of the Department.

A number of other departments occupied the second floor of the south wing. Opposite to our department was the women student's common room, to which all the girls retreated at the conclusion of their classes. At the other end of the corridor was the Teachers' Club, a single room with a small attached pantry, where teachers shared tea, singharas and gossip between classes. Classrooms on the ground, first and second floors shared space with the department offices.

The remainder of the Arts Faculty was located in a number of decrepit outhouses in the faculty grounds, adjacent to a large pond. These departments included Commerce, Political Science, Islamic History and Philosophy. For a while, the Economics Department was also banished to these outlands until the Arts Faculty was relocated to a newly constructed independent building opposite the Medical College. Adjacent to the old Arts Faculty was Madhu's canteen, the crucible for student politics at the University and close by was the historic *Amtala*[1] where student politics had expressed itself over the years.

At our first encounter, Huda assigned us our academic responsibilities. I was happy to be entrusted with the task of teaching economic history to the first-year honours students. This included the history of the USA and USSR. I had done papers on both these countries at Cambridge and could draw upon the works and excellent notes I had accumulated attending the lectures of Maurice Dobb on the USSR and Frank Thistlethwaite on US economic history.

Huda, however, caused me more concern by suggesting that I also lecture to the MA Final class on a compulsory paper on monetary theory. This was a more daunting challenge as my MA students were close to or even older than my 22 years, when I joined the University. I cannot claim to have been over-knowledgeable or enthusiastic about this responsibility and drew heavily on the Keynesian economics I had imbibed at Cambridge.

Around 1960 or so, Nurul and I persuaded Professor Huda to introduce a paper on development economics that was then assigned to me in lieu of my classes on Monetary Theory. This was far more congenial to me and enabled me to catch up with the emerging literature on a subject that was still in its infancy. In those days, we could draw on the textbooks on development written by Benjamin Higgins, Meier and Baldwin and on Arthur Lewis' *Economic Growth*. I also drew upon my old favourite, Ragnar Nurkse's *Capital Formation in Underdeveloped Countries*, which introduced me to the subject of underdevelopment in my classes at Cambridge.

Around 1961, Nurul Islam and I further persuaded Professor Huda to introduce a course on the Pakistan Economy that had surprisingly been missing from the syllabus. As a result, students

[1] Mango tree.

appeared to know more about the USSR or development in general than they did about the nature and state of the Pakistan economy. As there were few textbooks on this subject, apart from S.M. Akhtar's ancient text and a later, better, book written by Aziz Ali F. Mohamed, I had to undertake my own research on the Pakistan economy to continue my lectures based on the syllabus I helped draw up. Once research works from PIDE began coming on stream, our understanding of the national economy was greatly enriched. I spent the next decade giving courses on the Pakistan economy to a generation of third-year honours students who I exposed to a more critical perspective on the state and structure of the economy. In the process, I introduced the students to the issue of regional imbalance in the development of the Pakistan economy and its underlying political economy.

Engaging with My Students

When I entered my first class to lecture to a group of bright young students on USSR economic history, they too were having their first exposure to university life. This first batch included a number of young men who moved on to quite distinguished careers. The top three students of the class, who all earned first classes in both honours and the MA, included Fakhruddin Ahmed, who ended his career as Head of the Caretaker government that presided over Bangladesh's interrupted democratic journey in 2007–08, and Mirza Azizul Islam, who served in his cabinet as Finance Adviser. Fakhruddin and Aziz, who could have had promising careers as academics, opted to join the CSP.

The most illustrious among my first batch of students turned out to be Muhammad Yunus. He was a good student but did not obtain a first class. Since Yunus has emerged as a globally eminent person after he left the Economics Department with an MA in 1961, I do not need to retail his subsequent career path. While it will always be satisfying to know that I once taught a Nobel laureate, I cannot claim to have influenced the transformative trajectory of his life that owes entirely to his own sense of commitment. I did renew my connection with Yunus many years later when I was invited by the then Finance Minister, S.A.M.S. Kibria in 1996, to Chair the Board of Directors of the Grameen Bank, set up by Yunus in 1983.

It is notable that during my tenure at Dhaka University between 1957 and 1971, virtually all my best students, who were also recognized to be among the academic elite of Dhaka University, chose to join the Civil or Foreign Service in spite of advocacy, obviously infructuous, by me to persuade the best of them to pursue economics as a profession. The younger generation of that era viewed a Civil Service career as the apex of their social aspirations and marital opportunities. Their career path was encouraged by their families who did not recognize an academic career as the highest source of return on their investment in their children. Eventually, Fakhruddin, Mirza Aziz, along with a number of my best students such as A.M.A. Rahim, Abul Ahsan, Monwarul Islam, Mostafa Faruque Mohammad, Shamsul Alam, Farashuddin and Shah Muhammad Farid, who all scored first classes, chose to become civil servants. Some of them eventually acquired higher degrees abroad in the post-liberation period and a number among them moved on to seek careers as economists in various international institutions.

Among the few who opted for an academic life, Azizur Rahman Khan stands out, spending the best part of his career as a Professor of Economics at the University of California, Riverside, where he built up an international reputation as a development economist and China specialist. He initially joined us in the Economics Department at Dhaka University as a Lecturer but could not make this a career because all teachers needed to be politically 'cleared' by the intelligence agencies before they could be confirmed in their position. Aziz, along with his classmate Aminul Islam, had been active, as students, in the EPSU, which attracted students with a left-wing orientation. Both of them along with Swadesh Bose, who had invested his early life in political activism, though they had obtained first classes, were compelled to forsake teaching careers at Dhaka University and move to PIDE in Karachi.

Interestingly, some of my best students in the Economics Department who earned first-class firsts, such as Mirza Azizul Islam,

M. Farashuddin, later Governor of Bangladesh Bank, and Mujahidul Islam Selim, currently the Secretary General of the Communist Party of Bangladesh, were active in student politics that was then driven by a sense of idealism where academic merit more than muscle power was seen as an electoral asset. This tendency may be compared to the current domination of student politics by hoodlums who remain largely motivated by material gain rather than political principles.

Learning to Be a Teacher

My weekly teaching load consisted of six hours of lectures divided between the two courses assigned to me and six hours of tutorials also shared between the two subjects. The tutorials involved encounters with groups of seven to eight students drawn from a class cohort of about 50 students in the BA classes and around 60 to 70 in the MA class that received an additional intake from the MA preliminary class drawn from students who entered the University with a BA pass degree awarded by colleges affiliated to the University.

My initial approach to my students was at that stage part of a learning process for me as a young teacher and a person who aspired to influence the direction of the society where I had chosen to make my home. My recent exposure to the Cambridge style of education persuaded me to emphasize the importance of encouraging the students to think for themselves rather than to remain captive to the tradition of rote learning that was part of the academic tradition in our educational system. I sought to use the tutorial system, then in vogue at the university, to promote independent thinking. The tutorial system had been originally inspired by the Oxbridge tradition. But in Cambridge, this tradition was sustained by a rather better teacher–student ratio so that one tutor usually met one or two students, who spent an hour with them every week that encouraged strong interpersonal interaction. In my final year at Cambridge, I had the privilege of being tutored by Joan Robinson on a one-on-one basis.

The rather meagre teaching capacity of the departments at Dhaka University meant that my tutorial classes carried 8–10 students. I was budgeted to take six tutorials a week so that in an honours class of around 50, I needed to organize around six to eight tutorial groups to maintain this ratio. My approach in the tutorial was to invite one of the group members to present a paper, which was then opened up to discussion by the group and comments by me. This approach motivated the students to do some research and to articulate their thoughts in discussions before and with their teacher during the tutorial.

This task was more of a challenge than I had anticipated. The tradition of talking to/ before a teacher and to do so in English was a real burden on the students who were further intimidated by my presumed command of this foreign language. The few students who had been exposed to English medium education tended to be more articulate in my tutorials, but these were not necessarily the smartest in the group. Furthermore, the challenge of encouraging the paper writers to be creative in presentation, rather than reproduce material from one or another work I had recommended they read, was a further challenge.

These challenges were multiplied in the case of the few girl students who attended my classes. In those days, there were around four or five girls in a class. The prevailing convention was for the girls to enter the class after the boys were seated and usually to do so just after the teacher had entered. They invariably sat together in the front row. The moment the class ended, they followed the teacher out of the class and retreated to their common room, which served as a sort of prison cell for girl students, which could only be exited to attend classes or visit the library. If a boy wished to converse with a girl, he could only do so through some form of written permission from the Proctor. This rather monastic approach to co-education was perhaps instrumental in making girls particularly inhibited about speaking out in class or even in tutorials. I was happy to discover conspicuous exceptions to this rule but needed to organize a separate women's tutorial group to persuade them to speak out. Such a gender-segregated regime did not necessarily discourage student romances, some of which ended in early matrimony.

I was guilty of encouraging some element of elitism in organizing my tutorial groups. I consulted the intermediate exam results and the third-year honours exam results when I organized my tutorial group for first-year honours and MA classes, respectively. From these lists, I identified seven or eight students with the best results and located them in what I regarded as my A group. This was rather undemocratic but extremely rewarding because the A group was the best equipped to do quality research and also tended to be more articulate. Through this system, I could stimulate a capacity for research and challenging intellectual discussion among students. While the best discussion took place in the A group, as the year progressed, other tutorial groups organized on more democratic principles, began to throw up hitherto unexpected talents for both research and argument. The women's groups, in the process, proved to be no less capable of rising to my challenge.

Over the years, the tutorial system proved particularly effective in enabling me to establish a more intimate relationship with my students. Inevitably, the closest relationships tended to be developed with my A groups, most of whom remained connected to me over a passage of half a century. To this day, I am greeted by a progressively aging community of my students who remember me as their teacher, though whether with fondness or trepidation is not always made clear. I too remember them as individuals, though with the passage of years, names cannot immediately be attached to faces that were once part of my living memory.

University Life Outside the Classroom

The teachers' common room in the old building was where I came to meet and know colleagues outside the Economics Department such as Sir, Dr Sarwar Murshid, a Reader in the English Department, and Anisuzzaman and Munier Chowdhury from the Bangla Department. I became particularly friendly with Sarwar Murshid, some years older than me, who used to edit an *Encounter*-style, multidisciplinary journal, *New Values*, which faced perpetual financial constraints and thus enjoyed a rather interrupted journey. I occasionally contributed to the journal and joined with Murshid in organizing some dialogues. One such venture during the martial law phase of the Ayub regime was addressed by Sir on the theme of the 'military in politics' where he observed, inter alia, that as it was the less intelligent members of any family in Pakistan who were encouraged to join the military, this did not indicate that they were the best qualified people to run a country. Such subversive discussion did not lend itself to attracting a large audience, though some teachers, apprehensive of being associated with such seditious company, furtively followed our discussion from a safe distance.

Within two years of my entry into Dhaka University, I was becoming more visible within the University. Obviously, a person who drove his own car to the campus, lectured in a loud enough voice to attract the attention of not just my students but those unfortunate enough to be in the vicinity of my classroom and was also willing to take part in debates and discussions organized by the more active students tended to be more recognizable.

I also became more politically visible through my occasional journalistic writings and encounters with the high and the mighty. Around 1960, during the period of martial law, a number of central government ministers decided to visit the University to talk to the students and teachers in order to win them over to the so-called reforms being enacted by Ayub Khan. One of the visitations to the university was by a young Zulfikar Ali Bhutto, the then Minister for Energy. Bhutto believed his Oxford education, fluency in English, debating skills and radical rhetoric would impress the intellectual elite of Dhaka. In his meeting at the Arts Faculty, he was exposed to sharp questioning, both by the students and some of us teachers. As the questions on deprivation of the Bangalis and the return to democracy became sharper, Bhutto tended to take refuge in his putative commitment to radical solutions. Unfortunately, his rhetoric, replete with references to Lenin and even ancient philosophers, failed to impress us and he was compelled to beat a hasty retreat from the encounter.

My university life initially coexisted with my role as a quasi-businessman. In the years up to 1962, this meant driving away from the University around 2:00 p.m. to Armanitola where the offices for Dhaka Tanneries were located. Since my half day at the University was largely preoccupied with lectures and tutorial classes, this schedule left me with little time for serious research. I could only engage in such research by returning to the University after 5:00 p.m., but by then most of the teachers had headed home after their classes. Some of the teachers who lived in university quarters turned up at the Teachers' Club, particularly after a special building was constructed on Nilkhet Road, opposite the University Administrative Building. Here, enthusiastic chess players such as Sir and Qazi Motahar Hossian played chess while others engaged in games of bridge. The less gifted sat around a central common room to gossip, often about politics. Only the more serious-minded academics such as Muzzafer Ahmed Chowdhury and Nurul Islam spent time in the library or stayed up late at home to engage in research. But this was no easy task as teacher's quarters were constricted for space and family obligations also demanded attention.

I attempted to recreate the Cambridge institution of the Political Economy Club, which brought together the better qualified students with the teachers of the Economics Department to discuss a particular topic then being researched by one of them. We organized a few such discussions, but the project languished either because the research input tended to be weak or the teachers were unwilling to return to the campus in the evening for such academic engagements.

Travels of a Young Economist

Encounters with Our West Pakistani Colleagues

In my first year as a teacher, I was provided the opportunity to come into contact with economists in West Pakistan. Within two months of my joining the Department, Professor Huda included me in a group of teachers who were nominated to attend the biennial conference of the Pakistan Economic Association (PEA) in Lahore. All I needed to qualify was to invest Rs 100 to become a life member of the Association. I am presumably still a member of the PEA as well as its successor organization, the Bangladesh Economic Association (BEA), formally established in 1972.

In December 1957, in the company of more senior colleagues such as Nurul Islam, R.H. Khandkar and Shamsul Islam from Rajshahi University, I travelled to Lahore where we were accommodated in the only hotel of any quality, Faletti's. Unfortunately, due to budgeting constraints, if I recollect correctly, three of us were accommodated in one room. The conference itself was held on the campus of Punjab University.

At the conference, I met some of the senior members of the profession in West Pakistan such as Professor S.M. Akhter, the perennial Chair of the Economics Department at Punjab University, known for his one and only publication, a textbook on Pakistan Economics. Other senior teachers I met included Professor Q.M. Fareed, Chair of the Economics Department at Karachi University. None of these senior economists appeared to have engaged in serious research. I established a more congenial and durable relationship with Professor M. Rashid, the Chair of the Economics Department at the prestigious Government College, Lahore, who had been Mahbubul Haq's teacher. Another person I met was Dr Sajid Abbas, a Reader in Punjab University, who had earned a PhD in the Netherlands as a student of Jan Tinbergen, and was married to a Bangali from Dhaka, Rabeya Islam.

At the conference, I met Akhlaqur Rahman for the first time. He was then serving as a Reader in the Economics Department at Peshawar University, where I too had been offered a similar position by its Chair, Professor Wise. Akhlaq was an engaging personality, radical in his views, quick to anger whereupon he became extremely aggressive but always remained lovable and generous to a fault. Akhlaq eventually moved away from Peshawar to Karachi to become the first senior Pakistani economist to be recruited by PIDE.

To justify my travel, I presented a paper on the superiority of fiscal over monetary policy as an instrument of economic management. It was a rather immature exercise. The event offered me a first-hand opportunity to be exposed to the emerging debates on economic disparity and the growing divide between the economists of East and West Pakistan.

Over the next summer, in 1958, some of us were provided an opportunity to spend six weeks attending a summer school in the Punjab hill station of Murree. This was a unique event, organized by Professor Austen Robinson, one of my teachers at Cambridge University. This enterprise, along with the founding of PIDE, reflected Austen's lifelong love affair with the economics profession, first in Pakistan and subsequently in Bangladesh. Austen persuaded the International Economic Association to sponsor a refresher course for teachers of economics in Pakistan to update them on the latest developments in the discipline. Austen brought in an exceptional galaxy of well-known economists to lecture to us at Murree, which included Harry Johnson, Gerry Meir, Alan Brown, Brian Reddaway and even Peter Bauer, my tutor at Cambridge, among other stars. They provided us with a sumptuous intellectual feast to enrich our appetite for economics. In this environment, we managed to establish more congenial relations with the West Pakistanis attending the programme. I am not aware of another such feast being provided to us economists, at least during our association with Pakistan. Tragically, in the post-liberation Bangladesh, we failed to organize such an educational experience for the economics profession where conceptual skills tended to be rather impoverished.

Just after our return from Murree, martial law was imposed by Ayub Khan. Never again did another occasion arise where we could interact with our West Pakistani colleagues in such a relaxed environment. We did however encounter them in further conferences convened by Hyderabad University, and Peshawar University, which I particularly remember for our feasting on the cholesterol-enhancing *patay* tikkas[2] at Kisakhani Bazaar in the heart of Peshawar's old town.

[2] Lamb wrapped in fat.

Excursion to a New World

My days at Dhaka University not only provided me scope for travel to West Pakistan but created the ground for travelling to the USA, a new world that existed in my literary imagination but remained far outside my travel itinerary. In the first part of the 1960s, some of my evenings were taken up socializing with a few members of the then rather small international community resident in Dhaka. In the period 1957–60, as one of the more articulate young academics at Dhaka University, I came to be recognized among some circles as something of a stormy petrel, ready to criticize both the regime and its external patrons. This did not inhibit the more adventurous members of the international community from cultivating me and later Kamal, when he returned from Oxford. Our close friends in those days were Bill Hollinger, who was attached to the HAG then seconded to advise the East Pakistan Planning Board, and his wife Flora, as well as some of their colleagues.

Some members of the US consulate also sought out my company, possibly as part of a process of keeping in touch with dissenting opinion among the Bangalis. As a by-product of such interactions, I was invited to visit the USA under an exchange programme sponsored by the US State Department to educate up-and-coming intellectuals about the American way of life. This involved a four-month tour of the country, where I could travel to any place of my choice. I viewed the invitation as a good opportunity to travel and understand something about a country that was playing a significant role in influencing the course of events in Pakistan though not always in acceptable directions.

This visit to the USA was a useful learning experience for me. My first stop was in Washington D.C. for orientation at the State Department, where I was invited to spell out my preferences as to places and institutions I would like to visit as well as people I would prefer to meet. My programme was to be organized by the International Institute of Education (IIE) whose local offices would both arrange my programme as requested and identify a local host who may provide me with a home-cooked meal and even drive me around, if needed.

In Washington, I sought meetings with US congressmen, State Department and US Aid officials where I could learn and also argue with them on the direction of US policy. I am not sure what these more established and older figures thought of this precocious young man from an insignificant Asian country who was uninhibited in charging the US government with patronizing a military dictator in his own country.

During my stay in Washington, I undertook a short excursion to Tennessee to visit the Tennessee Valley Authority, then a global model for public sector intervention in the construction and management of major infrastructure projects. In my travels to the South, I had an exposure to the practice of racial segregation where toilets at bus stops were still segregated between 'coloured' and 'white'. I was placed in some tension as to whether I should publicly proclaim my solidarity with the 'coloured' population or challenge the local authorities by pointedly using the 'whites-only' facility. I cannot recollect whether I resolved this dilemma or merely exercised greater control over my bladder.

I travelled from D.C. to New York where I spent another fortnight. I used this visit to meet academics such as Ragnar Nurkse, the pioneer of Development Economics at Columbia University, talk to corporate leaders on Wall Street, argue with journalists at *The New York Times* and acquire a taste for Nathan's frankfurters located at Times Square. I even managed to indulge in the luxury of hearing one of the all-time greats of jazz, Dizzy Gillespie, perform at Yankee Stadium.

From New York I moved to Cambridge, Massachusetts, where I had programmed myself to spend most of my time interacting with professors at Harvard and Massachusetts Institute of Technology (MIT) as well as attending courses of my choice at the Harvard Summer School. Classes in Summer School were more of an academic 'smorgasbord' treat rather than a serious learning experience. I chose classes offered by well-known scholars and public figures and had one-on-one meetings with legendary economists such as J.K. Galbraith, Paul Sweezy, Alvin Hansen and John Dunlop. At MIT, I met Walt Rostow, Paul Samuelson and Charles Kindleberger whose works I had read at and after my years at Cambridge University.

Apart from academic encounters, I spent quite a bit of time at Harvard's Lamont and Widener libraries. I also tasted something of the rich cultural life on offer in Cambridge. I remember attending a concert at the Tanglewood Festival as well as listening to my all-time favourite folk singers, Joan Baez and Pete Seeger who were then at an early stage of their inspirational careers.

At that time, Anisur Rahman and Abu Mahmood were both completing their PhDs at Harvard, so I could also interact with them. I was so enthused by my stay at Cambridge that I programmed myself to return there in October, for the last two weeks of my visit when I stayed with Anis and his wife, Dora. At that time, I met Sukhamoy Chakraborty and Amartya Sen, who were both spending a year as visiting professors at MIT. Amartya had just married Nabaneeta, who I met for the first time and have been friends with her even since.

From Cambridge I travelled to Chicago, where I met my Cambridge contemporary, Jagdish Bhagwati, and his mentor as well as my teacher at Cambridge, Harry Johnson. We spent pleasant hours together, including a swim in the lake that abuts Chicago. At that time, the University campus on Chicago's South Side, close to the city ghetto, was reportedly a dangerous place, so I was advised not to roam around in public spaces in that area after dark.

From Chicago I had the opportunity to visit a small township in McCall, Idaho, the home of the parents of the programme officer at United States Information Services (USIS) in Dhaka, Ivan Evans, who had organized my US trip. It was a unique opportunity to taste something of small-town US life. I stayed with the senior Evans in their log cabin located on a lake, enjoyed barbecues where I met the very friendly townsfolk who had never heard of Pakistan and obtained a view of a world to which visitors are not normally exposed.

From Idaho I moved on to San Francisco, where I spent another two weeks. Of all the cities I visited in the USA, San Francisco was my favourite. Its congenial climate, undulating streets, continental-style tramcars, excellent seafood cuisine at Fisherman's Wharf and rich cultural life were a treat for me. While at San Francisco, I attended a concert of Beethoven music performed by the New York Philharmonic Orchestra conducted by Leonard Bernstein, attended a jazz concert presented by the legendary Kid Ory and even managed visits to the Hungry I cafe where the top comic satirist of the time, Mort Sahl, used to dissect the US political establishment every evening. For my academic education, I visited Berkeley regularly, where I met some of the economics faculty still available on campus such as Laurie Tarshis. I also attended a seminar at Stanford that gave me the opportunity to spend a few days with my Cambridge friend Dilip Adarkar, who had then just completed his PhD at Stanford and was living in nearby San José where he worked.

From San Francisco I went on to Los Angles, where my local hosts drove me all over the city, which did not readily lend itself to travel by public transport. They took me to Disneyland as well as Hollywood, the place of my dreams. The area turned out to be rather scruffy and not quite what I had imagined. From Los Angles I travelled via Texas to New Orleans, which was enjoyable for my exposure to Cajun cooking and jazz in the French quarter.

During my visit, the campaign for the 1960 presidential election was in full swing, where the Republican candidate, Richard Nixon, then serving as Vice President in the Eisenhower administration, was being challenged by an exciting young Senator from Massachusetts, John F. Kennedy (JFK), who was the favoured candidate of the Harvard academic community. During my stay, I witnessed two of the Kennedy–Nixon TV debates, the first of the 'presidential debates' that have since been institutionalized. I recollect that the younger Kennedy, well coached on the issues by his Harvard advisers, won handsomely over a perspiring Richard Nixon, sporting a '7 o'clock shadow' on his face. My education on US electoral politics had been whetted during my trips to the US Congress and discussions at Harvard which reached its culmination with my later reading of Theodore H. White's pioneering work on the 1960 election, *The Making of a President*.

During that period, global political events had also been infused into the election campaign. During my second visit to New York at the end of September, the UN General Assembly session was attended by the Soviet leader Nikita Khrushchev, who we all viewed on television banging his shoe on his desk at the General Assembly hall to register his objections to the address of a speaker from the USA at that session. Fidel Castro, who had then recently captured power in Cuba at the end of a long guerrilla insurgency, also attended the General Assembly. His arrival aroused particular hostility from right-wing circles who advised all the leading downtown hotels to deny accommodation to him and his delegation. Castro excited public imagination by opting to stay in a hotel in Harlem where the Afro-American population were far more receptive to him.

En route home I stopped off in London, where I had the good fortune of attending an epic theatrical performance of *Man of All Sessions* where Paul Scofield's performance as Thomas More surely serves as the greatest theatrical event I have ever witnessed. I returned home from the USA with a taste for hot fudge sundaes, Tad's steaks, Nathan's frankfurters as well as a lifelong interest in US politics.

10

Dhaka: Personal Encounters of the Close Kind

Early Encounters

Settling into professional life in Dhaka, along with my miscellaneous involvements, did not preclude the pursuit of a more personal life. Dhaka, in those days, remained less pressurized than today while the absence of traffic jams permitted much greater opportunities for casual socialization. I had some exposure to this leisurely lifestyle in my early years in Dhaka, but these spaces were narrowed by the return of Kamal to Dhaka from Oxford in 1960, whence our evenings tended to assume a more politically purposeful dimension. Fortunately for me, Kamal, on his return, joined Dhaka's leading law firm, Orr Dignams, and tended to work late into the evening so that my social life did not altogether close down.

In those days, my ports of call included some of my university colleagues such as Sir, Nurul Islam and Sarwar Murshid who then lived in the university apartments in Azimpur Colony. Outside the University, I had become close friends with Zeaul Haq Tulu, then a young bachelor and man about town who was embarking on a business career. Tulu lived on Green Road, with his father, Fazlul Haq, a much respected figure and a gracious host who periodically invited his friends to an epic feast of succulent fish dishes.

Another good friend of mine in those days was the journalist S.M. Ali. In those days, he worked as the principal correspondent in the *Pakistan Times* of East Pakistan, then owned by Mian Iftikharuddin. I had met Ali way back in 1953 when we were fellow voyagers on the *Batory* on our first journey to England. After I arrived in Dhaka, I revived contact with Ali, who was by then an established journalist who shared with me his aspiration of setting up an English-language daily or a weekly on the lines of the *New Statesman*. I had been an avid reader of this left-wing weekly and shared Ali's vision. We hoped to persuade Mian Iftikharuddin to underwrite our enterprise.

Ali also sought to mobilize some local funding for his prospective venture and took me to meet Mahbub Raschid, then the General Manager of the Sadarghat branch of the National Bank of Pakistan. We managed to also involve my friend Mosharaff Hossain in our journalistic aspirations. Raschid, who then lived in a small house in Segun Bagicha, was extremely well read and progressive in his outlook. We spent more time discussing politics than raising funds from him to sustain our venture.

Our *New Statesmen* venture came to an abrupt end in October 1958 with the enforcement of martial law by Ayub Khan and the takeover of *Pakistan Times*. Not only did this frustrate hopes of financing our venture but Ali lost all enthusiasm for working for *Pakistan Times* under its now official ownership. He managed to negotiate a job with, I think, the *Bangkok Post* and prepared to set out on a prolonged safari across South East and East Asia. He returned to Dhaka after an absence of 30 years and founded the *Daily Star* with Mahfuz Anam.

As Ali was preparing to leave Dhaka for Bangkok in 1960, he offered to introduce me to the famous sculptor Novera Ahmed. Ali had for some years been a close friend of Novera, who lived by herself in an apartment on New Bailey Road just across the road from Kamal Court. Though she was already making a name for herself, Novera led a very isolated life with few friends and had very limited links with her family, so Ali felt he should connect her with some of his own friends.

Ali took me over to Novera's apartment to introduce me. She always dressed in black, at least whenever I visited her. She was fair-skinned with East Asiatic features that gave her an attractive and rather ethereal look. She was not unreceptive to my intrusion into her secluded domain with its perennially subdued lighting. After Ali departed for Bangkok, I would periodically walk over to her apartment in the evening after phoning her to ascertain whether she was free. During the day, she usually worked on her sculptures at a studio she had established in her apartment. She was not particularly talkative, but we discussed various aspects of her life and her existential concerns.

Novera was an intensely emotional and highly sensitive person. I once brought over some of my long-playing records of Western classical music that she found evocative to her emotional needs. On one occasion, listening to a particularly moving piece of music, she fell into a sort of trance. This was rather alarming, and I had to be careful about my future selections of music. Occasionally, I took her out for drives and, on one occasion, escorted her to a play performed by a visiting theatre group hosted by the British Council. Our public appearance together occasioned some gossip. In those days, a bachelor regularly visiting an attractive single woman in her apartment was unusual. This aspect of our relationship was not publicized, but escorting Novera in a public place was hardly likely to escape notice.

My visits to Novera continued for over a year until I departed for London in May 1962 for my marriage to Salma. Around that time Novera also left Dhaka and travelled to Europe, from where she never returned. It would be dishonest if I were to say that I was not attracted to her or was not moved to take the relationship further. I cannot say whether Novera reciprocated my feelings or would have been inclined to move ahead with our relationship. I was not insensitive to her artistic temperament, but I was by then moving into the political phase of my life, and we recognized that our two worlds would always remain polarized.

As it transpired, our relationship remained at a platonic level, so there was no emotional baggage to jettison when I informed her about my decision to marry Salma. She realized that our relationship had to end. I took pleasure in her company and was sad to part from her. I learnt later that she had moved to Paris. As the years went by, I occasionally heard of her from her fellow artists.

Shahabuddin, one of our most eminent painters, who is settled in Paris, at a recent encounter with me in Dhaka, informed me that Novera still lives in Paris but was a virtual recluse. She passed away in Paris, in the summer of 2015.

Salma: Encountering a Life Partner

First Encounters

One of my favoured ports of call, where Kamal often joined me, was at the home in Paribagh, of Erfan Ahmed, an executive at Burmah-Shell. Erfan, whose family came from Khulna, had retired on health grounds from his position as a Commander in the Pakistan Navy. I found Erfan to be very well read and excellent company. He was married to a Sindhi, Khurshid Akhund, a charming person with a rather dry sense of humour. Erfan and Khurshid's home and our relationship with them incubated at least three marriages—mine to Salma, Khurshid's younger sister, Hameeda, to Kamal and that of her elder sister, Rasheeda, to Syed Akhlaque Hussain, a CSP officer.

I was, in fact, the point of connectivity between Rasheeda and Akhlaq, who was one of a number of non-Bengali CSP officers serving in East Pakistan with whom I became good friends. Rasheeda and Hameeda, who both worked at Oxford University Press in Karachi, occasionally visited Khurshid in Dhaka and met their respective life partners on these visits to Dhaka. Salma, who was a very close friend of Rasheeda, also visited Dhaka and stayed with Khurshid. I had known Salma, though only fleetingly, from our Cambridge days but had not encountered her once she returned home. Both Rasheeda and Akhlaq were the principal sources for reconnecting me to Salma.

Beyond Novera, there had so far been no occasion for me to come close to any woman. At the age of 26, I was under a certain pressure from my senior relatives, though less so from my parents, to consider marriage. I, thus, kept an eye open for an appropriate companion but did not pursue this issue with any seriousness.

When Akhlaque suggested that Salma was an exceptionally sweet-natured person who may be a prospective partner, I suspect he raised the issue more in a spirit of reciprocity because I had introduced him to his prospective partner, Rasheeda, than with any purposeful intent. I, therefore, decided on the occasion of a visit to Karachi, to reconnect with Salma, courtesy of Rasheeda.

Salma had arrived in Karachi with a reputation for exceptional intelligence. She had completed her BA honours in law from Girton College at Cambridge in the summer of 1958, where she had spent an enjoyable three years and accumulated friendships that have lasted a lifetime. Her father had been Pakistan's High Commissioner in London during her entire stay at Cambridge. He was advised that he would be recalled from London at the end of 1958 in order to once again take over as Foreign Secretary. Salma had been awarded her law degree in Cambridge in June and expected to spend a relaxed year in London studying at Lincoln's Inn for her Bar exams. Prospective barristers had to consume a number of dinners at the Inns of Court to be eligible to take the exam but eventually had to study hard to pass some tough exams to qualify as a barrister. Salma was rather unhappy when she was informed by her father that she was not going to be given a year in London to qualify for the Bar but had to appear for the exams in December so that she and her sister Naz, who was graduating from the Byam Shaw Art School in London, could return to Karachi with their parents.

Salma had to push herself to take the Bar finals within six months. In this short time, Salma appeared and passed the exams, thereby qualifying as a barrister at the age of 21. This made Salma the second Pakistani woman to qualify as a barrister and one of the youngest Pakistanis, of any sex, to qualify. On her return to Karachi, she joined the leading Karachi law firm, Surridge and Beecheno. Had Salma remained with the legal profession, she may well have gone on to become one of Pakistan's leading lawyers. Her uncle, Shaheed Suhrawardy, was keen to persuade Salma to join him as his junior, but his political involvements meant that her pursuit of law with him would always be something of a speculative proposition, even if he was recognized as one of the three or four top lawyers in Pakistan.

Salma's interest in pursuing a legal career in Karachi was never very strong. When she was offered a scholarship to spend a year at the Law School of the Sorbonne in Paris, she seized the opportunity with enthusiasm. Her great ambition was to live in Paris, perhaps work at a law firm there, but above all to settle down to write novels while she enjoyed life on the Left Bank of the Seine.

Salma's ongoing career and dreams of Paris were frustrated by my decision to lay siege to her emotions and to eventually propose marriage. Salma and Naz had been much sought after as brides in Karachi society and were under heavy pressure from their mother to take the plunge. Naz, a highly attractive and lively young woman, then establishing herself as painter of some promise, was much sought after, but Salma was also regarded as a good catch by prospective mothers-in-law. Salma was particularly reluctant to entertain suitors unless she could find someone of her choice. Salma, who was a great lover of Jane Austen's novels and knew every one of them, virtually by heart, frequently likened her mother's attitude to her daughter's marriage to that of Mrs Bennet, Elizabeth's mother in *Pride and Prejudice*.

Both Salma and Naz were eventually spared the fate of the Bennet daughters when her father, on his retirement as Foreign Secretary sometime in 1961, was invited to move to London to take up the prestigious post of the Chairman of the Commonwealth Economic Committee that later evolved into the Commonwealth Secretariat. Naz accompanied her parents to London along with their youngest sister, Sarvath, known to all as Bitlum, while Salma was left in Karachi with her older brother, Inam, at the family home, Kashana, in Clifton.

Life Choices

It is not clear to me, even today, why Salma decided to marry me rather than pursuing her aspirations to become a novelist living in Paris. Family-wise, I have already observed, the match was quite compatible. My own academic and hence professional credentials were not too deficient. Though my political involvements were viewed with some concern by Salma's father, my anti-regime stand was appreciated by her congenitally anti-establishment mother and approved by her uncle Shaheed. Their one concern was that my income as a teacher at Dhaka University was hardly likely to ensure that Salma would be able to live the life she had been accustomed to as the daughter of an ICS officer and a scion of the Suhrawardy family.

Salma herself was least concerned with my financial net worth and saw my preference for the teaching profession to be a plus point. Little did she realize that life as the wife of an academic in Dhaka University was hardly the same as life as a don's wife at Cambridge University. Neither did she appreciate the full implications of my political involvements, which first sent us off in self-exile to London in 1966, then almost led to her incarceration in the Cantonment in 1971 and again found her moving into exile in Oxford in 1975 after the assassination of Bangabandhu, nor did the degeneration of public life and social values that she witnessed in Dhaka after our return from Oxford in 1981 persuade her that life in Dhaka had turned out as I had promised.

Salma, in the last quarter of her life, went on to found Ain O Salish Kendro and emerge as one of the leading members of the global organization, Women Living Under Muslim Laws. She remains enshrined in the public mind as a person dedicated to the protection of human rights, particularly for women. But her unrealized ambition remained to be the wife of a simple academic who gave her space to pursue her great love for reading, gardening and her unrealized ambition of writing novels in the style of Jane Austen.

Whatever may have been the assumptions underlying Salma's fateful decision to be my wife, we were both quick to make up our minds by the time of my second visit to Karachi in October 1961. Salma was about to depart for the Sorbonne and was loathe to surrender her year in Paris on account of our prospective marriage. We therefore agreed that she should spend an academic year in Paris prior to our marriage in London in the summer of 1962 where her parents and also, as it happened, my mother, were then in residence.

The best-laid plans of mice and men do go astray. Salma departed for Paris via London in October just after she had accepted my proposal. When she reached London, she informed her parents of my proposal. They, in turn, paid me the compliment of finding me acceptable, particularly because of the long-established connection between our families. Tragically, the moment Salma arrived in Paris, she fell seriously ill. This was diagnosed as typhoid, a bacillus she must have carried within her from Karachi. In the Europe of those days, typhoid was taken as seriously as the plague and Salma had be to first hospitalized in Paris and then evacuated to the School of Tropical Medicine in London, where she had to spend an uncomfortable and tedious period of quarantine. The Sorbonne authorities, who had already registered her before she fell ill, generously permitted her to spend three months there following her recovery so that her life's ambition, however fleeting, did not remain completely unfulfilled. In this period, during both her hospitalization and her stay in Paris, we corresponded unendingly and at lengths that are now inconceivable in the days of email.

Joy and Sorrow

Our wedding in London on 17 May 1962 was organized with great fanfare by Salma's mother at the Islamic Centre in Regent's Park, followed by another grand reception at Marlborough House, the premises of the Commonwealth Secretariat. My father had travelled to London from Nairobi after relinquishing his office as Pakistan's Commissioner to British East Africa, while my mother had been living in South Kensington for the last six months. My younger brother, Farooq, was just completing his first year studying history at Queen's College, Oxford. I was the only person who needed to travel from Dhaka to London, along with my stepmother, Nayyar Begum, who was then in Karachi.

Salma's mother was determined to conform to every cultural norm associated with the marriages she had attended in Calcutta and Karachi, so our ceremony in Regent's Park was arranged as a cultural tableau where I turned up resplendent in a brocade sherwani and turban specially tied for me by my friend from Cambridge, Shahryar Mohammad Khan, who was then serving as Third Secretary in the Pakistan High Commission in London. Salma's parents had a wide cross section of British friends, accumulated from as far back as her father's tenure as Trade Commissioner for the Indian government in London from 1937 to 1939. The Ikramullahs had built up an even larger circle of friends in high circles while he was High Commissioner in London, which included an amicable relationship with the Royal family. My father-in-law was eventually knighted by the Queen. One of the signatories to the *kabin nama*[1] as witness to our wedding at the Islamic Centre was Sir Alec Douglas-Home, who was then the Foreign Secretary in the Tory government of Harold Macmillan and later became the PM of England. We subsequently spent an exceedingly pleasant honeymoon at the Lake District and eventually sailed back to Karachi on an Anchor Line boat, which served to prolong the honeymoon.

In Karachi, our main goal had been to call on Salma's uncle Shaheed, who was exceptionally fond of Salma but could not attend our wedding in London as he was under custody in Karachi Central Jail. When Salma and I returned to Karachi around July 1962, Shaheed was still under detention at Karachi's Central Jail. Salma was determined to meet her Shaheed *mumma*,[2] but this was not that easy as he was still deemed to be a threat to the Ayub regime. Fortunately, my colleague from Cambridge, Mujeebur Rahman, was then the Additional Deputy Commissioner (ADC) of Karachi. Mujeeb was happy to provide passes for Salma and me to undertake a couple of visits to her uncle in jail. We found him in poor health but making the best of his enforced leisure and, as usual, in good humour. He requested a long list of books and a fly swatter to take on the flies that plagued his life in jail.

[1] Muslim deed of marriage.

[2] Mother's brother.

While in Karachi, we visited Shaheed's residence at Lakham House, where we met a collection of opposition politicians who had managed to be elected to the National Parliament, in spite of the constraints imposed by Ayub's constitution. This group, which included Masihur Rahman (Jadu Mian), then a leader of NAP, claimed they were the 'B-team' of East Pakistani politics, as most of the major figures, such as Bangabandhu and Ataur Rahman, were disqualified from contesting the election. Most of these opposition figures had heard of me due to my writings but had never met me. To meet them in the home of Shaheed Sahib invested me with a special status in their eyes that gave me access to them whenever I sought them out in later years.

Our wedding had an unfortunate aftermath. My father had decided to sail back with his wife from Liverpool to Karachi on a later Anchor Line vessel. On the high seas, he suffered a heart attack and died instantly. Rather than returning to Karachi and then Dhaka, his remains were landed at Karachi, where I along with his elder brother, Fazle Haider, buried him at the PECHS graveyard.

Married Life in Dhaka

I had by that time begun settling down to married life in Dhaka. My father's unanticipated death was quite traumatic for all those close to him, but particularly for Nayyar and their son—my brother—Naveed, then only four years old. My father was just 57 and had a long life ahead of him. His passing, which coincided with the beginning of my life with Salma in Dhaka, had a transformative effect on my future. Salma could never understand how a university academic could live a dual life as a business person. She, herself, had no taste for such a life and rightly deduced that I didn't either. She suffered from no urge for us to become wealthy and was happy for me to live the life of a full-time academic managing on whatever income we could earn. As a result, in the months after my father's passing, I began to spend less and less time at Dhaka Tanneries.

Eventually, over the next two years, I stopped attending office, leaving the affairs of the Tanneries exclusively to our partners.

I was keen that Salma should lead an active professional life in Dhaka. This objective was not exclusively motivated by altruism. My abandonment of the world of business meant that our income needed to be supplemented by Salma re-entering the ranks of the working class. This was not greatly welcomed by her, particularly as she was then pregnant with Taimur. However, she had the qualifications to be immediately enrolled as a Senior Lecturer in the Law Faculty, which was then headed by Dr Dham, a German scholar. Dham was supported by two full-time teachers, one of whom was Shahabuddin who had been my contemporary at Cambridge, where he had passed his law tripos. Shahabuddin took over as Chair of the Faculty when Dr Dham returned to Germany.

The advantage of teaching at the Law Faculty was that classes were held in the evening as much of the remaining faculty consisted of practising lawyers. Many of the law students who were already graduates were also working. This meant that Salma could take care of her household chores and eventually her child-rearing tasks and then take off for her classes at the University just when I was returning home.

When Taimur was born on 2 March 1963, at the Holy Family Hospital on Eskaton Road, then most efficiently managed by Catholic nuns, my child-rearing skills could not be fully road-tested. Salma's mother had, fortunately for all of us, persuaded their long-serving nanny, an Anglo-Indian lady by the name of Helen D'Cruz, to come out of retirement, where she was living with her family in London, and join us in Dhaka to look after Taimur. Salma's induction into a teaching career was greatly eased by the fact that the University was still in a highly turbulent state following the student protests that had exploded in Dhaka on the arrest of Shaheed Suhrawardy in early 1962. The ongoing protests included long spells of hartals when classes at the University remained suspended.

Once my modest earnings from Dhaka Tanneries were no long available, even on two salaries our financial circumstances were rendered rather perilous. I attempted to supplement my salary by taking on some consultancy assignments and eventually research projects, but these were far from lucrative. Immediately after our return to Dhaka, we occupied the full premises at 831/833 Shantinagar, which I had only partially occupied before my wedding. The tenants, who were pilots in Pakistan International Airlines (PIA), vacated their share of the house, so I was left to pay the full Rs 600 rent of a house owned by Begum Naushaba Huda, wife of Shamsul Huda, who subsequently became a minister under Ershad. We lived there for the first two years of our married life until we moved to teacher's quarters at Dhaka University on Savage Road, which considerably eased the strain on our budget.

The struggle to pay rent for a larger establishment was not eased by the birth of Taimur. Contrary to family custom, Salma declined to travel to Karachi to stay in the family house in Karachi while the baby was born as she refused to be parted from me even for a few weeks. As a result, her mother felt obliged, somewhat reluctantly and unhappily, to travel to Dhaka and live under rather spartan conditions in our Shantinagar house. After Taimur was born, Salma's father also managed to travel to Dhaka to greet his first grandson. This was the last we saw of him. He returned to London, and, in the course of a holiday in Rome with Sarvath, he suffered a heart attack sipping tea in the living room of the residence of Pakistan's Ambassador, Begum Liaquat Ali, where he was a house guest. Both Salma and my father passed away within a year of each other. Salma's uncle Shaheed then died of a heart attack in Beirut in November of the same year. The year after our wedding took a heavy toll on our respective families.

The year 1964 proved a better year for us once we moved into our apartment in the Dhaka University teacher's quarters. We lived on the second floor in a rather austere two-bedroom apartment that Salma managed to furnish with some taste. I had, by 1964, more or less ended my engagement with Dhaka Tanneries and invested the next three years, until we left for London in November 1966, as a full-time teacher. Our social connections with our university colleagues were now strengthened. In the apartment opposite ours lived Sarwar Murshid, Munier Chowdhury and Ansuzzaman. Taimur soon became old enough to run around on his own and play in the open space between our apartments with the children of the teachers who lived around us.

Sir, who lived across the road in the teacher's quarters located close to Salimullah Hall, frequently dropped by in the morning equipped with a succulent fish or a juicy joint of meat that he had acquired for us on his morning visit to the market. He would breakfast with us while giving Salma and our cook, Saheb Ali, detailed instructions on how to prepare these choice cooking items.

My own routine was quite relaxed but structured. I went over to the Arts Faculty building that had initially moved out of the Medical College complex to a newly constructed building just opposite, where some of us had rooms of our own. After two years, we moved to the more spacious premises on Nilkhet Road, which to this day remains the home of the Arts Faculty. This new structure was quite close to our apartment on Savage Road, so I walked there every day, returning home for lunch around 2:00 p.m. In the afternoon, I worked at my desk at home until around 5:00 p.m. or longer. If Salma had evening classes at the Law Faculty, which remained located in the premises opposite the Medical College, I continued working at home unless some activity was scheduled at our place.

By that time, we had begun construction of our house at the northern end of Gulshan. A plot of land in Gulshan had been allotted to my father but had been taken back by the DIT at his death in August 1962 as he was no longer able to pay the due instalments. I protested about this to the DIT. Since I was by then quite well known, in my own right, to senior Bangali bureaucrats, they allocated me a plot of land at NW(A)8, Gulshan, on Road 69. At that time, north Gulshan was a rural retreat that Dhaka citizens visited for picnics and where jackals roamed freely at night. In our area, at the extreme end bordering the Cantonment, the only construction project had been initiated by Chief Justice Mahbub Murshed.

Our own construction venture was a rather heroic task as our resources were limited. Even though the cost of building a 2,500-square-feet house was then no more than Rs 100,000, we needed to supplement our House Building Finance Corporation loan with further bank loans and eventually rental advances from our first tenant. The house was completed in September 1966 just before I departed for London on a fellowship, but we did not get to occupy it until April 1969, following our return from London.

In 1964 when we began constructing our home, there were no such institutions as property developers, so the houses were built by contractors under the owner's supervision, which was itself a time-consuming affair. We were uniquely fortunate in persuading Mazharul Islam, then the leading architect in Dhaka, to design our house, which he did largely as a gesture of friendship towards an intellectual fellow traveller. The engineering designs and supervision were done for us by his partner at Vastukalabid, Engineer Shaheedullah, who also shared Islam's radical political views. On my periodic visits to Vastukalabid's premises at Paribagh, we spent more time discussing politics than the house construction plans. But this did not distract from the quality of work and effort invested by them in our construction for which we remain eternally indebted to both of them. Islam eventually joined the Muzaffer NAP, but Shaheedullah moved further left and joined the Matin–Alauddin faction of the Maoist-inclined Communist Party and spent some time in jail around 1970–71. Mazharul Islam and Shaheedullah did a great job. The house was built around a small courtyard hosting a *kamranga*[3] tree of immense fertility. Our home remained a centre of attraction for all visitors who saw the house as a tribute to Mazharul Islam's and Shaheedullah's simple artistry.

Road to Morocco

Prior to the completion of our home, Salma and I were provided with an opportunity to visit Morocco, a part of the world that I had never expected to visit, at least at that phase of my life. This opportunity owed to the changed fortunes of my mother-in-law, Begum Ikramullah. Salma's father had passed away in 1963, so her mother and sister had returned home from London to Karachi. It was a difficult time for the family as Salma's father was a pivotal

[3] Star fruit or carambola.

figure in the household, a tower of strength and much loved. For all Begum Ikramullah's public eminence and extraordinary intelligence, his departure weighed heavily upon her.

Quite unexpectedly for her, she was invited by President Ayub Khan to serve as Pakistan's Ambassador to Morocco. This was no special honour for her as she was a publicly eminent person in her own right. The family thought this may be just the stimuli she needed to rebuild her zest for life. Salma and I, as indeed her mother, were somewhat concerned that she would be serving a military dictator, but we felt we should not let our prejudices stand in her way.

Choosing a woman to serve as Ambassador to a Muslim monarchy was always likely to be a challenge. However, Salma's mother had a head start because she and her husband were already held in some esteem in Morocco. Mr Ikramullah, during his tenure as Foreign Secretary, had strongly championed Morocco's struggle for independence from French colonial rule. This gesture was remembered and appreciated by the Moroccans as was Begum Ikramullah's interventions in the UN General Assembly where she spoke out in favour of Morocco's independence.

Once Salma's mother was well established in Rabat, the capital of Morocco, she was keen that we visit her with Taimur. In the summer of 1965, Salma, Taimur, nanny and I first travelled to London, where we spent some time, before flying to Rabat via Paris. Taimur was just two years old but quite articulate and hyperactive. One of our English family friends evocatively observed that Taimur has sunshine coming out of his navel.

Morocco was another enriching experience. It had been independent for only a few years so that the French inheritance was still in place in the form of French-run pensions, *boulangeries* and other manifestations of their version of colonial management not just at the top but through *petit functionaries* who controlled the intermediate levels of the economy.

Rabat itself was more of a French colonial outpost as were Tangiers and Casablanca. But visits to Fez and Marrakesh were exceptional. These cities survived as ancient urban centres of a once rich Arab civilization that had retained their medieval character into the 20th century. Morocco was still waiting to be discovered as a global tourist destination, so life there in 1965 was a special pleasure.

I learnt a great deal about Morocco's politics and found myself engaged in debates over the issue of monarchial despotism and democracy. The democratic movement was then led by the grand old man of Moroccan politics, Allal al-Fassi, the leader of the Istiqlal Party, an old-style liberal party. We had several encounters with him via interpreters, where he impressed me and reminded me of the political discourse we had left behind in Pakistan.

Salma's mother turned out to be a great Ambassador but an unenthusiastic housekeeper. This task was fortunately taken over by her youngest daughter, Sarvath, who decided to forego her opportunity to go up to Cambridge in order to run the Ambassador's household in Rabat with exceptional efficiency, where her fluency in French proved to be a great asset.

We returned to Dhaka via Belgrade, where we stayed with Kaiser Morshed, then the First Secretary in the Embassy, where the Ambassador was Lieutenant General Sher Ali Khan. This was my second visit to a communist country since my visit to Prague in 1956. It was less drab than Prague but did not radiate the affluence that was now becoming more visible across Western Europe.

We spent some long evenings with the General who held Ayub Khan in rather low esteem. Sher Ali Khan, the younger brother of the Nawab of Pataudi, took much pride in his ancestry. He was a graduate of Sandhurst, as was Ayub Khan, but believed he was more able than Ayub to lead the army. At that time, Bhutto had initiated the strategy of infiltrating Pakistani army commandos into Kashmir in the guise of local insurgents. This was invoking strong retaliation by the Indian armed forces with threats to cross the border into Pakistani Punjab. Sher Ali rightly predicted that this strategy could precipitate a full-scale Indo-Pakistan war for which Pakistan was ill-prepared. Sher Ali's assumptions proved to be quite prescient and inspired his lifelong hostility to Bhutto. Salma and I managed to return to Dhaka just before full-scale war broke out between India and Pakistan in October 1965.

In Loco Parentis

After the tensions of the 1965 war, with its political fallout had subsided and some element of normalcy was returning to life in Dhaka, my brother, Farooq, somewhat unexpectedly, informed me that he was contemplating matrimony. There was nothing unusual about this as he was 25 years old. He had graduated from Oxford with an honours degree in history in 1964 and qualified as a CSP in the same year. He had subsequently entered the Civil Services Academy in Lahore that year as a member of the 1964 batch that gained distinction in later years for the high proportion of its alumni who were elevated to high office. While at the Academy, Farooq had met Nasreen Rasheed, then a student at the elite Kinnaird College in Lahore. Nasreen, an attractive and intelligent young woman, was the daughter of Commodore Rasheed, who had attained the highest rank among Bangalis who had served in the Pakistan Navy but had chosen retirement when he was superseded for the position of Naval Chief of Staff. He had, since, been appointed a Director at the EPIDC in Dhaka. Nasreen's mother, Shams Rasheed, in the later phase of her life, earned recognition as a writer of Bangla fiction.

As the elder brother, functioning in loco parentis due to the passing of our father, I voiced the usual caution, as did my mother, that they should wait until Nasreen, who was then only 19, graduated. But the young couple were in a hurry. Farooq had opted to move from the civil to the Foreign Service and hoped to be posted abroad at an early date. My mother was also preparing to move to Bangkok with her husband Syed Masood Husan who had, since his retirement as Chair from the EPIWTA, been appointed as a Division Chief at UNESCAP. We, therefore, decided to go ahead with Farooq's wedding which was thus organized, with much jollity, in mid-1966 at the Shahbag Hotel, which, in those days, was still Dhaka's premier hotel.

With my father, K.F. Sobhan,
just before I entered St. Paul's, March 1942, Age 7

Winning the Senior Marathon at St. Paul's in 1950

With my mother Hashmat Ara Begum and brother Farooq Sobhan, Nathiagalli, 1952

At my graduation from Cambridge University, June 1956

Engagement ceremony with Salma, London, 1962

Rear (L–R), my father, K.F. Sobhan; Salma's father, M. Ikramullah
Front (L–R) Salma's mother, Shaista Ikramullah; Salma; my mother, Hashmat Ara Begum

Wedding ceremony of my brother Farooq, Shahbagh Hotel, 1966

(L–R) Salma, myself, my mother, Farooq, his wife Nasreen Rashid, Shaikh Muhommed Alley, Qamarara Zaman

Calcatta South Club, December 1950

Myself, Age 15, sitting on the ground (4th from left); on the ground, 1st from left, Ramanathan Krishnan, future national tennis champion of India and semi finalist at Wimbledon; squatting just behind me, Jaroslav Drobny, Wimbledon Champion, 1955.

Pakistan Prime Minister's Secretariat, 1952

K.F. Sobhan (Political Secretary to PM, seated 3rd from left),
Khawja Nazimudddin, (grand uncle); Prime Minister (seated centre)

Aitchison College, Kelly House 1952

Myself (as house prefect), sitting front row fifth from right

Front (L to R) Makarand Dehejia, Iran Ispahani, Pandit Nehru, Shyam Sarda, Swaran Singh, Amal Bose

Rear (L to R) Minoo Tata, Lalit Jayawardena, Dilip Adarkar, Arif Iftikhar, Dipankar Ghosh, Rehman Sobhan, Harish Rana

11

Exposures to Political Activism at Dhaka University

Dhaka University's Political Inheritance

In the rather narrow social and political universe of Dhaka in the 1960s, Dhaka University could hardly expect to remain immune. Students at Dhaka University were inevitably drawn into the political process and were used by the political parties as the front-line soldiers for any street mobilization. Student activism served as an incubator for aspirant politicians, some of whom moved into prominence in various political parties. One of my students in the Economics Department, Rashed Khan Menon, was at that time also General Secretary of EPSU. He was detained in Dhaka Central Jail while he was appearing for his MA final exams in 1965 so that Abu Mahmood, Anisur Rahman and I had to conduct his viva exam within the jail premises. Menon stood fifth in his class but chose a political career and emerged as the leader of a faction of the NAP that is now known as the Bangladesh Workers' Party (BWP).

Within this vortex of political activity at Dhaka University, the teachers could not remain untouched. During the 1952 Language Movement, such teachers as Muzaffar Ahmed Chowdhury (MAC) in Political Science and Munier Chowdhury in the Bangla Department spent time in prison even though the Movement itself was largely located within the student community. These and other teachers never imposed their views on their students. Teachers who had their own political perspectives shared them with those of their students who sought them out, but this was done outside the classroom. Most teachers and indeed a large body of students tended to be apolitical so that in those days, student admissions, their exam results and also career advancement for teachers were not contingent on political identity as is reported to be the case today.

There were conspicuous exceptions to this norm where teachers did engage in drawing upon particular student groups as a political resource or were themselves directly drawn into particular aspects of student activism. In this chapter, I will discuss this political interface between teachers and students by drawing upon three episodes where I was a direct witness or was personally associated. In two cases, a student organization, the NSF, was used for instrumental reasons by teachers. In another case, I was both witness to and an indirect participant in an episode of student activism.

Teacher–Student Relations of the Fraught Kind Affair

During the initial years of martial law, political activism originating in the University had remained subdued and manifested itself, if at all, within the campus. One such episode that exposed a teacher's link with student politics was the Newman affair. Professor Newman, a political scientist of German origin, had for many years been Chair of the Political Science Department at Dhaka University. I do not know much about Newman's academic contributions, but he came to be known on campus for his right-wing views and consequential links with both domestic and possibly external intelligence agencies. It was believed across the campus that he displayed his political identity by informing on teachers and students of left-wing and radical views. In his own department, his bête noires were Razzaq (Sir) and MAC, while his great favourite was Ghulam Wahed Chowdhury who succeeded him as the Chair of the Department.

Professor Newman was reported to be one of the inspirations and also adviser to the notorious NSF, where its leader, A.R. Yusuf, was reported to be particularly close to him. While students recruited to the NSF were presumably meant to be pro-Muslim League or Islam-oriented, a substantial intake included a more muscular breed of students with a capacity and inclination to use violence in their practice of student politics.

Newman's rather sinister role at the University was quite well known but did not extrude itself into university affairs outside his department. It was thus somewhat unexpected that his presence should become more controversial during the tenure of an enlightened VC such as Dr Mahmud Hussain who had recently been appointed to the post by Lieutenant General Azam Khan, the Governor of East Pakistan. Azam Khan had been sent out by Field Marshal Ayub Khan in 1959 to take over from an ex-IG of Police, Zakir Hossain, as Governor. He was not overly intelligent but was a well-intentioned soldier who projected the Sandhurst tradition of the Pakistan army. His claim to fame originated in the ruthless way in which he dealt with the anti-Qadiani riots in Lahore in 1953 instigated by the Jamaat-e-Islami with the clandestine support of Mumtaz Daultana, the CM of Punjab.

On his arrival in Dhaka, Azam Khan sought to project himself as a friend of East Pakistan, determined to step up development in the once neglected province. With this end in mind, he periodically invited some of the Dhaka University teachers known to be speaking out on the deprivation of the Bangalis and sought our opinion on what he could do to reverse this process. Apart from discussing the issue of disparity, we also managed to inject the germs of democracy into Azam's political consciousness. By the time Ayub began to make his transition from military to civilian rule, Azam Khan appeared to have become critical of the regime's political direction. Unsurprisingly, he was recalled by Ayub to General Headquarters (GHQ). Just days before Azam relinquished office, he invited Kamal, Sir and me to dinner in Government House and informed us of his decision to resign from the army and speak out on the need for genuine democracy.

Azam Khan was, in some measure, influenced by some of the Bangali bureaucrats around him, such as Kazi Fazlur Rahman, who was then a Deputy Secretary in the Governor's Secretariat. Kazi, who was a Kali Narayan scholar from Dhaka University who had topped the Central Superior Services (CSS) exam in 1956, was a progressive-minded and dedicated officer. Azam had consulted Kazi on the appointment of the VC of Dhaka University. Kazi, in turn, consulted Sir, who he held in high esteem. He was advised by Sir to recommend the name of Dr Mahmud Hussain who had in earlier years been a Professor of History at Dhaka University and was much respected by his colleagues. Mahmud Hussain's brief tenure at Dhaka University between 1960 and 1963 was something of a golden age for the University. Not only were major development projects such as the construction of the new Arts Building in Nilkhet and the large-scale construction of teacher's residences around Savage Road taken up but academic standards were strengthened at the University.

The infamous Newman affair occurred in the first part of 1960 at a time when the campus appeared to be quite tranquil. In those days, the Economics Department had been demoted from our retreat in the old Arts Building to a few rooms in the outhouses overlooking the pond where we were neighbours to the Political Science Department. One morning in 1960, I had just arrived at my department for an early class when I noticed that Newman was walking towards his office besieged by a small crowd of students led by Maudood Ahmed, a leader of a minor student's party, the Pakistan Students Force, shouting slogans demanding justice for Talukdar Maniruzzaman, one of the top students of the Political Science Department, who had reportedly been deprived of a first class in the MA exam due to the presumed machinations of Newman. As Newman, pursued by this angry mob, approached the Political Science Department, I noticed a smaller group of students, with A.R. Yusuf at its epicentre, standing on the verandah outside Newman's office observing the scene. As Newman reached the department, Yusuf gave a signal and a group of more muscular NSF students, led by Abul Hasnat, a rather hefty youth from old Dhaka, jumped down from the verandah and launched an attack on Maudood and his motley crew. I personally witnessed Hasnat landing a few well-placed punches on Maudood's face that resulted in his moving around the campus for the next few days with a conspicuously swollen jaw. The crowd behind Maudood, whose fighting capacity did not match their shouting abilities, was soon put to flight. This episode not only provided tangible evidence of Newman's links with the NSF but demonstrated their commitment to serve as his sword arm on the campus.

The Talukdar incident, unfortunately for Newman, did not turn out to be his moment of triumph but served as his swansong at Dhaka University. The event was much publicized in the media where the Newman–NSF connection was highlighted. Azam Khan used his ex-officio position as Chancellor of the University to appoint an Enquiry Commission headed by a respected judge of the High Court, Justice Asir who, in his report, recommended Newman's removal from the University, which was acted upon and led to his return to Germany. The Newman affair, unfortunately, did not bring to an end the attempt to use the NSF for partisan ends on the campus.

Engagement with Student Activism

In the subsequent two narratives of the teacher–student interface, I was not just a bystander but more closely engaged with the process. In the first of these episodes, I was exposed to the ways in which national politics impacted on Dhaka University. During the period of martial law, political activism remained stifled and the politicians also remained silent. In such circumstances, some of us teachers, who wrote and spoke publicly on the political economy of Pakistan, were accorded a degree of political visibility that served to project our voices into the political domain. Once my writings on the political economy of Pakistan began to appear in the newspapers and I also addressed some seminars on such issues, not only political activists but some of my students sought me out to discuss the policy and political implications of my work.

Conversations with my students originally tended to be of a more academic nature but, occasionally, acquired a topical dimension as the political climate became more restive. Up to the end of 1961, the policy agendas of the regime had faced little challenge in any part of Pakistan. The once restive students had remained largely passive in the absence of any external political stimuli. By this time, Ayub was preparing to present his constitution to the country that had aroused debate and consternation on account of its undemocratic character. At that stage, the regime demonstrated no apprehension that dissent would move outside the academic arena and into an activist phase.

The catalyst for the first protests against the martial law regime was provided by the arrest of H.S. Suhrawardy. Initially, there was no strong public outcry, which surprised Kamal and me. We were not aware that the EPSU and EPSL had met on the night of 31 January and agreed to convene a *hartal* or general strike on the next day, 1 February, to protest the arrest of Suhrawardy. The strike was also intended to coincide with the arrival of Ayub Khan in Dhaka that day. The strike began with an incendiary meeting convened by the students of Dhaka University at the Amtala. Processions moved out of the campus and extended across the streets of old Dhaka, shouting slogans denouncing martial law and Ayub Khan. In response to this first public challenge to the martial law regime, many of the political activists in East Pakistan, including Bangabandhu, were arrested along with assorted fellow travellers, including journalists.

In the wake of these public manifestations of protest, I was warned by Akhlaq Hussain, who was then the Deputy Secretary, in the Home Department, that Kamal and I were potential candidates for preventative detention and might, thereby, consider making ourselves less visible. Excited by the prospect of our first exposure to the need to disappear 'underground', we took temporary refuge at the home of my cousin Akhter Morshed in Narayanganj. However, we did not stay long, deciding to take our chances with the law, and eventually returned to Dhaka. Fortunately, we were not deemed to be worthy of detention, which was rather deflating.

Student Activism of the Hostile Kind

My own notoriety with the intelligence agencies perhaps owed less to my writings, which were out in the open, than to my interactions with my students at Dhaka University who were leading the agitations against the Ayub regime. This view was given some currency as a result of the visit to the University on 3 February 1962 by Manzoor Qadir, the then Foreign Minister, who had accompanied Ayub on his visit to Dhaka. Qadir had been one of Pakistan's leading lawyers and prided himself on his erudition and eloquence.

Qadir recognized that the real challenge was to face the Bangali intellectuals who were presumed to be heavily concentrated in Dhaka University and were likely to be more critical, possibly because they were unaware of the merits of Ayub's constitution. To Qadir's credit, he believed in the force of argument. It was thus arranged that on his visit to Dhaka, he would address a meeting of teachers and students at one of the larger lecture halls of the old Arts Building. Unfortunately for Qadir, his visit to the University came in the wake of the students mobilization on 1 February so that the atmosphere on the campus, at the time of his visit, was highly charged.

Prior to the meeting, some of the more politically oriented of my students, led by Ziauddin Mahmud, an EPSU activist, came to me for a briefing on the questions they should put to Qadir. We had several exchanges on this issue, and I eventually drafted a set of questions for them which addressed both the issues of restricting the franchise to elect the President and legislatures as well as the deprivation of the Bangalis.

By the time Qadir presented himself at the Arts Building, Dhaka was already in turmoil not just over the undemocratic nature of the constitution but more so over the arrests of the leaders of the opposition and sundry fellow travellers. When I entered the auditorium in the mid-morning of 3 February, it was already packed with students. I sensed a certain tension in the air that did not augur well for a peaceable exchange of views among intellectuals. After a brief introduction by the Dr Mahmud Hussain, the then VC who was chairing the meeting, Qadir launched into an erudite defence of the constitution. While some of us were preparing a point-by-point refutation of his arguments, the students apparently had other plans. When the VC opened the discussion to questions from the floor, some of the students rose to ask their questions in a rather intemperate tone of voice. Qadir made some effort to respond to these questions, but the mood was far from conducive to public reasoning. Soon, many students were on their feet, shouting their own questions that escalated into slogans against the Ayub regime.

I observed that some students were gradually moving towards the speaker in a rather menacing mood. Some got close enough to Qadir to spit at him, and Ziauddin even tried to grab his collar. The VC immediately terminated the meeting and began to move Qadir out of the hall. Sir, who was sitting next to me, feared that Qadir could be assaulted at any moment by the students and suggested that the teachers form a cordon sanitaire around him as we escorted him down the stairs to his car. The journey down the stairs became more precarious by the step, so that by the time we descended to the porch, some of the teachers may even have taken a few blows on their back in their defence of Qadir. The VC put Qadir into his own car and drove off to his residence on Nilkhet Road.

While we were descending the stairwell, Qadir demonstrated an interest in continuing the debate if it could be held in a more peaceable environment. We accordingly suggested to the VC that, if Qadir was willing, we could immediately host an impromptu dialogue with him at the Teachers' Club, which had by then been relocated to a building next to the Sikh gurdwara opposite Rokeya Hall. Some of the teachers present at the Arts Building rushed off to the Teachers' Club to prepare for our encounter with Qadir.

The intrepid barrister turned up as promised, ready to join battle with us teachers. If I recollect correctly, the debate lasted for at least three hours. Sir, Abu Mahmood, Anisur Rahman and I, among others, engaged in the debate that inevitably focused on the issue of deprivation of the Bangalis, but the discussion covered a much larger landscape, including Qadir's favourite topic of the constitution where his defence of its undemocratic features was challenged by quite a few of us. As the evening progressed, Qadir's immaculate self-confidence as well as his good manners began to fray a bit, and he eventually begged leave on grounds of another official engagement. While we may not have convinced Pakistan's Foreign Minister of our concerns, we certainly educated him on our perspectives towards his regime. In turn, the teachers present experienced a certain catharsis at being able to express ourselves so freely before a person of high influence who had claims to be the principal intellectual of West Pakistan. Qadir himself is to be commended for exposing himself to such a risk-prone encounter. I cannot imagine any minister today in Bangladesh or Pakistan engaging in such debates in a politically hostile milieu.

Martial Rule in Civilian Garb

My third exposure to the interface between national and university politics had a more direct impact on my professional and personal life. The transition from a martial law regime to a military regime in civilian garb turned out to be no less subversive to the democratic process. A military regime usually needs to bring in 'respectable' civilians such as senior bureaucrats and well-regarded professionals such as Manzoor Qadir to leaven the military aspect of the regime. The Bangali members of Ayub's martial law regime included some eminently respectable public servants. One of these, Justice Ibrahim, who had previously served as VC of Dhaka University, began to stand up for the cause of the Bangalis in cabinet meetings, presenting written briefs to Ayub, prepared mostly by drawing on the assistance of Professor Nurul Islam. He eventually resigned from the Government on account of his objection to the undemocratic constitution about to be promulgated by Ayub.

Ayub's transition from a general in uniform to a political neta, now garbed in a sherwani and a karakul cap, transformed his image from a dictator ostensibly in office to establish a clean government into a patron of the more corrupt elements of public life. The newly included political elements of his Muslim League regime tended to practise corruption as a way of life. In East Pakistan, in particular, the regime used the Basic Democracies (BD) system to spread corruption right down to the village level to build a political support base. While much of the regime's corruption was documented in the more independent media such as *Ittefaq*, *Sangbad* and *Pakistan Observer*, I had generated my own insights into the process during research for my study on the book that I published in 1966, *Basic Democracies, Works Programme and Rural Development in East Pakistan*.

The principal instrument for Ayub's rule over the Bangalis was Abdul Monem Khan, a half-educated Muslim League district lawyer from Mymensingh. He never graduated beyond the culture of a district politician, using money and muscle to sustain his reign. Without the benediction of the Pakistan army, manifested in the presence of the Ninth Division located in the Dhaka Cantonment, his tenure at Government House would have been short-lived.

Lathials on the Campus

Monem Khan's malignant regime projected itself into Dhaka University in the most disastrous form and effectively pulled down the curtain on the golden age of Dhaka University. During this dark era, Monem made it his mission to recapture Dhaka University from the clutches of the pro-AL/NAP teachers who he believed had traditionally dominated the University since the Language Movement of 1952. This belief was a figment of his imagination since university teachers, even those who had political leanings, had little to do with driving student activism that was sustained by its own dynamic. As part of this agenda, Monem replaced the independent-minded Mahmud Hussain as VC with Professor Osman Ghani, a professor of Soil Science who had previously been the VC of the Agricultural University in Mymensingh. The Governor was not disappointed as Ghani served him loyally throughout his tenure. However, many former colleagues of Ghani at Dhaka University, where he was once a respected academic in his own right, did not expect him to become so deeply involved in the district-level *lathial*[1] politics that Monem Khan introduced into the campus.

To strengthen his hand in university affairs, Ghani built up a cabal of senior teachers who were willing to participate in the Governor's game. This group included Professor Aziz, the Chair of the Mathematics Department; Professor Mafizuddin, Chair of the Chemistry Department and Provost of Salimullah Hall; Dr Mushfiqur Rahman, a teacher in the Mathematics Department and Provost of Dhaka Hall; and, for a while, Professor Abdul Matin Chowdhury, Chair of the Physics Department. Matin Chowdhury sensibly saw the writing on the wall for the Monem regime and took up an assignment as member of the Atomic Energy Commission in Karachi. On the fall of the Ayub regime in 1969, he politically reincarnated himself and ended up being appointed by Bangabandhu to succeed Professor Muzzafer Ahmed Chowdhury as VC of Dhaka University in 1973. There were some other members of Ghani's inner group whose names escape my memory.

One of the early fallouts from the arrival of the Monem–Osman Ghani era was the fiasco of the first convocation ceremony of Dhaka University in 1964 to be attended by Monem Khan in his capacity as Chancellor. From 1962 onwards, Dhaka University had remained turbulent, reflecting the political climate in East Pakistan in the wake of the civilianization of the Ayub regime. By 1964, Monem Khan had emerged as a much reviled figure so that any presence by him on the Dhaka University campus was viewed by the students and many teachers as a provocation. The convocation was, thus, not just boycotted by the students but was disrupted by them and ended in pandemonium.

A number of students presumed to have been actively associated with the mayhem at the convocation, such as Fazlul Huq Moni of the EPSL, a nephew of Bangabandhu, along with one of my favourite students, Zakir Ahmed of EPSU, had their degrees withheld by the University. Zakir Ahmed, through Kamal Hossain, led by

[1] A distinct social group in the rural society of Bengal who practise *Lathi kela*, a Bangladeshi martial art. Eminent people hire them for security and as a symbol of power.

a senior lawyer, S.R. Pal, legally challenged this arbitrary decision and managed to have his degree restored through favourable judgements, first by Justice Sattar in the Dhaka High Court and eventually at the Supreme Court of Pakistan. The case of *Zakir Ahmed v. Dhaka University* is inscribed in the law reports. Zakir Ahmed eventually opted for the legal profession where he was appointed as judge of the Dhaka High Court during the 1980s but died prematurely during his tenure on the bench.

Whatever may have been Monem Khan's obsession with the sinister role of the teaching community, he recognized that the students of Dhaka University were one of the principal threats to his regime and set out to tame them as a political force. Monem's main instrument for tackling the students and capturing the University remained the NSF, which was created to serve as a counterweight to the EPSU/EPSL influence over the student community. However, using an ideologically motivated political strategist such as A.R. Yusuf to organize the NSF did not fit well with the *lathial*-style politics of Monem Khan. Thus, a new generation of NSF leaders were deployed in Dhaka University who tended to be outright hoodlums, motivated largely by money rather than politics. The now ubiquitous tradition of pressurizing university authorities to award contracts for implementing various development projects originated in the 1960s with this new gang of State-patronized NSF student leaders.

The new group of NSF hoodlums were chosen for their muscular qualities and willingness to use force, including lethal weapons, to impose their will on the student community. Their leader was a university-level athlete, Jahangir Faiz, who ran Dhaka Hall as a mafia fiefdom. His regime in the hall was patronized by Dr Mushfiqur Rahman, the Hall Provost. As a teacher, I was formally affiliated to Dhaka Hall, which, in practice, meant that I was called upon, once a year, to supervise the polls for the elections to the Hall student's union. I used to witness Jahangir, under the benediction of the Hall Provost, overseeing the polls with a practised eye. At the end of the day, he would cast his own vote. Each student, before he voted, needed to be identified by a teacher. On one occasion, when I enquired as to who would identify Jahangir from among the teachers, he contemptuously retorted, "None present are big enough to identify me. I can be identified only at the highest level!" Needless to say, the students' union at Dhaka Hall tended to end up under the control of the NSF.

Other hoodlums around Jahangir included a muscleman, Sayeedur Rahman, known by the nickname 'Paspartwo', so-called because when he was asked to indicate his educational qualifications, which were non-existent, he rather enigmatically replied 'Passed part two'. Another character in Jahangir's gang was Khoka, who used to roam around the campus with a snake, presumably non-poisonous, draped around his neck. These hoodlums remained under the protection of Monem Khan through a student of mine in the Economics Department, Jomir Ali, who kept a close liaison with the two sons of the Governor who oversaw the more criminalized aspects of the regime.

These colourful characters and a few others imposed a reign of terror on the campus that culminated in a physical assault on my colleague, Abu Mahmood, Chair of the Economics Department. This infamous episode occurred in February 1966 after around two years of Osman Ghani's regime as V.C. Ghani had set about cleansing the University of those he deemed to be more conspicuously hostile to the ruling order. Abu Mahmood, who was an ideological Marxist, regularly wrote, along with me, articles in the newspapers, which were critical of the regime but particularly of the existing social order. He was targeted because he chaired the Economics Department, which was singled out by the Monem regime as the trouble spot of the University. Mahmood, who had returned with a PhD from Harvard in 1962, had succeeded to the Chair of the Department in 1965 when Nurul Islam departed for Karachi to take over PIDE. Mahmood was at that time, by age and length of service, the senior most member of the Department.

At that time, Abu Mahmood, Dr K.T. Hossain, a demographer with a PhD from Duke University, and I were the three Readers at the Department. The other Reader in the Department, Anisur Rahman, was abroad on a sabbatical. I could hardly be deemed a politically appropriate replacement for Mahmood. Ghani therefore decided to supersede Mahmood and appoint K.T. Hossain to take over as the Department Chair. As Hossain was many years junior to Mahmood in both years and service to the Department and was not known for any noticeable academic publications, this was a manifestly unfair and even unprecedented decision. Mahmood decided to challenge his supersession and filed a writ in the High Court. The writ was heard by the Chief Justice of the East Pakistan High Court, Justice Mahbub Morshed, a jurist of the highest calibre, integrity and independence of mind. It says something of the state of the judiciary, even under a militarized regime, that such judges could remain free to challenge the illegal acts of the State.

The case for Mahmood was prepared by Kamal Hossain and effectively argued by S.R. Pal before the bench that issued a stay order on the University to desist from superseding Mahmood with K.T. Hossain. The University, presumably under pressure from Monem Khan, went ahead and appointed K.T. Hossain as Chair of the Economics Department. Mahmood, under advice from his lawyers, immediately filed a 'contempt of court' petition against VC Ghani. The writ was also argued by Pal before Murshid, who, in a landmark judgement, found the VC of Dhaka University, Dr Osman Ghani, guilty of contempt of court. I was present in court, along with Mahmood and a few others of my university colleagues, to witness this landmark judgement. For all of us, but particularly Mahmood, this was a great victory, both for the Department and indeed for the independence of the judiciary, and was greeted with some jubilation in the courtroom.

Our jubilation did not last long. It was then reported that on the night before the court judgement, which was anticipated to go against Ghani, a meeting was held where it was decided that if the verdict was awarded in favour of Mahmood, he was to be taught a lesson by the NSF goons. After the verdict, around noon of 15 February 1966, we dispersed to our various residences. Mahmood drove to his apartment in the teacher's quarters on Savage Road in his small Fiat 600 car. As he alighted from his car in front of his apartment block, a group of six NSF goons, Jahangir Faiz, Aftaf Hussain, Paspartwo, Khoka and two others, assaulted Mahmood with hockey sticks and also damaged his car. The assault was sufficiently ferocious as to inflict severe bodily injuries on him that required his hospitalization in the Dhaka Medical College for several weeks.

The news of the assault spread rapidly across the campus and was communicated to me in my apartment across the road from the British Council while I was sharing the good news of the verdict with Salma. I rushed to Mahmood's apartment where I found him in a rather battered condition but alert enough to recount the details of the assault and to identify his assailants.

The NSF gang were known to everyone on the campus and had some months earlier assaulted one of our students, Mahbubullah, then an activist with the pro-Chinese wing of EPSU, on the premises of the Arts Faculty. After the assault, Mahbubullah had taken refuge in Mahmood's office in the Arts Building and narrated his encounter with the NSF before some of us teachers. It was reported at that point that the goons had also threatened to sort out the anti-regime teachers of the Economics Department.

I stayed with Mahmood until an ambulance arrived to take him to hospital and then went over to the apartment of Sir, which was located in another building on the same campus. Sir was so traumatized by the unprecedented news that a teacher of Dhaka University had actually been assaulted by students that he vomited all over the floor and was then rendered speechless for the next few days.

Around the campus, all hell broke loose. Violent fights broke out between the NSF and the EPSU/EPSL. The NSF goons, though outnumbered, were better armed and fighting fit, so they retained control of the campus. First information reports (FIRs) were lodged with the police against Mahmood's assailants who, in the spirit of the times, refused to take cognizance of the case. The political opposition and media made the Mahmood assault into a cause célèbre and demanded the dismissal of the VC. We also took up the case with the administration. I remember personally raising the issue with Karim Iqbal, a senior CSP officer who was then the Secretary to the Governor. I was given some sense of which way the wind was blowing, when Iqbal, an otherwise highly capable officer, admonished me with the quote "he who sows the wind must reap the whirlwind." I deduced from this that Mahmood could expect no justice from either the law enforcement agencies or the administration.

Some days after the incident, Monem Khan, in his capacity as Chancellor, summoned the senior teachers to Government House. Those of the senior teachers who sat in the front row were permitted to speak, with some seeking justice for Mahmood. Monem roundly admonished them, implying that Mahmood got what he deserved. Monem appeared to suffer from an inferiority complex in the presence of us teachers over his lack of educational qualifications and defended himself with the risible observation that his educational deficits were not important as Rabindranath Tagore also had no university education.

Some weeks after the Mahmood episode, with the whole of Dhaka in ferment, President Ayub Khan visited the city. A delegation of citizens led by Begum Sufia Kamal, which also included Kamal Hossain, called on Ayub in a rather optimistic belief that he would intervene to restore peace and justice to Dhaka University. Ayub had been well briefed by the Governor and went on the offensive against the delegation, accusing the Dhaka University teachers of being politicized, anti-regime and even anti-Pakistan. Begum Sufia Kamal, who spoke fluent Urdu, in parting requested Ayub to do something in the name of *insaniyat*[2] to resolve the situation, to which Ayub replied, also in Urdu, that the anti-regime elements involved were not *insan* but *haiwan*.[3]

A Period of Withdrawal

Following the Mahmood assault, the categorical refusal of the administration to take any action against his assailants and the military supremacy established by the NSF over the campus, darkness descended over Dhaka University. Despite the court ruling

[2] Humanity.
[3] Animals.

K.T. Hossain continued to Chair the Economics Department. The marginalization of the anti-regime teachers was extended to Sir through action initiated by the University administration, who sought his dismissal as a teacher of the University. With the prospect of further litigation ahead of him, Sir decided to take an extended leave from the University and moved to England around 1967. Abu Mahmood, without further legal recourse and under constant threat of assault, resigned from the University and went abroad to take up an assignment with the UN in Bangkok. My colleague Muzaffer Ahmed was so disgusted with this turn of events in the Department that he too resigned and took up an assignment as an Economic Adviser to the United Bank, at its headquarter in Karachi, from where he then returned to Dhaka to join the EPIDC as its Chief Economist. My other senior colleague, Anisur Rahman, who had been associated with the anti-establishment image of the Economics Department, had taken up an academic assignment at Yale University sometime around 1965 and had moved abroad.

As the Mahmood affair ended in ashes and Sir came under attack from the University administration, I found the atmosphere becoming increasingly inimical both to academic work and to the pursuit of any form of political activism. Teachers loyal to Monem Khan ruled the campus. The NSF, who had established their immunity from the rule of law in spite of their widely publicized assault on a university teacher, had enforced their own reign of terror over the University. EPSU/EPSL students, who had once been the dominant force on the campus, found it difficult to even organize public meetings.

Within the suffocating environment, which prevailed not just in Dhaka University but across East Pakistan at that time, I felt it was time to take a sabbatical from political involvement and apply myself more exclusively to academic pursuits. I availed of the opportunity provided by Nurul Islam to take up a Ford Foundation fellowship then administered by PIDE, in order to go abroad to work on my PhD. I had never really aspired to seek further degrees after my return from Cambridge and had hoped to remain continuously engaged in teaching as a route to my further involvement in politics.

Salma was not at all interested to go abroad at that stage as she was well settled in our university apartment, enjoyed her teaching in the Law Faculty and was fully immersed in learning Bangla through classes at the Bangla Academy. I prevailed on her to take our excursion abroad as a break from the tensions of life at the University and in the political world around us. I hoped to return to Dhaka once the political situation improved, but at the end of 1966, this did not promise to be anytime soon.

I registered myself as a PhD student at LSE with the intent of writing a thesis on the issue of regional imbalance in Pakistan. It remained ambiguous as to whether I would see this project to its conclusion or merely write a publishable book on the issue and return when the winds across Pakistan changed. I was clearly ill-prepared for serious academic pursuits. However, the two years I spent at LSE were academically useful to me even if they ended infructuously. This outcome owed in no small measure to the tension that prevailed between my aspiration to be a scholar of political economy and my graduation to the role of politician economist through my involvement in the struggle for self-rule for the Bangalis.

12

From Political Economy to Politician Economist

Insights into the Political Economy of Pakistan

First Lessons

It had become apparent from my initial exposure to the practice of political economy at the East Pakistan Planning Board, engagement in discussions at Dhaka University and even my limited involvement in business that the central theme of Pakistan's political discourse was the unequal and unjust relationship between West and East Pakistan. I had, in my own small way, been sensitized to this issue as far back as 1959 when I was invited by Professor Kabir Chowdhury, who then worked at the Bureau of National Reconstruction (BNR), an entity established to propagate the various policy reforms emanating from the Ayub regime, to contribute a paper on the economy in a special volume on East Pakistan being published by the BNR. The volume was intended to present an upbeat perspective on East Pakistan consistent with Ayub's vision of a united, forward-looking nation.

My paper on the economy of East Pakistan turned out to be rather less positive, though far less so than in my later writings, and drew out the issue of economic neglect of the province. Kabir Chowdhury had assured me of complete freedom of expression, so he had no problem in including the paper, as submitted by me, in the volume that was published early in 1960. When I visited the

BNR a while later to pick up a copy of the volume, I was flattered to learn, from an obviously embarrassed Kabir Chowdhury, that his superiors at the BNR had taken sufficiently strong objection to the critical tone of my article to demand that the large numbers of copies already in print should be withdrawn from circulation. The volume was republished some months later, this time with a more positive article on the economy of East Pakistan, written by a Dhaka University colleague, Abdullah Farouk, based in the Commerce Faculty.

By 1961, the issue of regional disparity and the search for political solutions, recognizing the distinctive structural features of the two economies of East and West Pakistan, had begun to gain stronger traction. As political leaders of both wings were silenced by martial law, those among the academic community who were willing to speak out on these subjects in public fora and to write in the media began to attract a degree of public attention that was rather disproportionate to our years or professional standing.

Apart from the episode of the BNR publication, I had already been involved in a number of less publicized engagements with policymakers. Late in 1959, Mosharaff Hossain, who had just joined the newly established Economics Department at Rajshahi University, Akhlaqur Rahman, who had just joined PIDE in Karachi, and I were invited to be part of an advisory panel set up by the East Pakistan Planning Board, to help them to provide inputs to the Second Five-Year Plan, which was then under preparation. As I was then only 25 years old, for me this was a rather elevated responsibility that I nonetheless happily accepted.

One of our associates in this rather assorted advisory group was the late Fazlul Qader Chowdhury, then a labour leader from Chittagong and a Muslim League politician whose association with our enterprise seemed to us to be rather bizarre. Chowdhury, a large man, with a booming voice, whenever he was given the chance to speak within our small group sitting in a small conference room of the Eden Building, tended to address us as if we were an audience at Paltan Maidan. While we were sufficiently bemused to let Chowdhury indulge himself, he, on occasion, aroused the ire of Akhlaq who was no less irascible in temperament, which led to some shouting matches that promised to have a more fearsome outcome.

Our group's more radical recommendations did not greatly influence the Second Plan document that was premised on the notion that West Pakistan, as the engine of growth, should be encouraged to grow and that this would spill over to stimulate growth in East Pakistan. These rather weakly documented and manifestly tendentious arguments were roundly criticized by the Bangali economists in the media and in academic gatherings. Nurul Islam has addressed these issues more satisfactorily in his memoirs, so I will not elaborate on the professional aspects of these debates.

When the Second Plan was eventually published in mid-1960, a number of Bangali economists were invited to Rawalpindi for a conference to discuss the Plan. We did so, quite intensively, over three or four days with the Finance Minister, Mohammed Shoaib, the Deputy Chairman of the Planning Commission, Syed Hasan, along with sundry Secretaries of the Central government and the senior staff of the Planning Commission, in full attendance. Their team was joined by Mahbubul Haq, who had recently returned with a PhD from Yale and was then an Assistant Chief Economist at the Commission.

The Bangali team which, inter alia, included Nurul Islam and me from Dhaka, stated our positions quite strongly, without pulling any punches. Interestingly, this did not invoke charges of talking treason or, in today's parlance, such favoured epithets by our economics czars as 'rubbish'. These government figures, senior to us in years and at the apex of their power, were willing to sit patiently with us and engage in reasoned argument. I suspect this indulgence originated in their awareness of the unequal relations of power between young academics located in a powerless corner of Pakistan and those who wielded unchallenged power which they then believed would be further consolidated over the years.

During 1961, as the Bangalis became more restless over the denial of democracy, their frustrations increasingly found outlet in the escalating debate over economic disparity that was deemed to originate in the undemocratic and unjust nature of a Pakistan State ruled by an elite of West Pakistani generals, senior bureaucrats, feudal landlords and affluent businessmen, where Bangalis were completely excluded. Whenever opportunity presented itself, the Bangali academics spoke out on these issues, though most were reluctant to do so before any public gathering.

Two Economies and All That

I remember Nurul Islam and myself organized a seminar on the theme of 'two economies' in Curzon Hall, at Dhaka University, around June 1961, which was addressed by us along with Dr Habibur Rahman, then a Deputy Chief in the Pakistan Planning Commission. Rahman, the father of my BIDS colleague, Sultan Hafeez Rahman, had himself written a number of papers on the theme of two economies that had come to the attention and aroused the ire of President Ayub. As a public employee, he was, thus, reluctant to publicize his views, except at small academic gatherings such as the one convened by us.

On that occasion, I too presented a paper on the theme of two economies. Though both Rahman and Nurul Islam also spoke on this issue, for some unaccountable reason, it was my presentation that attracted much media attention. The next morning, I opened the *Pakistan Observer* to read a front-page headline, "Rehman Sobhan says Pakistan has two economies." My presentation gained further notoriety owing to the presence of Ayub Khan, then visiting his colony. On his departure from Dhaka on the same day as our Curzon Hall seminar, he was asked by the journalists about his views on two economies. His response, which was also emblazoned on the *Observer*'s front page, adjacent to my own remarks, stated, "Ayub Khan says Pakistan has only one economy." This bizarre juxtaposition of the remarks of an all-powerful military ruler with those of a 26-year-old university teacher reflected the changing climate of opinion in the Pakistan State that eventually culminated in an independent Bangladesh.

Later that year, around October, possibly, on the strength of the exposure provided to me, courtesy of the *Pakistan Observer*, I was invited to present a paper at a national seminar organized by the BNR on the theme of 'How to build Pakistan into a well-knit nation'. The BNR, to which I had earlier exposure, was one of the dedicated institutions established by the martial law regime to project its image as reformers and nation builders. However, as Ayub moved to politicize his regime, the BNR appeared to assume a more political role premised on the assumption that a significant number of citizens, mostly presumed to be Bangalis, were being alienated from the idea of a Pakistani nation state constructed around its Islamic identity. This alienation, it was believed, owed to false propaganda spread by a small class of intellectuals. To correct this mischief, the BNR became more active in promoting the 'ideology' of Pakistan through specially commissioned publications and national seminars that brought intellectuals from both wings together to better understand each other as well as the rationale of the Pakistan State.

It was perhaps presumed that Rehman Sobhan was merely a misled intellectual rather than an agent of sedition and could thus be salvaged to serve the cause of national integration through closer interaction with more loyal West Pakistanis. The title of the seminar was intended to provide the terms of reference for my paper. So that I could not move off-message, I was programmed to present a paper on 'The indivisibility of the national economy of Pakistan'.

The BNR must have been shocked to read my paper which argued that the integrity of Pakistan would be best preserved by investing its two regions with the maximum policy autonomy, which located within it the power to, inter alia, raise its own taxes, retain control over export earnings where, up to that point, East Pakistan accounted for more than half of the country's foreign exchange receipts.

I concluded my presentation at the relevant session of the seminar, which was not presented in the written text of my rather academic paper, with the observation that if full regional autonomy was not conceded to East Pakistan and disparities continued to grow over the years, this would, in the future, jeopardize the integrity of Pakistan and defeat the objective of building Pakistan into a well-knit nation.

My argumentation, and particularly the off-text conclusion, was totally out of step with the ethos of the seminar. A Justice of the West Pakistan High Court who presided over my session sought out my good friend Iftikhar Bokhari, who had accompanied me to the seminar, to enquire as to who was this young man and whether I was unaware that Pakistan was still under martial law!

The consternation of the BNR and its political masters was exponentially aggravated when they discovered that my presentation in Lahore, largely ignored in the West Pakistan media, was emblazoned across the front page of some of the leading papers of Dhaka. The *Pakistan Observer* reproduced my paper in full in their issues of 23–25 October 1961. This publicity elevated me on to the political radar screen of the government and its intelligence agencies. I was informed some years later by Dr Aneesa Farooqui—who was an economist in the Planning Commission—whom I came to know well when she was working for her PhD at the LSE, that some staff members in the Planning Commission were even assigned to track my writings in order to refute them.

All this attention to a 26-year-old university teacher did not adequately appreciate that my views were neither unique nor original but had been articulated with varying degrees of intensity and sophistication by a broad range of Bangali economists, which included Dr A. Sadeque, a pioneer in this dialectic; Dr Nurul Islam, Dr Habibur Rahman, Dr Akhlaqur Rahman, Dr Mosharaff Hossain, Mr Abdur Razzaq; and even Professor M.N. Huda and Professor A.F.A. Hossain. An articulation of the concept of two economies was, indeed, incorporated in an unofficial report prepared by the Bangali economists on Pakistan's First Five-Year Plan in 1956 during the tenure of AL rule when much greater freedom of expression was possible. During the era of martial law, from October 1958 to mid-1962, academics tended to be more inhibited about publishing their views on more controversial subjects mostly preferring to use the medium of seminars or academic papers to express themselves.

Economists as Political Combatants

Our views on disparity gained resonance in the 1960–61 period because it projected the growing political dissent across East Pakistan with the anti-democratic and discriminatory character of the West Pakistan dominated martial law regime. Ayub was then moving towards the presentation of a new constitution for Pakistan that was designed to perpetuate his military regime under a civilian façade. The Bangali politicians who were then embargoed from addressing public meetings found our potentially subversive ideas of political relevance and sought out some of us, along with sympathetic Bangali civil servants, to educate them on the policy dimensions of the autonomy agenda.

We have already observed that in the martial law phase of Ayub's rule, it was the University teachers and other intellectuals who had given voice to the deprivation of the Bangalis within the framework of the Pakistan State. However, as there was no visible political force to respond to our efforts, the Ayub regime could afford to be indulgent at our provocations. The articles we wrote, the arguments we presented at seminars or in our encounters with ministers and senior bureaucrats between 1960 and 1962, were quite bold for their time. Such efforts would be rather less tolerated in today's independent and democratic Bangladesh. I have come to recognize since those days that strong responses from any government to criticism originate less in the strength of these criticisms and more in the sense of weakness and insecurity of the concerned regime.

Tolerance of criticism from economists did not lead to indifference. The regime's spokesmen would periodically launch tirades against us. I remember one such assault when the then Deputy Chairman of the Planning Commission, Syed Hasan—a civil servant—in a public address on Radio Pakistan argued that disparity was a 'dead horse' and accused the Bangali economists of being 'mediocre minions of foreign power.' Anis, Abu Mahmood and I retaliated in kind. I wrote a piece in response for the *Dhaka Times* titled 'Disparity: A Dead Horse or a Live Problem?', which took Hasan's arguments apart.

I have already referred to Ayub's unscheduled confrontation with me when he observed that Pakistan has only one economy. This statement of his was followed by my widely publicized speech on 'two economies' at the Lahore seminar on October 1961. When Ayub visited Dhaka a few weeks after my presentation, he addressed a public meeting in Dhaka, where he officially took cognizance of the issue of economic disparity by announcing the launch of a Finance Commission to address the issue of how public resources should be allocated between the two regions.

On the occasion of that visit to Dhaka, Ayub had solicited a meeting with the Bangali economists in order to ascertain their views about disparity. M.N. Huda, A.F.A. Hossain, Mazharul Huq, Abdullah Farouk and Nurul Islam were invited to the meeting, which was held in a rather cordial atmosphere, according to Nurul Islam. On Ayub's request, the Bangali economists sent him a strongly worded memorandum prepared by Nurul Islam on the issue of correcting East Pakistan's economic deprivation.

The setting up of the Finance Commission was indeed a tribute to the efforts of the Bangali economists at putting the issue of disparity at the centre of the political stage. Ayub felt compelled to respond to this issue as he was about to present a new constitution to the country that would provide a legal basis for his transition from a martial law to a civilian presidency. In the 1960s, Ayub was one of the earliest of those generals who were in the process of conquering democracy to establish what Professor Samuel Huntington at Harvard then conceptualized, as the developmental state. Ayub was followed by Generals Park Chung-hee in the ROK; Suharto in Indonesia; sundry caudillos in Latin America and soldiers of various ranks across Africa. Virtually all these soldiers recognized the need to eventually shed their uniform and civilianize themselves if they aspired to rule their people for any length of time. Ayub was again one of the earliest to develop a constitutional model that would ensure his rule in perpetuity and to do so in the name of the rule of law and democracy.

Encounters with Ayubian Democracy

Ayub had accordingly established a Constitution Commission, chaired by Justice Shahabuddin of the Supreme Court with sundry jurists and academics of a politically convenient disposition, such as G.W. Chowdhury, who would be receptive to his guidance. Ayub termed this a constitution suited to the genius of the people, though what he actually sought was a document suited to his own genius and urge for self-perpetuation. This was ensured by limiting the franchise to elect the President as well as a national parliament and two provincial legislatures for East and West Pakistan. This electorate was constituted by 80,000 Basic Democrats (BDs) divided between East and West Pakistan. The BDs were, in turn, directly elected by voters as representatives of the lowest administrative tier, the Union Council.

The first book I ever published, in 1966, based on a research project for the Bureau of Economic Research at Dhaka University, was titled *Basic Democracies, Works Programme and Rural Development in East Pakistan*. The book was distributed by Oxford University Press and attracted a small but select clientele who, after all these years, surface to cheer me up by claiming to have read this work. The thesis of the book was built upon the argument that the Ayub regime had constructed their political constituency around a manageable number of 80,000 BDs drawn from a more privileged segment of rural society. The loyalty of this class was secured by channelling public resources into their hands as patronage. The principal resource for patronage was provided through a rural public works programme (RPWP) funded by a massive injection of external resources underwritten by the USA under its Public Law (PL) 480 aid programme. The project was designed to use the vast reserves of surplus food, originating in public subsidies provided to US farmers, as aid to feed the needy around the world.

Pakistan, and within it East Pakistan, was then possibly the world's largest recipient of PL 480 wheat. This wheat was sold in the local market and served to keep food prices down while generating public revenues to underwrite public works designed to construct infrastructure in the rural areas. This investment was intended to provide much-needed employment to the rural landless during the dry winter season in East Pakistan that would relieve rural poverty while it would ensure the enduring political loyalty of the BDs.

The political economy underlying my hypothesis was validated when the BDs twice elected Ayub as President in 1962 and 1964. The elections to the national and provincial legislatures also ensured handsome pluralities for the party set up by him, built around the rump of the Muslim League. In the 1964 elections, Ayub contested and defeated the candidate of the Combined Opposition Party of Pakistan (COP), Begum Fatima Jinnah, the sister of Pakistan's founding father, Mohammed Ali Jinnah.

My research, focused on the BD system in East Pakistan, established that the RPWP, which largely invested its resources in constructing rural roads of indifferent quality, had become a source of corruption which enriched rural elites in the expectation that they would thereby identify their own prosperity with the continuity of the Ayub regime. My work was well received by both academics and opposition politicians as it sought to challenge the myth of Ayub's economic successes and exposed the political opportunism underlying its principal development project. The Government of East Pakistan's response was quite instructive. Obeidullah Khan, who was then possibly a Director in the Department of Basic Democracies, was instructed to ensure that no copies of the book would be made available to any government official or diplomat. Obeidullah was somewhat embarrassed by this responsibility, which he faithfully discharged, as he had given me access to some of the official reports, which I used in my research and also shared his own insights as a public official associated with the BD and the RPWP, on the corruption inherent in the system.

Encounters with the HAG

My work also aroused the ire of the HAG that had, through the 1960s, assembled a group of economists to serve as resident advisers to the Pakistan Planning Commission and the two Provincial Planning departments. The HAG was so-called because the US government had contracted with the Development Advisory Centre (DAC), the consultancy wing of Harvard University, to provide advisory services to the Government of Pakistan. The HAG advisers mostly consisted of mid-level professionals recruited from around the world by DAC but had initially been headed by a faculty member from Harvard, David Bell.

The HAG enjoyed a larger-than-life role in driving Pakistan's development strategy and had played a critical role in designing Eastern Pakistan's RPWP that they considered critical to rural development and poverty alleviation in East Pakistan. Their enthusiasm for public works was, to some extent, inspired by the work and writings of the legendary Akhter Hameed Khan whose commendable work with rural cooperatives through the Bangladesh Academy for Rural Development (BARD) in Comilla had become a place of pilgrimage for aid donors as well as academic researchers searching for developmental success stories built around the rural poor. I was, myself, one of Akhter Hameed's admirers and visited BARD several times. Unfortunately, Akhter Hameed could not influence the actions of the Ayub regime when they sought to selectively take to scale and thence abuse some of his ideas, including those related to the use of rural public works. Akhter Hameed had argued that investments in rural water control and irrigation projects should be prioritized but such projects tended to be neglected under the RPWP.

More than the government, which rarely read any non-official works and could afford to ignore the efforts of a teacher at Dhaka University, the HAG appeared to have been particularly incensed by my work. One of the younger members of the HAG, John Thomas, made the RPWP the subject of his PhD thesis at Harvard, which he projected as a great developmental success story. Thomas and I had a scholarly, if rather sharp, exchange on our contested views of the RPWP in the columns of the *South Asia Journal* published in London.

The relationships of the Bangali economists with the HAG leadership, located in the Pakistan Planning Commission, tended to be somewhat fraught. We regarded the HAG as the ideological inspiration of the state-sponsored capitalism and West Pakistan–centric policy priorities of the Ayub regime. This perspective towards HAG was strengthened when the Deputy Leader of HAG, Gustav Papanek, a Harvard-trained economist, wrote a book validating the development philosophy of the Ayub regime and argued in favour of the 'social utility of greed'. Anis and I wrote rather critical reviews of the work and frequently cited it to emphasize our argument about the policy influence of the USA and World Bank over Pakistan's development policy.

Then and to this day, I continue to have cordial social relations with Gus and his wife Hannah, who is a good friend of Rounaq from their involvement in gender equality struggles. I also had amicable relations with the head of the group, Richard Gilbert, who was more of a politician than an economist and was a special target for our attacks. The intimacy of HAG with the Ayub regime was reaffirmed when, after the downfall of Ayub, the successor Yahya regime declined to renew the Planning Commission's contract with HAG. I wrote a short piece on this in the columns of *Forum*, a weekly I then edited, which they did not appreciate and provoked a letter of protest from Gus Papanek that I published.

Encounters with the Planning Commission

The real battle waged by the Bangali economists was, however, directed at the Pakistan Planning Commission, who we saw as the source of the growing economic disparity between East and West Pakistan. A good part of my journalistic writings, first in the columns of the *Pakistan Observer* or *Dhaka Times* and then more regularly in the columns of *Forum*, targeted the Commission. The Planning Commission was indeed the font of development policy and remained a significant player in designing the political economy of the Ayub regime. We took the Commission to task on the allocative priorities for distributing public expenditure, first in the Second Five-Year Plan (1960–65) and then in the Third Five-Year

Plan (1965–70). Economic policies designed to implement the Plan were also seen as biased towards West Pakistan and the business and feudal elites from the region who dominated its politics and appropriated the gains from development that were inequitably distributed at both the interregional and interpersonal level.

The Planning Commission of the 1960s was a powerful body that not only presided over the development process but was also responsible for aid negotiations. In those days, the Deputy Chairman of the Commission, Syed Hasan and subsequently M.M. Ahmed—a senior member of the Ahmadiyya community, which is today effectively outlawed in Pakistan—were seen as much more powerful figures in the direction of economic policy than the Finance Minister. The Commission was a large, well-staffed organization served by a number of able economists. Bangalis who served there included A.F.A. Hossain, who was appointed a member in the final years of a united Pakistan. Other Bangalis, such as Dr Habibur Rahman and Dr R.H. Khandker, as well as bureaucrats such as A.M.A. Muhith and Dr M.A. Sattar, served there. The professional head of the Commission was Dr M.L. Quereshi, a chemist by training, who was more familiar with the discipline of political economy than economics.

The conspicuous star of the Commission was my Cambridge contemporary, Mahbubul Haq, who began his career there as an Assistant Chief Economist. He rose rapidly in the ranks and was finally elevated to the position of Chief Economist around 1968. Mahbub was a highly capable policy economist with a creative mind. He was soft-spoken but articulate in both debate and writing and sought to get along with everyone. This occasionally required that he tailor his intellectual positions to the views of his interlocutor. In Cambridge, Mahbub had never been active in the Majlis or in political engagements with Amartya or even Arif and me, but we enjoyed an amicable relationship. Whenever I visited Karachi, I called on him at the office of the Commission, and he invariably invited me home to share a meal with him and his wife, Khadija Haq, known to her friends as Bani, a Bangali economist working at PIDE with whom he shared an excellent marriage until he prematurely passed away while in his sixties.

Notwithstanding Mahbub's commendable interpersonal qualities, the Bangali economists saw him as our principal protagonist and singled him out for criticism in our writings, but he rarely responded, even in face-to-face encounters in seminars. In 1965, when work on the Third Five-Year Plan was nearing completion, on the occasion of a visit by me to Karachi, he suggested that he would like to invite Mosharaff Hossain and me to serve as members of the Panel of Economists to review the Plan. The Panel was traditionally designed to seek an external endorsement for the Plan from a panel of independent experts. My senior colleagues, M.N. Huda and A.F.A. Hussain, had provided such an endorsement as members of the Panel of Economists on the Second Plan. Mahbub indicated to me that Pakistan's development, while successful in terms of growth, had tended to be inegalitarian in its incidence, and he thought that our presence in the Panel would highlight these issues and argue for more equitable distributive strategies.

When Mosharaff and I turned up in Karachi for the first meeting of the Panel, we immediately took the offensive on the issue of the allocative injustices still victimizing East Pakistan. This was a familiar theme with the Planning Commission so that the debate was contested but remained manageable. When we moved the discussion towards issues of social inequality, the issue proved more problematic. We argued for agrarian reform and for countervailing the concentration of wealth with the 22 leading business families of Pakistan through extension of the public sector and other such policy interventions to promote greater social justice.

Interestingly, raising issues challenging the economic power of the West Pakistan elite proved more provocative than arguing for ending regional disparities. In the second or third meeting of the Panel, our Chair, M.L. Quereshi, informed us that the Deputy Chairman of the Commission, Syed Hasan, had received a phone call from the Governor of West Pakistan, the fearsome Nawab of Kalabagh, whose son Muzaffer Khan, had been my class friend in

Aitchison. The Nawab, who was one of the biggest landowners in the Punjab, ran his estates as he did West Pakistan, as a feudal overlord. He was thus, incensed to read in the newspapers that the Panel of Economists was discussing the issue of land reform. The Nawab advised Hasan that land reform was none of the business of the Planning Commission so he should order the Panel to exclude this from its agenda. Quereshi, rather embarrassed, requested the Panel to take account of political realities and move on to other less controversial issues. While our colleagues, particularly from West Pakistan, were happy to do so, Mosharaff and I felt no such compulsion and turned to Mahbub to back us up. Mahbub, diplomatic as always, avoided the issue with an inscrutable smile so that the two recalcitrant Bangalis were left on their own to challenge the obiter dicta of the Nawab. The meeting ended inconclusively with Mosharaff and I promising to present a paper on the need, scope and possible contours of a land reform programme for Pakistan.

No further meetings of the Panel were convened, and I was unsurprised to receive a cryptic message from M.L. Quereshi that the Panel had been wound up. The Third Plan was, thus, the only one of four Plans to appear without an accompanying report of its Panel of Economists. When I subsequently challenged Mahbub on his silence on the subject and inability to keep the Panel in business, he observed that he was but a humble minion of the Government of Pakistan and his interventions on our behalf were overridden by more powerful forces. This episode, I thought, was typical of Mahbub's working style and explained how he could so effectively serve military dictators pursuing inegalitarian development strategies while being recognized as a development radical, which he undoubtedly was, before the global development community. Among all of my colleagues from Cambridge, including Manmohan Singh, later PM of India, Mahbub had the greatest understanding of the discipline of political economy backed by enormous skill in interpersonal communications, for which he is widely respected. May his soul rest in peace.

The Emergence of a Politician Economist

Encounters with a Political Icon

In one of the meetings of the Panel of Economists on the Fourth Five-Year Plan of Pakistan, convened in 1970, one of the West Pakistani members observed that I was no longer engaged in the study of political economy but had evolved into a politician economist. I accepted this as a compliment, though it was not thus intended, perhaps because it flattered my aspiration to be more directly engaged in the political process.

My engagement in the world of politics turned out to be a long-drawn-out and rather unstructured process. My journey from a young teacher of economics into a combatant in the debates on the deprivation of the Bangalis was part of such a process whereby I discovered, from first-hand experience, that in the Pakistan of the 1960s, the dividing line, between writing about the deprivation of the Bangalis and a world where deprivation was the central issue of politics, was quite fluid. My involvements with the political process are, thus, not part of a sequential narrative but ran concurrently with my engagements in the teaching and practice of political economy.

In most countries, teaching and discussing political economy tends to be far removed from the real world of politics that underlies such a discourse. When I arrived in Dhaka at the beginning of 1957, I knew little about the real world of politics in Pakistan beyond what I had read in a few articles and books or had learnt from my brief political excursions, largely in a touristic capacity, which I have discussed earlier. I realized that if I aspired to more fully understand the political component of what little I had learnt about the discipline of political economy, I needed to attend primary school in the real world of Pakistani politics.

My political education had been interrupted by the declaration of martial law in October 1958, which denied me further opportunities for political tourism. It did however provide some opportunity for me to interact with political leaders, now rendered largely underemployed, who were more readily available for political conversations. My political education was particularly enhanced by my contacts with H.S. Suhrawardy, the president of the All Pakistan AL. HS, as he was known to many of us had, along with a number of political leaders, been disqualified from participating in politics by a special act legislated during the martial law regime under the acronym of EBDO (Elective Bodies Disqualification Order). HS had been in the front line of Bengal and national politics for 35 years. His political experience and sophistication had few equals. He commanded the unique distinction of being a Bangali leader of the then strongest political party in East Pakistan, but was an Urdu speaker who lived with his daughter, Akhter Sulaiman, in Karachi. HS joked that Pakistan was held together by only two institutions, PIA (the national airline) and himself.

During the period 1959–61 when he was embargoed from engaging in politics, HS could give more attention to his profession as a barrister-at-law where he was one of Pakistan's most distinguished and highest earning lawyers. He would thus travel regularly to Dhaka to represent clients from Dhaka before the itinerant Supreme Court and the East Pakistan High Court. He always stayed at the residence of Manik Mian, the Editor of the leading Bangali daily, *The Daily Ittefaq*, which had been set up drawing heavily on the legal earnings of HS. At Manik Mian's residence in Kakrail, usually propped up in his bed surrounded with legal briefs, HS held court with his AL acolytes.

HS frequently visited Kamal Court, the home of Kamal Hossain and his parents, as Kamal's father, Dr Ahmed Hossain, was his physician. Kamal and I thus had occasion to interact with HS and various AL leaders, including Bangabandhu, who assembled regularly at Manik Mian's residence but also came over to Kamal Court to meet him. I recollect one such interactive episode at Kamal Court when HS was projecting some films of his tenure as PM that showed massive crowds in attendance to hear him speak. HS remarked, rather sadly, "Where are these crowds today?" Bangabandhu's immediate response was "Boss, just give the call and they will all be there again."

Kamal and I learnt much from HS about politics; he was a giant among politicians in Pakistan, with a stature attained only by Jinnah and Fazlul Haq. He had an exceptionally sophisticated mind, was enormously well read, had a delightful sense of humour and a great zest for life. Conversations with him were an integral part of my primary schooling in politics. Later interactions with Bangabandhu and Tajuddin elevated my education to the secondary level. Having spent the whole day working on his briefs, appearing in court and meeting with his party colleagues, at around 10:00 p.m., HS would retain enough energy to turn up at a party, where he could relax in the company of a younger, less serious crowd.

Throughout the martial law regime, HS remained politically inactive, but the Ayub regime always regarded him as a threat because of his political stature and more particularly because of his leadership of the largest mass-based political party in East Pakistan, the AL. The decision to arrest HS in early 1962, however, owed less to any political action by him than to the regime's sense of threat perception. Ayub eventually agreed to release HS on the understanding that he would go abroad for treatment. On his release, HS moved to organize a combined opposition alliance to the Ayub regime where various parties, including the AL, subsumed their political identities within a National Democratic Front (NDF). He could not provide leadership to the NDF as he was again taken ill. The last time Salma and I met him, he was in a hospital bed in Karachi. He recovered sufficiently to travel to London, where he spent the next year living with his son Rashed at Brookland Rise down the road from Salma's parents' house during which time he wrote what turned out to be highly informative and readable but alas, unfinished memoir.

On his way home from London, HS suffered a heart attack in Beirut and passed away on 5 December 1963. His final return to Dhaka invoked one of the largest mobilizations ever seen in the city in recent years to attend his *janaza*[1] at the Race Course Maidan, I sat with his son Rashed, in an open jeep at the head of a motorcade escorting his father's cortège that took many hours to travel from

[1] Islamic funeral prayer.

the old airport to the Race Course. We were received at the Maidan by Bangabandhu, who was totally overwhelmed with grief. HS was buried next to his great rival in Bengal politics, Sher-e-Bangla Fazlul Haq, where he was then joined a year later by yet another of his political rivals, my grand-uncle, Khwaja Nazimuddin.

Nearly a decade later, on 17 March 1972, when the nation was celebrating Bangabandhu's first birthday in an independent Bangladesh, myriad well-wishers had inundated him with flowers. That evening, when the crowds had departed, Bangabandhu quietly took this mountain of flowers to the national mausoleum and placed them on the grave of his Boss. Bangabandhu also acknowledged his debt to Boss in his recently published diaries that provide one of the most insightful accounts of HS' early political role.

Early Encounters with Bangabandhu

Bangabandhu never had much faith in the NDF but, as always, deferred to his Boss. The passing of HS inspired Bangabandhu to initiate the exit of the AL from the NDF and commit it to contest the 1964 election to the national and provincial assembly under its own banner. As a consequence, some senior AL party leaders who believed that AL should remain within the NDF broke away from the party, whereby Bangabandhu effectively assumed the leadership of the party. Bangabandhu invited Kamal and me to advise the AL on the drafting of a manifesto for contesting the 1964 elections to the central and provincial legislatures. At that stage, the 6 points were yet to be formulated, but our discussions with Bangabandhu educated us to recognize that full democracy, along with the struggle for provincial autonomy, was the paramount concern of these leaders.

In response to a public statement by Ayub Khan to announce his candidacy for the 1964 elections, where he extolled the achievements of his regime since he assumed power, Bangabandhu issued a strong counterstatement challenging Ayub's record. Kamal and I were again invited to contribute to the drafting of his response.

My input was reflected in the strong economic content of the statement that questioned the alleged developmental achievements of the regime. These encounters with Bangabandhu and his colleagues in the AL served as the beginning of a deepening engagement for Kamal and me with the political process and the related struggle for national self-assertion.

Bridging the Gap between Academe and Politics

NASEP: A Pioneering Think Tank

Once Kamal returned from Oxford to Dhaka in 1960, we sought more direct engagement with the political process. Our encounters with HS facilitated our endeavours. The HS connection, in a political culture where personal linkages counted for much, enhanced our acceptability within this closed community. However, we also learnt that proximity to HS was something of a political liability in our interactions with the left-oriented intellectuals of Dhaka with whom I was building up ties through Tulu and Mosharaff. The pro-American direction taken by the AL during the tenure of HS as PM in 1956–57 and the hostility of the party to the foundation of the NAP had made HS and his party anathema to many from this constituency.

In order to institutionalize the linkages between the political and intellectual communities, as also to bridge the intellectual divide between the AL and NAP supporters, Kamal and I decided to establish a policy study group to explore and devise viable solutions to the major problems facing East Pakistan. We rather unimaginatively titled this group the National Association for Social and Economic Progress (NASEP).

NASEP had, in part, been catalyzed by my reading of the book by William H. White, *The Making of the President*, based on an insightful account of the election of JFK to the US Presidency in 1960. It was a brilliant book and set the stage for a series of such books by White which spawned a thriving cottage industry on the subject that prospers even today. What particularly impressed me in White's book was his articulation of the close relationship between Kennedy and a brilliant community of intellectuals such as William Schlesinger, J.K. Galbraith, McGeorge Bundy and many others identified in a far from flattering account by the journalist David Halberstam, as *The Best and the Brightest.* What particularly impressed me was Kennedy's willingness to draw on this community to provide him with ideas for setting a new direction to US politics and, when elected as President, to subsequently bring them into his administration. Kamal and I believed that politics in Pakistan was driven more by rhetoric than substance where power rather than policy change motivated political action. We believed that democratic politics needed to focus on policy issues that would guide their campaign and actions when elected.

This presumption on our part was not without foundation. The victory of the Jukta Front in the 1954 provincial elections had been influenced by a clearly defined 21-point policy agenda. Bangabandhu's agenda for advancing Bangali nationalism was constructed around a well-conceived and argued 6-point programme for realizing full autonomy for East Pakistan. Some intellectuals from the Dhaka University may have contributed to the '21 points' and had also involved themselves in the Language Movement of 1952.

Establishing regular links between academics and politicians in the pre–martial law period had been limited in its incidence, but it was at least recognized as a legitimate relationship. The Ayub regime introduced legislation which, in effect, sought to bar university teachers from being associated with politics. The only person who challenged this law was Sir, whose case was argued before the Dhaka High Court by the eminent jurist A.K. Brohi, with Kamal Hossain as his junior. A bench headed by Justice Sattar ruled in favour of Sir, but did so only on the legal grounds that such a restraint was a violation of his terms of appointment when he joined the University as a teacher in 1935. The judgement accordingly applied to all teachers including me, who had entered service prior to the new legislation, which however, remained enforceable on all teachers recruited in the wake of the new law enacted in 1961.

NASEP's sustainability in such an inhospitable political environment was always rather tenuous. We had no access to funding so that all its activities were inspired by a sense of public service. As our founding members, Kamal and I drew in Mosharaff who had by then moved to Rajshahi University as a Reader in Economics. Mosharaff, in turn, persuaded his colleagues from Rajshahi, Professor Salahuddin Ahmed, who was then Chair of the History Department, and Badruddin Umar, who had an honours degree in politics, philosophy and economics (PPE) from Oxford and taught political science at Rajshahi, to join us in NASEP. Both of them were strongly secular and left oriented in their outlook. Umar, in particular, inspired by the Marxist tradition, was a dedicated disciple of the politics of Lenin, Stalin and Mao Tse-tung. Sir, who was by then a guru to all of us, was brought in as a mentor. He was, inevitably, rather cynical about our venture within the prevailing political circumstances and sceptical about our understanding of the real world of politics.

Outside the academic world, we drew in Erfan Ahmed, who shared many of our concerns, and Ziaul Haq (Tulu), who was then a struggling businessman but retained a strong commitment to the Bengali nationalist cause. Tulu was extremely well connected with left-secular intellectuals drawn from the literary, artistic and journalist community. We also involved Qamruddin Ahmed, who had been actively associated with the AL. His seminal work on the *Social and Political History of Bengal* had been read by all of us and served as a non-academic history of the origins of the nationalist movement.

NASEP met episodically in the living room of Kamal's ground-floor apartment at Kamal Court on New Bailey Road or our house at 831/833 Shantinagar Road around the corner from Bailey Road. Our discussions were rather open-ended, so we felt that we needed to give it more focus and outreach through some policy-oriented publications that we could place in the hands of the political community. Our initial and, as it turned out, only output emerged in the form of three pamphlets on the themes: 'The Challenge of Democracy' by Kamal, 'The Challenge of Education' by Mosharaff and 'The Challenge of Disparity' by me. The pamphlets were published in English and printed on cheap newsprint at *Sangbad*. I had, by then, become a good friend of Ahmedul Kabir (Monu) and his wife Laila, who generously agreed to print the pamphlets free of cost, as a contribution to our endeavour. Sir advised us to either prepare the pamphlets in Bangla or have it at least translated into Bangla, if we expected to reach a significant political audience. For some reason, the translation process was overtaken by events so that the audience for our pamphlets remained narrow. A few faded copies of this endeavour of our political adolescence remain today, but their contents remain quite prescient.

Janamaitri Parishad: Witness to a Schism

NASEP as an entity did not last more than a couple of years and was superseded by the Janamaitri Parishad (JMP). This organization was built upon NASEP but drew in Muyeedul Hasan, a former student of mine in the Economics Department who had established himself as a bold journalist at *The Daily Ittefaq* and had already faced imprisonment during the first political agitation against the Ayub regime in 1962. Muyeed, in turn, introduced us to Salahuddin Mohommed, a charismatic Bihari, who was then the President of the East Pakistan Journalist's Union. Salahuddin also worked in *Ittefaq* but was underwritten by Manik Mian to establish an English-language weekly, *Dacca Times*. Salahuddin's English-language skills were rather shaky, so the editorial pen was weakly wielded. However, *Dacca Times* did give voice to some bold journalism, highly critical of the then Ayub regime. I wrote a number of pieces for the weekly but preferred to publish my pieces in the *Pakistan Observer*, the most widely read English daily then edited by another journalistic legend, Abdus Salam.

Salahuddin, who was then much admired not just by us but within the journalistic community, was politically well connected and introduced me to the three historic figures of the Baluch nationalist struggle, Ghous Bakhsh Bizenjo, Sardar Ataullah Khan Mengal and Sardar Khair Bakhsh Marri during their visits to Dhaka to participate in sessions of Ayub's first parliament. They were impressive figures with a strong commitment to assert the national identity of the Baluch people. The tribes of Mengal and Marri eventually engaged in a tribal insurgency against the Ayub regime that was brutally suppressed by General Tikka Khan and earned him the title of 'Butcher of Balochistan'.

We parted company with Salahuddin after the 1965 Indo-Pakistan War after we learnt that he appeared to be moving in questionable company. Salahuddin remained out of sync with the intensification of the nationalist struggle in East Pakistan prior to and after the fall of the Ayub regime. He eventually moved to West Pakistan with his family in 1971.

Muyeed and Salahuddin had suggested that NASEP's reach was too narrow while its title was too academic. The JMP title was designed to reach out to a more politically active constituency drawn from among left and nationalist circles. JMP's main role was to organize discussions on various political and policy issues, usually held either in Kamal Court or in my living room at my Dhaka University teacher's quarters on Savage Road, opposite the British Council, where I had moved with Salma in 1964.

JMP drew in a broad spectrum of radicals that included Enayetullah Khan, who was yet to set up *Holiday*; Siraj Husain Khan, a labour leader; and Anwar Zahid and Ahmedur Rahman, both then journalists at *Ittefaq* and active in the NAP. Some active politicians such as barristers Abdul Haq of Kushtia, a member of NAP; and Muntaqim Chowdhury from Sylhet, associated with the AL, who had both been elected to the National Assembly in 1962 on the basis of the limited franchise of 80,000 BDs also joined us. Haq and Muntaqim regularly met us, prior to sessions of the National Assembly, for briefings on questions to be asked and on legislative interventions. A number of other opposition members of the National Assembly (MNAs) episodically dropped by our apartment to solicit briefings prior to sessions of the National Assembly.

JMP eventually became a casualty of the split within the political left in Pakistan, precipitated by the growing divide between Beijing and Moscow over the direction of the world Communist movement. As a number of our members were active in left politics or were at least fellow travellers, the emerging divide in the movement manifested itself in some tensions within our group.

Interesting paradoxes emerged from the divisions of the left where again JMP served as a microcosm to these conflicts. We were surprised to note that some of our associates, active in the Bhashani (pro-Beijing) NAP, were becoming more muted in their criticism of the Ayub regime and more openly hostile to the nationalist agendas articulated by Bangabandhu through the 6-point programme. Badruddin Umar, in volume 2 of his highly informative work on *The Emergence of Bangladesh*, writes that Bhashani was invited to visit China in September 1963 and met Ayub Khan in Rawalpindi on the way, where they reached some political understanding in the context of Ayub's changed attitude towards the USA.

6 Points: The Beginning of the End

From the mid-1960s, the struggle for self-rule had emerged as the dominant political agenda for Bangalis. Bangabandhu grew to apotheosize this struggle after the presentation of his 6-point programme to the nation on 23 February 1966. The 6 points were hardly an original agenda but eventually played the role of a Magna Carta for the Bangali's struggle for self-rule. Most of the points had already been articulated in the 21-point election manifesto of the Jukta Front in 1954. Four of the 6 points were of an economic nature and drew on the writings of the Bangali economists against the economic deprivation of the Bangalis and for full autonomy in policymaking for the East Wing.

In later years, and particularly in the post-liberation period, I have been flattered by ascription to the authorship of the 6 points. Regrettably, I can claim no such credit, though, along with fellow economists such as Nurul Islam, Mosharaff Hossain,

Habibur Rahman, Akhlaqur Rahman and Anisur Rahman, I did contribute to the intellectual sources of the document.

The moment Bangabandhu launched a political campaign to propagate the 6 points through a series of widely attended public meetings across East Pakistan, he was arrested. To protest his arrest, the AL called for a general strike on 7 June 1966 that mobilized not just the traditional student and urban protestors but drew in large numbers of workers and urban poor. I recollect the air of tension and excitement that prevailed across the city before and on 7 June. The ferocity of their agitation unnerved Monem Khan's government and led to State violence that culminated in a large number of deaths among the workers. Bangabandhu was arrested. Large-scale arrests of other AL leaders as well as numerous lesser activists from all over the province followed.

By the end of 1966, a large swathe of AL leaders and activists were in custody. Thereafter, the Bangalis entered a long night of oppression exercised on behalf of Ayub by his satrap, Governor Monem Khan. Any political or professional voice of consequence was silenced. This phase lasted from around mid-1966 to October 1968 when the anti-Ayub agitation was launched, first in West and then in East Pakistan. As has happened in other phases of history, not just in Pakistan but in many other countries, the night was at its darkest just before the break of dawn. I was fortunate enough to sit out this worst phase of the Ayub dictatorship. I have already reported that I had moved to London in November 1966 and only returned to Dhaka in March 1969 after the fall of the Ayub regime.

13

Engagement with the National Struggle

End of an Era

The Uprising against Ayub

It took some years for the first light of dawn to appear on the Pakistani landscape. In the period 1967–68 when Bangalis were suffering under a repressive regime, fissures also began to appear on the once solid edifice of the Ayub regime in West Pakistan. Bhutto, in the hope of politically exploiting the latent hostility to the Tashkent Agreement in West Pakistan, had resigned from the Ayub regime. He was exploring his political options which improved greatly once Ayub was stricken with a pulmonary embolism that required treatment abroad and left him both physically and mentally weakened.

During his rather unaccustomed experience of being out of power, Bhutto visited London, sometime in mid-1968, when I was living in London. My friend Neville Maxwell, a much respected correspondent of the *London Times*, had come to know Bhutto well during his long tenure as the *Times*' South Asia correspondent based in New Delhi, where I too came to know him on account of his periodic visits to Dhaka. Neville offered to take me along to meet Bhutto at his apartment in London, where I had my first direct exposure to his arrogance as well as his intelligent, incisive yet unprincipled mind. I was amazed at the contemptuous way in which he referred to Ayub, a leader he had so slavishly served for close to a decade. He indicated that the time was mature to challenge Ayub through a mass-based political party committed to socialistic policies and an independent foreign policy. When I questioned him on his ability to challenge the traditional dominance of the feudal lords in Punjab and his own state of Sind, he indicated that they were paper tigers who would crumble against a challenge from a popular party. As far as the Punjab was concerned, he was not off the mark and destroyed the traditional feudal political overlords of the province, such as Mumtaz Daultana, in the 1971 elections. However, while Bhutto's Peoples Party also triumphed in Sind, it did so by drawing in a variety of no less feudalistic elements, to represent his party.

On the issue of the Bangalis' demand for self-rule, Bhutto tended to be more equivocal, arguing that a broader, shared commitment to socialism would subsume the autonomy demand. He was sceptical of Bangabandhu's willingness to commit himself to progressive causes and appeared to regard Maulana Bhashani as a more ideologically sympathetic ally in East Pakistan. We had some sharp exchanges over his inability to recognize the significance and urgency of the autonomy demand and his undervaluation of the political significance of Bangabandhu. This exchange was repeated again, rather more acrimoniously, when Bhutto visited Dhaka early in 1970, when Kamal and I met him at the Hotel Intercontinental and challenged him on his long service under Ayub Khan. On his return home from London, Bhutto initiated the process of forming the PPP, which aspired to mobilize the people but ended up in 1971 as the Pakistan General's Party.

At the zenith of its power, when the Ayub regime was celebrating its decade in power, incipient challenges on the ground slowly gained in intensity and spread across West Pakistan. These agitations eventually spilled over to East Pakistan, gaining in amplitude until they eventually threatened the very foundations of the regime. The fast-changing political situation in Pakistan inevitably intruded into my academic haven at the LSE. As the anti-Ayub movement spread rapidly across Pakistan, I found myself spending a great deal of time travelling to the Pakistan High Commission at Lowndes

Square in Knightsbridge to keep abreast of the political developments through reading the slightly dated newspapers arriving at their library. I was also approached by various papers and journals to write on these latest developments and wrote articles on the unfolding Pakistan crisis for the *London Times*, *New Statesman*, new society and academic journals, one of which was *Round Table*. I also addressed a seminar on the Pakistan crisis at the weekly round table on South Asia, convened at Chatham House, which I had addressed earlier on my book on the theme of BD.

My sense of excitement at the prospective demise of the Ayub regime stimulated my urge to return home to engage with this historic political transition. This mood was totally at variance with any concentrated effort to finish my thesis that required some more months of work. Much to Salma's irritation, I decided to abandon my academic enterprise and return to Dhaka. Salma, who had never wanted to move to London in the first place, perhaps rightly felt that if I did return home without a PhD, these would serve as wasted years in our lives, and I could not entirely disagree with her. This was not the only time that I was to disappoint Salma and return home at a time when she had settled in to a rhythm of life abroad and had no strong desire to return home. My selfishness in prioritizing my own political agendas over her preferences for family stability, even today, hangs heavy on my conscience.

We were not the only Bangali 'political' refugees in England. Mosharaff had taken time off to accept a fellowship at York University and spent two years there in 1968–69 with his family so we could get together at both London and York. Sir also turned up in London and stayed with us at Brookland Rise until we left for Dhaka in March 1969. He then moved in with Arjun Sengupta, an exceptionally talented economist located at the Delhi School of Economics (DSE) who was a visiting lecturer at LSE. During our stay in London, Salma and I had become close friends with Arjun and his young wife, Jayshree, another relationship that has endured over the years.

Our two years in London were not entirely unfruitful from the perspective of an enjoyable life style. We appreciated the relaxed pattern of life, with frequent visits to the theatre, movies and concerts. England in the late 1960s was in the midst of its own cultural revolution with the liberalization of social values and the radicalization of political consciousness among the young. The anti-Vietnam mobilizations in Britain were at their peak and such figures as Tariq Ali, the son of Tahira and Mazhar Ali Khan, who led these demonstrations, had emerged as household names.

The Pakistan cricket team toured England in the summer of 1967, so I could renew my love affair with cricket. I dropped in to Lord's to see the Pakistanis play Middlesex. A friend from Aitchison and Cambridge, Fakir Aizazuddin, was, somewhat surprisingly, chosen as a member of the team, so I also hoped to meet him. After watching him open the innings with a rather defensive display of batsmanship, I went round to the famous Lord's Pavilion and sent up a note to the player's dressing room announcing my presence to Fakir. This message was greeted by the prompt arrival of Fakir at the entrance where he greeted me with a great bear hug. He then took me up to the players' balcony of the Lord's Pavilion to rub shoulders with his more distinguished colleagues such a Saeed Ahmed, Asif Iqbal and Intikhab Alam. Thanks to Fakir, I had the historic experience of sitting not only in the players' balcony at Lord's but also in the Pavilion at the Oval in the final Test, where I witnessed Asif Iqbal's epic innings of 147 that saved Pakistan from the ignominy of an innings defeat.

Another sporting bonus was provided to me, thanks to my uncle Sayeed Shahabuddin, who was visiting England in 1968. He managed to obtain two tickets to watch the finals of the European Cup at Wembley, where Manchester United were playing Benfica from Portugal. Man U were then at their prime having topped the First Division League and won the FA Cup. Their team was led by an inspirational forward line that included Bobby Charlton, Dennis Law and the magical George Best. Benfica also had one of the all-time great forwards, Eusébio, to lead their attack. It was a great game that Man U won, thereby bringing the European Cup to England for the first time.

My weekly encounters with the South Asia group at Chatham House were a stimulating experience and proved serviceable to the Bangladesh cause in 1971 as did the journalistic contacts I developed during this period. I also renewed connections with Cambridge contemporaries such as Tam Dalyell, who represented Labour in the House of Commons, so that I had some access to the Labour Party, which was also helpful to our cause in 1971.

At a personal level, our son Babar was born in London on 22 July 1967. We were fortunate that Nanny D'cruz was still with us and could take care of Babar in his first year. But she chose to stay back in London with her family when we departed for Dhaka, thus bringing to an end our golden years of child-rearing. From then on, it was Salma who had to assume the primary responsibility of looking after our sons, which she did with great love and care, with a modest, less skilled, backup from me.

We eventually returned to Dhaka via Amman, Jordan, in March 1969, shortly after the fall of Ayub and the reimposition of martial law by Yahya Khan. Our trip to Amman originated in the marriage of Salma's youngest sister, Sarvath, to Prince Hassan bin Talal, the Crown Prince and younger brother of King Hussein of Jordan, in Karachi around October 1968. Hassan and Sarvath had known each other from their childhood when Salma's father, Mohammad Ikramullah, was Pakistan's High Commissioner in London in the mid-1950s. During that period, Begum Ikramullah had invited Hassan, then a young student at prep school in England, to come over and have tea with her children at the High Commissioner's residence at 56 Avenue Road, Swiss Cottage. During a State visit by Hussein to Pakistan in 1968, Hassan remembered this kindness and paid a courtesy call on Begum Ikramullah, where he met Sarvath, now a beautiful and vibrant 20-year-old, who was preparing to attend Cambridge University later that year. King Hussein invited Sarvath and her mother to visit Amman, and the rest, as they say, is history. Sarvath, instead of moving to Cambridge in October 1968, married Hassan, who was her age, 21, but had already completed his degree in Oriental Languages at Christchurch College, Oxford. I found him to be an intelligent, modest young man, who appeared to be mature beyond his years with a lively sense of humour.

On our way back to Dhaka, we had travelled through Austria, holidaying at St. Wolfgang, and then travelled to Istanbul, where I recollect wheeling Babar around the Topkapi Palace Museum in a pushchair. Arriving in Amman, which was then a small, provincial town with an airport not much bigger than Dhaka's, we were received by Hassan and Sarvath and driven to their residence that had once belonged to the British High Commissioner and was well appointed but hardly palatial. Travelling through Amman, we noticed that the Palestine Liberation Organization's (PLO) armed forces were ubiquitous across the town with many checkpoints set up by them in the style of a parallel government. It was apparent that serious tension prevailed between the Royal government and the Palestinians. It came as no great surprise to me when the Jordanian army, which was manned largely by Bedouin troops loyal to the Hashemite family, in September 1970 launched a surprise assault on the PLO encampments across Jordan in what infamously came to be known as 'Black September', killing a large number of their militia and expelling Arafat and the PLO from Jordan.

The Last Days of the Ayub Raj

From Amman we returned to Karachi, where I found a totally transformed climate of opinion compared to when we left for London in November 1966. In the months before we returned, the eye of the cyclone threatening the beleaguered Ayub regime had moved from West to East Pakistan. The initial mobilization in East Pakistan against the regime, spearhead by the students of Dhaka University under the *Chattro Sangram Parishad*,[1] had broadened to draw in both peasants and workers. The uprising in the rural areas was mostly targeted at the BD who had grown fat on the corruption originating in the RPWP. The prognosis and the

[1] Students mobilization front.

consequential political fallout from the project, which I had articulated in my first published volume, was satisfying, at least for me, as it played itself out in real life. The workers, who had been exposed to a decline in real wages within an industrial regime dominated by non-Bengali capitalists, were resorting to gheraos or siege tactics of their employers, to extract higher wages. These three streams of resistance—students, workers, peasants—merged into a single and quite formidable force that West Pakistanis viewed with trepidation as presaging both revolution and the separation of East Pakistan. Maulana Bhashani, who had hitherto enjoyed a certain licence from the Ayub regime due to his lukewarm support for the AL's 6-point programme, now attempted to project himself as the vanguard of this revolutionary upsurge.

In reality, the principal beneficiary of the upsurge in East Pakistan turned out to be Bangabandhu as the focal point and spokesperson of Bangali nationalism. The notorious Agartala Conspiracy Case accusing Bangabandhu, along with several Bangali bureaucrats and military persons, of plotting with the Indians to create an independent Bangladesh had become politically counterproductive. Kamal had been actively involved in organizing Bangabandhu's defence and has written about the trial as have others. Bangabandhu was elevated into a national hero and potential martyr in the eyes of the Bangalis. The *Chattro Sangram Parishad*, chaired by Tofail Ahmed, an activist in the EPSL and the sitting Vice President of Dhaka University Central Student's Union (DUSCU), had tabled an 11-point programme. The 11 points expanded on Bangabandhu's 6 points, to incorporate a further 5 points, which took into account the more radical concerns of the left movement, that then may have been electorally insignificant but commanded a strong presence within the student community.

Sometime in 1968, prior to the launch of the anti-Ayub agitation by the students in East Pakistan at the end of the year, the EPSU and EPSL, often at loggerheads with each other, had joined hands to confront the menace of the NSF hoodlums who had ruled the campus with the full patronage of Governor Monem Khan since their assault on Abu Mahmood in early 1966. In an encounter between some activist EPSU students and the NSF, the most violent of the hoodlums, 'Passpartwo', was grievously injured, thereby requiring hospitalization, where he eventually expired.

The demise of Passpartwo changed the balance of power on the campus. The remaining NSF hoodlums disappeared from sight. A while later, the dead body of another of the more violent elements, Khoka, was discovered in the Suhrawardy Udyan. Some of the more politically oriented NSF leaders found it expedient to associate themselves with the anti-Ayub movement. The eclipse of the NSF as an instrument of terror once again re-established the EPSU/EPSL as the voice of the student community and gave them the courage to launch the anti-Ayub movement from within the University. Since Dhaka University had in those days served as the inspiration for student activism across East Pakistan, the movement, led by the Sangram Parishad, spread across the campuses of East Pakistan with the ferocity of a forest fire.

As Ayub's regime crumbled in both wings of Pakistan, he attempted to buy time by convening a round-table conference (RTC) in Islamabad at the end of February 1969. The intensity of the movement across East Pakistan was such that the political element of the Ayub regime had totally disintegrated. His ministers had disappeared from public view, their houses were being set on fire and any flag car became a target of the rampaging mobs in Dhaka. Mujib was eventually released from his Cantonment Jail, from where he emerged to address a mammoth public meeting in the Dhaka Race Course, convened by the *Chattro Sangram Parishad*, where he was invested by Tofail Ahmed, its convenor, with the title of 'Bangabandhu' (friend of Bengal).

When Bangabandhu travelled to Islamabad, he did so as a triumphant hero who believed that the winds of history were behind him. While a variety of issues informed the anti-Ayub mobilization, Bangabandhu had the political vision to recognize that the dominant concern in the minds of the Bangalis was the realization of self-rule from a quarter of a century of Pakistani dominance. Democracy was seen as instrumental to this transcendental mission. Thus, when Bangabandhu sat down at the RTC table, he tabled his 6/11 point agendas as the principal demand of the people of East Pakistan. In order to project his demands to the RTC in more professional terms, he took Kamal Hossain, as well as Sarwar Murshid and Muzaffer Ahmed Chowdhury from Dhaka University, along with him to Islamabad. He also brought in Nurul Islam from Karachi, along with Anisur Rahman and Wahedul Haq who were then both professors at the Department of Economics in Islamabad University, to help him prepare his presentation.

Most of the other participants at the RTC from West Pakistan, and also the non-AL members from East Pakistan, were content to settle for the exit of Ayub Khan and the holding of elections, based on direct franchise, to a new constitutional assembly. However, Bangabandhu sought acceptance of his 6-point agenda as a pre-condition for signing on to an all-party agreement to mark the transition from the Ayub regime. Bangabandhu's demands were acceptable neither to Ayub nor to the West Pakistanis leaders, except for the Pathans and the Baluch who had articulated their own demand for autonomy from Punjabi hegemony.

Bhutto and Bhashani had kept away from the RTC. Bhutto was alerted by his friends in the military that Ayub's days were numbered and that he would eventually hand over power to Yahya Khan. He thus, realized that the RTC was a sideshow where participation would dilute his putative revolutionary image. Bhashani may have been similarly advised through his lieutenant Masihur Rahman (Jadu Mian) who had his own serviceable links with the military.

Reportedly, Yahya had also established contact with Bangabandhu when he was in Islamabad and indicated to him that when he took over from Ayub, he would concede to an election based on 'one person one vote' that would give Mujib the opportunity to establish his political strength and use it to pass a constitution of his choice. With the principal political players of Pakistan now signed on to a post-Ayub regime, albeit under martial law, presided over by yet another general, the RTC ended with a whimper. Bangabandhu returned home as the uncompromising and uncompromised leader of the Bangalis and prepared to wait another day for contesting for power through the electoral process.

A New Dawn

Homecoming to a New Political Era

By the time we arrived in Karachi at the end of March 1969, the Ayub raj had ended and yet another martial law regime, headed by General Yahya Khan, was in office. Unlike 1958, Yahya's martial law regime did not greatly disturb us. We were more inclined to seek inspiration from the new balance of forces unleashed in East Pakistan by the anti-Ayub uprising and the political ascendance of Bangabandhu.

At a personal level, I was surprised to learn from my friends and relations in Karachi that I was viewed with both alarm and occasional admiration by my Pakistani friends. I had written an article for the *New Statesman* just before departing London, indicating that if the demand for full autonomy for East Pakistan was not accepted, this could culminate in a liberation struggle. This article somehow acquired publicity in Pakistan, which came as a surprise to me, since I assumed that few people here had heard of this highbrow left-wing weekly. I was advised that the powers that be in Islamabad viewed my writing as potentially seditious. In my prevailing euphoric mood, I viewed this warning as a compliment rather than a cause for concern.

In Karachi, I observed that Bangabandhu was regarded as the messenger of doom for Pakistan. Those who knew something of politics were more nuanced in their concerns. My friend Kamal Azfar, an intelligent, articulate young lawyer who I had come to know well in the 1960s, and my St. Paul's friend Rafi Raza, who had established himself as a successful lawyer in Karachi after his return from Oxford and was now active in the PPP set up by Bhutto, enquired as to whether Bangabandhu would compromise on 6 points. They were not greatly assured by my suggestion that a constitution based on 6 points would possibly be the last hope for preserving Pakistan as one country. The less politically aware among Karachi society were, no doubt, either praying for a solution imposed under martial law by Yahya Khan or exploring opportunities for investment and relocation outside Pakistan.

While in Karachi, I touched base with Nurul Islam and the Bangalis at PIDE. Nurul updated me on his summons to Islamabad by Bangabandhu and his inputs, along with Kamal, Anis and Wahidul Haque, to the presentation at the RTC that had effectively foreclosed the political transition envisioned by Ayub. Nurul, as always the sceptic, believed that the handover of power by Ayub to Yahya was preordained and that the main political players, Bangabandhu and Bhutto, were privy to this agenda. On the longer-term issue of the realization of 6 points through an electoral process, he was again sceptical not, I suspect, due to great political insight but as part of his naturally pessimistic perspective on the human condition. As often happens in the real world, pessimists are more likely to be vindicated by events. However, what Nurul's pessimism could not anticipate was the possibility that sometimes the sun does shine through the clouds and that, within three years of our encounter at PIDE, he would be invited by Bangabandhu to serve as Bangladesh's first Deputy Chairman of the Planning Commission in the People's Republic of Bangladesh.

Over the next year, Nurul provided further service to the cause of Bangladesh by negotiating the transfer of PIDE from Karachi to Dhaka. In this endeavour, through Kamal, he drew on the support of Admiral Ahsan, the Governor of East Pakistan, and some of the Bangali members of the Yahya cabinet. As the Yahya regime was already under pressure to move some central government institutions to the East Wing, it was resolved that PIDE, as a low return asset, could be painlessly ceded to East Pakistan. As a result, by around November 1970, PIDE was moved from Karachi to Adamjee Court, Motijhee in Dhaka, bringing with it the entire faculty plus its invaluable library of development literature. When Bangladesh eventually emerged, PIDE, along with its rather modest assets, was the only central institution that was inherited by the country.

Home for Life

I returned to Dhaka at the beginning of April to find a new spirit of optimism among those who were close to the AL such as Kamal and apprehension from the 'left' that Bangabandhu had sold out the revolutionary upsurge of the students, workers and peasants that could have led to both independence and social revolution.

My most immediate task was to move into our newly built home at House 9, Road 69, Gulshan, which we had leased to tenants when we departed for London in November 1966. When we eventually moved into our house in April 1969, it was a unique and exhilarating experience for me as this was the first time in my 34-year lifespan that I enjoyed the luxury of living in a home of my own. From my birth, family circumstances had condemned me to a nomadic existence where I occupied innumerable places of residence, distributed across Calcutta, Darjeeling, Lahore, Karachi, London, Cambridge and eventually Dhaka but none that I could call home. Salma and I furnished our home with love and care, making good use of the beautiful Lazarus furniture inherited from 53 Elliot Road.

Moving into the northernmost part of Gulshan early in 1969 was something of an adventure as the only other house in our immediate environs belonged to Justice Mahbub Murshed. Our friend Alijoon Ispahani was then building his house, also designed by Mazharul Islam, just next to us, but they did not move in for another year. In those days, we could not afford security guards or even a durwan, so we placed our faith in the intelligence of prospective dacoits that they would have the good sense to bypass the home of an indigent university teacher for more lucrative pickings. Fortunately, in those as yet, less avaricious days, my faith in my fellow man was sustained, so we lived there in complete security throughout our lives. The only time my house was invaded was by the cohorts of the Pakistani army in 1971, when they first came to arrest me in March and later when we had abandoned the place, to comprehensively loot our possessions.

I lived at 9, Road 69, Gulshan for the next 46 years. Salma and I made it into a much loved home and a landmark for visitors. Our sons grew up in this house; Zafar was born when we were resident there. Over the years, Salma planted a variety of trees that provided us with good-quality mangoes, jackfruits and even lychees. Salma eventually passed away in this house on the fateful night of 29 December 2003 in the very bedroom we slept in when we first moved into our home in April 1969.

Dhaka University under the New Order

Apart from settling into our home in Gulshan, my immediate task was to rejoin my duties in the Economics Department. Professor M.N. Huda had resumed his position as Chairman of the department after an absence of nearly a decade, first in Karachi and later as Minister of Finance in the East Pakistan provincial government under Monem Khan. In the last few weeks of the Ayub regime, under pressure from the political forces besieging the President, he had reluctantly sacked Monem Khan and replaced him as Governor, with Huda. This elevation proved rather fleeting as Yahya Khan, after a short time, replaced Huda with Admiral Ahsan, the Naval Chief of Staff, who he entrusted to oversee the critical transition from martial law to some form of electoral democracy.

Ahsan was quite well known to me as he was one of the closest friends of Erfan Ahmed, Kamal Hossain's brother-in-law. Ahsan and Erfan had been close colleagues in Erfan's years in the navy. We came to know Ahsan more closely when he came to live in Dhaka for a couple of years when he took over from my stepfather, Syed Masood Hussain, as Chairman of the EPIWTA. In our earlier encounters with Ahsan, who came from Hyderabad in India, he came across as an enormously decent, well-read person of genuinely liberal views that appeared to be totally at variance with the militarist world view we associated with the Pakistan armed forces. Ahsan had been appointed Naval Chief of Staff around the time Yahya took over as Chief of Army Staff in 1968 and along with Air Marshal Nur Khan, the Chief of Air Staff, had been appointed Deputy CMLA after 26 March 1969.

Significantly, Ahsan's position as Governor was not made coterminous with that of CMLA for East Pakistan. Instead, Yahya sent over Lieutenant General Sahibzada Yakub Khan, reputedly the premier intellectual of the Pakistan army, as General Officer Commanding (GOC), East Pakistan and CMLA. Yakub, who came from a landed family in the princely state of Rampur in India, where his sister was married to the Nawab, took great pride in his erudition and linguistic skills. He reportedly spoke eight languages, including Russian and French in which he was quite fluent. On arrival in Dhaka, he immediately engaged Professor Rafiqul Islam, from the Bangla Department of Dhaka University, as his tutor and, by the time of his exit from Dhaka on 8 March 1971, had become quite proficient in our mother tongue.

From the moment of his arrival, Ahsan recognized that the only hope of preserving the integrity of Pakistan lay in coming to terms with Bangabandhu through a democratic transition realized through an electoral process. Without sounding vainglorious, Ahsan's political consciousness was possibly raised through his close encounters with Erfan, Kamal and me. Kamal served as his conduit to Bangabandhu, which helped to contain a number of dangerous confrontations during the 1969–71 period that had the potential of escalating into open clashes between the martial law authorities and the democratic movement.

My encounters with Ahsan and the martial law regime remain in the future tense. At that initial phase, I needed to get back into a teaching mode, an exceedingly difficult task when my own attention, as well as those of my students, was focused on the highly fluid political situation. The Economics Department in April 1969 was seriously understaffed as some of its more senior teachers such as Mahmood, Muzaffer Ahmed, Anisur Rahman and me had been away. On my return, I advised Professor Huda to reach out to Anis and Wahidul Haque, who were both professors at Islamabad University, and to offer them professorships in the Department as an inducement to return to Dhaka University.

The regime in Government House had also served to facilitate the appointment of a more acceptable VC at Dhaka University. Governor Ahsan was persuaded to take the safe route and appoint an interim VC while he searched for a credible choice from the academic community who was expected to be a distinguished scholar as well as politically uncontroversial, a challenge of some complexity. Ahsan chose Justice Abu Sayed Chowdhury, then a judge of the High Court, who had distinguished himself for his independent judgement in the case of Abu Mahmood. Chowdhury turned out to be an excellent choice and served the University through the dangerous years of 1969–71 with much skill and sobriety.

While I went about my duties in the Department, teaching courses on the Pakistan economy to the third-year honours class and on development economics to the MA class, I was spending quite a bit of time with the senior students who were seeking guidance on the possible course of events in the country and how they may relate to it. I was at that stage not much more knowledgeable about the course of events than my students or any of my colleagues. However, my awareness was moderately enhanced once I came into contact with the political community and particularly Bangabandhu. Kamal was my immediate link to Bangabandhu, who had come to invest great confidence in him due to his central role in organizing his legal defence in the Agartala Conspiracy Case.

Days of Hope

Political Involvements

After the reimposition of martial law, Yahya committed himself to the holding of elections on the basis of 'one man one vote', which provided the possibility of East Pakistan holding a majority of seats in the prospective CA, that would frame a new constitution for a democratic Pakistan. Bangabandhu recognized the risks and challenges that lay ahead in the uncertain path to elections under a martial law regime. Nor did he have any illusions that success in the elections would provide any assurance that his goal of full self-rule for East Pakistan, expressed through the 6-point programme, would be realized. In discussions with Kamal and me, he advised us that, within the prevailing circumstances, he needed the time and space to mobilize total support behind 6 points and looked to an election campaign to enable him and his party to politically reconnect with the Bangali people in order to engage them in the struggles ahead.

Today, much is said from the perspective of the left intelligentsia, about Bangabandhu being an instrument of the aspirant Bangali bourgeoisie. Whatever may have been the political prehistory underlying this perception, the reality of 1969 East Pakistan demanded that Bangabandhu must reach out to a broader national constituency where the great majority of households were working people. The subaltern classes had been the principal victims of years of subordination and deprivation, initially in British India and subsequently through 22 years of Pakistani rule. It was this large constituency of the deprived who could invest him with the massive mandate he needed to politically challenge the military and who would stand by him if this confrontation could not be resolved through the democratic route. In such a confrontation, Bangabandhu, more than any radical politician, realized that the emerging Bangali bourgeoisie, who were rapidly climbing on to his political bandwagon after 1969, were important but unreliable allies. He apprehended that when the moment of truth arrived, to stand up to the military might of the Pakistan army, this class would be the first to press for a compromise on the struggle for self-rule.

Kamal took me over to Road 32, shortly after I returned. I was no stranger to Bangabandhu, who knew me through our shared encounters with his boss, Shaheed Suhrawardy, as also on account of my writings and our meetings in the 1960s. Bangabandhu, who never forgot a face, in our first meeting immediately reminded me of our first encounter in the summer of 1957 at Baitul Aman, at the dinner hosted by my nana, Khwaja Nazimuddin. Notwithstanding his many years of antagonism to the Muslim League, he spoke with affection about my nana's integrity as a human being and his heroic role in the last days of his life in associating himself with the combined opposition movement to defeat Ayub Khan in the 1964 elections.

I spent many of our early encounters in simply educating myself on the state of politics and Bangabandhu's perception of the days ahead. In these encounters, I became more closely exposed to the political acuity and intellectual depth of Tajuddin Ahmed, who I had met briefly in 1964 during the preparation of the AL manifesto. Every meeting with Tajuddin enhanced my political education and respect for him. Bangabandhu loved, trusted and respected Tajuddin. Between them, they provided the formidable and indestructible core to the direction of the liberation struggle. One of the post-liberation period's deepest tragedies, culminating in the assassination of both Bangabandhu and Tajuddin in 1975, was the conspiracy by Tajuddin's enemies to divide him from Bangabandhu. But this remains part of another tale about a darker phase of our history.

Bangabandhu's greatest quality lay in his ability to reach out to people and draw upon their perceived capabilities in serving his immediate political goals. He had already recognized and used Kamal's skills as a lawyer and perceived his integrity as a political comrade. He persuaded Kamal to formally become a member of the AL so he could establish his acceptability within the party. Bangabandhu wanted to bring Kamal into the Parliament with him. He eventually vacated his seat in Dhaka, one of several seats he had won in the 1970 election, for Kamal.

In my case, Bangabandhu was conscious of my linguistic inadequacies and cultural distance from the ordinary Bangali but appreciated that some of my skills could be serviceable to the realization of his political goals. In various ways, given the centrality of economic issues, where I had been engaged with Nurul and others, in the validation of his 6-point programme, he hoped to draw upon our services in operationalizing this agenda. He recognized the importance of projecting 6 points as an arguable and viable programme that could be politically and professionally defended both domestically and internationally.

He was also aware of my left-wing intellectual leanings and saw me as a useful resource who could coherently link the 11-point agenda of the left with his 6-point programme. In reaching out to his worker/peasant constituency, he recognized the importance of the more progressive components of the 11-point programme. As a result, he drew me in to work with Kamal, who he saw as having a sobering influence on my more radical positions, in drafting a number of important political speeches he made at critical periods.

Designing an Agenda for a Just Society

The election manifesto of the AL, prepared for the forthcoming elections in December 1970, was intended to serve as the final expression for ratifying Bangabandhu's political agenda. The document was prepared by Kamal Hossain and me in close consultation with Tajuddin Ahmed. Prior to preparing this document, Kamal and I flew over to Karachi in April 1970 to sit at PIDE with Nurul Islam, A.R. Khan, Swadesh Bose and Hasan Imam to prepare the manifesto. Anis flew over from Islamabad to join us in this task. The draft we took back to Dhaka was discussed with and refined by Tajuddin and finally with Bangabandhu, who carefully scrutinized the key features of the draft and suggested modifications where he felt the programme was politically unfeasible. Bangabandhu signed off on the final document that was presented before and approved at the AL's historic council meeting in Dhaka on 6 June 1970.

The manifesto, reportedly one of most thoughtful documents produced so far by any party in Pakistan, was possibly more radical than those published by any of the left parties. The document proclaimed a vision of a socialist economic order in which economic injustice will be removed, economic growth will be promoted and provision shall be made for the just distribution of the fruits of such growth among all sections of the people and the different regions of the country. To realize these objectives, the manifesto proposed certain measures of "nationalisation and the extension of public sector by the development of cooperative enterprises and by the evolution of new institutional arrangements such as worker participation in the equity and management of industrial enterprises." The manifesto went on to propose

1. total abolition of the *jagirdari*,[2] zamindari and *sardari*[3] system prevalent in West Pakistan;
2. orientation of the land system to serve the best interests of the actual tillers of the land;
3. setting a ceiling upon landholders and redistribution of land that exceeds this ceiling to landless cultivators;
4. a massive programme for the establishment of multipurpose cooperatives;
5. that all holdings of up to 25 bighas (8.33 acres) throughout Pakistan shall be exempt from the payment of land revenues and arrears in respect of such plots shall be written off.

At the foreign policy level, the AL manifesto stated that "the continued participation in SEATO, Central Treaty Organization (CENTO) and other military pacts is against our national interest and therefore favours the immediate withdrawal of Pakistan from SEATO, CENTO and other military pacts."

The manifesto was approved without contest at the AL council meeting. This surprised its draughts people who expected more of a challenge from the so-called bourgeois elements of the AL leadership. However, Bangabandhu presented the document to the council as reflecting his own vision that brooked no challenge then or later when he was in power. This may have pleased his advisers but was not a good omen for the party where policy proposals needed to be exposed to debate before being adopted. I attended that council meeting, accompanied by Nurul Islam, who was then visiting Dhaka. We were somewhat concerned at the lack of debate on a document with such far-reaching political implications.

[2] Holding a place.

[3] Sardari system means survival, and they depend on Sardars. It is prevalent in Baluchistan.

The articulation of Bangabandhu's vision through the manifesto helped the AL to radicalize the election campaign that was designed to reach out to the working masses of Bangladesh. Bangabandhu's presentation of his vision, on the eve of the December election, was prepared by Kamal, me and Tajuddin for a 30-minute broadcast on radio and television on 28 October 1970. The ultimate compliment to this speech was provided by Badruddin Umar, one of the most unreconciled critics of Bangabandhu, in his exceedingly valuable volume, *The Emergence of Bangladesh: Volume 2: Rise of Bengali Nationalism* (1958–71):

> Mujibur Rahman—spoke as a person who was expecting a serious electoral battle and that he would win the battle. It was true that most of what he said was routine promises, but it was clear from his speech that he or his advisors knew the kind of problems that they would have to address if they happened to win the election and form the government.

The radical ideas that were incorporated into the political agenda of the AL through the manifesto responded to the politically felt needs of Bangabandhu. It was recognized by him that if millions of working people were to be actively engaged in the struggle for establishing self-rule, his appeal to them would need to move beyond 6 points and hold out the prospect of building a more inclusive society. While such a vision was fully shared and possibly influenced by Tajuddin, his most trusted comrade, it was less clear how far Bangabandhu's other senior colleagues shared his concerns for the deprived majority. The agenda, however, appealed strongly to the student and working-class component of the AL that were emerging as critical elements in delivering Bangabandhu's message to the masses.

A Forum for the Future

Our efforts to contribute to the policy agenda of the AL through our close interaction with Bangabandhu and Tajuddin were one part of my engagement with the nationalist movement. Both Kamal and I recognized that we needed to initiate public discussion on the implications of framing a constitution based on '6 points' and beyond this to address the more fundamental problems of poverty and social injustice that would need to be tackled by a democratically elected government. We were keen to draw in not just thinking people in East Pakistan but to persuade West Pakistanis to join the debate. To realize this goal, we decided to publish a weekly journal of quality that would promote such debate and could incubate policy agendas for the future. While our primary goal was to influence policymaking in East Pakistan, we also hoped to discuss the broader problems of Pakistan, including the component provinces of West Pakistan.

Establishing, publishing and sustaining a weekly journal, to be published in English, was more challenging than designing its contents and lining up contributors. It was easy enough to set up the journal under the name of *Forum*. Kamal, Hameeda, Ziaul Haq Tulu and I were identified as its founding members. The declaration under the Publications Ordinance was obtained in the name of Kamal Hossain. Hameeda was designated as its Editor, and I was to be the Executive Editor. We established a small one-room office located in the servant's quarter above the garage of Kamal's residence at 3 Circuit House Row, off New Bailey Road, which is today the office of the Press Institute. In this room, Hameeda and I set up our desks and tables, which also provided space for an experienced journalist from *Sangbad* who worked at *Forum* on a part-time basis, to proofread the copy which was hand composed at another desk by Akhtar Mian, who was also loaned to us from *Sangbad*.

Ahmedul Kabir, *Sangbad*'s owner was one of the mainstays of our venture. *Sangbad* not only provided us with the professional staff who were, of course, paid modest salaries by us but also printed *Forum*, free of cost, on the *Sangbad* presses at their Bangshal office. The hand-composed typeset for each page was taken over on a rickshaw to *Sangbad*, the day before *Forum* was to appear. That same night, Hameeda and I relocated ourselves to the print room of *Sangbad* to personally proofread the page proofs of the weekly, which were then printed, bound together and distributed by the newspaper hawkers on Saturday morning. Hameeda and I stayed on at *Sangbad* until the late hours of the night when *Forum* was put to bed. For the year and a half that *Forum* remained in business, I remember driving home through the darkened streets from Bangshal to Gulshan in the early hours of the morning, animated by a minor sense of achievement that one more issue of *Forum* was about to hit the streets.

Publishing *Forum* was perhaps the easier part; keeping it in business with little capital at our disposal was the more difficult task. Our office was run on a shoestring where neither Hameeda nor I took any remuneration, but we needed to pay a modest wage to our proofreader, compositor and peon, Zainul Abedin. Ever though *Sangbad* did not charge us for the use of their press, we needed to pay for the weekly consumables such as newsprint, printer's ink and related costs. We regrettably remunerated none of our quite distinguished contributors who were persuaded by us to share in our adventure as an act of love, out of a sense of public purpose.

Forum's alumni were in some ways exceptional. Our principal asset was Mazhar Ali Khan, from Lahore, who sent us a weekly column under the caption of 'Between the Lines'. Mazhar Ali Khan was arguably one of Pakistan's most outstanding and respected journalists. He came from a distinguished Punjabi family and was married to Tahira Mazhar Ali Khan, the daughter of Nawab Sir Sikander Hayat of Wah who had been the CM of undivided Panjab in the 1940s and was one of the founders of the Unionist Party. Both Mazhar and Tahira were part of that old school of leftists of the 1930s and 1940s who were motivated by an authentic progressive sensibility that prioritized the concerns of the less privileged who dominated India's landscape. Immediately after the establishment of Pakistan, Mian Iftikharuddin, who I have mentioned in my chapters on Aitchison College and Cambridge, decided to invest part of his landed fortune in setting up Progressive Papers, the mother organization headed by Faiz Ahmed Faiz, the distinguished progressive poet who published both the English-language daily, *Pakistan Times* edited by Mazhar, and the Urdu daily *Imroze*, edited by Ahmed Sibtain.

The *Pakistan Times* certainly reflected the progressive stance of its owner and editor, but above all, it was, qualitatively speaking, perhaps the best paper ever published in Pakistan. Mazhar Ali Khan had a superior command of the English language, an acute political mind and superb editorial skills. One of the first targets of Ayub's martial law regime was to take over Progressive Papers in 1959. Mazhar was driven out of journalism and never chose to return to what he believed was a media-held captive under cantonment rule. Our perhaps greatest achievement was to persuade Mazhar to re-enter journalism through his weekly column for *Forum*. Not once in our short life did he miss his deadline, nor did he accept any payment for his services. For all his strong left-wing views, he was a gentleman of the old school, decent, honourable, expressing strong views with felicity and restraint.

In contrast to Mazhar, Tahira was full of fire, angry at the injustices of society. She was one of the few voices in West Pakistan who had the courage to publicly denounce the genocide committed by the Pakistani army on the people of Bangladesh. She continued to passionately embrace progressive concerns until a few years ago when she was silenced by a stroke. Their son, Tariq Ali, has retained their commitment to progressive causes but preferred to live out his life in London, where he has established himself as a well-regarded writer of fiction as well as on political affairs.

Apart from Mazhar, *Forum*'s other regular contributor from West Pakistan was M.B. Naqvi from Karachi, a much respected journalist with a progressive and secular outlook. Our regular columnists from Dhaka included A.B.M. Musa, then a senior journalist at the *Pakistan Observer*, who wrote a column for us under the title of 'Renegade', discussing the weekly contents of the Dhaka press. A.L. Khatib, another senior journalist who worked for *Morning News*, contributed a column titled 'Sunshine and Clouds'. Our literary columns were contributed by Razia Khan Amin, who provided us with a series of brilliant articles on Bangla literature that could serve as source material in any literature class. Sirajul Islam Chowdhury was another of our contributors who wrote some excellent literary commentaries for *Forum*.

Others who wrote periodically on politics included Mayeedul Hasan, Maudood Ahmed and Siraj Hossain Khan, the labour leader. My economist colleagues, Nurul Islam, Anisur Rahman, Akhlaqur Rahman, A.R. Khan and Kabiruddin Ahmed, periodically contributed articles. Muzaffer Ahmed Chowdhury contributed a series of erudite articles on constitutional and administrative reform. K.G. Mustafa and A.R. Khan both wrote some extremely informative pieces on the left in East Pakistan. Wajihur Rahman of Dhaka University wrote columns on educational reform. Mumtaz Iqbal, a banker, but with some interest in military affairs, contributed interesting pieces on the goings-on in the Pakistan army, including a column that appeared in the final edition of *Forum* titled 'Who's who in the aviary', on the hawks in the military high command who were getting ready to pounce on Bangladesh.

Harouner Rashid, my contemporary at Aitchison and Cambridge, then in the Civil Service, initiated a series on investigative journalism that appeared in our inaugural issue, under the rather fanciful logo of the Forum Research Unit (FRU) titled 'The Spectre of Famine'. The front page of this issue was adorned with a print of one of Zainul Abedin's famous 1943 famine pieces. Another, FRU investigative article was contributed by the atomic scientist Dr Anwar Hussain, who then worked for the Pakistan Atomic Energy Commission, on the theme 'Roopur Odyssey', about our first flirtation with setting up a nuclear power plant in Roopur with funding from the USSR. Hamza Alavi wrote some long pieces for us from West Pakistan, on his reform experiences with Nur Khan. Amartya Sen sent us a piece from the DSE on bank nationalization in India, while his colleague at DSE, Arjun Sengupta, sent us several columns on Indian politics and economics. My friend Neville Maxwell sent us an occasional piece from London, including one on the Indo-China war and a brilliant book review of J.K. Gailbrath's memoir, *Ambassador's Journal*. Looking through the yellowing pages of the few collections of *Forum* that survive today, I am consumed with pride and wonder that we could assemble together such an exceptional list of contributors for a new weekly of ideas, in so short a time.

As inevitably happens in such shoestring enterprises, the main load was carried by Hameeda and me. Hameeda managed the office, performing heroic feats in editing the copy that went into each issue, and occasionally wrote her own column. I was the odd-job man of the weekly. I too did some editing that often involved rewriting entire articles contributed by some of our distinguished columnists who retained a rather notional command of the English language. But my main task was to write the weekly editorial, plus a column, sometimes more than one, with the second appearing under various pseudonyms, the most frequent of which was Rashed Akhter. I also doubled as field reporter and investigative journalist. This involved attending public meetings, which included the peasant rally in Santosh, organized by Maulana Bhashani, on 19 January 1970. My piece 'Red Dawn for the Red Caps' in *Forum* drew on a long background briefing provided to me by Abdul Haq who had been the General Secretary of the Krishak Samity until he broke away with Toha to form a faction of the Communist Party dedicated to a hard Maoist line.

My research on this piece was supplemented by a field trip to Santosh to attend the rally and its follow-up meeting in Paltan Maidan. In the same way, I attended various political rallies in Paltan Maidan, including the *Jamaat*[4] meeting that came under attack from the public where I had to escape from the battlefield and view the events from the DIT (now Rajuk) tower. I attended all the major meetings of Bangabandhu at the Suhrawardy Udayan, then the RaceCourse, and accompanied him on his boat safari to Ghorasal to address a public meeting. I visited the cyclone-affected areas of Manpura in the company of Tajuddin and travelled to the remotest char, Kukri Mukri in a two-seater plane. These visits inspired two articles from me, 'Outposts of the damned' and 'Journey into hell'. All these field encounters ended up as columns in *Forum* as did accounts of my visit to West Pakistan. Some of my most effective field reporting was based on my observation of the events of March 1971 and my own personal involvement in the first period of self-rule by Bangalis since the Battle of Plassey.

[4] Assembly.

My most regular columns related to the economy for which I paid regular visits to the Secretariat to be briefed by Dr Rabbani, Secretary of the Planning Department, or Dr Shahadatullah, a Deputy Chief Economist in the department, on their encounters with the central government in Islamabad at various meetings to discuss the budget or the Five-Year Plan. Many of my current reports on these meetings were thus based on first-hand accounts provided by Bangali friends in the government who shared our commitment to self-rule. I also wrote longer analytical pieces on 6 points and other policy issues. Many of my columns and editorials in *Forum* appear in volume 2 of my collected works, *Milestones to Bangladesh* (published by the Centre for Policy Dialogue in 2008).

Apart from my role as editor, columnist and investigative journalist, I was also engaged in raising funds to cover the modest running costs of our journal. This mostly involved visiting business houses to solicit advertisements. In this task, I was helped by Tulu who drew on his extensive business connections. Tulu had recently joined the ranks of an emergent Bangali bourgeoisie, where he was one of the beneficiaries of support from EPIDC to establish a jute mill he had set up in partnership with Zahurul Islam, Sonali Jute Mills, of which he was the CEO.

I cannot claim that my role as marketing manager was as effective as my role as columnist, but we did generate a modest though insufficient revenue to meet our full costs. Selling the paper through news agents was not a great revenue earner as our circulation rarely exceeded a thousand copies. We managed to secure some regular subscribers, including a category optimistically classified as 'lifetime subscribers', who paid Rs 1,000 for the promise of a lifetime delivery of *Forum*. Our first such subscriber was none other than Bangabandhu who was recruited and immediately paid his full subscription at the launch of *Forum* on the evening of 22 November 1969 at Ramna Green. *Forum*'s demise on 26 March 1971, when it was banned under a martial law order, preceded that of Bangabandhu by several years. But I still feel I remain in his debt not just fiscally but for his act of faith in our infant enterprise.

An English-language weekly, published in Dhaka, with a circulation of less than a thousand was not likely to set the world on fire. Our readership was inherently limited but did include a segment of thinking people, policymakers, which included members of the Yahya regime and particularly the military intelligence (MI) agencies. As I wrote my columns with a complete absence of caution, which occasionally even alarmed Kamal, I was periodically called up by the CMLA's Press Chief, Major Siddik Salek, who eventually wrote a book on the events leading to 1971, *Witness to Surrender*, and warned that I was crossing the line. I was even privileged with an official encounter with the CMLA, General Yakub, who, knowing of my relationship to Begum Ikramullah, was more discrete in his warnings to me.

Since I was now recognized as a working journalist, I was invited every year with a group of Bangali editors to attend the presentation of the annual budget at Islamabad. This included encounters with M.M. Ahmed, the then economic czar of Pakistan. While I was still a junior in the company of senior editors such as Zahur Hussain Chowdhury of *Sangbad*, Abdus Salam of the *Pakistan Observer* and Badruddin of *Morning News*, my reputation for writing on the economy persuaded my seniors to push me forward to lead the interrogation of M.M. Ahmed and his colleagues in their post-budget press conference. I was by then, quite well known to the economic establishment in Islamabad, so they handled my queries with some caution.

In my journalistic capacity, I was once invited to an encounter between Yahya Khan and the local editors on the occasion of his visit to Dhaka, where I asked him why he did not appoint a Bangali to become Deputy Chair of the Planning Commission. Yahya was not without a sense of humour and proceeded, tongue in cheek, to offer me the job. I replied that if he needed my advice, he could get it through a weekly subscription to *Forum*! At the end of the day, the Pakistani military establishment took *Forum* more seriously than we had imagined as we were one of the three papers banned by Tikka Khan at the outset of the launch of their genocide.

While editing *Forum*, I continued to discharge my responsibilities as a teacher and meet with all the classes assigned to me. In those fraught days, I cannot claim that I discharged these responsibilities as diligently as I should. But then in those days, my students remained no less distracted than I was. Some like Mujahidul Islam Salim and Mahfuz Anam, who were my students in the MA class in development economics, were active in EPSU and preparing for an eventual showdown with the military. Mahbullah, then an activist with the Matin-Alauddin faction of the Communist Party, was in jail for his involvement in some arms related episode against the military and wrote to me from Dhaka Central Jail.

Such acts of confrontation and violence became a periodic occurrence that made life unpredictable. On one occasion, the students of Dhaka University threatened to bring out a procession from the Arts Building to challenge some act of the martial law authorities. When I drove to the campus to take a morning class, I found the gates to the campus barred by soldiers of the Ninth Division with machine gun nests posted on top of the Arts Building. Confronted with this show of force, along with Kamal, I sought a meeting with Admiral Ahsan at Government House, where I strongly protested this act of aggression on the campus. Ahsan indicated that this action did not originate from his administration but directly from the CMLA headquarters. He pointed out that the action was intended as a warning to students not to seek a confrontation with the military which would interrupt the progress towards resumption of normal political activities that would be permitted from 1 January 1970. I was not much placated by this assurance, but the troops were indeed withdrawn from the campus. It is also likely that Bangabandhu intervened to advise caution on the more militant members of the EPSL as he had decided to commit himself to the electoral route and did not want any such confrontation to derail the process.

Debates on the Political Economy of Pakistan

The Final Round

During 1969–70, apart from my involvement at Dhaka University, *Forum* and with the political leadership of the AL, I continued to be active in the debates on economic disparity. Up to March 1969, the voices of the Bangali economists largely registered in Islamabad as cries in the wilderness that could be debated academically but were politically ignored. After the fall of Ayub, with Bangali nationalism now an ascendant political force, our views, however unwelcome, were accorded more attention in Islamabad. My columns on the economy, the development budget and eventually the Fourth Five-Year Plan, were read regularly in the Planning Commission and presumably by the intelligence agencies, as were the more scholarly writings of my colleagues such as Nurul Islam, Anisur Rahman, A.R. Khan and Swadesh Bose. There was some presumption, not always justified, that our views on the economy projected the opinions of Bangabandhu and his party. Senior bureaucrats from the central government occasionally sought me out to discuss the 6 points and obtain some insight into the thinking of the AL leadership.

Our final encounter within a united Pakistan, with the Pakistani development establishment took place when I was invited to serve as a member of the Panel of Economists to review the Fourth Five-Year Plan of Pakistan. I have already written of my aborted involvement, along with Mosharaff Hossain, with the Panel on the Third Plan that was largely on our account, dissolved. The Panel on the Fourth Plan commanded a more robust Bangali presence, which included Nurul Islam, Akhlaqur Rahman, Anisur Rahman and our senior colleague, Dr Mazharul Huq, in his capacity as president of the Pakistan Economic Association. The West Pakistan contingent included Professor Matin, the Chair of the Economics Department at Peshawar University; Professor Mukhtar, the Director of the Institute of Business Administration at Karachi University; Dr Perveze Hasan, the Chief Economist of the West Pakistan Planning Department; Dr Moen Baqui, the Chief Economist of the State Bank of Pakistan; and Dr Mahbubul Haq, who had been elevated to the position of Chief Economist of the Pakistan Planning Commission, as the Chair of the Panel.

I had already written critically in *Forum* on the initiative of the Planning Commission to frame a Fourth Plan on the eve of a national election. I had indeed introduced such a thought into Bangabandhu's address to the AL Council meeting on 6 June 1970, where he regretted that the Fourth Plan had been prepared by a military government despite the demand that it should be left for the future government. Bangabandhu had declared that the Fourth Plan would be scrapped when a newly elected government would assume power. The Bangalis were therefore, in some doubt, as to whether they should serve on such a Panel. I discussed this with Tajuddin and among ourselves, where it was decided that the Panel would serve as a good platform to further bring to public attention the critical importance of the economic deprivation of the Bangalis that had inspired the 6-point agenda of Bangabandhu.

At our first meeting in Islamabad, the Bangalis took a collective position that they would not serve in a Panel chaired by Mahbub because of his intimate association with the Ayub regime and its economic policies. Mahbub was enough of a gentleman to withdraw himself, and we then agreed to invite Mazharul Haq, by virtue of his role as President of the PEA, to assume the Chair. Mahbub had already been discomfited with the fall of the Ayub regime and the exit of his strong supporters from the HAG from Pakistan. He had, accordingly, decided to take up an offer to serve in a senior position at the World Bank, then headed by Robert McNamara. He took with him to the Bank some of the best and brightest elements from the Pakistani policy establishment such as Perveze Hasan, Shahed Javed Burki and Khaled Ikram. Another of his close associates in the Commission, Sartaj Aziz, also moved abroad, but to Rome not Washington D.C.

At the Panel, the Bangalis were in an elated and fairly uncompromising mood where Anis and I were at our most provocative. At one of the sessions of the Panel in Karachi, I so incensed Perveze Hasan with my verbal aggressions that he burst out, rather prophetically as it transpired, "if you go on like this, we will do such things to you that it will make you shiver."

Nurul Islam has written more comprehensively in his memoirs (*An Economist's Tale*) on the disputations within the Panel, so I address this episode in a more cursory form. I recollect that while our West Pakistani counterparts were willing to make some accommodation to the allocative needs and policy concerns of East Pakistan, even at that late stage of the political game, they remained unwilling to accept a strategy for the Plan that would explicitly reverse the widening of economic disparities. Faced with a prospective deadlock, we decided to publish two separate reports from the Panel, one reflecting the views of the West Pakistan members and one written by the Bangalis. The Bangali report remains, even today, a definitive statement on the nature and circumstances that contributed to the widening of economic disparity between East and West Pakistan and what might be done to reverse this process. All of us, from both sides, knew well that our reports were academic exercises that would serve no purpose except to provide material for economic historians. The document serves as an intellectual requiem on two decades of conflict between the academics as well as policymakers of East and West Pakistan.

The Last Farewell

Another such farewell encounter with our erstwhile compatriots occurred shortly after the completion of the Panel's work. I was invited by Dr Khaled bin Sayeed, a distinguished political scientist who had once been a teacher at Dhaka University but now taught at Queen's University in Canada, to a conference at Rochester University in upper New York State, in August 1970, to discuss the present state and future of Pakistan. Dr Rashiduzzaman from the

Political Science Faculty at Dhaka University and I were the only invitees from Dhaka. I have already mentioned my first encounter with Rounaq Jahan at this event. The other Bangalis at the conference mostly consisted of my ex-students, such as Abu Abdullah and Mohiuddin Alamgir, who were studying for their PhDs at Harvard and other US universities. The Harvard Bangalis all spoke out boldly and articulately at the meeting, on the injustices of the Pakistan State.

At Rochester, I was impressed to note that many of my adversaries from the Planning Commission, now relocated at the World Bank, turned up for the conference, along with some American sparring partners such as Gus and Hanna Papanek. Away from the battlefield, Mahbub and his colleagues were more conciliatory and anxious to learn what might be done to bridge the widening divide between East and West. In contrast, having sailed on the rising tide of Bangali nationalism, I was at my rhetorical best and did little to alleviate their concerns. Whether they saw me as a prospective occupant of chairs recently vacated by them as part of an incoming AL-led regime in Islamabad or as a foolish Bangali who did not know what was in store for him, must remain part of their memoirs.

As prophesied, I was indeed, given reasons to shiver at the genocide unleashed by the Pakistan army on the Bangalis and narrowly escaped becoming a part of this process. When I met Mahbub again in the company of Nurul Islam, in the coffee shop of the Roger Smith Hotel in Washington D.C., sometime in 1971, I was by then an envoy for the provisional government of Bangladesh. Mahbub was now anxious to rebuild bridges. But, as I advised him in our rather uncomfortable exchanges, those opportunities were left behind in the years of intellectual turbulence in the 1960s. As we talked that day, genocide was being inflicted on the Bangalis by the Pakistan army that had irrevocably destroyed every bridge between us.

14

Fulfilment: Witness to the Birth of a Nation

The Renaissance of the Democratic Process

The High Tide of Electoral Democracy

Yahya adhered to his commitment to Bangabandhu that he would open up space for the political parties to resume political activities in anticipation of the forthcoming national elections. He spelt out his road map to the elections, which was scheduled for October 1970, through the enunciation of a Legal Framework Order (LFO). This imposed a number of conditions to be realized before power would be handed over to the elected representatives. The LFO generated protests by the students and much critical comment in the media, including in the columns of *Forum*. Bangabandhu preferred to ignore these potential roadblocks. He calculated that the immediate priority was the need to resume open political activities so he could reconnect directly with the people through initiation of his election campaign.

As with everything in Pakistan's history, it is not the written word that counts, but what is written between the lines that needs to be deciphered. The short unwritten message from the LFO was that the military retained the final decision on whether and when power would be handed over to the elected representatives. Bangabandhu could also read the message between the lines. He believed that the campaign and its electoral outcome would establish its own political dynamics that would determine the political balance of power between him and Yahya Khan. This assumption was fully validated by events, but its final outcome took a different turn, which had little to do with the words.

Bangabandhu had of course remained politically active, largely behind closed doors, in meetings of his party to evolve their strategy for the future campaign. His main concern was that no impetuous actions by his rather volatile followers should prematurely trigger off any confrontation with the army. He maintained a regular dialogue with Governor Ahsan, who had the political good sense to remain generally receptive to his concerns.

Once Yahya permitted the resumption of open politics from 1 January 1970, the political scenario in East Pakistan underwent a sea change. Bangabandhu's political stature had already been elevated to a high level in the wake of the Agartala Conspiracy Case. Now, with the prospect of contesting the first general election in Pakistan's 22-year history before him, Bangabandhu came into his own. The AL was not a revolutionary party but had deep roots with the people who served as an asset in contesting elections. All that Bangabandhu needed was the opportunity to reconnect with the people and mobilize their support.

In the next 11 months, Bangabandhu surged across the province like a tidal bore sweeping all before him. Well before the election day, it was apparent to most people in Bangladesh that the AL would win the elections by a landside. When I enquired from Tajuddin, as we travelled by car to the cyclone-affected area of Manpura in November, as to how many seats the AL would win, he counted on the fingers of one hand the possible seats they might lose. As it transpired, the only two seats they lost were to former CM Nurul Amin of the Council Muslim League in Mymensingh, and to Raja Tridiv Roy, the Chakma Chief, an independent candidate in the Chittagong Hill Tracts.

During the months of 1970, Bangabandhu was elevated to iconic status and loomed over the entire election campaign. We calculated in an article in *Forum* that every constituency visited by Bangabandhu added 10 per cent to the vote tally of the AL candidate. I recollect a conversation with Barrister Amirul Islam, a first-time AL candidate from Kushtia, who told me that when he asked an ancient peasant in his constituency whether he would vote for him, he replied "I'm sorry I cannot vote for you, I am voting for 'Mujeebuddin'."

I travelled with Bangabandhu from Dhaka to Kaliganj, where he was to address an election rally in Tajuddin's constituency. En route, at Adamjee Nagar, the entire workforce in the industrial area had assembled en masse to greet Bangabandhur and pledge their support to him. From Narayanganj launch terminal to Kaliganj, the riverbanks were packed with cheering crowds along every inch of the route. The belief in those days held by some left party supporters that Bangabandhu was the candidate of the Bangali bourgeoisie appeared totally at variance with the mass support he commanded from among ordinary working people. In the minds of the common people, Bangabandhu had been transformed from a political leader into the personification of their hopes and dreams. This was a heavy burden for any person to bear, and Bangabandhu shared his concerns with us on the implications of such a mandate.

About the only people who did not fully recognize the emerging political scenario in Bangladesh appear to have been Pakistan's unintelligent intelligence agencies. Lieutenant General Umer, the head of National Security and political strategist of Yahya Khan, was deluded by Sabur Khan, Waheeduzzaman and Fazlul Qader Chowdhury—leaders of the Qayyum Muslim League (QML)—into believing that their party along with Bhashani's NAP, would win enough seats from East Pakistan in the National Assembly to ensure that Mujib would not have an overwhelming majority and would have to compromise on 6 points if he aspired to emerge as the PM of Pakistan. To this end, large sums of money were invested by Umer from the coffers of the Pakistan army on the QML, where it was also believed that Abdul Qayyum Khan, of the NWFP, the president of the All Pakistan QML, could be used to neutralize Bhutto's electoral offensive in West Pakistan. When the votes were counted, Sabur, Fazlul Qader and most of their party candidates had forfeited their security deposits in the election where Qayyum's party was wiped out by Bhutto in Punjab and was also defeated in the NWFP.

Throughout the 1970s, we lived in apprehension of a conspiracy to derail the electoral effort. This prospect never materialized, perhaps because of the misinformation fed to Umer by Sabur and gang, for which the people of Bangladesh owe them a small debt of gratitude. However, whenever nature intervened, as in the case of floods in August 1970 and the epic cyclone in November of 1970, Bangabandhu apprehended that this could be used as an exercise to delay the elections.

The floods in August persuaded Yahya to postpone the elections scheduled for 5 October to 7 December, and Bangabandhu went along with it. A final attempt to defer the election was made in the wake of November cyclone and tidal bore of 12 November that swept across the coastal areas of Bangladesh. The initiative did not originate from Yahya but from the rival political parties in East Pakistan contesting the AL, with Maulana Bhashani taking the lead. By the time of the elections, the only parties that eventually boycotted the elections were Bhashani's NAP, Ataur Rahman Khan's minuscule National League, the Jamaat Ulema-e-Islam and the KSP. However, their withdrawal came too late so that the symbol of these four parties remained on the ballot paper, which ensured that their respective candidates were exposed to the ignominy of forfeiting their deposits.

It is more likely that the decision of the Maulana and other leaders to withdraw from the polls was predicated on their realization of such an imminent electoral debacle. Bangabandhu was however apprehensive enough about a postponement to issue a public statement declaring that if the polls are frustrated, "the people of Bangladesh will owe it to the millions who have died to make the supreme sacrifice of another million lives, if need be, so we can live as free people and so that Bangladesh can be the master of its own destiny".

A protracted election campaign, which extended through 1970, worked to the advantage of the AL. Every day invested in the campaign enabled Bangabandhu and his party to deliver their message of national assertion to more people. By December, there was not a single household in Bangladesh that did not know what the election was all about and who was Bangabandhu. The overwhelming victory of the AL in the December elections, which gave them an overall majority in the National Parliament, invested him with an unchallenged mandate to speak for the Bangali people not just with Yahya but to the world. This authority was crucial in unifying the country to establish a sovereign Bangladesh in March and to collectively resist the military aggression of the Pakistani army on the night of 25 March 1971.

The elections held in December 1970 were the very first national elections, held on the basis of direct franchise, since the emergence of Pakistan on 14 August 1947. While the Yahya junta invested some effort in influencing the outcome by backing some parties, the elections were largely recognized as being free and fair. The Chief Election Commissioner, Justice Sattar, a Bangali who was later elected President of Bangladesh in 1981 through a somewhat less free and fair electoral process than he had ensured in 1970, was given a free hand to ensure the integrity of the electoral process.

The decisive outcome of the elections of December 1970 was apparent to any who could gauge the political mood of the Bangalis. However, all except perhaps Bangabandhu and Tajuddin must have been surprised at the final outcome, with the AL winning 160 out of 162 seats from East Pakistan, that provided it with an absolute majority of the 300 seats in the National Parliament. In contrast, Bhutto's PPP won 83 out of 138 seats from West Pakistan, largely from Punjab and Sind.

I had been invited by Radio Pakistan to be one of the live commentators on the elections and thus spent the night of 6 December at the studios of Radio Pakistan on Mymensingh Road, watching the results being reported in by the Election Commission and periodically commenting on the trends. As the night progressed and the electoral avalanche in favour of the AL became fully apparent, it became difficult to conceal the jubilation I felt at that historic moment. I also realized, though I may have been less explicit in recording this on the air, that such an overwhelming mandate may have strengthened Bangabandhu's negotiating capacity, but it had also seriously narrowed his political options.

On that historic night, we also noted that the political calculations of the junta had been undone in West Pakistan. Zulfikar Ali Bhutto had led the PPP to a historic victory over the feudal-based parties that had traditionally dominated the politics of Punjab and Sind. The PPP's slogan of *roti, kapda aur makan*[1] had excited the imagination of the ordinary people who chose to repudiate the traditional authority exercised over them by their feudal lords at the polls. The victory of the NAP and its allies in NWFP and Baluchistan had further upset the junta's maths.

A Prisoner of Democracy

Having publicly committed himself and his party to proclaiming a constitution for the Pakistan State, based on 6 points, Bangabandhu now had to face up to the implications of his commitment. While the 6-point programme provided the core of the AL's election campaign, there were many and more radical features of their election manifesto we had prepared that did not disturb the sleep of the military regime or the West Pakistani parties. All their attention was focused on the operationalization of the 6 points through its incorporation into the constitution, which was to be framed by the CA, elected in December 1970. Neither the Military Junta nor indeed the West Wing political parties had any clear idea as to whether Bangabandhu would stand by his election pledge and insist on reconstructing the federal polity on the basis of the 6 points. The Pakistani political establishment, led by the junta, believed 6 points was a code word for secession or at least they sought to project it as such. No major political player in West Pakistan was willing to recognize the 6 points as a legitimate, politically mandated basis for framing the new constitution.

Bangabandhu himself, initially did not appear fully convinced that the 6 points provided a practical basis for reconstructing the Pakistan State. He had adopted the 6 points because it precisely articulated his commitment to an autonomous East Pakistan and could be presented in the form of concrete demands both to the electorate and at the negotiating table. It was not clear to me as to how much homework Bangabandhu had himself done on

[1] Food, clothing and shelter.

understanding the full legal, economic and political implications of the demand. Both the military and the West Pakistani politicians thus assumed that the 6 points were designed as a basis for negotiations. It was believed by them that, in the established traditions set by earlier Bangali leaders, Bangabandhu would, through a process of political bargaining, be happy to secure a bigger share of power in the Centre in lieu of compromising on his demand for 6 points.

Most of my economist colleagues were in the ranks of the sceptics but were willing to put their pens at the service of the cause. As the perennial optimist among our tribe, I remained the most hopeful and had argued in my writings, on the favourable conditions, following the downfall of the Ayub regime, in realizing the cherished goal of self-rule for the Bangalis.

Bangabandhu's personality and leadership style eschewed the elitist style of politics conducted behind closed doors that could be easily pressurized and lent itself to compromise. He firmly believed that the Bangali masses needed to be mobilized in any struggle that fundamentally challenged the hegemonic rule of the Pakistan State over the Bangalis. He sought to reach out to mobilize this mass base in the campaign for contesting the 1970 elections. I have already indicated the depth and breadth of his political appeal that made a massive victory in the December elections a certainty. But I suspect even Bangabandhu may have been awed by the totality of his electoral mandate. As a political leader whose sensitivity to the pulse of the masses had no equal, he recognized immediately that his victory had made him captive to his own agenda and that there was little, if any, scope of negotiating a compromise on the 6 points.

Bangabandhu was less confident about the commitment of many of his own party members who had been elected to the CA. He feared that some of them, tantalized by the prospect of sharing national power after spending 13 years in the political wilderness, may be in the mood for a negotiated settlement. One of his first acts after the elections was to convene a mass meeting in the Dhaka Race Course grounds at the beginning of January 1971, where he compelled all the AL members elected to the CA to take a collective oath, in the presence of the masses assembled there, that they would not compromise on 6 points. This public affirmation of their loyalty to 6 points imposed on them by Bangabandhu aroused some resentment, particularly among the more senior members. I managed to infiltrate myself on to the dais from where I had a bird's-eye view of the mammoth audience. We could sense the mood of expectation that animated the crowd and felt both elated as well as uneasy about the challenges ahead in responding to their mandate.

Constitutionalizing the 6 Points

In anticipation of the convening of the first session of the CA, Bangabandhu decided to move ahead with the task of framing a viable constitution that fully incorporated the provisions of the 6-point programme. He wanted to discuss in detail the implications of putting such a constitution into operation so that the 6-point programme could be taken beyond the level of election rhetoric and be presented at the negotiating table and to the CA as a seriously thought-out and workable constitutional programme for the country.

In the weeks after the election, Bangabandhu convened a series of meetings to discuss the constitution. These meetings were attended by the high command of the AL made up of Tajuddin Ahmed, Nazrul Islam, Captain Mansoor Ali, Qamruzzaman and Khondkar Mushtaq Ahmed. In order to expose them to the technical problems involved in constitution making, Bangabandhu invited Dr Kamal Hossain, now an AL member who he had nominated to fill the Dhaka CA seat vacated by him, Nurul Islam, MAC, Sarwar Murshed, Anisur Rahman and me. While Kamal and the economists had already been activated by him during the RTC and the framing of the AL manifesto, MAC and Sarwar Murshid were intellectual fellow travellers of the AL leadership from the days of the Language Movement where MAC had been jailed for his involvement. Murshid's wife Nurjehan, had been elected to the provincial legislature on an AL ticket in 1954 and was again elected as a

Member of the Constituent Assembly (MCA) on their ticket in the 1970 election.

The meetings were kept out of the public eye, though its assembly and purport were hardly unknown to the intelligence agencies of the Yahya regime. To avoid media attention, the meetings were held at the residence of a jute trader by the name of Hameed who was a friend and loyal supporter of Bangabandhu. Hameed's house was located on the banks of the Buriganga, halfway along the road between Old Dhaka and Narayanganj. We were taken there in convoy in the morning and kept captive there until well after nightfall. These extended dialogues were punctuated by a massive lunch of the most delicious, freshly caught fish dishes.

In those days of long and intensive discussions, the academic participants, including Kamal Hossain, played the most active role. However, Tajuddin Ahmed was quite as fertile in his contribution as any of the academics, demonstrating deep political insight, dialectical skill and an extraordinary capacity to absorb and break down complicated technical issues to their basic essentials. Bangabandhu was himself an active participant, giving us the benefit of his political experience and shrewd common sense.

One of the critical questions we debated was the issue of whether the 6-point demand was tantamount to de facto secession by East Pakistan or could be accommodated within the framework of a united Pakistan. The Pakistani ruling elite viewed 6 points as a thinly veiled blueprint for secession. Its economic czars such as M.M. Ahmed and Qamrul Islam were reported to have advised Ayub and Bhutto accordingly. Very recently, these apprehensions of our Pakistani adversaries were validated in an article by Professor Nurul Islam in *Daily Star*, who pointed out the separatist agenda implicit in 6 points.

At that time and particularly during our intensive debates, what Bangabandhu needed to understand from the academics assembled on the shores of the Buriganga was whether the 6 points could indeed be accommodated within the constitutional framework of a united Pakistan. Our arguments indicated that a valid constitution, which accommodated the 6-point demands, could be made operational, provided that the military were sincere about seeking a constitutional solution to the political crisis. Our affirmation contributed to strengthening Bangabandhu's resolve to stand firm on 6 points as a credible negotiating option. This awareness did not prejudice Bangabandhu's scepticism over whether the realization of 6 points would be peacefully conceded by the Pakistani junta. By the time our group had finished our exercise, the AL had a constitutional draft and a fully worked out negotiating position for any future political dialogue that may have ensued.

In the later days of these discussions, our draft was reported on in some sections of the media. Bangabandhu suspected that our discussions and draft had been leaked to the intelligence agencies by a participant who he indicated might be Khandkar Mushtaq. Mushtaq was believed to favour a compromise on 6 points and was unhappy that the economists had gone to such lengths to persuade Bangabandhu as to its viability. Mushtaq lacked the competence as well as courage to challenge our arguments but suggested to Bangabandhu that he explore alternative opinions from other economists. Bangabandhu appeared unimpressed by this suggestion. He advised us to hand over all copies of the draft and our notes of discussion to him at the end of the day so this could be kept secure in his custody. In a telltale confession of guilt, Mushtaq was the only one among our group to protest at this lack of trust in his colleagues demonstrated by Bangabandhu.

In Quest of a Democratic Solution

Once the AL had prepared its own constitutional draft, we needed to know the position of the other political players. Bangabandhu was particularly interested to ascertain the political position of the PPP after its somewhat unexpected triumph at the polls in Punjab and Sind. He wanted to explore whether the PPP had given any serious thought to the constitution and their position on 6 points as they had chosen to downplay this issue in their election campaign. I was requested by Bangabandhu and Tajuddin Ahmed to pay an informal visit to West Pakistan in January 1971 to explore the mind of the PPP leadership. As I regularly travelled to West Pakistan for academic meetings, it was assumed that my visit there would not merit any special attention. I also personally knew some of the key personalities of the PPP which gave me easier access to their thinking and leadership.

I contacted Mazhar Ali Khan, our colleague at *Forum*, who had intimate links with the top PPP leaders in Lahore, to organize my mission there. He invited me to stay with him and his wife, Tahira, in their small but warm, tastefully decorated home in Gulberg. Mazhar organized my programme in Lahore and usually drove me to my important appointments. Through him, I met separately with Dr Mubasher Hasan and with Mian Mahmud Ali Qasuri of the PPP, who were its two founder members and reported to be the leading brains of the party. Qasuri was one of Pakistan's most famous lawyers who had been a member of the NAP and so was known to be a man of the left. His radical credentials had been internationally recognized, and he had been invited by Bertrand Russell, the philosopher and Nobel laureate, to be a member of the International War Crimes Tribunal on Vietnam, set up by him. Mubasher was less known but was an eminent engineer with strong left-wing views that he put into effect when he was appointed the Finance Minister by Bhutto in his first cabinet in 1972.

My meeting with Mubasher involved discussions on economic policy rather than the 6 points. I discovered in my conversations with Mubasher that what was deemed as the left wing of the PPP, which included J.R. Rahim, a retired diplomat who was the Secretary General and reported ideologue of the PPP, as well as younger stalwarts such as Meraj Muhammad Khan of Karachi, evaded discussion on the issue of 6 points. They tended to argue that the primary mission of the democratic upsurge in both East and West Pakistan was to end feudalism and capitalism, and this revolution would inevitably lead to the restoration of the usurped rights of the Bangalis. I found these rather academic discussions with these leftists quite frustrating because it diverted attention from what at that time had emerged as the principal contradiction in Pakistan politics, the East–West divide.

I did not realize that Mian Qasuri's Punjabi loyalties would override his long commitment to human rights. Even though he was an eminent lawyer, Qasuri gave me the impression that he had not given serious thought to the task of constitution making and had little to offer but rhetorical posturing on the subject of national unity. I was interested to learn after liberation that some of my remarks, then made in conversation with Qasuri at an exclusive dinner at his home, about the need for the AL and PPP to work together to end military rule, were subsequently passed on by him to MI. This was revealed by the MI in their subsequent interrogation of Kamal Hossain when he was held in custody by them in Haripur jail, near Abbottabad, during the Liberation War. Kamal's interrogators reported back to him that his cousin, Rehman Sobhan, was attempting to engage the PPP in a conspiracy against the army. So much for a man of honour from the left!

When I moved from Lahore to Karachi, I first contacted my St. Paul's friend, Barrister Rafi Raza. I had renewed contact with Rafi in March 1969 on my way back from London. Rafi had come to know Bhutto over the bridge table and had then been motivated by him to participate in joining him to found the PPP. After the PPP's electoral victories in West Pakistan, Rafi had been designated as the constitutional adviser to Bhutto.

From my talks with Rafi, I learnt that he had been entrusted by Bhutto with formulating the constitutional position of the PPP for the forthcoming CA. On the basis of the dialogues on the shores of the Buriganga with the AL leadership, I tried to engage Rafi in discussing some of the practical aspects of preparing a constitution based on 6 points. I wanted to learn from him and his PPP colleagues, including Bhutto, what were their specific objections to the 6 points. Rafi could not respond to my queries as he had done little work on these issues largely because Bhutto was himself disinclined to go into the fine points of constitution making. Rafi subsequently told me that his English wife, Rosemary, who sat in on some of our discussions, later pointed out to Rafi that the AL had demonstrated professionalism in their constitution making while the PPP were a bunch of amateurs. Further discussion with one of Bhutto's principal lieutenants, Barrister Abdul Hafeez Pirzada, confirmed this point.

I also had discussions with Barrister Kamal Azfar whom I had also encountered in March 1969. At that stage, Kamal had rather unwisely joined the Muslim League, headed by Mian Mumtaz Daultana who was perceived by many to be the principal political figure to emerge from any election in the Punjab. This illusion was shattered when the PPP trounced the Muslim League at the polls. Kamal, without much embarrassment, transferred his loyalties to the PPP, drawing on his intimacy built up with Bhutto over the bridge table. Bhutto himself had, at the young age of 32, been brought into the martial law cabinet of Iskander Mirza and Ayub Khan in 1958 due to his acquaintance over the bridge table with Nahid Mirza—the young second wife of Mirza. It appears that this noble game has played an important role in Bhutto's political life.

Kamal was now also a member of Bhutto's inner circle, so I hoped that he or Rafi would arrange for me to meet Bhutto. I had pointed out to Rafi and Kamal that after the elections there had been a qualitative change in Bangladesh's political perspective. The 6 points was now the conservative position as more radical opinion was building up for establishing an independent Bangladesh. If the junta and PPP were unwilling to concede 6 points, they had better be aware of the possibility of having to cope with a separatist movement in Bangladesh. My views were conveyed to Bhutto by Kamal Azfar with the suggestion that he might meet with me to discuss the post-election mood in East Pakistan. Bhutto was disinclined to do so, dismissing me and my views as unrepresentative of mainstream political thinking in Dhaka, indicating that I was known to be a hot-headed radical. He perhaps recollected the heated exchange Kamal Hossain and I had with him in his rooms at the Hotel InterContinental during his visit to Dhaka prior to the election.

The Larkana Conspiracy

On my return to Dhaka, I had reported to Bangabandhu that the PPP were far from prepared for serious constitutional discussions and that Bhutto's own political agenda may be elsewhere directed. This agenda became more apparent in the course of Yahya's visit to Dhaka around 12 January 1971. He chose to play his own games with Bangabandhu and his colleagues rather than engage in serious discussions on constitutional issues. What Yahya possibly confirmed for himself during these meetings in Dhaka was that Bangabandhu was politically committed to frame a constitution based on 6 points. Yahya accordingly based the subsequent actions of the junta on this understanding.

In a revealing memoir by Major General Khadim Hussain Raja, *A Stranger In My Own Country*, which provides a first-hand account of his tenure as GOC of the 14th Division at Dhaka from October 1969 to April 1971, he reports on Yahya's response to this meeting on 12 January 1971.

> Sheikh Mujib was not prepared to concede any ground and the President closed the meeting in disgust. He left Dhaka in some anger and went to Larkana where he was Bhutto's guest. They were joined by General Abdul Hamid Khan (Army Chief of Staff). During the next two days momentous decisions were taken about the fate of the country.

Raja's telling prelude and conclusion about the Larkana meeting was personally confirmed to me some four decades later when I was provided with a unique insight on the outcome of the Yahya–Bhutto encounter in Larkana. This evidence was provided to me on a visit to Lahore in 2011, by an Aitchison friend of mine who reported to me that he had recently encountered one of the principal players of the drama of 1971, Lieutenant General Ghulam Umer, who was then the Head of National Security and was used by Yahya to manipulate various politicians in both East and West Pakistan. Umer, long since retired, now an elderly man but still equipped with a sharp memory, was challenged by my friend to spell out his role in the events leading up to 25 March.

Umer confided to my friend that he had accompanied Yahya to Dhaka for his talks with Mujib. At the end of the talks, Yahya instructed Umer to immediately contact Bhutto and set up a meeting in Larkana. The press were to be told that Yahya was taking time off for a hunting vacation at Bhutto's feudal estate. This level of apparent intimacy between Bhutto and Yahya was the outcome of the junta's post-election strategy. The junta, who had invested in defeating Bhutto in the elections, now sought to use him as an ally in frustrating the emerging ascendency of the Bangalis in the political arena, posed by the massive victory of the AL in East Pakistan. Yahya's principal aide, General Pirzada and Umer, had accordingly directly established contact with Bhutto to make common cause against Mujib.

Yahya travelled directly from Dhaka to Larkana, where he was met by Bhutto. In the first exchanges with Bhutto, Yahya burst out, "We must fix this bastard, Mujib." At the Larkana meeting, a strategy was laid out as to how Bhutto would set up the political preconditions for a postponement of the CA session, scheduled to be convened in Dhaka on 3 March. The idea was to use this postponement to pressurize Mujib to compromise on 6 points, though Yahya had not indicated to Mujib during their talks with him the specifics of such a compromise.

The Larkana plan was, however, kept on hold until Bhutto, towards the end of January, visited Dhaka, ostensibly for talks with Bangabandhu, where he had the opportunity to make his own assessment of the AL's position. Bhutto was accompanied by a large PPP entourage. From what I learnt of these talks from Tajuddin, Bhutto appeared to be more interested in negotiating a share of power with Bangabandhu rather than discussing the implications of implementing a constitution based on 6 points. I, therefore, once again sought to engage myself in discussions on the acceptability of 6 points with Rafi Raza and Mubasher Hasan at my home in Gulshan. At the meeting, Rafi and Mubasher requested Kamal for a draft of the constitution that we had prepared for presentation at the forthcoming session of the CA. Kamal consulted Tajuddin, who suggested that it may be unwise, at this stage, to show the AL's hand. It was evident from the available media reports and political speculation about the Larkana meeting that Bhutto was in close touch with the military junta and could use any information derived from our document to influence Yahya's strategy in the days ahead.

The specifics of the PPP–AL talks have been revealed by Kamal Hossain, in his recently published memoir (*Bangladesh: Quest for Freedom and Justice*), so I will not dwell on this. My own impressions were that neither the PPP nor Yahya Khan had made any effort, prior to 1 March 1971, to define a serious negotiating position on the subject of 6 points. As far as I know, no discussion ever took place between the AL and any of the political leadership of West Pakistan on the concrete problems involved in implementing 6 points. When detailed discussions did get underway at five minutes to midnight, in March of 1971, the constitutional issue had moved beyond 6 points and the Generals had already decided to settle the issue by blood and fire.

The game plan to operationalize the Larkana agenda was put into motion after Bhutto's return from Dhaka, where he had personally confirmed for himself that Bangabandhu was not interested in making any private deals with him. Bhutto, unlike the Jamaat or Muslim League politicians of West Pakistan, had been rather silent on the issue of 6 points during the election campaign. At the time of his departure from Dhaka, he had indicated to Bangabandhu that they would further discuss the scope for framing such a constitution during the forthcoming Dhaka CA session. In early February, Bhutto appeared to suddenly change his public stance on 6 points which was elevated into his principal political concern. He now threatened to boycott the assembly session on 3 March unless Mujib agreed to compromise his position on 6 points. Bhutto went on to publicly threaten to break the legs of any non-PPP MCA who dared to travel to Dhaka for the prospective assembly session.

Bhutto's rather crude provocations to frustrate the convening of the assembly session had generated both alarm and some surprise in Dhaka. In the Dhaka meetings, Bhutto had at no point indicated that he was faced with such an intractable political stance by the AL as to warrant assuming a confrontational posture. His blusterings at his public meetings were thus viewed by the AL leadership as a confirmation of the possibility that Bhutto was part of a conspiracy with Yahya that had originated in the Larkana meeting. Bangabandhu finally issued a public warning to Bhutto not to play with fire through his provocative acts and statements. Our concern that a conspiracy was afoot were aggravated by the sudden appearance of military bunkers, posted with automatic weapons, which suddenly greeted Dhakaites as they drove past Dhaka airport one morning in mid-February.

Closure of the Democratic Route

Notwithstanding the mounting tension, no one anticipated that the CA would actually be postponed. West Pakistani MCAs, other than the PPP, began arriving in Dhaka in the last few days of February to attend the prospective session of the CA on 3 March, in spite of Bhutto's threat to breaks their legs. I had conversations with several of those known to me who had checked in to the InterContinental Hotel. At that stage, they expected that Bhutto would eventually turn up once the CA was in session.

Wali Khan, the leader of the West Pakistan NAP, and Ghaus Bakhsh Bizenjo, a NAP leader from Baluchistan, who I met several times at the residence of Ahmedul Kabir in Indira Road, were less sanguine and reaffirmed the belief that a conspiracy was being plotted by Yahya with Bhutto to frustrate the transfer of power to civilian rule. Both Wali and Bizenjo argued that the conspiracy by Bhutto and Yahya was not just targeted towards Bangladesh but also directed at frustrating the national aspirations of the Pathans and the Baluch, particularly as Bhutto had won few seats from these two provinces. I recollect, with sadness, those long and increasingly melancholy discussions with the NAP leaders, sitting in the tranquility of Laila Kabir's garden at Indira Road, where she attempted to illuminate the unfolding darkness with her incandescent charm and insightful interventions.

Up to the eve of the CA session on 3 March, Yahya was expected in Dhaka. Generators had been installed outside the President's House that was located at the juncture of Hare Road and Bailey

Road and was later used as the Bangladesh PM's office in the initial years after liberation. It was reported around 27 February that Yahya had departed from Islamabad to Karachi to embark on his flight to Dhaka. Later, we learnt that he actually reached Karachi but then flew back from there to Islamabad.

I learnt some years later, in conversations in London in 1977 with Admiral Ahsan and later with Lt General Yakub in New York in 1993, that at some crucial meetings in Islamabad they had both attempted to persuade Yahya to go ahead with the session on 3 March and that any attempt to postpone the session could provoke the most severe reaction among the Bangalis. Their views did not prevail.

The conclusions from my own discussions with Ahsan and Yakub have been confirmed, again in Raja's memoir, where he reports that Yakub was informed at a meeting with Yahya in Islamabad of his decision to postpone the convening of the CA in Dhaka on 3 March. According to Raja, by early February, Yahya had already drawn up a contingency plan, Operation Blitz, for a military crackdown accompanied by suspension of all political activity, whereby the armed forces would move against defiant political leaders and take them into preventive custody. Operation Blitz had been passed on to the CMLA in Dhaka to be activated when ordered. Yakub, on his return to Dhaka from his abortive mission to dissuade Yahya from his folly, instructed his commanders on 26 February to be ready to put Operation Blitz into action if called to do so after 1 March. The timing of the preparation of Operation Blitz suggests that it coincided with the return of Bhutto from Dhaka and was part of the operationalization of the Larkana agenda.

Apart from Yakub, Governor Ahsan also made a last-minute dash to Islamabad to avert Yahya's march of folly. Yahya was not persuaded by Ahsan's arguments and, instead, dismissed him from the post of Governor. Yakub was then ordered to take over as Governor of East Pakistan. Ahsan will be remembered by history as a genuinely decent man who did all in his power to not only ensure a free and fair election in December 1970 but tried, until the last moment, to work for a peaceful democratic transition.

Nothing of this ongoing drama in Islamabad was known to us in Dhaka so that the announcement by Yahya on 1 March to postpone, sine die, the assembly session on 3 March was greeted with universal anger in East Pakistan. When the postponement was announced over the airwaves, a cricket match was in progress between Pakistan and the MCC at the stadium on Bangabandhu (then Jinnah) Avenue. The crowd spontaneously raised slogans of protest and walked out, en masse, from the stadium, heading towards the Purbani Hotel next door, where an AL Presidium meeting, convened to discuss a response to Yahya's decision, was in session. Bangabandhu greeted the mob with the declaration that Yahya's act would not go unchallenged and announced an indefinite hartal.

On the afternoon of 2 March, the *Chattro Sangram Parishad* convened a massively attended public meeting on Paltan Maidan, which I attended, that was addressed by various student leaders. All speakers proclaimed that we should now fight for independence and proceeded to unfurl the green and red flag of an independent Bangladesh. The next day, an even larger meeting was addressed by Bangabandhu, where he spelt out his defiance of Yahya and the launching of a programme of total non-cooperation.

The initial phase of non-cooperation was far from peaceful. General Yakub did not fully activate Operation Blitz that involved the arrest of major political leaders including, presumably, Bangabandhu. Under the prevailing political circumstances, Yakub sensibly realized this would be an unfeasible and senseless act. He did, however, move to impose curfew, backed by a sufficient show of military force, which he thought would be enough to calm down the situation and buy time for some sort of political deal between Yahya and Mujib. Yakub's military and political calculations did not add up. The Bangalis, who were reputed to run away at the first sight of the army or the sound of gunfire, proved to be sired from another breed. They unprecedentedly defied the curfews, demonstrating willingness to face up to the guns of the army and risk death. Many were indeed killed in confrontations with the army as the local police force refused to fire on Bangalis at an early stage of the non-cooperation movement. All offices and institutions, both public and private, all factories, educational establishment and even the law courts came to a standstill.

When General Yakub realized that no military solution was possible, he recalled his troops to the cantonments around 4 March 1971. At that point, he effectively relinquished Pakistan's sovereignty over Bangladesh, thereby drawing down the curtain on 24 years of imperial rule. When he failed to persuade Yahya to travel to Dhaka to deal with the situation in person to seek a political solution, he chose to resign as CMLA and Commander, Eastern Command. Yakub, in his resignation letter sent to Yahya on 5 March informed him that

> the control of the administration had passed on to Sheikh Mujib who was now *de facto* head of government and controlled all public life. … I am convinced there is no military solution which can make sense in the present situation. I am consequently unable to accept the responsibility for implementing a mission, namely military solution that would mean large scale killing of unarmed civilians and would achieve no sane aim. It would have disasterous consequences. (Khadim Hussain Raja)[2]

Yahya accepted Yakub's resignation and immediately sent out General Tikka Khan, the Butcher of Baluchistan, to take over as both Governor and Chief Martial Law Administrator. Tikka's arrival in Dhaka on 7 March indicated that much blood would need to be shed before the Bangalis attained self-rule.

The Birth of a Nation

The Bangabandhu Regime

The withdrawal of the troops to the cantonment around 5 March set the stage for a non-cooperation movement of historic proportions the like of which had never been seen before. The entire civilian bureaucracy, the police force and all components of the provincial

[2] Khadim Hussain Raja. (2012). *A Stranger in My Own Country, East Pakistan 1969–71.*

and central government ceased to extend their services to the established government. The apogee of the non-cooperation movement was reached when the then Chief Justice of East Pakistan, Badruddin Siddiki, declined to swear in General Tikka Khan as the new Governor of East Pakistan.

The non-cooperation movement graduated to a qualitatively different level, when all the different echelons of the machinery of government sent their representatives to Road 32, Dhanmondi, to pledge their allegiance to Bangabandhu. The bureaucrats were shortly followed by the business community, then dominated by non-Bengalis, who also pledged their support. The world has witnessed many such movements but, to the best of my knowledge, none has reached a point where the administration, the police force and the law courts have decided to not only disobey the orders of an incumbent government but have gone on to pledge allegiance to a political leader who held no formal public office.

At the much anticipated meeting of 7 March at the Race Course, where Bangabandhu made his historic declaration, *Ebarer Sangram Amader Muktir Sangram, Ebarer Sangram Swadhinatar Sangram*,[3] many anticipated that he would declare the independence of Bangladesh. It was at the same time believed that were he to do so, the Pakistan air force stationed at Kurmitola had been instructed to bomb the meeting as the prelude to a full-scale genocide to be launched by the army. This apprehension has since been confirmed in the memoir by Khadim Hussain Raja, who reports that he had sent a warning to the AL leaders that any move to declare independence would invoke a full-scale offensive by the Pakistani armed forces.

I learnt from Kamal Hossain that a fateful meeting of the AL high command had taken place before 7 March at Road 32, and continued through most of the day and night, to discuss the line Bangabandhu should take at the public meeting the next day. It was argued by the more senior elements, led possibly by Bangabandhu and Tajuddin, that a declaration of independence was premature

[3] This struggle is for freedom, this struggle is for our independence.

and more time was needed to mobilize public consciousness before committing the people to such a struggle with the costs in blood that this would entail. The AL leadership, at that time, had little knowledge of the capacity of the ordinary people to actually engage in an armed struggle and were far from sure of the possible response of the Bangalis in the armed forces then serving in the cantonments of Bangladesh.

In contrast to the doubts of the more senior members of the AL younger stalwarts, such as Sirajul Alam Khan known as Kapalik Siraj, argued for an immediate declaration of independence to inspire a full-scale liberation war. Prior to attending the meeting on 7 March, Nurul Islam and I drove to Iqbal Hall to gauge the mood of the younger generation. We ran into Kapalik, who appeared depressed and indicated to us that no dramatic declaration of independence may be expected. As it transpired, Bangabandhu made the most masterful speech of his political life where, without actually declaring independence, he spelt out that the Bangalis should be prepared to commit themselves to a struggle for independence and freedom. This left open the scope for a negotiated pathway to independence or at least a form of independence in substance, if not in law.

In the tense period prior to 1 March, I put some of the concerns indicated above into print in my writings for *Forum*. In this I tried to spell out in more explicit terms the implications of implementing 6 points and the issues at stake for the political leadership in West Pakistan. The universal theme of my writings in the columns of *Forum* was that the 6 points were the last chance for a political resolution to the Pakistan crisis. Beyond this lay the path of mass struggle and independence for Bangladesh. Few Bangalis at that time retained any sentimental attachment to the Pakistan concept. The only question appeared to be whether the parting of the ways would emerge through a process of constitutional evolution or through armed confrontation.

The decision by President Yahya Khan on 1 March 1971 to postpone the meeting of the CA sine die, in my mind, marked the watershed that constituted the political independence of Bangladesh.

The non-cooperation movement, which was initiated on that day throughout Bangladesh, at the call of Bangabandhu Sheikh Mujibur Rahman, repudiated the political authority of the Pakistan government within the territory of Bangladesh. This political authority was never again restored. All subsequent attempts by the Pakistan junta after 26 March 1971 to restore their authority were seen by the masses of Bangladesh as acts of forcible usurpation by a foreign military occupation power.

The totality of the success realized by Bangabandhu's call for non-cooperation immediately created a crisis for maintaining essential civic and economic services within Bangladesh. Once the entire labour force, administration and law-enforcing authorities had answered Bangabandhu's call for non-cooperation, the writ of the Pakistan government in Bangladesh quite literally ceased to run outside the military cantonments. This vacuum had to be filled if economic and social life in the country was not to break down completely. Bangabandhu had, therefore, to assume both political and administrative authority throughout the country once Yahya had concurred with his local Corp Commander, General Yakub's suggestion that the Pakistan army be withdrawn into the cantonments from 5 March 1971. From that day, Bangladesh attained self-rule for the first time since the Battle of Plassey in 1757.

This unique transference of authority, outside of the perimeters of the cantonments, within the boundaries of Bangladesh, from the sovereign government of a militarily-ruled Pakistan to Bangabandhu, on 5 March, renders contemporary political discussions on the declaration of independence both mindless and pointless. Whatever may be the date of a formal declaration of independence for Bangladesh by Bangabandhu or anyone else, the effective independence of Bangladesh could be dated from 5 March 1971 when political authority over Bangladesh was devolved on Sheikh Mujibur Rahman. After this date, any move by Yahya Khan, through the deployment of military force, was deemed by all Bangladeshis as an act of armed aggression against a sovereign country. This emergence of a national consciousness among Bangladeshis was reflected in their response to the events of 25 March 1971.

People's Raj

Once the Pakistan government effectively surrendered its authority to Bangabandhu, a variety of economic problems of some complexity had to be resolved on a daily basis in order to keep the economy viable. Such questions as the enforcement of exchange controls on remittances to West Pakistan, the limits on the stocks of Pakistani currency arising out of the cut-off of supplies of cash from the mint in Pakistan, policies towards export consignments and modes of payment for import of essentials and raw materials had to be worked out.

To address such problems, Tajuddin Ahmed and Kamal Hossian were commissioned by Bangabandhu to assume responsibility, drawing on the group of economists who had already associated themselves with Bangabandhu. The rented residence of Nurul Islam on Road 6, Dhanmondi, was established as a sort of economic secretariat for the government of Sheikh Mujibur Rahman centred on Road 32, Dhanmondi. Kamal Hossain's residence on Circuit House Row was the other centre of administration. Some of us met daily at Nurul Islam's residence with some of the Bangali civil servants and bankers to review specific problems. Those consultations were then distilled into decrees or instructions, which were passed on to the civil servants, business leaders, bankers and for press circulation, every evening by Tajuddin Ahmed and Kamal Hossain either at Road 32 or at Kamal Hossain's residence.

Apart from reviewing the state of the local economy, another task that devolved on the economists was to brief the international press. Every day, the elite of the foreign press corps came to these sessions at Islam's house. These well-known journalists included Tillman and Peggy Durdin of *The New York Times*; Sydney Schanberg of *The New York Times*, whose coverage of the Liberation War had him expelled from Dhaka by the Pakistan military authorities and almost won him a Pulitzer Prize; Peter Preston, later Editor; Martin Woollacott and Martin Adeney of *The Guardian*; Peter Hazelhurst of *The Times*, Simon Dring of *The Daily Telegraph*; Selig Harrison for *The Washington Post*; Henry Bradsher of *The Washington*

Star; and Arnold Zeitlin of Agence France-Presse (AFP). All these experienced journalists had gravitated to Dhaka, where the possible emergence of the independent State of Bangladesh was seen by the global media as the breaking story of the time, eclipsing the Vietnam War that had continued to dominate the news. These news-hungry journalists were keen to file regular copy from Dhaka to their newspapers to keep their readers abreast of the unfolding drama in Bangladesh.

In retrospect, what was interesting and perhaps special about the Bangladesh story was the extent to which a number of these event-hardened journalists graduated beyond their search for a good story from Dhaka into making an emotional investment in Bangladesh's struggle for liberation. Seasoned journalists such as Woollacott, Sydney Schanberg, Selig Harrison and Simon Dring went beyond the call of professional duty in projecting the struggle of the Bangalis before their readers. I remember hearing a story in London about Nicholas Tomalin who had been one of the luminaries at Trinity Hall when I entered the college, who had gone on to become a renowned correspondent of *The Sunday Times* and had made a reputation covering the Vietnam War. Tomalin, in his address to a teach-in on Bangladesh convened at Cambridge, informed his audience that he had covered many major political stories including Vietnam, but none had so emotionally engaged him as had events in Bangladesh.

Several of these journalists provided me with ready access to their columns when I was campaigning in London, New York and Washington, which enabled me to write about the Bangladesh struggle in the columns of *The Times*, *The Guardian* and *New Statesman* in London and *The New Republic* and *The Nation* in the USA. Some among them, in return, served as valuable conduits of information to us about what was going on in the ranks of the Pakistani ruling elite. It was Peter Hazelhurst who told me, over a cup of tea at the residence of Kamal Hossain in March 1971, that he had recently interviewed Bhutto in Larkana who contemptuously told him that this agitation in Bangladesh was a storm in a tea cup led by a few urban-based politicians who knew nothing about armed struggle. A whiff of grapeshot from the army that killed and terrorized the demonstrators in Dhaka and jailed many of the leaders would lower the tempo of the agitation and create a climate for more reasonable negotiations. This piece of intelligence seemed to have a prophetic quality that Bhutto may have shared with Yahya Khan at their Larkana meeting as it was this false assumption that may have contributed towards the army's military adventure on 25 March 1971.

During this period, Nurul Islam's now historic Dhanmondi residence, which had gained notoriety as the secretariat of an insurrectionary government as well as a media briefing centre, also came to be viewed by the MI as a den of treasonous conspiracy. This owed to the fact that Col Yasin of the Pakistan Army and Mr S. Huda, then in the Telephone and Telegraph (T&T) department, both brothers-in-law to Nurul Islam, were regular visitors to his house. Col Yasin was in charge of supplies to the Pakistan forces in Dhaka. He was therefore, in a position to prepare a list of the food suppliers to the Pakistan Army in Dhaka. This list was passed on by us to the AL leaders, who then instructed their workers to visit these suppliers and persuade some of them to cut off supplies to the cantonment. This strategy proved to be quite effective. Khadim Hussain Raja, in his memoir, reports on the complete interruption in the supply of fresh foodstuffs in March and the consequent hardships faced by the inmates of the cantonment.

There was a more sinister aftermath to these exchanges. After the army assault on 25 March, both Col Yasin and Huda were picked up by the army. Huda was kept in custody in Dhaka, where he was interrogated and asked to confess to conspiring with Professor Islam and me for acting on behalf of the AL to set up a telecommunications link with India. This totally fabricated charge found its way into the charge sheet for treason drawn up against Bangabandhu, for which he was put on trial for his life during 1971. Col Yasin faced a worse fate. He was taken into custody. But in his case, he was transferred to Lahore, where he was interrogated under torture with a view to forcing him to bear false witness against Bangabandhu in his trial and also against Brigadier Mazumdar, who had been the Commandant of the East Bengal Regimental Centre in Chittagong prior to 25 March and was being separately interrogated under torture in Lahore (Brig. Mazumdar's interview with journalist Ruhul Motin, 1999).

In those twilight days when most vehicular traffic was suspended due to the ongoing hartals, I could move around freely in my Volkswagen due to my privileged journalist's sticker, courtesy of my editorship of *Forum*. I could thus, divide my days as a part-time economic administrator and a full-time editor as well as a field reporter and an op-ed writer of *Forum*. Hameeda and I managed to turn out some of the sharpest copies of the journal right up to the crackdown by the army.

Due to the continuous hartal, no one actually worked in those days. Much time was spent in casual visiting in one's neighbourhood where everyone constantly speculated about the dangers to come. In the first part of March, these concerns, particularly among the Gulshan–Banani set of non-Bangalis and elite Bangalis, remained in abeyance as much of Bangladesh was exceptionally peaceful. Non-Bangalis were less assured and remained concerned about their future. Our particular concern at home related to the prospects for Salma's younger sister, Naz, her husband, S.M. Ashraf, and their newborn daughter, Amina. Ashraf, a Canadian citizen since the 1950s, where he worked as civil servant, had negotiated a senior executive position with a foreign company in Dhaka and had moved with Naz and their newborn daughter to Dhaka around October 1970.

This sea change in Pakistan's political circumstances after 1 March was a traumatic experience for the Ashraf family. Ashraf, who normally had a brilliant sense of humour found the occasion far from humorous. As the crisis reached its denouement in March, with the promise of a possible civil war, foreign nationals were gradually being repatriated out of Dhaka by their respective embassies. Ashraf could thus arrange for repatriation for himself and his family to Karachi via Bangkok, through the courtesy of the Canadian High Commission in Dhaka. Ashraf's good humour did not desert him altogether. At the closing stage of the conflagration where he had earlier witnessed the lighting of the match, when Karachi was being bombed by the Indian air force in December, he quipped to a circle of friends, "I am the only true son-in-law of

Begum Ikramullah, Prince Hassan is above the law and Rehman Sobhan is an outlaw."

As long as Bangabandhu exercised effective authority across Bangladesh, law and order was being enforced either by the AL workers or ordinary citizen's groups. This was facilitated by the response of ordinary people themselves who appeared to be more law abiding. There were occasional reports of attacks on non-Bangalis, particularly in Chittagong, but such episodes were on a small scale that was later exaggerated by the Pakistan army to justify their subsequent massacre of Bangalis.

Whatever may be the extent of the tribulation of the non-Bangalis, a steady exodus of the better off among them to West Pakistan was discernible after 1 March. At one point, the AL leadership feared that some of those leaving Dhaka might be escaping with moveable wealth in the form of cash and jewellery. Some AL volunteers began, without authority, to intercept and search cars perceived to be heading to the airport. The AL administration was compelled to issue orders discouraging such actions as they were contributing to panic and further alienation among non-Bangalis whose fears were aggravated by rumours of violence against those who did not speak Bangla.

It was reported that various student groups were undergoing military training, but the only weapons on display appeared to be at military drills by students bearing wooden rifles. We heard a few .303 rifles were being stolen from armed guards at offices for possible action and that chemicals were being stolen from the University chemistry labs for preparing explosives. These amateurish efforts of our youth did not inspire any confidence that we were anywhere near prepared for an armed struggle.

More typical of our culture and history, our colleague Anisur Rahman, in company with the artist Qamrul Hasan, organized meetings of cultural activists at his University apartment to keep up the morale among this community through sessions of *gano sangeet*.[4] Anis was rightly fearful that genocide was imminent and wrote letters to his academic friends abroad to launch a global

[4] Popular protest songs; also commonly known as people's songs.

campaign to build opinion in their respective countries against such an event.

By mid-March, some hopes of a peaceful resolution of the crisis were held out with the arrival of Yahya Khan in Dhaka, who claimed to be seeking a peaceful solution to the crisis through negotiations with Mujib. Bhutto shortly followed him to Dhaka to participate in these negotiations, though some believe that he came to Dhaka to frustrate any hope for a bilateral settlement between Mujib and Yahya.

The Last Charade

From the time that negotiations were begun between Yahya and Mujib, some of us were drawn in to back up the AL team which consisted of Nazrul Islam, Tajuddin Ahmad and Kamal Hossain. The team was supposed to be negotiating an interim constitutional arrangement with Yahya's team of experts, made up by Major General Pirzada, Justice Cornelius, M.M. Ahmed and Col Hasan, who was reported to be the legal draughtsman of the government. Since some of the trickiest points in the negotiations related to the economic components of the 6 points such as East Pakistan's control over its export earnings, monetary policy and right to negotiate foreign aid, the services of the AL's team of economists were much in demand. We would accordingly, sit with the AL team after each session of negotiations to take note of suggestions made by M.M. Ahmed, Yahya's principal negotiator on economic issues, and put forward our responses or present our own substantive suggestions. These back-room efforts involved long sessions, including some with Bangabandhu.

In the last days leading to 25 March, there was one climactic session which went on in the conference room of the law chambers of Kamal Hossain in Motijheel, where Bangabandhu along with the AL high command and its advisers worked all night to formulate the final negotiating position for the talks the next day. The economists were confined to Kamal's office to be available when needed. I remember Anis stretching out on the floor of the office to catch up on his sleep. Our last contribution to the talks, around 22–23 March, was to sit over the handwritten amendments of M.M. Ahmed to the proposals prepared by us the night before. If I recollect, we concurred with these amendments and went home thinking that an agreement had been reached.

The final position taken by Yahya's team indicated that, at least on economic issues, an agreement could be reached. The expectation was that on 24 March, General Pirzada would convene the final session of the negotiations, following which an announcement of an agreement would be made to the press. The next two days passed by waiting for a phone call from General Pirzada to convene this final session. It was only on the 25 March that we learnt that M.M. Ahmed and Cornelius had already left for West Pakistan the night before.

I met M.M. Ahmed again in 1977 in Washington D.C. while he was a senior adviser of the World Bank. Ahmed informed me that in those fateful days of March 1971, he too had been waiting for the meeting with the AL team where it was expected that a public announcement on the interim agreement on the constitution would be made. Instead, he was abruptly told by General Pirzada that his work had been concluded and that, along with Justice Cornelius, he should immediately fly home from Dhaka. The substance of the negotiations is not discussed here as I have given my own indication of what went on in my article 'Negotiating for Bangladesh', which I wrote for *South Asian Review* later that year to put my knowledge, while still fresh, on the record. Kamal Hossain has separately given his own more authoritative version on the negotiations.

The negotiations discussed above were going on against the backdrop of a progressively mounting environment of tension, created by the daily reinforcement of the Pakistani garrisons in Bangladesh via Colombo since India, after the hijacking of an Indian Airlines Corporation (IAC) flight by Kashmiri terrorists who then landed the plane in Lahore, had suspended inter-wing flights over their territory. This build-up by the army was matched by the growing political consciousness and militancy of the Bangali masses.

Around mid-March, a friend of ours, Muyeedul Hasan, informed me he had an urgent message to deliver to Bangabandhu from sources within the Cantonment. I took Muyeed to Bangabandhu's residence at around 10 p.m. one night where he passed on the message that the Pakistan army was preparing to strike and was going into a state of combat readiness. Bangabandhu took note of this but said that he was already informed of these preparations.

The relevant point of the message from within the Cantonment was to alert Bangabandhu about the real danger of a crackdown by the army and the need for a pre-emptive response from the Bangladesh side. The Bangali soldiers were seeking guidance from Bangabandhu as to whether the Bangladeshi members of the armed forces, distributed across the various military cantonments in Bangladesh, should go on the offensive.

A similar question was posed to Kamal and me around 23 March when we had a visitation from M.R. Siddiqui, a leading businessman and President of the Chittagong District AL, and A.R. Khaled, a banker, who had driven up from Chittagong with a message from Brig. M.R. Majumdar, the Commandant of the East Bengal Regimental Centre in Chittagong and the senior most Bangali military officer serving in the East Wing. Majumdar has stated in his interview with Ruhul Motin in 1999 that he sought directions from Bangabandhu as to the future course of action by the serving Bangali troops in Chittagong. He claimed that the Bangalis, including those in the EPR, outnumbered the Pakistani troops in the cantonments and should thus strike first to gain the advantage since the Pakistanis were preparing to strike. They reported that the MV Swat had just landed in Chittagong with a shipload of arms and troops from West Pakistan and the Bangali troops had to either attack the vessel or obey orders and help to unload the equipments that would then be used by the Pakistanis to kill them.

Kamal took Siddiqui to Road 32 to meet Bangabandhu, who advised him against immediate action by the Bangladeshi forces and indicated that they should wait for further signals from him. Siddiqui, thus returned to Chittagong without a clear message to the Bangali forces there who were left to their own resources to respond to the military build-up by the Pakistan army.

There has, in later years, been much speculation over whether Bangabandhu should have responded to messages from within the cantonment and ordered a first strike by the Bangali armed units in the Pakistan army and EPR. Whether these forces could have used their numerical superiority to overwhelm the Pakistani troops stationed in each of the cantonments remains open to debate. Subsequent writings from Pakistan indicate that the military leadership were not unaware of such possibilities and might have had potential insurgents under their intelligence scrutiny. Raja, in his memoirs, repeatedly refers to the concerns of the Pakistani officers about the loyalty of the Bangalis serving with them. At one stage, as GOC he secretly advised all West Pakistani officers to carry their side arms with them at all times in case of a sudden attack on them by their Bangali troops.

The scope for an organized and coordinated first strike by Bangali units dispersed across Bangladesh would have posed major security, organizational and logistical challenges for the Bangladesh cause. The failure, at the end of such a strike, to overwhelm the Pakistani forces dispersed across the region and their incapacity to cut off the inevitable military reinforcements sent from Pakistan would have embroiled Bangladesh in an open-ended civil war initiated through a unilateral declaration of independence (UDI) underwritten by a mutiny of Bangali soldiers. Bangalis may have eventually prevailed in such a struggle, but in the eyes of the world community, Bangladesh would have been viewed less favourably as secessionists and mutineers on the same lines as Biafra's ill-fated attempt to secede from Nigeria. I recollect that one of our themes in international advocacy was to persuade people that 'Bangladesh was not Biafra'.

Bangabandhu was not unaware of the prospective hazards, both domestic and global, of proclaiming a UDI. In the Pakistan era, a political leader of the opposition had little opportunity to cultivate the military, let alone conspire with Bangali officers. Bangabandhu could, thus, never be completely sure whether all Bangali armed elements would join such an insurgency or have the military capacity to carry this through to final victory. In such circumstances, he was reluctant to be the initiator of a UDI, and the consequential civil war needed to sustain it that would expose the people of Bangladesh to unlimited bloodshed.

Bangabandhu and his party had won all their victories in the political arena and had led the people of Bangladesh to the point where they had peacefully, through the democratic process, established their sovereignty over Bangladesh. He believed that the unprecedented support publicly demonstrated by all Bangalis for self-rule would both pressure Yahya Khan to seek a peaceful solution and earn the respect and sympathy of the world for the Bangladesh cause. This latter part of his strategy did indeed serve its purpose and invoke sympathy for our struggle. Across the world, it was perceived by most people that Bangalis were victims of a genocide inflicted on a peaceful movement in order to frustrate their democratic aspirations.

Tragically, this global sympathy was gained at a heavy cost in Bangali lives. Bangabandhu's gamble of pressuring Yahya, through one of the most comprehensive democratic mobilizations in contemporary history, proved to be infructuous. Yahya had no compunction about shedding large torrents of Bangali blood because he and his armed hordes regarded us as alien enemies, not fellow citizens. Yahya was also led to believe that Bangalis could not and would not put up much resistance so that Bangabandhu and his movement could be easily crushed and forced to compromise. When the initial acts of terror by the Pakistan army failed to intimidate the Bangalis into compromise and instead provoked mass resistance, genocide followed. Today, some may question whether our nationhood could have been achieved at a lower cost in blood. At a remote and safe distance from such epochal events, any amateur historian remains free to sit in judgement on the past. But, the moving finger having writ has moved on and not all the treasures on earth can bring back half a line.

During the period of the negotiations, I was meeting with some of the NAP leaders from West Pakistan, such as Abdul Wali Khan of NWFP and Ghous Bakhsh Bizenjo of Baluchistan at the residence of Ahmedul Kabir. Both Wali Khan and Bizenjo conveyed their apprehensions to me that the talks between Yahya, Mujib and Bhutto were likely to override the interests of the smaller provinces of West Pakistan. The Pathan and Baluchi apprehension arose from the fact that Bhutto had come over from Karachi to join in these discussions so he could demand a free hand in West Pakistan on the strength of his electoral majorities in Punjab and Sind. His offer of a deal to Mujib through his famous public pronouncement, *Idhar hum, udhar tum*,[5] gave substance to the fears of the Baluch and the Pathans.

On the Eve of Genocide

I subsequently acquired some insight into the duplicity of the Pakistani generals who, it appears, were conducting the negotiations to buy time to reinforce their garrisons in Bangladesh. On 24 March, the NAP leaders and other political figures from the smaller West Pakistani parties left Dhaka. When I met them at the Hotel InterContinental just prior to their departure, they indicated that they had been advised to do so by Yahya and that army action was imminent.

In the days prior to 25 March, Mazhar Ali Khan turned up in Dhaka from Lahore. He and Tahira were deeply distressed that a confrontation with the army was imminent which would precipitate a bloodbath. Mazhar felt that he could use his connections with the PPP, who were now in Dhaka to try and build links with the AL, to avert this tragedy. Mazhar arrived in Dhaka and stayed with me at our home from where I took him to meet various AL leaders.

As the days slipped away, Mazhar became even more concerned at the possible failure of the negotiations and the prospect of a full-scale military assault on the Bangalis. In these last days, as a last resort, he insisted I take him to meet Bangabandhu. This was not possible until the final hours of a united Pakistan, around 5:00 p.m. on the fateful night of 25 March, when we managed to meet Bangabandhu at Road 32. At that time, the house was besieged by journalists, who had presumably sensed that the crackdown by

[5] We rule here, you rule there.

the Pakistan army was close. Large numbers of AL workers as well as hangers-on, including members of the intelligence agencies, were adding to the congestion.

Bangabandhu had known Mazhar from the days when he was the Editor of *Pakistan Times* in the days when it was owned by Mian Iftikharuddin. They had travelled on a delegation to visit post-revolution China in 1954. He greeted Mazhar warmly and emptied the room so that there were just two of us with him. Bangabandhu told us that Yahya had decided to take the path of war. He went on to say, I quote from memory, "Yahya thinks that he can crush the movement by killing me. But he is mistaken. An independent Bangladesh will be built on my grave." Bangabandhu appeared to have a rather fatalistic attitude to what he seemed to accept as his imminent death. He suggested that a new generation would carry on the liberation struggle.

With his worst fears now confirmed, Mazhar Ali Khan wanted to find out what some of the PPP leaders had to say about the impending bloodbath. From Road 32, I drove Mazhar directly to the Hotel InterContinental to meet the PPP leaders known to him. We found the hotel in a state of ferment with journalists, politicians, military personnel and ordinary residents milling around. I remember a passing encounter with Brigadier Siddiqui, the principal media person for the Pakistan army who I had met as part of my *Forum* persona. Siddiqui was evasive and distracted during our brief encounter in the hotel lobby and appeared to be slightly inebriated.

Mazhar and I ascended to the top floor to meet Qasuri, his special friend. In his usual rather blustering tone, Qasuri immediately greeted me with the charge that, "It appears the Awami League do not want a settlement." As to my knowledge a draft agreement was already there waiting to be announced to the press, I asked him where he had received this confirmation. He told me that General Pirzada had told him this. As again it was General Pirzada who had been a key figure in the negotiations, it was evident that they were feeding a different story to the West Pakistani political leaders while preparing the ground for a crackdown. Qasuri went on to say that the unity of the country was at stake and that, if necessary, blood would have to be shed in the same way that Lincoln had fought a civil war to preserve the integrity of the USA. This irrelevant and politically mendacious reference to US history showed up Qasuri's chauvinist colours. I left Qasuri with the rhetorical observation that he was a well-known jurist who had served on the Bertrand Russell War Crimes Tribunal to expose US genocide in Vietnam. As the Pakistan army was about to launch a genocide on the Bengali people, I hoped that he would raise his voice in the same way that he did for the Vietnamese.

Following this confirmation of the duplicity of the Pakistani generals, I went on with Mazhar to the house of Kamal Hossain on Circuit House Road to pass on the message that Pirzada had obviously fed a concocted version of the talks to the PPP and that the ground was now set for action. Kamal appeared to be also taken by surprise at this news. We had, rather optimistically, planned to host a dinner that night for Mazhar at our home in Gulshan, which included the Hossains along with Laila and Ahmedul Kabir. This dinner had to be cancelled and I had to drive Mazhar home before all the roads were blocked. The reports of impending army action were given substance by the spectacle of some AL volunteers putting up makeshift barricades on some of the roads.

As we sped home to Gulshan, through darkened, deserted streets, I remarked to Mazhar that we were about to witness a great tragedy where the Pakistani army was preparing to launch a genocidal war of aggression on the Bangali nation. When and at what cost Bangladesh would establish its sovereignty remained, at that stage, incalculable.

15

Fulfilment: From Politician Economist to Political Combatant in the Liberation War

The Death of a Nation

The War Begins

For the citizens of Dhaka, the first salvos in Bangladesh's war of national liberation were fired sometime around 9:00–10:00 p.m. on 25 March when we heard the sound of artillery fire. This signalled that action by the Pakistan army against the EPR and police barracks had begun. I phoned up a direct number I had to Road 32 to enquire after the welfare of Bangabandhu. I do not know who answered the phone, but the voice at the phone indicated that he was there. Later calls went unanswered. After that all lines went dead.

For the next 36 hours, we heard the sound of artillery and automatic weapons fire. From the roof of my home in Gulshan, we could see the glow in the distance from fires started by the army action. The sound of artillery sounded like the thud of a giant's fist on a large pillow. With each thud, we realized that we were hearing the sound of nails being hammered into the coffin of Pakistan's corpse.

The next morning, on 26 March, we listened to Yahya's broadcast over the airwaves announcing the banning of the AL along with a tendentious account of the direction of the negotiations. He emphasized that his primary mission was to restore order. Bangalis, on the other hand, recognized this action by Yahya as a military invasion on an independent Bangladesh by a foreign army and responded accordingly. It was clear to all of us that the Liberation War had begun. It was less apparent when it would end.

For the next 36 hours, confined to our house in Gulshan and cut off from telephonic contact, we could only hear the sounds of genocide. On 26 March, Mazhar decided to walk across to the Russian consulate across the road from us on Gulshan Avenue, to explore if some of his contacts there could arrange for him to get to the airport. This mission proved fruitful and Mazhar obtained a ride with a consulate official to the Kurmitola airport, where he negotiated a flight back to Lahore. We parted company in the knowledge that we may never meet again.

On the morning of 27 March, the curfew was lifted. Up to that time, I had not regarded myself as a combatant. Therefore, the first thing I did that same morning was to walk across to the Ford Foundation guest house in Gulshan where Daniel Thorner, who was a Visiting Scholar from Sorbonne at the PIDE, was staying. I had been particularly concerned about Nurul Islam, whose house in Dhanmondi had been a hive of activity during the 25 days of March that could have made him a target of the military. I, therefore, urged Daniel to immediately drive over to Dhanmondi to ascertain if Nurul and his family were safe.

When I returned home, I found my friend Muyeedul Hasan waiting for me with the message that if I valued my life I should immediately leave my house. According to him, the army had already begun killing people on a large scale. He had contacted Kamal Hossain's house and had heard that the army had been there to pick him up but that Kamal had not been in the house at that time. Muyeed's commitment to the safety of his friends extended to Nurul Islam and a few others. In those early days, he engaged himself in securing their safety and, where required, arranging for their escape from Dhaka across the border. In the period before he left Dhaka, Muyeed, along with our close friend Zeaul Haq (Tulu) and Mukhlesur Rahman (Shidu Mian) who both stayed back, set up a system for gathering intelligence and transmitting it to key people in Mujibnagar.

I had thus far, quite naively, failed to appreciate that I may be a target for the army because, for all my pretensions as a politician economist, I did not appreciate that the army may also recognize me as a political activist and thereby treat me as a combatant. Muyeed pointed out the folly and dangers of my thinking and suggested I should move out of my house without delay. I was reluctant to do this, feeling that this would leave my family exposed to danger, but Salma felt that, if anything, my presence could be a risk to them and that it would in any case be easier for her to get out of Dhaka so that I could be free to contribute to the Liberation War.

With much reluctance, I left my family and was driven by Muyeed to the house of my cousin Sarwar and J.R. Khan. However, we found their home filling up with fugitives from the centre of Dhaka who hoped that Gulshan would be a safer refuge from the guns of the military than Ramna or Dhanmondi. I met Hameeda Hossain there, accompanied by her two young daughters Sara and Dina and her niece Fawazia Ahmed. Hameeda told me that Kamal had left their house shortly after my visit on the night of 25 March to go to the house of Tajuddin in Dhanmondi, whence they could together connect with Bangabandhu. Later that night, in the early hours of the morning, their house had been attacked by a posse of soldiers searching for Kamal. They spoke aggressively to Hameeda, terrorized the girls and their commanding officer slapped Fawazia when she questioned their actions; so much for military chivalry and discipline. Not finding Kamal there, they left them but promised to return. Hameeda was not too anxious for a second such visitation and had decided to move to Jamil's the moment the curfew was lifted.

JR advised me that if I wished anonymity, his house, which was filling up rapidly with downtown refugees, was not the safest place. I then suggested to Muyeed that he take me to the residence of another of our friends, Barrister Viqarul Islam and his wife Salma, who had a house in Gulshan between Circle 2 and Circle 1. Viqar advised me that his house was not too secure as it was overlooked by the apartment of a Pakistani of unproven provenance who may report on my presence. Viqar then took me to the home of John Rhode, an American who worked in the Cholera Research Laboratory (CRL) at Mohakhali. The Rhodes lived in a small house across Gulshan Avenue. The Rhodes welcomed me without hesitation and gave me refuge for the next two nights. Subsequently the Rhodes, along with other American colleagues at CRL such as William Greenhough and David Nalin, were repatriated to the USA, where they proved to be some of Bangladesh's most vocal and active friends, providing testimony on the genocide in Bangladesh before the US Congress and publicizing our situation in the US media.

Muyeed reported back to me in the afternoon that he had been to the Dhaka University teacher's quarters where there was evidence of a massacre. He had visited the block of flats occupied by Professor Abdur Razzaq and Professor Anisur Rahman, opposite Jagannath Hall, where he saw pools of blood on the floor and staircase of the now deserted building. There were reports that Professor Razzaq had been killed by the army. This knowledge deeply disturbed me not only because he was one of our closest friends but because this indicated that the army had widened its target to include people who were not directly involved in current events.

From Economist to Combatant

I spent the night of 27 March in my new refuge. That night we tuned in on the radio and heard a faint broadcast by Major Ziaur Rahman, proclaiming the independence of Bangladesh. We wondered who was this Major Zia and hoped that his declaration would not create confusion in the minds of both citizens and the world, who only recognized Sheikh Mujibur Rahman as the spokesman of Bangladesh.

Any doubts I may have retained about my non-combatant status were dispelled the next morning by Muyeed who visited me after calling on Salma at our house. Salma had informed him that the previous evening, just after curfew was restored, I had been formally upgraded to the status of a combatant in the Liberation War, courtesy of one Captain Sayeeduddin who, backed by a posse of troops, had come to our house to pick me up. Sayeeduddin claimed the distinction of having been one of the leaders of the assault party that took Bangabandhu into custody from his house on Road 32, Dhanmondi, on the night of 25 March.

My oldest son, Taimur, who was then just eight years old, was alone in our house, lying on the floor of his room reading a book when it was invaded by the troops of the Pakistan army. He was asked by Sayeeduddin about my whereabouts and appears to have handled himself quite coolly in the face of these gun-toting soldiers marauding around our house. Salma was next door with Babar, having coffee with Amineh and Alijoon. Our houses shared a wall that had a small connecting gate. Our maidservant who had Zafar, then aged nine months, in her arms and was standing outside our garage rushed next door, thrust Zafar into Salma's arms and blurted out the message that Pakistani soldiers had entered our house. Salma's immediate concern was for Taimur, alone next door, so she dashed, barefooted, back to the house through the common gate but was prevented at gunpoint from entering it. Sayeeduddin let her in and first questioned her about my whereabouts. When he heard that I had only left the house this morning, he told Salma that I must be either a brave or a foolish man to have lingered for so long at my house. He thought I could not have gone far and observed that if he took my wife and sons hostage to the cantonment, 'this would flush me out'.

Sayeeduddin's calculations were quite accurate because I would have immediately surrendered myself to the military if this could secure the freedom of my family. This horrendous scenario was averted through the intervention of Amineh and Alijoon who promised to stand security for Salma's presence next door. Sayeeduddin was willing to accept such an assurance as he knew that General Yakub had been a regular visitor to the Ispahani home. I owe a blood debt to Amineh and Alijoon that I have never been able to repay.

The knowledge that the Pakistan army had paid me the compliment of wanting to pick me up within the first 48 hours of their operation indicated that I was now a designated target. Muyeed advised me that I should get out of Dhaka as there would be house-to-house searches that would put at risk anyone who gave me shelter. Salma also sent a note to me with Muyeed, suggesting I should get out of the country as fast as possible as that would reduce their vulnerability. There was at that stage no foreknowledge of what course the war would take or our role in it. I sent a note to Salma asking her to get away from Dhaka and preferably abroad so that I could be more freely active in the cause of the liberation struggle.

Salma's exit from Dhaka to Karachi was facilitated by another friend, Akhter Ispahani, then married to Alijoon's cousin, Isky Ispahani, who had been in school with me in St. Paul's. Akhter invoked her own connections in the cantonment to get Salma and our sons' permission to fly to Karachi, on the plea that she was a patriotic Pakistani who had innocently married this subversive, Rehman Sobhan, knowing little of his heinous associations! Happily, this argument did the trick and Salma and the boys could fly out to Karachi within a week of my departure, where they stayed with her mother. When this news reached me in Delhi, this was a source of enormous relief, but I still wanted Salma to get out of Pakistan, beyond the reach of the army.

Moving into the War Zone

Muyeed took me over to the residence of Shidu Mian in Gulshan who, he believed, would be able to arrange for my exit. Shidu Mian's home had also become a magnet for fugitives seeking refuge or guidance on where to go. He directed me to move across the river from Gulshan to the village of Baraid, to the home of his father-in-law, Matin Sahib, a well-known political figure of the old school and great personal friend of Professor Razzaq. Walking across the fields from Gulshan to the village of Baraid, I merged with the vast exodus of the population of Dhaka fleeing the city and heading for the villages. In this exodus, I ran into Anisur Rahman, who introduced himself with a fictitious nom de guerre of Abdur Rashid and suggested that I assume a similar pseudonym, which he hoped would conceal our identities from the Pakistani intelligence. I was accordingly, assigned the name of Deen Mohomed. Anis' penchant for such nominal changes of identity extended across the border into India, where he changed his name to Ashok Roy, cleverly maintaining on both occasions the same initials as his original name while I was denominated as Mohan Lal. I do not know if these changes in nomenclature deceived Pakistani intelligence, but it certainly confused me as I tended to forget not only Anis' new names but mine as well and occasionally confused our respective appellations.

Anis gave me a first-hand account of the horrors he had lived through on the night of 25–26 March. He narrated how the army had invaded their block of flats and killed Professor Jotyrmoy Guha Thakurta of the English Department of Dhaka University, who lived on the ground floor, as well as Professor Maniruzzaman of Statistics, who lived on the top floor of the building. Professor Razzaq was spared only by providence. Some Pakistani soldiers banged at the door of his flat on the first floor of the building. As he took some time to reach the door, they took this to mean that the flat was empty and moved on before he could open it.

Anis, who lived opposite Professor Razzaq, was spared by the fact that he had—as a precaution—put a lock on one of the doors leading into his flat, which again suggested from the outside that it was empty. Anis had spent two nights and a day on the floor of his darkened flat with his wife Dora and their two daughters, with the army going up and down the stairs carrying out the bodies of their victims. He managed to escape with his family from this house of death the moment the curfew was lifted on the morning of 27 March. Anis' family had advised him to get out of Dhaka, so he had first sought out Shidu Mian for assistance. Shidu bhai's role in 1971, ably assisted by his wife Rosebu, in providing refuge, help and even safe passage to many like us seeking to move out of Bangladesh, is one of the less told stories of heroism in 1971.

At the village home of Matin Sahib in Baraid, we came across a number of other friends such as Mostafa Monwar of Dhaka Television. Matin Sahib's house was inundated with an assortment of middle-class Dhaka residents who sought an interim refuge there while they decided whether to go back to Dhaka or move on to their village home or abroad. At Baraid, it was decided that as I was a direct target of the army and so might Anis be, we should get across the border into India and then launch a campaign to seek international support for the cause of Bangladesh. Matin Sahib accordingly arranged for our safari.

In the early morning of 30 March, Anisur Rahman, Mostafa Monwar and I, escorted by a relation of Matin Sahib, Rahmatullah, a 21-year-old college student, and Rasheed, who was a school teacher in the area, set out for Agartala across the border. This duo subsequently escorted Nurul Islam and various other people to the border. Rahmatullah has, since those days, moved on to become a successful businessman. He has also been elected an MP from Gulshan, first on the Jatiya Party ticket in 1986 and then as an AL-er in 1996, 2008 and 2014. Rasheed was given an administrative position at the BIDS after liberation and remained there until his retirement when he began practice as an advocate in the High Court until his untimely death.

We were escorted by Shidu bhai across the fields to the banks of the Sitalakhya. I was rather bizarrely clad in a khadi kurta, check lungi held up by a belt as I had never worn such a garment before and Pathani chappals. This comical fancy dress was possibly suggested by Anisur Rehman to enable me to merge with the fleeing masses but cast me in the garb of a non-Bengali *kasai*[1] from Chowk Bazaar in Old Dhaka and served to flaunt my alien appearance.

From Baraid we crossed the Sitalakhya by *nauka*[2] and headed for Narsingdi by bus. Along the way, we came across people fleeing from Dhaka. At Narsingdi, we were to take a launch across the river to Brahmanbaria from where we could move across the border. Up to this point, we had only seen a demoralized population fleeing army terror in Dhaka. We had heard rumours of resistance in Chittagong but nothing more to indicate that a full-scale war of resistance had begun. The first direct signs of this resistance

[1] A butcher.

[2] Boat.

appeared before us when we sighted the Bangladesh flag flown by the launch that came across the river Meghna to pick up passengers at Narsingdi.

Same Side Goal

On the launch, some students tried to engage me in conversation, but I kept silent and Anis told them I was unwell. After a while, we found the launch pulling into the riverbank across the river but a long way from Brahmanbaria. Here some students from the launch approached us and asked us to accompany them off the launch. As at that stage both Anis and I still remained anxious not to reveal our identities lest Pakistani intelligence operatives had been moving in these crowds, we were hesitant to so expose ourselves but eventually went ashore. Here we found ourselves in an unanticipated situation because some of the people there, mystified by my *obangali*[3] appearance and outlandish garb, suggested I might be a Pakistani intelligence agent. Bigger crowds surrounded us on the shore front and some pushing and shoving took place where Anis, unfortunately, took a few punches, including one on the jaw, which led to a swelling that interfered with his eating for a few days. I was perhaps, more fortunate in not having my skills as a boxer put to the test or perhaps I did not register in my memory any of the blows directed to me. I remain indebted to Anis for tolerating these assaults on account of his *obangali* friend. In the process, I was deprived of my bag that had been sent to me by Salma containing a change of clothing, some money and my spectacles. Mostafa Monwar's assertion that we were Dhaka University teachers elicited some let up in the pressure building up around us.

We were initially taken to a tea shop just off the riverfront, but crowds were milling around outside demanding action. At the centre of the shop, I noticed a person with a large moustache, who was slicing fish or meat on a table with a large, nasty-looking

[3] Non-Bangali.

knife. At that point, I apprehended that my attempt to join the Liberation War may come to an untimely end and a phrase passed on to me by my brother-in-law, J.R. Khan, 'same side goal', kept flashing through my mind. JR had heard this phrase at a Mohun Bagan–Mohammedan Sporting football match in Calcutta when the Mohammedan's full back had inadvertently turned the ball into his own goal, to be greeted by the cry of 'same side goal'. I was rather bemused to think that here was I, seeking to escape from being shot by the Pakistan army, meeting my end at the hands of my fellow Bangalis, in a remote village whose name I did not know. Apprehending that this situation might yet take a dangerous turn, Mustafa Monwar, with some presence of mind, asked some bystanders if there were any students of Dhaka University in the vicinity and if they were that they should be sent for immediately as they would be sure to establish the identity of their teachers.

Anis and I asked that we be taken before the local leader of the Sangram Parishad. These citizen groups had been set up all over Bangladesh at the call of Bangabandhu to respond to any prospective crackdown by the army. We indicated that we would reveal our identity in confidence to its leader rather than in the middle of a big mob. At that stage, a peon at Oxford University Press, Dhaka, who had identified me from my visits there, spoke up declaring that he recognized me. This persuaded some of the mob leaders to at least wait for the arrival of the SP leaders. We were then taken to the local school by the head of the Sangram Parishad, an AL-er, who had by now arrived on the scene. There we sought to reveal our identity but still had no way of confirming that we were who we claimed to be. Anis, to proclaim his Bangla identity, sang a few verses of *Rabindra Sangeet*, which may have improved our prospects or merely served to soothe our interrogators. Some of the SP members there recognized my name, but it took longer discourse with us for them to finally be convinced that we were the people we claimed to be.

Once our credentials had been established, it was decided that we should go out and address the crowd. As we went out, we came across Mohammed Muqtada, who had been the direct student of Anis and me in the Economics Department at Dhaka University, and his cousin Mofakkher, a student of the History Department. They lived in the next village, and when Mostafa Monwar's message to search out some Dhaka University students had finally reached them, they ran all of several miles to get to us in order to proclaim our identity. Both had immediately assumed that one of the teachers would be their 'Sir' who spoke little Bangla and that consequently his life may be in danger.

Once our bona fides had been firmly established by Muqtada and Mofakkher, we became instant celebrities in the area. We were moved to the house of the local AL leader. At that stage, a rumour began to circulate in the village that Bangabandhu had arrived in the area! Large numbers of people from the area began descending on the place where we were staying. This rumour was eventually dispelled, but any hope of retaining our anonymity had vanished and it was felt that we should move on.

We were told by the local leaders that the village masses had been in a state of alert to apprehend Pakistani saboteurs and paratroopers. The local population had armed themselves with whatever weapons came to hand and were in a state of high vigilance. This again, albeit at our own expense, was reassuring first-hand evidence that the village masses of Bangladesh had in these last four weeks been sufficiently conscientised by Bangabandhu during the March mobilizations to a point where they were willing to engage in an armed struggle, however unequal, against the Pakistan army to defend Bangladesh's sovereignty. Under local leadership, they had mobilized themselves all over the country, but their military capabilities, though heroic, did not look too reassuring. Villagers were standing by in the fields with sharpened bamboo staves to spear Pakistani troops who may be parachuted into the area!

From this area, Muqtada and Mofakkher took us to their nearby village, to the home of Mofakkher's brother, Professor Noman, a professor of English and later Principal of Dhaka College. There it was decided that we should head for Brahmanbaria and should travel late at night by river as there was some apprehension the Pakistan army may be patrolling the rivers. We set out for Brahmanbaria by nauka in the early hours of 31 March accompanied by Muqtada, Mofakkher and his older brother, Mohaddes, who was then working for Radio Pakistan. We bade farewell there to Rashid and Rahmatullah and asked them to take messages back to our families that we were about to cross the border into India.

The nauka which carried us was a sailboat that needed a supporting breeze to determine its speed. When there was no breeze, the boatmen had to debouch onto the riverbank and themselves pull the boat through an attached rope, a process known as *gun tan*. It was a moonless night, deadly quiet, so that a strange tranquility prevailed even though danger hovered around us.

As we travelled through the night down the river, I had time to reflect on my situation. I had abandoned my family, home and all my worldly possessions and had no idea whether I would ever be reunited with them. I felt strangely liberated at having relinquished my material possessions as I now felt I had nothing to lose. But the biggest fear of loss was for my family, where I recognized that unless they were out of harm's way outside Pakistan, I would never feel free or brave enough to fully involve myself in the liberation struggle.

First Encounters with the Liberation Warriors

We landed in Brahmanbaria early in the morning of 31 March. One of the first things we noticed, patrolling the streets of the town, was an army jeep flying the Bangladesh flag. At that time, Brahmanbaria was part of liberated Bangladesh. It appeared that the town was in control of freedom fighters. We were given the opportunity to meet some of them. We took rickshaws to the rest house of Titas Gas Company in Brahmanbaria. Once there, we freshened up and were having tea in the lounge when a handsome man, barely in his thirties, walked in. He wore a smart short-sleeved check shirt, khaki slacks and sported a revolver at his side. He looked more like an action hero from Hollywood than a soldier, but turned out to be Major Khaled Mosharraf, Second in Command of the Fourth East Bengal Regiment, located at Brahmanbaria.

Mosharraf spoke with great confidence. When they heard of the army assault in Dhaka, he had spontaneously arrested their Pakistani commanding officer, Lt Col Yakub Malik and two other officers, who Khaled claimed were now the first prisoners of war in the liberation struggle. He handed them over to the Indian army at Agartala for safe custody, whence they were eventually repatriated, unharmed, to Pakistan with the other Pakistani prisoners of war. Khaled's troops had then moved to establish control over Brahmanbaria, which they were now planning to defend against attack by the Pakistani army forces located in Comilla Cantonment.

Major Mosharraf took us on an inspection of the defences of Brahmanbaria and then, as night approached, took all three of us to his command post which he had set up at the nearby Teliapara Tea Estate that he had taken over. The whole area was in darkness as a precaution against air attack by the Pakistan air force, and armed troops were posted in readiness across the estate. In their headquarters at the garden manager's bungalow, all lights were blacked out. There, Major Mosharraf narrated the odyssey of his battalion and informed us of the massacre of those of his Bangali colleagues who had remained in Comilla Cantonment, where he had originally been based. He was not in close contact with other areas of the resistance and appeared to have only some knowledge from his signals and the radio of the battle in Chittagong and of Ziaur Rahman's two proclamations of independence, the second, in the name of Bangabandhu.

That night at the tea estate we heard together over the radio that overseas Bangalis were trying to collect money to buy arms for the liberation struggle. Mosharraf suggested that we should go across the border and carry their request for the supply of more weaponry to the Indian authorities and should also seek their help in the procurement of arms overseas from funds raised by the *probashi*[4] Bangalis. He felt that while their resistance was strong, the freedom fighters would be outgunned by the Pakistan army if they did not very soon get access to more arms and ammunition.

[4] A Bengali living outside Bengal.

Mosharraf further told me that as of now, he and his officers were in a state of insurgency and, if captured, could be shot as mutineers. He and his forces had once been commissioned into the Pakistan army but now their resistance needed to be legitimized through a proclamation of independence by a legally constituted sovereign civilian authority who could give them directions. He suggested to me that in the name of a sovereign government of Bangladesh, all officers and men of the Bengal Regiment should be recommissioned into the army of an independent Bangladesh. Khaled was in as much ignorance as I was over who could constitute such an authority, but suggested that if I met with any of the elected political leaders, I should communicate this message to them. We were all at that stage deeply impressed by the commitment of these soldiers who had pledged their lives and risked the safety of their families, left behind in the cantonments, to fight for the liberation of Bangladesh.

We spent the night of 31 March in the staff quarters of Teliapara Tea Estate. Early next morning, on 1 April, Major Mosharraf provided us with a jeep to take us across the border to Agartala in Tripura state. It seemed that by then the border had become quite porous and people were moving across it with impunity. I could only feel confident that we were in India when I came across a Sikh guard of the Border Security Force (BSF) that patrolled India's borders.

The Man in the Red Dressing Gown

Once we reached Agartala, we were not sure where to go. I suggested that the most proximate source of authority might be the local DC. As it was still not yet 8:00 a.m., we sought directions to get to the DC's bungalow, which was situated on a hillock. We arrived there to find a rather surprised young man of fair complexion, clad in a red silk dressing gown, sipping his morning tea on the verandah of his bungalow. He was not too surprised to see these Bangladeshi professors as he had already had some exposure to the hordes of Bangladeshis steaming across the border seeking shelter, food and, in some cases, arms, to fight the Pakistanis. He told us that he was an IAS officer from northern India and had only just been posted to Agartala as DC. He felt quite helpless at this sudden, fairly traumatic disturbance in the routine of a DC. He had little idea on how to cope with this onrush of Bangalis, let alone respond to their request for arms to fight the Pakistan army, and had been making frantic efforts to seek guidance from Delhi. He felt that those who could speak for Bangladesh should instantly fly to Delhi in order to make contact with the Indian leadership. He told us that he had heard that some Bangladeshi leaders might be flying to Delhi that evening escorted by the CM of Tripura and that we should immediately connect with these leaders who were holed up at the Agartala stadium along with a large contingent of Bangladeshi refugees.

We bade farewell to the DC and headed for the stadium. By a strange coincidence, I ran into this same DC and his family in 1973 at a ferry crossing between Comilla and Dhaka, where he was headed from Agartala to a newly liberated Bangladesh on a vacation. We exchanged nostalgic greetings as I welcomed him to a now independent Bangladesh in whose emergence he too had contributed. We never met again, but the image of that young man, in his red silk dressing gown, has remained, through all these years, embedded in my memory.

Engaging with Our Allies

In Quest of Leaders

At the sports stadium, we met M.R. Siddiqi, Taheruddin Thakur and a number of other AL MPs, student and workers from the districts of Chittagong, Noakhali and Comilla. Among them was

Captain Amin Ahmed Chowdhury who had been one of the few Bangali soldiers who had managed to escape from the Dhaka Cantonment. The group at the stadium were in some state of shock, looking more in need of relief than as the forerunners of a resistance struggle. Siddiqi confirmed the DC's information that he, Thakur and advocate Sirajul Huq of Comilla, subsequently the Chief Prosecutor in the Bangabandhu murder case, were flying that evening to Delhi with the CM of Tripura to put the facts of the genocide before the Indian government and to request help so that the resistance could be sustained. I learnt from Siddiqi that he had no knowledge whether other AL leaders were alive or their whereabouts. He himself had been involved in organizing resistance at Chittagong and had only just come over to Tripura to seek military assistance to enable the defence of Chittagong to survive.

At the meeting with Siddiqi and Thakur, it appeared that they themselves had never visited Delhi and knew few people of consequence there. They felt that the contacts that Anis and I had with some eminent Indian economists might help in securing an effective hearing for the Bangladesh cause. I offered to write a letter of introduction for the group to Ashok Mitra or P.N. Dhar, two eminent economists now close to the centres of power in Delhi. Siddiqi suggested it might be more productive if we joined them on the flight to Delhi that same evening. Thakur dropped out to make way for the two of us. We were escorted on the flight by the CM. We flew from Agartala to Calcutta and then took a connecting flight to Delhi. To appear more presentable for such a historic mission, Anis and I, who both looked quite dishevelled, bathed, shaved and had to be fitted out in borrowed punjabis and pyjamas, which were the only assets we carried with us on the flight from Agartala to Delhi.

On the flight, I chatted with Siddiqi, who I had last met in Kamal's residence on the eve of the Liberation War. I knew him as a decent, capable businessman who, as the son-in-law of A.K. Khan, had been more associated with business than politics. Siddiqi filled me in on the battle for Chittagong and gave me an account of the now politically contested issue of the declaration of independence. He indicated that the first declaration by the local

AL leader Hannan, made from a local relay station with a weak transmitter, was barely audible. Local party people requested Major Ziaur Rahman—whose force had by that point taken control of the Radio Pakistan station at Kalurghat—to make an announcement of the declaration of independence by Bangabandhu. However, Zia in his first broadcast omitted any reference to Bangabandhu and proclaimed himself as President, which confused everybody, as Zia at that time was an unknown army major who had no authority to broadcast such a historic message. A.K. Khan and M.R. Siddiqi, thereafter, prepared a fresh draft of the proclamation of independence in the name of Bangabandhu that was rebroadcast the next day by Zia.

The current controversy over who declared independence is thus a somewhat meaningless exercise as, at that time, only one person's declaration could convey both legitimacy and authority before the people of Bangladesh and the rest of the world—Bangabandhu Sheikh Mujibur Rahman. In my subsequent meetings with Zia, first in Calcutta in 1971 and subsequently in Dhaka between 1972 and 1975, he never once made reference to being the proclaimer of independence, nor did he ever make such a claim to the nation during his lifetime.

Siddiqi, a thorough gentleman, who was by nature a modest and rather reticent person, shared with me his discomfort at having to present himself to Indira Gandhi as a leader of the AL who was qualified to speak on behalf of the Bangladesh liberation struggle. He claimed he was only the district president of Chittagong AL. He had been compelled to assume the mantle of leadership as the CM of Tripura needed a Bangladeshi political leader of some standing to be by his side as they negotiated Delhi's direct support for the liberation struggle that had spilled over into his state. Siddiqi confirmed that he had no idea who among the AL leadership was alive or how they would react to his assumption of the role of spokesman before the Indian government. I attempted to persuade Siddiqi that this was not the time for demonstrations of personal modesty as the Indian leadership needed to meet someone who could speak with authority on behalf of Bangladesh and he was the closest such figure at hand. I am not sure if Siddiqi actually met Indira Gandhi, as this responsibility was lifted from his shoulders once Tajuddin Ahmed made his appearance in Delhi.

FIRs

On landing in Delhi on the night of 1 April 1971, Anis and I accompanied the CM and our colleagues to the state guest house of Tripura, where we were expected to stay. When we reached the guest house, I managed to obtain the home phone number and called my Cambridge classmate Amartya Sen, who was at that time a Professor at the DSE. He was surprised and much relieved to hear from us, fearing we were both dead. He and his wife Nabaneeta, immediately drove over to Tripura House and took us to their residence near the Delhi University campus located in Old Delhi. That night we had our first hot bath and a relaxed meal in three days. Nabaneeta prescribed us sleeping pills, which ensured a good night's sleep.

The next morning, 2 April, Amartya took us to the Lodhi Estate residence of Dr Ashok Mitra, later Finance Minister in the CPM government in West Bengal, who was then the Economic Adviser in the Ministry of Finance, Government of India. On hearing our narrative of events, Mitra immediately called up Professor P.N. Dhar, a well-known academic economist, who had recently taken over as Secretary to the PM of India, to come over and meet us. To Dhar, Anis and I provided a full account, as best known to us, of the background to the genocide, the accounts of the massacres in Dhaka and the state of the resistance by the people of Bangladesh. Dhar felt that our narrative needed to be heard at the highest level.

That same evening, Ashok Mitra drove us to the residence of Mr P.N. Haksar, then the Principal Secretary to the PM. Haksar, a former diplomat, was a leftist of the old school. As a student in London in the 1930s, he had campaigned, alongside Krishna Menon, for the independence of India. Haksar was a person of exceptional intelligence and erudition, informed by a profound sense of history. We repeated our narrative of events to Haksar, who was deeply moved by our story. I thought I detected some tears of emotion in his eyes. He came across as a person of considerable authority as well as commitment and indicated that he would immediately convey this intelligence as well as the urgent need for support to the Bangladesh cause to Indira Gandhi. As Haksar was reported—due to his proximity to Indira Gandhi—to be the second most powerful person in India at that time, we felt comforted that Bangladesh had acquired an invaluable friend in our forthcoming struggle.

Since that historic encounter, I remained friends with Haksar up to his passing in the late 1990s and invariably called on him at his home in Santiniketan whenever I was in Delhi. In his later years, he lost his beloved wife and later his eyesight and had become rather disillusioned with the passage of events in both India and the world. He, however, remained deeply interested in Bangladesh. Our meditative conversations never failed to educate and inspire me. I was much comforted when his no less committed activist daughter, Nandita Haksar, was invited to Dhaka in March 2012 to receive an award on behalf of her father from the Government of Bangladesh in recognition for his services to our war of liberation. Haksar's confidential papers have been recently made available and have served as an important resource for recent books on the emergence of Bangladesh by Bass and particularly Raghavan. Regrettably, I could not draw on these papers while I was writing this memoir.

We are not sure if our encounters with Dhar and Haksar were the first full account of the background to the Liberation War that had been communicated to the upper reaches of the Government of India. Haksar's reactions suggested that this was his first such exposure to these events. I recollect that both Anis and I were surprised at how little was known by the highest levels of the Government of India of the specifics of the drama unfolding next door that had culminated in the launch of a genocide by the Pakistan army. The idea of a pre-planned Indian conspiracy to break up Pakistan appeared to us, from our direct exposure to the responses of those in authority in India, to be a figment of the Pakistani imagination.

Around the time, Anis and I were briefing Haksar Tajuddin Ahmad, accompanied by Barrister Amirul Islam, also reached Delhi.[5] However, Amirul Islam informs me that they did not meet Indira Gandhi until the evening of 3 April, which is now also confirmed by Raghavan in his recent book. Once Tajuddin reached Delhi, he was clearly the best person to speak authoritatively on behalf of the Bangladesh movement. However, when he arrived in Delhi, this may not have been so obvious to the Indian leadership who appeared not to have heard of, let alone know of any major political figure from Bangladesh apart from Sheikh Mujibur Rahman, who was in any case, now a globally recognized figure.

Recognizing Bangladesh's First PM

I had some indication of this lack of knowledge about Bangladesh's political leaders. On the morning after I met Haksar, Anis and I were asked by some Indian officials sent by Haksar to accompany them to a house somewhere in Delhi, where we were surprised and delighted to meet Tajuddin Ahmed. But it took us some time to identify a clean-shaven, handsome, young man who was also there. This turned out to be none other than Amirul Islam, sans his famous piratical beard that he had shaved off in order to disguise himself. My first feeling after meeting Tajuddin was one of overwhelming relief that the person, who I felt was the best qualified to speak for Bangladesh after Bangabandhu, had now arrived in Delhi and could interact with full authority with the Indian leadership.

What occurred to me somewhat later was that both of us may possibly have been taken to the house to provide further authentication as to the identity of Tajuddin whose face was unknown to the Indian leaders. Tajuddin's first possible contact and even visit to India was on the morning of 30 March 1971 when he stepped

[5] Srinath Raghavan. 2013. *1971: A Global History of the Creation of Bangladesh.* Cambridge: Harvard University Press.

across the border at Kushtia in the company of Amirul Islam. Two of my students—Towfiq Elahi Chowdhury, then the SDO (Subdivisional Officer), Meherpur, and Mahbubuddin Ahmed, SDPO (Subdivisional Police Officer), Chuadanga, located on the Kushtia border with India—had actively joined the liberation struggle and had already established contact with the BSF across the border. Having received Tajuddin and Amir, they were in a position to introduce them to the local BSF commander.

In my meeting with Haksar, he had enquired about the potential leaders from the AL who could provide leadership to a liberation struggle in the absence of a towering figure such as Bangabandhu. I had observed, without any knowledge of his concurrent arrival in Delhi, that Tajuddin could possibly play such a role and briefed Haksar on the full political biodata of Tajuddin, including the high trust invested in him by Bangabandhu. Given the lack of information of the Indian authorities on Bangladesh's political dramatis personae, I had to invest some time on educating Haksar on the who's who of Bangladesh politics. Haksar must have known of Tajuddin's presence in Delhi but had not yet met him and needed to know more about him before he could advise his PM on her interactions with the prospective leaders of Bangladesh's Liberation War.

We should keep in mind that at that stage in time, the Indians were far from clear as to the course of our liberation struggle and whether all the principal political elements engaged in the struggle had the stamina and commitment to fight on until independence was attained. They were particularly apprehensive over the issue of who would lead the struggle in the absence of Bangabandhu and whether such a leader would command the capability as well as authority to sustain such a struggle.

At our first encounter, Tajuddin told me that he himself had no knowledge about which of his colleagues were alive. He told me how he and later Amirul Islam along with Dr Kamal Hossain had met Bangabandhu on the night of 25 March, after the reports of imminent army movements had come in, and had tried to persuade him to accompany them to a more secure place. But Bangabandhu had refused to accompany them and advised them to go underground and carry on the struggle for an independent Bangladesh. Tajuddin and Islam had parted company with Kamal Hossain, who apprehended that three of them, moving together, would be a more conspicuous target for the Pakistan army. Kamal had accordingly asked to be dropped off at the Dhanmondi residence of one of his relations, from where he would then rendezvous with them. Tajuddin and Islam had taken refuge in Old Dhaka.

As Kamal could not reconnect with Tajuddin and Amir, the two had subsequently made their way across the border via Kushtia on 30 March, where they were eventually received by Golok Majumdar, a senior official of the BSF who drove them to Calcutta airport in the evening to meet his boss, K.K. Rustamji, who had flown in from Delhi to meet them. After intensive debriefing by Rustamji, Tajuddin and Amir were flown to Delhi on 1 April and ensconced in a BSF safe house where I subsequently met them, on the morning of 3 April, the day after I met Haksar.[6]

Tajuddin was scheduled to meet Indira Gandhi on the evening of 3 April. The Indian authorities, it appears, needed at least two days to persuade themselves that Tajuddin was the appropriate person with whom the PM of India could initiate a serious conversation about the course of our liberation struggle. I spent the remainder of the day with him and Amir, discussing his prospective strategy at this historic meeting with the PM and the eventual course of action and support we may expect from India.

Of immediate importance was the issue of the political identity that Tajuddin should assume in his meeting with Indira. I conveyed to him the concern registered by Haksar in our meeting of the previous evening on who could assume a leadership role in the absence of Bangabandhu. Amir and I advised Tajuddin that this was no moment for self-doubt. He was manifestly the best equipped to lead the struggle, given his intimate association with Bangabandhu and the role he had already assumed in running the Bangladesh administration in March. I alerted him that I had argued before

[6] Srinath Raghavan. *1971: A Global History.*

Haksar about his qualifications and authority to be recognized as the interim leader of the liberation struggle so we should do nothing to introduce ambiguity over his credentials. I imagine that my modest and unsolicited role in this small historical cameo would not have endeared me to those from among his party who subsequently contested Tajuddin's assumption of leadership.

While we were in the safe house with Tajuddin, we were deeply disturbed to hear over the radio that Kamal Hossain had just been captured by the Pakistan army. However by then, we were also getting news that one by one, members of the AL high command had been making their way across the border. Tajuddin Ahmed was thus anxious to fly immediately to the border to meet with his colleagues whereby they could collectively constitute the government of an independent Bangladesh to give leadership to the Liberation War.

Once Tajuddin learnt that his senior colleagues had reached India, he became even more concerned about projecting himself as the principal spokesman for the liberation struggle. He pointed out that in the AL party hierarchy, he was the General Secretary of the provincial AL while Syed Nazrul Islam was the vice president of the national party. Other leaders such as Khondkar Mushtaq, Qamruzzaman and Mansoor Ali may also feel they outranked him, so any assumption of leadership by him would be resented. Tajuddin's apprehensions were subsequently validated when he met them on his return from Delhi, where they challenged his right to project himself as a prospective PM. Nazrul Islam, having been proclaimed as Acting President of the Mujibnagar government, was more reconciled to Tajuddin's elevation but Mushtaq remained mightily displeased.

The critical issue at that time was to proclaim an independent Bangladesh State before the world led by an elected government. In order to proclaim such a government, we felt that a formal proclamation of independence should be drafted. The declaration of independence authorized by Bangabandhu that had been transmitted over the radio at Chittagong—first by Abdul Hannan of the AL and then by Major Ziaur Rahman—now had to be incorporated into a formal proclamation of independence.

Along with Amirul Islam, I was entrusted by Tajuddin Ahmed with the task of drafting the independence proclamation. Amirul, by virtue of his qualifications as a barrister, took on the substantive responsibility for preparing the declaration and with subsequent inputs from some senior lawyers in Kolkata, such as Barrister Subroto Roy Chowdhury, completed this historic task. As far as I was concerned, I can only lay claim to two inputs that found their way into the eventual proclamation. As I recollect, I suggested the insertion of 'Peoples' into the proclamation of the 'Republic of Bangladesh', inspired as much by my ideological predilections as by a recognition, shared by all three of us present, that if a liberated Bangladesh was to emerge, it would do so as the end product of a people's struggle. My other input came—thanks to my encounter with Khaled Mosharraf, who had insisted that such a declaration of independence must formally recommission all those Bangali soldiers fighting the war—as soldiers in the service of an independent Bangladesh. The declaration accordingly commissioned the sector commanders, who were leading the struggle across Bangladesh, to serve as commissioned officers of the Bangladesh army. Beyond these two modest contributions to our constitutional history, I claim no further role.

As there was scant knowledge or awareness across the world about the background and immediate circumstances leading to our liberation struggle, I suggested that we prepare a separate statement setting out the background to the proclamation. Tajuddin requested me to prepare such a statement. I undertook this task with some trepidation as this was also likely to be a historic document.

I took some pains over the preparation of this declaration and was in a position to have the accuracy of its factual contents checked by Tajuddin. I had to be somewhat guarded in my use of language as I did not want my identity to be recognized through the draft because my writings in *Forum* and other publications had been widely read in Pakistan, including its intelligence agencies. I remember eliminating a concluding para in the draft because it sounded too recognizable as my style, where I warned the people of Pakistan that the same fate awaited them at the hands of this army if they succeeded in crushing our struggle. Happily, my first draft on the background to the events was kept intact and presented to the world, as the declaration broadcasted by Tajuddin Ahmad, PM of an independent Bangladesh, after the swearing-in ceremony of his government at a mango grove in Kushtia on 17 April, which is now known as Mujibnagar. One of the phrases in the statement that has since been frequently quoted, "Pakistan lies dead and buried under a mountain of corpses," reflected concisely my sentiments at that time and constituted the basis of all my subsequent actions.

16

Fulfilment: Envoy Extraordinaire

Mandate from the PM

Defining My Mission

While I was with Tajuddin and Amir, we heard over the BBC that M.M. Ahmed, Economic Adviser to Yahya Khan, was flying to Washington on an emergency mission to seek renewed aid from the consortium of aid donors to Pakistan. Tajuddin felt that any attempt to finance Pakistan's war machine through aid must be resisted with all the political resources at our disposal. I was accordingly commissioned by Tajuddin to proceed to London and Washington as fast as I could to initiate a campaign on behalf of the Bangladeshi government to seek the stoppage of aid to Pakistan by its principal donors. My second brief was to persuade all Bangali officers serving in the diplomatic missions of Pakistan to defect and proclaim allegiance to the Government of Bangladesh. My particular target was the mission in the USA, where some of the most able of the Bangali service holders were located. Their defection would be of tremendous political value as well as service to the Bangladesh cause.

Tajuddin requested Haksar to arrange for my travel to the UK and USA as his special envoy. My credentials as his envoy were rather theoretical as neither had the Bangladesh government yet been established nor was Tajuddin its anointed PM. My initial diplomatic career in the service of Bangladesh was thus entirely self-proclaimed and needed large dollops of chutzpah to be carried off. We were, however, much encouraged by reports of the response of probashi Bangalis all over the world who were rallying to the Bangladesh cause, demanding global action to stop the genocide in Bangladesh while also seeking recognition for our sovereignty and were raising funds in support of the liberation struggle.

Shortly after our encounter, Tajuddin and Amir flew back to Kolkata to establish contact with his various colleagues, who had now come across the border, so that they could begin the task of constituting a government and assuming leadership of the Liberation War. While I waited for my travel arrangements to be completed, I stayed with Ashok Mitra and attempted to quietly engage with those Indians, at the political as well as academic level, who were better positioned to be more serviceable to the Bangladesh cause.

Considering our close proximity to India, I found few people in Delhi who were knowledgeable about our affairs or had heard of any Bangladeshi apart from Bangabandhu. Furthermore, it should be remembered that in those early days of April 1971, Indians at various levels, however outraged they may have been at Pakistan's genocide, were far from convinced that Bangladeshis were fully committed to fight a war of liberation to its conclusion nor were they persuaded that this was a realistic aspiration. My initial exercise in public education, thus, involved meetings with senior media people such as George Verghese, Kuldip Nayar, Inder Malhotra, Pran Chopra, Ajit Bhattacharjee and others who were best positioned to propagate the Bangladesh case before the Indian people. This task was readily assumed by these media giants who remained steadfast in their loyalty to the Bangladesh cause throughout the Liberation War.

Haksar suggested I should reach out to the USSR government to persuade them to support our cause and suggested I meet the Soviet Ambassador, Pegov, a senior figure in the diplomatic corp. As Salma was still in Dhaka, I was not keen to expose myself to the prying eyes of the Pakistani intelligence services who we, perhaps exaggeratedly, presumed to be everywhere. P.N. Dhar, therefore, set up an early morning appointment for me with Pegov and agreed to personally drive me to the Embassy and pick me up after an hour. This cloak-and-dagger enterprise went off with clockwork efficiency and I spent a productive hour with the Ambassador where a full account of our situation as well as the importance that the People's Republic of Bangladesh attached to a strong relationship with the USSR was conveyed to Pegov. The Ambassador appeared both impressed with my argument and emotionally moved by Bangladesh's circumstances and promised to convey the message to his leaders in Moscow.

USSR subsequently emerged as one of the most powerful voices against the genocide of the Pakistan army and eventually took the momentous political decision to stand by India when Indira Gandhi finally committed her government's full support to Bangladesh's liberation struggle. The Indo-Soviet Treaty of Peace, Friendship and Cooperation signed in August 1971 was a landmark event in the liberation of Bangladesh as it militarily insulated India from any possible intervention by China in support of Pakistan. These historic decisions emerged out of the geostrategic compulsions of the relevant countries. My initial encounter with Ambassador Pegov on an April morning in 1971 was perhaps one of the first tiny steps in setting these historic events in motion.

P.N. Dhar subsequently put me in touch with Clovis Maksoud, who was then Ambassador for the Arab League, later to represent them at the UN. Clovis, a socialist by persuasion, was thought to be amenable to indoctrination about the emergence of an independent Bangladesh as part of the anti-imperialist struggle. Tajuddin had been worried that Pakistan would invoke the support of the Islamic countries including Iran, then under the Shah, to rally round to preserve the integrity of the then largest Islamic State. We therefore needed to build a bridgehead in the Arab world and Clovis Maksoud was seen as a prospective ally. Clovis may have shared some of my views, but I suspect in those days he had little influence among Arab leaders who remained lukewarm, if not outright hostile, to the Bangladesh cause during 1971.

While I was at Ashok's, Nurul Islam arrived from Bangladesh, looking much the worse for wear. He had been escorted to the border by our guides, Rashid and Rahmatullah, and was accompanied on his journey by Obeid Jagirdar, a politically oriented businessman, and the painter Debdas Chakraborty. They had been exposed to the added hazard of being strafed by Pakistani Sabre jets while passing through Narsingdi and Nurul was much shaken up. He had left his family behind in the care of Daniel Thorner, who remained behind in Dhaka and had promised to personally escort his wife Chuni, and her children, Roumeen and Naeem, out of Pakistan. Nurul was keen to get out of India and to the USA and was in correspondence with professional colleagues there to find him an academic billet. This was eventually provided by Yale University, which had a strong PIDE connection through Gus Ranis and Mark Leiserson who had preceded Nurul as Directors. Nurul eventually departed for the USA but not without some drama when he found that his Pan Am flight from Delhi had been routed through Karachi. He feared he would be detained at the airport and eventually managed to board a more congenial flight to the USA.

Nurul and Anis shared one guest room at Ashok's while I occupied the other room. Anis, in my memory, was quite understandably becoming increasingly concerned over the fate of Dora and their daughters, particularly after he learnt of Nurul Islam's airborne hazards in his crossing of the border. Anis suffered from some intestinal disorder possibly brought on by tension and ate little, subsisting mostly on diluted khichri prepared by Gouri, the wife of Ashok Mitra, who had established herself as the Florence Nightingale of her small brood of fugitive Bangali economists. For a while, Anis spoke little and confined himself to his room, writing a diary of his experiences. He eventually took himself to Kolkata to wait for his family but gave this up and proceeded to the USA through the intervention of academic friends such as Wassily Leontief, his PhD supervisor at Harvard, and Gus Papanek. Dora and their two daughters were eventually taken across the border all the way to Kolkata by Rosebu, from whence they eventually joined Anis in the USA.

First Stop in Paris

My air ticket was eventually arranged for a flight to Washington DC, routed through Paris, London and New York. I needed to visit Paris to touch base with my brother Farooq who was posted there as Second Secretary in the Pakistan Embassy. I departed Delhi around mid-April with a wardrobe of borrowed clothes supplied by my friend Arjun Sengupta, by then back in residence at the DSE, which included a brown Harris tweed coat that served as my combat uniform throughout 1971. I was provided by friends with the princely sum of £30 to serve as pocket money and hoped to survive off the land as I went along.

I arrived in Paris unannounced and headed for Rue de Bellechasse, where my brother Farooq lived. When I knocked at their door, Nasreen, his wife, greeted me with some amazement, as I was then a fugitive with some rumours in circulation of my untimely demise. Farooq had left for office, so she called him and simply asked him to come home as there was a domestic emergency. The knowledge that he was harbouring a fugitive of the government he served would have come as a bit of shock to S.K. Dehlavi, the Pakistan Ambassador in Paris who, ironically, happened to be an old friend of my late father. I did not have much to do in Paris but wanted to touch base with my brother prior to moving to London and then Washington. I rang up my friend Neville Maxwell in London and alerted him that I was alive and more to the point, that I was expecting refuge from him and his Uruguayan wife, Evelyn, in their Highgate home.

At Heathrow, I was received by Neville and Evelyn, who were warm and also helpful hosts during my stay with them for the next few weeks. I have already mentioned how in the 1960s, I had come to know Neville both as a personal friend and as a former newspaperman. When Neville had served as the Delhi-based correspondent of the *London Times*, he had, along with Selig Harrison of *The Washington Post*, hypothesized that the seeds of disintegration were present within the South Asian nation states. On his periodic visits to Dhaka, Neville had been sufficiently influenced by me and other Bangalis, to believe that this disintegration was likely to be initiated by the break-up of Pakistan. As my presence in London now gave substance to his cherished theory, almost as part of a self-fulfilling prophecy, his professional instincts were stimulated by my presence, particularly because I was fresh from the battlefront in Bangladesh.

I was keen for my sister-in-law, Sarvath, in Amman to use all her influence to get Salma and our boys out of Pakistan, as I felt deeply inhibited about surfacing in public as long as they were there. I had called Sarvath from Paris, and she had already advised me that Salma was expected soon. Salma eventually reached Amman when I was in London, staying with Neville. When I heard her voice over the phone and talked to the boys in Amman, it was as if a boulder had rolled off my chest, and I went a bit berserk in the aggressive way in which I openly entered the political arena in London.

In Paris, I had maintained a virtually invisible profile. The only person I visited was Alice Thorner in her apartment on Rue Guy de Labrosse. She had come out leaving her husband Daniel behind in Dhaka, where he was determined to do what he could to get some of his colleagues at PIDE, Dhaka, out of the country. In that period, Daniel was instrumental in getting Nurul Islam's family out of Dhaka to the USA and then bringing Hasan Imam, a research economist of PIDE, with him to Paris, where he gave him refuge until Hasan Imam's wife and daughter could join him. Daniel had, on his way out of Pakistan, travelled to Delhi, where he had activated his old leftist Indian contacts, now in high places, with the likes of P.N. Haksar, D.P. Dhar and Ashok Mitra. In Delhi, Daniel came across our friend Muyeedul Hasan whom he had met in our company in Dhaka and provided him *entré* into the power centres of the Indira regime. When I was in Paris, Daniel was still in Dhaka. I did, however, brief Alice to present her story on Bangladesh to the French press.

Early Footsteps in Diplomacy

In London, I sought out Justice Abu Sayeed Chowdhury in his North London house, as he had been the first major Bangali figure outside Pakistan to declare himself for the Bangladesh cause. As he was on a visit to London and had his whole family with him, he was a free agent to act boldly. His presence became the rallying ground for the UK probashi Bangalis and was probably crucial in building and maintaining a façade of unity in the highly fractured and quarrelsome community. Without his presence, there is little doubt that the internal political and personal differences within the UK Bengalis would have come to full flower through speaking out in many, and no doubt discordant, voices. His eminence could subsume these divisive trends so that whatever may have been the less publicized internecine quarrels, publicly we tended to speak with one voice.

In London, I touched base with my journalist friends such as Martin Woollacott, Peter Preston and Mark Arnold-Forster at *The Guardian*. Mark, who was then a senior presence in *The Guardian*, not only let me write a short piece on Bangladesh but gave extensive exposure to the events. Martin Woollacott had been in Dhaka at the time of the crackdown and had then, and in subsequent visits to Bangladesh, exposed quite effectively, the crimes of the Pakistan army. Through Neville, the *Times* had also hosted a piece from me, while *The New Statesman*, where I think at that time, Richard Crossman, a former cabinet minister in the Labour government, was the Editor, also gave us good coverage.

The Labour Party was, ab initio, sympathetic to the Bangladesh cause. Another journalist friend, Brian Lapping, put me in touch with the Foreign Policy Committee of the Labour Party, and I had an intensive and fruitful session with this group followed by a personal meeting with their shadow Foreign Secretary, Dennis Healy. The Labour Party was, from that period, fully sold to the Bangladesh cause, and some of the alumni of that first meeting in late April, such as John Stonehouse and Toby Jessup, became vocal spokesmen on the issue in the House of Commons. I had also managed to meet Judith Hart, who was the Labour Party spokeswoman on Foreign Aid. She received me at her home in Richmond and after that meeting, took the lead in supporting a private member's bill, sponsored by Stonehouse for stopping aid to Pakistan.

Unfortunately, for us, the Tories were in office. I was keen to meet the then Foreign Secretary, Lord Home. I entertained such expectations on account of the fact that Home had been a close friend of Salma's parents and had not only attended our wedding in 1962 in Regent's Park Islamic Centre but had been one of the signatories to our marriage document. Furthermore, Home's then Private Secretary was Nicholas Barrington, who was known to me from his tenure at the Pakistan High Commission in Islamabad. Unfortunately, neither family friendships nor Nicholas could get me an interview with the good Lord, who was conscious of the protocols involved in trafficking with a representative of a separatist movement threatening the integrity of a fellow member of the Commonwealth. Nicholas did however ensure that Home had a full exposure to our position.

Another route used to access the Tory high command was through Douglas Dodds-Parker, another close friend of my in-laws, who was an influential Tory MP with impeccable connections. My own pioneering efforts were of course greatly strengthened by the full mobilization of the Bangali community in the UK, so that by May we had virtually the entire British press on our side, the Labour Party committed to stoppage of aid and the Tory's sufficiently constrained from endorsing aid flows to Pakistan at the Paris consortium meeting.

In London, I came to see a good bit of Tassaduq Ahmed, whose office room above The Ganges Restaurant in Gerrard Street, Soho, became my campaign headquarters. Tassaduq was an old-time leftist who had been actively involved with Hamza Alavi in the 'Campaign for Restoration of Democracy in Pakistan' during the 1960s, from where I came to know him and his German wife Rosemarie, quite well. During 1971, Tassaduq was particularly helpful in bringing me together with a variety of people from

Bangali activists of all classes, to local journalists and British activists such as John Stonehouse and Donald Chesworth, who was a well-known social worker.

Tassaduq managed to set up meetings for me at his office with historic subcontinental figures such as Wali Khan, who was in London claiming to be opposing Yahya's actions in Bangladesh. Again at The Ganges, I met the historic Naga leader Phizo, in the expectation that through him we could persuade the Chinese to qualify their support for Pakistan and accept the Bangladesh liberation struggle as an authentic freedom struggle rather than a part of India's regional ambitions. The dialogue with Phizo did not get too far as he argued, largely through his daughter, that he would help us with the Chinese if the Bangladesh leadership could, in turn, persuade Delhi to grant independence to Nagaland. This rather surreal exchange, carried out in the midst of the grocery provisions of The Ganges Restaurant, was rendered even more bizarre by the fact that Phizo suffered from a rare ocular disorder whereby his eyeball tended to slip out of its socket and then had to be pushed back again by hand. By the end of our exchanges, which focused on the Naga's right to national liberation, my own attention had been totally distracted by Phizo's unstable eyeball and I hurriedly terminated the exchange before his eyeball ended up amidst the vegetables and spices in the Ganges storeroom.

During that initial sojourn in London, Tassaduq alerted me about a breaking story that would transform the whole British public perspective on the liberation struggle. This turned out to be the famous exposé by *The Sunday Times* of the Pakistani army's atrocities in Comilla and Noakhali written by Anthony (Tony) Mascarenhas who had been eyewitness to these events. I did not then know much about Tony beyond the fact that he was a Karachi-based Goan journalist with a reputation for having close links with MI. This, no doubt, earned him his tour with the homicidal Pakistani officers who felt free to gun down Bangali civilians in cold blood in the presence of a well known journalist. Mascarenhas, who was a Pakistani national, sensibly negotiated with *The Sunday Times* that as his life would not be worth a cent in Pakistan once his story broke in the *Times*, its management should guarantee safe exit and asylum in Britain for him and his family as well as a regular job with *The Sunday Times*. This seemed a modest price for the story of the year, which could give eyewitness accounts of these Pakistani killers in full cry, and *The Sunday Times* gladly paid it.

Through Tassaduq, I got to meet Mascarenhas shortly after the story broke. When I met him at the Ganges, he was in residence in London and on the way to securing a British passport. During our meeting, he shared further details of his gruesome adventures that did not reach the *Times*. Shortly after Liberation, we appeared together on a Bangladesh television programme, filmed in Dhaka, one of the few they did in English. We met again in Oxford around 1977 when he turned up with a film where he had interviewed Col Farooq Rahman, one of Bangabandhu's self-confessed killers. In that film he had placed on record Farooq's confession about planning and carrying through the murder. This film was, I believe, an important piece of evidence used by the prosecution in the trial of Farooq, so that Mascarenhas, now demised, could bear witness from the grave in sending Farooq to the gallows.

New York: Rediscovering Old Friends

My initial stint in London was a prelude to my invasion of the USA, which was my primary destination as commissioned by Tajuddin. I landed in New York wearing Arjun Sengupta's brown tweed jacket, a grey trouser I had acquired in London and other borrowed garb that made me look like a walking ad for a jumble sale. I was to spend a night in New York before moving on to Washington D.C. I could only afford a cheap room in a hotel near Times Square but was able to indulge myself by renewing my appetite for the excellent beef frankfurters on offer at Nathan's which was down the street. I had gone into a nearby Woolworths store on Times Square to make some purchases when I was greeted by my Indian nom de guerre, Mohan Lal. Who do I see looking happily relaxed, smiling, but Anisur Rahman and not far behind him Nurul Islam, looking much less haunted and hunted than he did in Lodhi Estate. I am not quite sure what brought them to New York. They had both headed for the USA from Delhi and their good cheer owed to the fact that Daniel Thorner had managed to get Nurul's wife and two children out of Pakistan. As Daniel tells us, this was an adventure not far removed from spiriting Resistance fighters away under the nose of the Gestapo, particularly as Daniel suspected anyone who came near the Islam family at Dhaka airport of being an agent of the Pakistanis.

Dora and her two daughters had come out of Dhaka the hard way. Rosebu, Shidu Mian's wife, personally escorted them to Agartala and reached them to Calcutta, where Anis caught up with them. The Rahmans were now together as a family in the USA, where Anis had been offered a fellowship at Williams College. Nurul had been offered a similar appointment at Yale. The old boys' network of the economists served us well, though in the case of both Anis and Nurul, their professional credentials were such that offers of fellowships were doing them no favours. During their stay in the USA, both Nurul and Anis remained active in their various ways, on behalf of the Bangladesh cause.

In New York, I also ran into Haroun-er-Rashid. This was over-straining the bounds of coincidence for me to meet three close friends by sheer happenstance within 24 hours. I took this as a good omen. Haroun had indeed been in school with me in Aitchison College, Lahore, and was also in Cambridge. Around 1970, he had landed a job with the World Bank and I had stayed with him in their home in McLean in Virginia when I visited Washington on my way back from the famous Rochester conference in 1970. Haroun had from the beginning, become active on behalf of the Bangladesh cause and throughout 1971 served as a mole of the liberation movement in the World Bank. During 1971, even though he was an employee of the Bank, most of his energy appeared to have been invested in working for Bangladesh. He had recently been sent out by the Bangladeshi community in Washington to visit Calcutta and make contract with the Mujibnagar government.

Washington D.C.: A Spokesman for Bangladesh

Discharging Tajuddin's Mandate

When I met Haroun in New York, he had just returned from Calcutta. We travelled together to DC and were received at the airport by Abul Mal Abdul Muhith. As Muhith was a senior diplomat at the Pakistan Embassy, his public meeting with a now proclaimed offender such as me was a potentially hazardous act as long as he remained in the mission. I moved in with Haroun at his home in McLean, where I spent the next month, using his living room divan as my bedroom, his phone as my point of contact, his car as my taxi and his office in the Bank as my campaign headquarters.

That very night, the Bangali community in the Washington Embassy assembled at the home of Enayat Karim, to meet their first emissary from the Mujibnagar government. This somewhat overstated my credentials, as at the time I left Delhi, the government had not yet been constituted so that all I had was Tajuddin's verbal command that I should set out for Washington, frustrate M.M. Ahmed's mission to solicit aid from the donor's consortium and particularly the USA, organize the defection of the Bangladeshis in the embassies in Washington and New York, and while I was about it, I was to convey his message to the US government to recognize the sovereignty of Bangladesh. This somewhat improbable mission was to be accomplished by a 36-year-old Reader in Economics at Dhaka University, wearing borrowed clothes, with $30 in his pocket and a reputation for being the most undiplomatic economist in South Asia!

The audience assembled to meet me at Enayat Karim's was indeed a blue-ribbon gathering. Enayat Karim was the Deputy Chief of Mission in the Pakistan Embassy in Washington. He was one of our brightest officers in the Foreign Service and would have soon made Ambassador. Next to Karim, S.A.M.S. Kibria, another of our proudest sons, was Counsellor (Political Affairs) in the Mission. While Enayat and Kibria were both in the PFS, Muhith, who was in the Civil Service, was on secondment to the Washington Embassy as Counsellor (Economics). Muhith was again one of our best products in the Civil Service with excellent academic credentials. Apart from Muhith, another eminent person at the mission was the Educational Affairs officer, Professor Abu Rushd Matinuddin, who was a well-known literary figure. Others at the mission included Moazzem Ali, the younger brother of my journalist friend S.M. Ali, who was Third Secretary, and a number of non-PFS recruits such as Rustam Ali, Razzak Khan and Shariful Alam who were in the administrative staff of the Mission.

On that first night, the atmosphere was rather tense. All those present in Enayat's house were in the service of the Pakistan government, who paid the salaries that kept them in comfortable homes in Bethesda, Alexandria and McLean, sent their children to good schools and still held out prospects for secure employment and career advancement within the service. All of them knew me personally or by reputation, and knew of my proximity to the AL leadership, so they received me with more respect and intimacy than may be warranted for someone younger than most of them and of a less elevated status. I spent the first part of the exchange narrating to them the events leading to the military assault, my own adventures, my encounter with Tajuddin and his message through me to the Bangalis in the USA.

This was my first attempt at dealing with officials, and when I communicated to them Tajuddin's request that they throw in their lot with the Bangladesh cause, I realized both the enormity and improbability of my request. Here was I, a vagabond in borrowed clothes, of no fixed address, wanted by the Pakistan army for unspecified acts of treason against the Pakistan State, conveying a verbal message from a PM of an as-yet hypothetical State, to put at risk all they had worked for in their service lives to get to Washington. I am not sure if I smiled when I made this request, or did inwardly, at my impertinence. But in those days, I could communicate a good deal of passion into my dealings with people and more authority than was justified by either my years or status in life.

The Bangalis in the Mission were all dedicated patriots who were outraged at the atrocities being inflicted on their people by the Pakistan army and, in principle, committed to the emergence of an independent Bangladesh. They also recognized the electrifying impact their defection, en masse, to the Bangladesh cause would have not just on US public opinion but around the world.

Openly declaring themselves to such a cause at this early stage held practical implications for the Bangalis before me. Such constraints did not apply to other Bangalis, then resident and working in the USA, or proclaimed offenders such as Rehman Sobhan, who was already at war with the State of Pakistan. These officials had to think about the livelihood of their families, the ongoing education of their children and the then not inconsequential issue of their fate in the event that this struggle was aborted through a negotiated settlement within the framework of Pakistan or indeed continued for many years without a clear end in sight. I personally had no categorical answers to their concerns beyond large doses of bravado fuelled by strong optimism that not only was Bangladesh totally committed to independence but that this would be realized within a year.

I am not sure how many of those present shared my optimism, but we did spend some time in subsequent meetings, discussing the operational implications of all the Bangalis in the mission in DC as well as in New York, proclaiming their allegiance to Bangladesh. This related not just to issues of financial support but of timing as well as their subsequent status in the US and relations with the host administration.

Some of these concerns had already been addressed in their earlier encounters with representatives of the Bangali community who had come to Washington to lobby them to proclaim their allegiance to Bangladesh. The community had promised to raise funds for the sustenance of their families. The fact that six weeks had gone by without a response from the Embassy was already contributing to some bad blood with the community. This came to my notice when I later returned to New York from DC and had a session with some members of the community at the Queen's residence of Dr Alamgir, a Bangali medical doctor of strong left-wing views. The community were quite angry at what they perceived was the reluctance of the Bangali diplomats to sacrifice their comfortable lifestyles. I attempted to reassure them of the patriotism of these noble sons of Bangladesh and engaged them in practical discussion of the funds that were needed to support them in the event of their defection. I recollect we sat through the night at Alamgir's residence negotiating salary scales for the various members of the Bangladesh mission along with establishment costs for an office they would occupy once in the service of the Government of Bangladesh.

I had, when in DC, worked out such a budget with our diplomats that I used as the basis of our discussions. The salaries involved substantial cuts in the lifestyle of the diplomats who were then living in quite comfortable circumstances. But even these scales were deemed too high for a community that had to raise resources from among others, taxi drivers and restaurant waiters. My somewhat bizarre involvement, sitting in a New York borough, in a Pay and Services Commission exercise, on behalf of the elite of the Bangladesh Foreign Service, involved hard bargaining and a firm demand from the community that the entire Bangali staff publicly defect to the Bangladesh cause not later than 1 July.

In actual practice, the defection took place around 1 August where the Bangladeshis in the Washington and New York missions publicly proclaimed their allegiance to Bangladesh in a globally publicized ceremony. As it turned out, the Mujibnagar government persuaded the Indian government to cover the costs of the prospective Bangladesh mission about to be established in the USA. This ensured a more comfortable lifestyle for our diplomats than would have been possible, based on the constrained and somewhat uncertain sources of funding promised by the Bangladeshi community. However, their allegiance to Bangladesh did require some cuts in their lifestyle. All had to move into more modest accommodation, and quite a few of their wives had to seek employment to support the family budget.

The first overseas mission of the provisional Bangladesh government was formally established in an apartment on Connecticut

Avenue, and M.R. Siddiqi was sent out from Kolkata by the Bangladeshi government to head the mission. Our first embassy was staffed by some of the most able officials of Bangladesh such as Enayat Karim, S.A.M.S. Kibria and A.M.A. Muhith. The mission, when it began functioning, was, thus, a formidable diplomatic resource at the service of the Bangladesh cause.

S.A. Karim, then Pakistan's Deputy Permanent Representative in the UN, who had defected at the same time as his DC colleagues, had established a small office in New York along with Abul Hassan Mahmud Ali, a former student of mine in the Economics Department and a university contemporary of Rounaq Jahan. Mahmud Ali had been serving as the Deputy Consul General for Pakistan in New York and was the first among the Bangali diplomats, then serving in the US, to proclaim his allegiance to Bangladesh at the end of April 1971. Mahmud Ali has served as the Foreign Minister of Bangladesh since 2013.

Building Alliances with the Media

The above narrative relates to the future. At the beginning of May, there were no such designated spokesmen for the Bangladesh cause in Washington so that individual members of the Embassy were engaging in private diplomacy in support of Bangladesh. Muhith was particularly active in visiting the Hill, ostensibly to work for Pakistan but, in practice, using his connections there to speak for Bangladesh. Others in the Embassy did their own lobbying for the cause but with greater discretion.

During this period, Razzaque Khan and Shariful Alam, non-diplomatic officers from the Embassy, quite publicly worked with me and functioned as a sort of secretariat for me, thereby putting their jobs at the Pakistan Embassy at risk. I was also assisted in my mission by two Bangladeshi students, Mohsin Siddiqui, the brother of civil servant Dr Kamal Siddiqui, and Dr Enayat Rahim, a historian who at the end of his life, among others, helped to edit

Bangabandhu's recently published diaries. This support staff of four was most helpful to me through chauffeuring me around Washington and in lining up contacts for me with the press, TV and Congress so I could talk to them about Bangladesh. I was connected by Razzaque to Warren Una, a well-known journalist and TV commentator who set up a number of prime-time TV appearances for me that gave valuable publicity to our cause. This was the first time I had ever appeared on TV, so I do not recollect if I had the makings of a media star. But in those days, I was seized with a fire that made me feel I could climb mountains so that my multidimensional role as media star, journalist, diplomat, academic and political rabble-rouser came quite easily to me.

On the press front, my task was facilitated by the fact that a number of US journalists such as Sydney Schanberg of *The New York Times* and Tony Clifton of *Newsweek* had already made Bangladesh front-page news in the US press. My mission was to reach out to the press in Washington to conscientise them, in anticipation of the arrival of M.M. Ahmed in the USA, to stop aid to Pakistan. I accordingly met Henry Bradsher of *The Washington Star*, Lewis Simons of *The Washington Post*, Adam Clymer of *The Baltimore Sun*, Ben Wells of *The New York Times* (Washington office), and Gilbert Harrison, editor of the prestigious weekly, *The New Republic*. These were the main papers read in Washington, and these columnists and their leader writers exercised considerable influence in shaping Congressional opinion.

My task was to educate the media on the background to the Liberation War, the facts and extent of the genocide, the inevitability of the liberation of Bangladesh and, finally, the importance of the USA in taking the lead in refusing to underwrite Pakistan's genocide through continuation of their foreign aid. It was therefore a major coup for the Bangladesh cause when, more or less simultaneously, all four papers then read in Washington D.C., came out with editorials, to coincide with the arrival of M.M. Ahmed in Washington, requesting the US government to suspend their aid commitment to Pakistan as long as the genocide continued in Bangladesh.

Reaching Out to the US Congress

Given the reluctance of the US administration to respond to Bangladesh's concerns, we were advised by friends to turn to the US Congress where the Democrats were the majority party. Before I arrived in D.C., Muhith had already been quite active on the Hill, where he had built up good connections that enabled him to put me in touch with two of the most effective supporters of the Bangladesh cause during that period, Senator Edward Kennedy and Senator Frank Church, who was a ranking member of the Senate Foreign Relations Committee. Tom Dine, aide to Senator Church, was Muhith's principal contact on the Hill. Dine, in turn connected us to Gerry Tinker and Dale Diehan, aides to Senator Kennedy. Tom, Gerry and Dale eventually became our close friends and active spokesmen for the Bangladesh cause. Through them I met not only Church and Kennedy but a number of other senators.

At that time, led by Kennedy, Church, and Gallagher in the House of Representatives, Congressman and Senators had begun to speak out on the floor of the House to denounce the genocide and to demand that US aid to Pakistan be reviewed. Both Church and Kennedy had been motivated by the messages and eventually the historic telegram sent to the US State Department by Archer Blood, the US Consul General in Dhaka, reporting on the genocide underway in Bangladesh and the failure of the US administration to restrain Yahya. The volume, *The Blood Telegram* by Gary Bass, provides much evidence of the impact of the telegram and its aftermath. Further statements, along with documents and letters sent by American civilians who had come out from Bangladesh after 26 March, were entered into the Congressional Record. Here, my host in Dhaka, John Rhode and his colleagues in the CRL, such as David Nalin and Bucky Greenhough, were particularly active.

At that stage, I was informed that some old-time friends of Pakistan in the US Congress, led by Senator Symington, were intending to organize a tea party for M.M. Ahmed when he arrived in DC so he could put his views on the events in Pakistan to the Senators. Ahmed's event yielded a small turn out, but it was felt by our friends on the Hill that we should match this. As Church and Kennedy were leading figures of the Democratic Party, it was felt that a less partisan figure in the Senate might be mobilized to host a lunch for me that could attract both Republicans and Democrats. Tom Dine contacted Mike Gertner, aide to William Saxby of Ohio—a respected, middle-of-the-road Republican—who agreed to host such a lunch for me. This managed to attract a larger and more distinguished collection of Senators than had turned up to hear M.M. Ahmed. I had as my audience, among others, Senators Church, Fulbright, the Chairman of the Senate Foreign Relations Committee, and Senator Scott, who was the Senate Minority Leader of the Republican Party. These distinguished figures of the American political establishment gave a patient hearing to the full facts behind the Pakistani genocide and the complicity of the US government in this act as long as they remained the principal aid donors to Pakistan. Out of these early initiatives in the Senate emerged the Saxby–Church amendment to the US Foreign Aid Bill, which aimed to stop US aid to Pakistan as long as the genocide in Bangladesh continued. But this is part of a later story and required a much larger mobilization.

I recollect, as I sat at the head of the lunch table next to Saxby, with an array of political figures before me who would normally only turn out to dine with eminent visitors such as ministers, at this extraordinary elevation in my fortunes. Here was I, an unheard-of teacher of economics from an obscure university, presenting the first public case for an as-yet-unknown country, Bangladesh, before the elite of US politics. I suspect when Tom Dine and Mike Gertner set up this VIP lunch, they must have marketed me as a figure of some significance in the Bangladesh establishment, which I was not. So I had to project myself as a person of authority by speaking with a degree of confidence and erudition. I must have managed to thus project myself as I was advised by my friends that my effort was well received and contributed towards motivating Congressional opinion, which eventually emerged as one of Bangladesh's principal sources of support.

A less relevant challenge before me at the lunch, where I had to not only make a speech but also converse with and answer questions from the Senators, was to also ingest some of the excellent lunch that was placed before me. This included the most delicious hot fudge sundae I have ever had. The Senate cafeteria that served this was a mandatory port of call for me whenever I visited the Hill.

Following our success in the Senate, we heard that M.M. Ahmed was scheduled to address a press conference at the National Press Club. We decided to beat him to it and managed, through the intervention of our friends on the Hill and the efforts of Razzaque Khan and his associates, to organize our own conference. This was well attended by the press, radio and TV media. Voice of America carried excerpts from my speech, which were heard around the world. Nasim Ahmed, correspondent of the *Dawn*, who later became Information Secretary, under Bhutto, had been sent by Pakistan, along with another senior journalist, Qutubuddin Aziz, to counter our campaign. Nasim Ahmed was at my press conference but appeared more interested in monitoring who was there than in putting any serious questions to me. The success of the conference and the favourable publicity that Bangladesh was attracting in the media sufficiently discouraged M.M. Ahmed who subsequently cancelled his own press conference.

What was again significant about my appearance before the National Press Club was that it traditionally invited Heads of State and similar distinguished foreign public figures to address them. I am not sure how many, if any of Bangladesh's PMs or senior ministers have since been invited to address the National Press Club. But again, here was I, a nobody, appearing before this elite establishment. I then came to appreciate that the liberation struggle served to encourage people to appear bigger than they were. Tragically, post-liberation Bangladesh has tended to be preoccupied with making people feel smaller than they actually are.

Waking up Henry

Our more challenging task lay in persuading the Nixon administration, with Henry Kissinger as his National Security Adviser, to not only stop aid to Pakistan but to come to terms with the emergence of an independent Bangladesh. At that time, we had little idea that a major strategic game was afoot where Pakistan was a critical player in Washington's opening to the People's Republic of China (PRC), then still led by Mao Tse-tung, who was engaged in pushing through the Cultural Revolution. Given the importance of the Yahya regime in this great game, Nixon, inspired by his éminence grise, Kissinger, was in no mood to displease Yahya, in spite of the globally visible genocide inflicted on the people of Bangladesh and the clear messages on this issue, sent by Archer Blood and his colleagues in the US consulate in Dhaka, to the US State Department. Not only were Blood's messages shelved on the advice of Kissinger but he was taken to task, first by US Ambassador Farland in Islamabad and then by Kissinger himself, on his ostensible partisanship in the cause of Bangladesh. Under the circumstances, no one from Bangladesh was given access to anyone of consequence in the US administration at that time.

At that stage, we had as yet not been exposed to the underlying background to Kissinger's great game and assumed that the administration needed to be better informed than they appeared to be. We were thus somewhat surprised to find that while the US Congress and media had given us a favourable hearing, it remained much more difficult to get through to the upper echelons of the Nixon administration. We had set our sights on making contact with Henry Kissinger, who had taught a number of Bengalis, including Dr Kamal Hossain, in his international seminar at Harvard and was presumed to be more familiar with the background to the liberation struggle. We soon learnt that the US administration was a closed door to Bangladeshis.

I was advised to fly to Cambridge to meet with Kissinger's former colleagues at Harvard to see if they could get me an audience with him. Apart from some of the ranking economists such as Professor

Dorfman, I met with a distinguished colleague of Kissinger in the department of Government, Professor Samuel Huntington and with Professor Lodge at the Harvard Business School, supposedly another close friend of Kissinger. None of these contacts proved particularly useful. At one point, a number of Kissinger's former colleagues at Harvard—which included Gus Papanek, then with the HAG—which had spent a decade in Pakistan advising the Planning Commission, travelled to Washington and picketed Kissinger's office shouting, "Wake up, Henry." A testimony before the US Congress was provided by three of Harvard's most eminent economists, Edward Mason, Robert Dorfman and Stephen Marglin, which had been prepared with support from Mohiuddin Alamgir, then finishing his PhD at Harvard, and fellow doctoral student, Shankar Acharya from India, drawing on material from Rounaq Jahan's thesis 'Pakistan: Failure in National Integration'.

As Bangladesh was off-limits to the US administration at the official level in Washington, the best I could do was to meet at the home of Enayet Karim, with Craig Baxter, who was then the Bangladesh desk officer at the State Department. I eventually secured a meeting with Anthony Quainton, then a junior officer in the US State Department, who met me on 14 May 1971. Quainton's report to his superior, Van Hollen, was recently made available to me by a Bangladeshi journalist of *Prothom Alo*, who had secured access to recently declassified documents of the 1971 events, and has been presented in the Annexure in this book. The report provides a faithful reproduction of my views that makes me appear more mature than I then imagined I was.

At a later date, along with Nurul Islam who was visiting Washington from New Haven, we met, through the good offices of Tom Hexner, a consultant to the World Bank, with Maurice Williams, who was then the Deputy Director, US Aid. I remember this meeting for the message communicated by Williams, that if Bangladesh expected its cause to be taken more seriously in Washington, it must demonstrate its military capability—an odd observation by an aid administrator but reflective of the realpolitik of the Nixon administration.

Ascending to Olympus

My other target in Washington was the World Bank who had till then been the leader of the Pakistan aid consortium and served as its principal spokesman within the international development community. My first contact in the Bank was with the Englishman, I.P. Cargill, who was then a vice president in charge of South Asia and the person who chaired the Pakistan consortium. He was a close friend of M.M. Ahmed from their shared ICS days and the most knowledgeable about affairs in Pakistan. He had for the last five or six years projected himself as the Bank's proconsul, dictating Pakistan's development strategy and was treated as royalty whenever he visited the country. We therefore apprehended that he would emerge as a firm supporter of his former fiefdom and go out of his way to accommodate the requests of his friend M.M. Ahmed.

Cargill's reaction surprised us. In the May meeting of the consortium in Paris, the members, under advice from Cargill, had suspended further consideration of aid to Pakistan, until the Bank–Fund mission to Pakistan had reported on its field visit to review the situation in Bangladesh. At an early stage of my arrival in D.C., Cargill, unexpectedly gave me a long hearing and conveyed the impression that new aid commitments were unlikely to be forthcoming until military activities in Bangladesh were stopped. It appeared that he was unhappy with Pakistan's military actions and was interested in building ties with Bangladesh whose independence he believed to be inevitable.

Beyond Cargill lay the Olympian figure of Robert McNamara, president of the World Bank. I was told that after much effort by friends within the Bank, McNamara had agreed to meet me. I was advised that his computer-oriented mind only absorbed facts that were presented as concisely as possible. To prepare for this, aided by other Bangladeshis in Washington, including Muhith, I put together a paper, arguing for the stoppage of aid to Pakistan. This paper was subsequently printed and widely circulated. I think the paper was titled 'Aid to Pakistan: Background and Options'. In our short meeting, McNamara appeared to be more moved by the human dimensions of the problem and gave me the impression of having genuine concern for the horrific nature of the crisis in Bangladesh.

It is difficult to isolate the impact of McNamara's response to the Bangladesh situation on the Bank's role in the Pakistan aid consortium. All that can be observed is that the Bank did send out a mission to Pakistan and that this mission submitted a devastating report on the atrocities of the Pakistan army in Bangladesh and the complete breakdown of the development process in that area. The report of the mission was leaked by Haroun-er-Rashid to *The New York Times*. This hugely informative report served as an important aide to lobbyists within the USA for the Saxby–Church amendment and in dissuading members of the Pakistan aid consortium from making fresh aid pledges in their meeting in Paris in June 1971.

Itinerant Diplomacy

Outside of my meetings with Congress, the World Bank and the media, I was also in contact with some of the groups that had sprung up among the large Bangladeshi community resident in the USA. The main group among the Bangalis was chaired by the late F.R. Khan, the famed architect from Chicago who had designed the then world's tallest building, the Sears Tower. Khan was involved in mobilizing public opinion within the USA in favour of the Bangladesh cause and in fundraising for supporting the Liberation War.

Apart from these major involvements, I used whatever residual time I had to meet with individuals or groups who might in any way be mobilized in support of the Bangladesh cause. In New York, I met with Jim Brown of *The New York Times*, who subsequently wrote some important pieces critical of Pakistani actions in Bangladesh. I also made some further TV appearances. I made a very valuable visit to Philadelphia at the invitation of Sultana Alam, a teacher at Pennsylvania University and friend from our Dhaka days, where I addressed a group that she had formed to support Bangladesh. Other such groups, either Bangalis or Americans who had been mobilized by the Bangalis, provided a ready audience.

A tape of my address at this Philadelphia meeting was preserved by a Bangladeshi in the audience and presented to me many years later as a testimony to my then prowess as a speaker.

While in New York, I stayed with S.A. Karim, the then Deputy Permanent Representative in Pakistan's UN mission, and his attractive, lively wife Ayesha, at their Upper East Side residence. Karim was still serving Pakistan, so the presence of a person then under indictment for treason as his house guest was a risky proposition for him. As I was also openly contacting members of various UN missions then sitting in the Security Council, this was doubly risky for Karim. But encouraged by Ayesha, Karim decided to take his chances. Karim also managed, in his own low-key style, to convey to UN colleagues in various missions the wide gap between the propaganda fed to them by Pakistan and the reality of events in Bangladesh.

At the end of my stay in the USA, I flew into Ottawa for a day, at the request of a Bangali action group there, who felt that my presence as a spokesman for the Bangladesh government may be of some value. On arrival in Ottawa, I addressed a well-attended press conference. Following this, I had lunch with some MPs in Ottawa, chaired by the shadow foreign minister from the opposition bench. In the afternoon, I was taken off to a private club for a clandestine rendezvous with a member of the Cabinet. As a minister, he was reluctant to meet me openly but gave me a sympathetic hearing. In the evening, I met with the Bangali community in Ottawa. My one-day visit to Ottawa was one of the most productive days I had spent on this campaign.

European Diplomacy

Reuniting with the Family

I returned to London at the end of May. While I was in the USA, Salma and the boys had come over from Amman to London and were staying at the residence of Mark and Val Arnold-Forster, at Clarendon Road, West London. They had generously taken them in even though they had a large family of their own. The sheer exhilaration, tempered by huge relief of having my family with me cannot be described in words. Salma spent long hours narrating her adventures on the way to and in Karachi. She had observed the indifference and callousness of the behaviour of those of her class in Karachi, including her friends, towards the atrocities in Bangladesh. The only person in Karachi who visited her to enquire after my well-being was my St. Paul's school friend Rafi Raza. Her experience in Karachi persuaded her that if people in West Pakistan could be so insensitive to the genocide being visited on those who they claimed to be their fellow countrymen, then indeed Pakistan was dead. She attempted to get this message across to her brother-in-law in Jordan, Crown Prince Hasan, as his government had historically been a strong sympathizer of Pakistan.

Once in England, I had to also address some of the practical problems of how to maintain my family while I travelled the world. Fortunately, Paul Streeten, then Warden of QEH, offered me a research position in his institution. This enabled Salma to set up an establishment in Wolvercote in North Oxford, where we rented a miniscule house. In my absence, she had to look after our three sons. Taimur was then eight and could attend the local school on his own. But Salma had to escort Babar, who was only four, to his nursery school in Summertown, pushing Zafar, then just a year old, in a pram. Babysitting and shopping assistance from Akbar Noman, a graduate student at Oxford, and his Norwegian wife was thus particularly helpful. My mother turned up in England from Bangkok and spent some time in Oxford, backstopping Salma. In order to supplement our limited resources, Salma took up a part-time teaching position at the Oxford College of Further Education. This was made possible by the babysitting services of the Nomans, my mother and later, my uncle K.G. Morshed, who came over from London to visit us.

While in Oxford, I cannot claim to have done much justice to my research responsibilities at QEH. I was away most of the time in the service of my country and, when in my office at QEH, spent time keeping in touch with Bangladeshis campaigning in London or in writing articles on the Liberation War. A.R. Khan, then a Visiting Fellow at Nuffield College, provided me with opportunities to discuss possible strategies for the future of an independent Bangladesh.

Reaching beyond Home

My primary mission, while in England, remained to mobilize opinion in favour of Bangladesh. I, thus, continued where I left off, before I had travelled to the USA with the task of stopping aid to Pakistan. By the end of May, I found that the climate of public opinion in the UK had moved much more strongly in favour of Bangladesh. I again met with Judith Hart. She was the Labour front-bench spokesman on foreign aid and subsequently became Minister for Overseas Development in the next Labour government. Following our meeting, she had made a powerful speech on the floor of the House of Commons, where she demanded, on behalf of the Labour opposition, that aid to Pakistan from the UK be suspended and that the UK government should pledge no further aid to Pakistan until the genocide in Bangladesh was stopped and a dialogue opened with the elected leaders of Bangladesh.

I also had an occasion to communicate my views to a number of Tory and Labour MPs and to again use my acquaintance with Nicholas Barrington to get our views across to Sir Alec Douglas Home, who was still disinclined to give me a hearing. I did however speak to some of the officials from the Ministry of Overseas Development in the UK delegation to the consortium meeting in Paris and gave them our memorandum on stopping aid to Pakistan. As in the USA, the reluctance of the UK government to receive, at a higher level, any spokesman for the Bangladesh cause was compensated by the positive response of public opinion that was moving strongly in favour of Bangladesh.

This same proposition to cut off aid to Pakistan, which had been argued in our presentation to McNamara in Washington and with the US Congress, had become the main campaign theme among the Bangali community in the UK. The UK Bangalis were the most numerous of the probashi Bangali communities and were active in raising funds and mobilizing public opinion in the UK against aid to Pakistan. Justice Abu Sayed Chowdhury had by then been officially designated as the chief spokesman for the cause and had set up offices for the movement near Liverpool Street station in East London. During my stay, I attended a mammoth meeting in Trafalgar Square, addressed by Justice Chowdhury, where the Bangladesh cause was articulately presented.

I took the opportunity of my stay in the UK to do some further writing on the Bangladesh issue. I renewed my old contacts with the left-wing weekly, the *New Statesman*, and offered them an article on the genocide in Bangladesh and the role of foreign aid in sustaining the Yahya regime. The editor of the *New Statesman* ultimately decided to use the material from my article as the substance for a front-page editorial in his weekly that demanded suspension of all UK aid to Pakistan. At the request of its editor, I also wrote a piece for *South Asian Review*, which for the first time put on record a full account of the negotiations leading to the army crackdown.

During my visit, I participated in a largely attended teach-in at the Oxford University Union organized by two sympathetic Pakistanis, Akbar Noman and Tariq Abdullah. It was largely attended and addressed by Professor Daniel Thorner, who had been witness to the Pakistan army genocide while with PIDE in Dhaka and had, on his return to the Sorbonne in Paris, become a leading spokesman there for the Bangladesh cause. Apart from Daniel, A.R. Khan also spoke along with others. This included another Pakistani, Tariq Ali, the son of Tahira and Mazhar Ali Khan, who was bitterly critical of the Pakistani army action and spoke in support of an independent Bangladesh. He, however, somewhat imaginatively, saw this as a prelude to a revolutionary upsurge where the two Bengals may unite to form a Socialist State. During his rather harsh remarks about the Pakistan army, he was heckled from the gallery by someone who appeared to be a Pakistani MI officer. The meeting was also addressed by a representative of Bhutto's Peoples Party. As may be expected, the Pakistani cause did not get a very sympathetic hearing. I was the last speaker and received a fairly enthusiastic response from the audience. This was our general experience at all such public gatherings. Akbar Noman and Tariq Abdullah, as Pakistanis, took some risks in openly organizing a potentially treasonous public event. After the emergence of Bangladesh, Akbar faced quite a few problems when he visited his family in Karachi.

The Paris Consortium

From London I moved on to Paris for the crucial meeting of the Pakistan Aid consortium scheduled, if I remember, for 7 June. The Pakistanis were banking on this meeting to get a large new pledge of commodity aid as their current import capacity had been seriously constrained by the collapse of jute exports due to the war.

In Paris, I stayed with Daniel and Alice Thorner at their home in Rue Guy de Labrosse, rather than with my brother Farooq. I met Farooq occasionally so he could brief me on Pakistan's strategy at the consortium meeting, which appeared to rest heavily on US support to keep aid flowing to them. Also staying with the Thorners was Dr Hasan Imam, who had been with PIDE and had recently come over to Paris via India. Daniel, Hasan Imam and I prepared a memorandum for the consortium based on my original memo presented to McNamara. On the night before the meeting, Daniel drove me and Hasan in his small Volkswagen, to the various hotels where delegates to the consortium were resident, to distribute our paper to the leader of every delegation to the consortium. We also attempted to meet with the respective delegations. Some gave us a hearing. Others were inaccessible. I met with the Deputy Head of the World Bank delegation, an American, the night before the meeting. He told me that it was unlikely the consortium would pledge any new aid. I spoke over the phone to Peter Cargill, the vice president of the World Bank. He had just returned from Pakistan. He confirmed the view of his deputy but asked me to see him after the meeting was over.

On the morning after the consortium concluded, I met with Peter Cargill over a luxurious breakfast at his five-star hotel, the Royal Monceau. He informed me that the consortium had declined to make any new pledges until normalcy was restored in Bangladesh. They were influenced by Cargill's report of his visit to Dhaka and Islamabad. In the meeting, he confirmed the highly unstable nature of the current situation in Pakistan. Some other members made stronger observations at the meeting. But most, reacting to mounting domestic public pressure at home against the atrocities of the Pakistan army, were happy to use the excuse of the prevailing inhospitable climate for development in Pakistan to withhold new aid pledges. The US delegate made a moderating plea for some support to Pakistan but did not argue the case very strongly and went along with the decision of the consortium.

The consortium meeting was a serious setback for Pakistan and a modest triumph for the international mobilization that had taken place around the world in support of Bangladesh's liberation struggle. However, their decision did not mean that all aid flows into Pakistan came to a standstill. Aid, already pledged and in the pipeline, continued to flow into West Pakistan. The brunt of any shortfall in aid was inevitably borne by Bangladesh, but West Pakistan's own economic position was rendered quite precarious and unsustainable as one of its main exports, jute, had also come to a standstill.

Apart from our work with the consortium, Daniel used my presence in Paris to present the Bangladesh cause to influential French intellectuals. I had some useful meetings with journalists and some leading figures of the French intellectual establishment such as Raymond Aron, the political philosopher; Louis Dumont, the social anthropologist; and Maxime Rodinson, the Arabist. I also presented a seminar at the Sorbonne on the Bangladesh issue.

We learnt that the French government had been an important source of arms supplied to Pakistan. Our target was to mobilize some influential opinion in France to get these sales suspended. As it turned out, the more decisive influence on the French government was the attempt by Pakistan to renege on their payment for the arms by seeking a rescheduling of their debt. This eventually led to a cut off in arms deliveries from France.

Roman Excursions

From Paris I moved to Rome. During a short stay there, I delivered a memo to the World Food Programme (WFP) suggesting that food aid to Pakistan, ostensibly meant for Bangladesh, would be misused to feed West Pakistan and the troops engaged in committing genocide in Bangladesh. We suggested that this aid should be diverted to the Mujibnagar government who would supply it across the border to inhabitants in adjacent areas. The WFP appreciated my argument but did not feel that my suggestions were feasible for an international organization mandated to operate through recognized sovereign governments.

Apart from my role in aid diplomacy, I also met with officials of the three major Italian political parties, the Christian Democrats, Communists and Socialists, to seek their support in securing a cut-off in Italian aid to Pakistan. This was meant more as a gesture because at that time, the Italians had never been particularly large aid donors to Pakistan or any other developing country. These political encounters were set up for me by a sister of Eva Colorni—who later married Amartya Sen—who had been so helpful to me when I was in Delhi. Eva's family had deep political connections in Italy that provided me with a level of access I could never have attained on my own.

Reporting Back to Tajuddin

Rediscovering Calcutta

I travelled from Rome to Delhi at the beginning of July. I did not spend much time there as my final destination was Calcutta, where I was expected to present a report on the mission assigned to me by Tajuddin Ahmed when we were together in Delhi in early April. I again stayed with Ashok Mitra and travelled with him to Calcutta.

I had no concern about blending into the Calcutta scene, which was after all my birthplace. I had expected to stay with either Dipankar Ghosh, my Cambridge friend in their Lansdowne Road home, where I had spent many days during my bachelor years, or with another close friend from St. Paul's, Monu Palchaudhuri, in their home at the Calcutta lakes.

Unexpectedly, both Monu and Dipankar were out of town, so this ready refuge was not immediately available to me. Ashok consequently took me along to the home of a close family friend of his, Arup Chowdhury. Arup lived with his wife Paromita, in an apartment on Belvedere Road, Alipore, in one of those old-style colonial houses with high ceilings and polished red floors. I had lived in such a house on Belvedere Road in the 1940s when my father was D.C., Ports.

Arup was a complete stranger to me but welcomed me into his home with exceptional warmth and evicted his newly born daughter Smita, from her recently decorated bedroom to provide me with an exclusive room to myself, which I occupied as his guest, for nearly a month. Arup was an exceedingly decent, pleasant, young man in his early thirties, who worked with his father. He had already engaged himself in the Bangladesh cause, contributed funds and had hosted a number of Bangladeshis at his home before I arrived. Paromita, his wife, was an extraordinarily attractive and intelligent young woman who had starred in a Satyajit Ray film, *Company Limited*.

Arup and Paromita treated me as family, thanks to the introduction by Ashok, so I spent my days in Calcutta in great comfort and even managed to attend my very first football match on the Calcutta maidan, courtesy of Arup and his father, who took me to watch East Bengal play Mohun Bagan. Arup drove me to the offices of the Mujibnagar government at 12 Theatre Road on the day after my arrival and continued to drive me there every morning during my stay with him. Arup had already met a number of people involved in the liberation struggle such as Mayeedul Hasan, Nurul Qader Khan and Jamil Chowdhury and hosted a number of dinners for me where I met this group along with a variety of Calcutta intellectuals who had committed themselves to the Bangladesh cause.

First Exposures to Mujibnagar

My first visit to Mujibnagar on Theatre Road was not too promising. Much water and blood had flown down the Meghna since my historic encounter with Tajuddin. There was now a formally constituted government in office. Syed Nazrul Islam was the Acting President. Tajuddin was the PM, Khondkar Moshtaq was the Foreign Minister, while Qamruzzaman and Mansoor Ali headed sundry ministries. Col. Osmani was the designated C-in-C of the Mukti Bahini.

These leaders presided over a rather improvised administration, headed by a number of bureaucrats who had heroically pledged their loyalty to Bangladesh. These were mostly junior civil servants serving in the border districts that had initially been taken over by the Bangladesh freedom fighters at the outset of the Liberation War. The group included bright, committed CSPs such as H.T. Imam, a student of mine, Nurul Qader Khan, Abdus Samad, S.A. Samad, another student of mine, Kamal Siddiqui and Akbar Ali Khan, among others. Two more of my students, Towfiq Elahi Chowdhury, a civil servant, and Mahbubuddin Ahmed from the Police Service, who had escorted Tajuddin across the border in March, had been commissioned as officers in the Mukti Bahini. The senior most among the officers, H.T. Imam and Nurul Qader, had been serving as DCs, but the others served at the level of ADCs or SDOs. The strong presence of my former students among the officials who chose to serve the Bangladesh cause is entirely coincidental but tantalizes me with the thought that they may have absorbed more from my classes with them than just Keynesian theory.

This group of ministers and administrators presided over a rather loosely structured administration where it was difficult to establish who did what or to locate any chains of accountability. When Arup dropped me off at 12 Theatre Road, I immediately recognized this as the residence of my nana, Khwaja Nazimuddin, from 1943 to 1945, when he was still CM of Bengal. I had attended his daughter Zafar's wedding there, played badminton on the lawn and spent nights with my nana's son, Saifuddin, in what was now the office-cum-bedroom of the first PM of Bangladesh. The central, rather largish, living room where the CM used to entertain official guests had been partitioned with particle boards into a large number of cubicles. The rooms abutting off this central space were designated as offices for the ministers. While the young administrators did their best to reproduce the discipline of a functioning secretariat, the problems of establishing order over large numbers of people who were brought up in the tradition of district politics rather than service in a functioning administration was more than challenging.

The first person I sought out was Tajuddin as he was the person who had set me off on my brief diplomatic career. Through Arup, I had already made contact with Muyeed who was staying at the Ramkrishna Mission hostel in Gariahat, and he had agreed to meet me at Theatre Road. We had last met at Baraid and had much ground to cover. Muyeed eventually took me in to meet Tajuddin whose office entrance was guarded by a Major Nurul Islam Shishu, who was rather grandiosely designated as Military Secretary to the PM. The other interlocutor was Dr Towfiq Aziz Khan, a well-regarded scientist, who was identified as the PM's Secretary.

The PM himself occupied a largish room that then served as the office and informal residence of the PM of Bangladesh. It consisted of a small table, a bed and a clothes horse that carried the PM's sparse wardrobe. I exchanged reminiscences with Tajuddin and commented on his austere surroundings. He told me that each of the ministers had been assigned small apartments for their accommodation. He had persuaded his cabinet colleagues that these apartments should be kept for the exclusive use of their respective families but the ministers should set up residence in their office in Theatre Road for the duration of the Liberation War. Tajuddin had taken the lead in this sacrificial enterprise; hence his presence in an office that looked like a college student's residence. However, he sadly reflected that his gesture was not emulated by his colleagues who preferred to retire to their apartments every evening while Tajuddin, no doubt, worked through the night at his desk.

I gave a brief account of my mission to Tajuddin, who suggested that because there was much to report which would be of relevance to the foreign policy concerns of his government, I should prepare a more substantive report that could be presented to the Cabinet. I invested the first part of my stay in Calcutta working on this report, though given the limited administrative resources of the Mujibnagar government, it took almost as long for it to be typed out for purposes of circulation. The original draft of the report, painstakingly prepared by me, resides as an exhibit in the Liberation War Museum.

Having met Tajuddin, I made formal courtesy calls on Nazrul Islam, Qamruzzaman and Mansoor Ali. When I met Nazrul Islam, he educated me to the fact that he was related to me, as his wife was a younger sister of my *khaloo*,[1] Syeduzzaman, married to my aunt, Sikander Begum. The remaining minister, Khondker Mushtaq, was the Foreign Minister. He and the then Foreign Ministry were located in another building at Park Circus, which had once been the office-cum-residence of the Pakistan Deputy High Commissioner (DHC) in Calcutta. This DHC, by the name of Hossain Ali, along with his Bangali colleagues had, from the onset of the Liberation War, pledged themselves to Bangladesh and had taken over the DHC premises. The seizure of the premises of the DHC had been recognized by the Indian government, which then placed it at the disposal of the provisional Bangladesh government.

I did not get to call on Mushtaq until some days later where I met Mahbub Alam Chasi, then designated as Bangladesh's first Foreign Secretary who along with Taheruddin Thakur, had come to be identified as part of Mushtaq's gang. At that stage, I had no idea of the intrigue building up between Theatre Road and Park Circus, which acquired serious political dimensions in the final stages of the war. The final denouement of this struggle did not materialize until 15 August 1975, when Mushtaq, Chasi and Thakur conspired with the army majors in the assassination of Bangabandhu that ushered in 15 years of cantonment rule for Bangladesh.

[1] Uncle.

Reconnecting with Old Friends

Having discharged my formal responsibilities, I spent the best part of the morning and a subsequent lunch with Muyeed at Sky Room on Park Street, a restaurant much patronized by me in my bachelor days. Muyeed filled me in on the tensions within the Mujibnagar government associated with Tajuddin's assumption of the PM's portfolio. I filled in Muyeed on my own modest contribution to these tensions. Muyeed sensibly advised me not to publicly talk about this episode in Delhi when I had encouraged Tajuddin to assume his role as PM unless I wished to incur the enmity not just of the rest of the Cabinet but of the band of young Turks, led by Sheikh Fazlul Haq Moni, who had also challenged Tajuddin's credentials.

Before I settled down to the task of drafting my report, I was keen to locate my friends, Mosharraf, Sarwar Murshed, Anisuzzaman and Swadesh Bose, who were all reported to be in Calcutta. My first target was Mosharraf, who was one of my closest friends. With some difficulty, I located his residence in a less salubrious segment of Park Circus. I arrived unannounced, to find Mosharraf, clad in a *ganji* and lungi, sitting with Inari and his two sons, Zafar and Razzaq, on the *chattai*[2]-covered floor of a single room that clearly looked like the servant's quarter of the apartment house. Mosharraf and Inari were pleasurably surprised at my unexpected appearance.

We spent the afternoon exchanging our wartime reminiscences. This included Mosharraf's escape, well after the army crackdown, from the Rajshahi University campus, just as the Pakistan army was approaching. Mosharraf had played a rather prominent role on the campus, during March 1971, and was an obvious target for betrayal to the Pakistan army, by these on the campus who were opposed to the liberation struggle. He and his family had spent close to a month moving from village to village in the environs of Rajshahi before they decided to travel across the charlands of the Ganges to cross over to Murshidabad in India, my ancestral home. En route, they had been waylaid by dacoits who were unimpressed

[2] Bamboo floor mat.

by the unfolding drama of the Liberation War and saw Mosharraf and his foreign wife as fair game. Mosharraf scolded them so loudly at their worthless conduct that they were shamed into letting them move on and even escorted them to the border.

Planning for a New Bangladesh

Once in Calcutta, no one in the fledging Mujibnagar government took much notice of Mosharraf, who had set up his modest home, based on some funds remitted to Inari by her family in Finland. Mosharraf told me that the Mujibnagar government should aim to put him and other professionals like him to work rather than leaving him to idle away his time reading about the war through newspapers and socializing with his many friends in Calcutta. I narrated Mosharraf's circumstances to Muyeed who had established a good working relationship with Tajuddin. We discussed the issue, and he confirmed that others such as his class friend, Swadesh Bose, had also registered similar concerns.

We subsequently took up the issue at our next meeting with Tajuddin and suggested that a Planning Board be established by the government, centred around the professional talents among Bangladeshis located in Calcutta. The Planning Board had the dual task of suggesting how the problems of the growing tide of refugees streaming across the borders could be addressed and could, concurrently, start planning for the myriad problems that would have to be addressed in a post-liberation Bangladesh. Tajuddin suggested I prepare a proposal on the Board, suggesting its role and composition, which he could present to the Cabinet. The preparation of the proposal became my second designated responsibility during my stay in Calcutta, where I drew upon an earlier note prepared on this issue by Muyeed and suggestions from Mosharraf.

My proposal for the PB was eventually presented to and approved by the Cabinet. Mosharraf, Sarwar Murshed, Anisuzzaman, Swadesh Bose and I were designated as its members. As I had by then been formally assigned as 'Envoy Extraordinaire', designated to work with the overseas campaign to stop aid to Pakistan, I suggested that Mosharraf be assigned the position of Acting Chair of the Board. He was not well known to the AL leaders, being located in Rajshahi, so I had to undertake some intense marketing to ensure his acceptance. I did not communicate Mosharraf's less than complimentary views of the Mujibnagar government to the Cabinet. Such were Mosharraf's people management skills that it did not take him long to establish relations of some intimacy with the Cabinet and particularly with his compatriot from Rajshahi, Qamruzzaman, also known as Henna Mian.

Murshed and Anis could only make limited contributions to the planning process as they were deployed on other fronts. The burden of managing the Board, within a miniscule budget as well as administrative support and the limited interest in its work on the part of the Cabinet, devolved on Mosharraf, supported by some younger colleagues such as the economist Q.K. Ahmed, who had been working at PIDE with Nurul Islam.

I also managed to track down Sarwar Murshed and his family. As Nurjahan Murshed was an elected AL MP, he received more attention from the government than Mosharraf. But this did not enhance his confidence in the state of governance at Mujibnagar. Anis and Murshed were separately engaged in winning friends for Bangladesh among the cultural fraternity of Calcutta. They both lived austerely with their families and remained optimistic, if somewhat cynical, about the political establishment.

Meeting with Our Liberation Warriors

At the time that I was in Calcutta, the first conference of the nine sector commanders had been convened by Tajuddin at 12 Theatre Road to discuss the direction, strategy and organization of the Liberation War. Interestingly, this was the first time that all the sector commanders had assembled under one roof, and some were meeting their colleagues for the first time. Each had until then been spontaneously fighting the war in their respective enclaves, though some such as Safiullah, Khaled Mosharraf and Ziaur Rahman, who were all Majors in the Bengal Regiment, had conducted joint operations in various theatres of war. Details of this famous conclave have been discussed elsewhere as have issues relating to the conduct and course of the war, so I will not pursue this beyond my own personal exposure to the event.

The first person I sought out from among the sector commanders was Khaled Mosharraf, my comrade from Teliapara. I pointed out that his message through me, to the Mujibnagar government to commission them into the army of an independent Bangladesh, had been duly inscribed in the declaration by Tajuddin on 14 April. Khaled shared with me some of the concerns on the conduct of the war but, as always, sounded upbeat and confident of eventual victory. He gave me his account of the Battle of Belonia, where his formations, along with those of Zia, had forced the far stronger Pakistani army to withdraw from the Belonia bulge that spills out of Comilla into Tripura. He had, as witness, a British television journalist, Vanya Kewley, who had been advised by me earlier in London to meet Khaled if she wanted to see some action. Vanya was quite overwhelmed by the handsome Khaled who she viewed as a romantic hero and conveyed to me, when we later met up in London, her fascination for this heroic figure.

During this visit, I met for the first time with Major Ziaur Rahman, who was another of the sector commanders. Muyeed arranged a lunch for me with Zia at Sky Room. Zia was then a much more withdrawn personality than Khaled but was always keen to elicit the opinion of others. This aspect of his personality was reaffirmed to me in our occasional encounters in Dhaka during the 1972–75 period when he was the Deputy Chief of Staff in the Bangladesh army. From Zia, I heard his account of the battle for Chittagong and his analysis of the present war.

I also met with General Osmani, the C-in-C of the Mukti Bahini, and with Group Captain Khandker, who was Deputy Chief of Staff. I spent a long afternoon with Muyeed and Khandker at his room in a hotel in Sudder Street, discussing the war. Through these encounters, I gathered that there were many concerns over the leadership of the war and that none of the sector commanders held the military leadership qualities of Osmani in high esteem. They believed that his more conventional, outdated, ideas of command were quite unsuited to the conduct of a guerrilla war.

All those whom I met with from the Mukti Bahini spoke of the impressive mobilization of youth who were streaming in to join the resistance. The Majors told me of their discomfort at the way in which the war was being organized. They were all unanimous in their complaints that inadequacy in the quantity and sophistication of arms was the principal constraint in the build-up of the resistance. From what I learnt later, it was only in August that the policy decision was taken by the Indian government to step up the flow of weapons to the Mukti Bahini and to improve their fire power. However, in this intervening period, some tensions had been built up between the sector commanders and their Indian counterparts over the inadequacy of weapons reaching the Mukti Bahini.

The Park Circus Conspiracy

While preparing my reports, I spent a fair bit of time at Theatre Road, where I could sense that all was not well among the various political players. As I was serving as a designated envoy of the government, I assumed that I should report to and take some guidance from the Foreign Ministry, located at Park Circus. Tajuddin did not sound too enthusiastic at this idea. When I eventually did call on Mushtaq, I met first with Mahbub Alam Chasi, the senior most among the Bangali officials to join the struggle, who had resigned some years earlier from the PFS. When I met Chasi, I sensed there was some distance between Park Circus and Theatre Road. Mushtaq was even more guarded in our encounter. He held me in some suspicion for being part of the group of economists who encouraged Bangabandhu to take an uncompromising position on 6 points and therefore presumed that I was a loyalist of Tajuddin, committed to the full independence of Bangladesh.

When I met Mushtaq, I had no idea that he was embarking on a conspiracy patronized by Henry Kissinger. Raghavan, in his volume, 1971, cites State Department files reporting discussions, initiated around 30 July, between Kazi Zahirul Qayyum, an AL MP, close to Mushtaq, and George Griffin, the Political Officer at the US consulate in Kolkata, to discuss a political settlement with Pakistan, short of full independence for Bangladesh. These discussions were fortunately uncovered and reported to Tajuddin, who frustrated the process. At the time of the first contacts between Qayyum and Griffin on 30 July, I was in Kolkata, but these interactions between Park Circus and the US consulate remained completely unknown to me. In hindsight, it becomes clearer to me now why relations between Park Circus and Theatre Road were so fraught and why Mushtaq was rather cagey during his encounter with me.

I had hoped to return to the overseas campaign by the end of July. However, such were the preoccupations of the Mujibnagar government that I was not given any time to make the presentation on my overseas mission and on the Planning Board, until the beginning of August. Following my submission, the Cabinet decided to establish the Planning Board along the lines suggested by me. Mosharraf descended from his retreat in Park Circus and brought the Board to life. When MAC, a figure held in high esteem by the AL, finally surfaced in Kolkata in October, he was designated as Chairman of the Board. However, Mosharaff continued to provide the substantive leadership until the liberation of Bangladesh on 16 December. When liberation became imminent, he worked closely with Qamruzzaman to prepare a rehabilitation plan for the 10 million refugees who were expected to return to their homes in a war-devastated Bangladesh.

The other outcome from my meeting with the Cabinet was my formal assignment as 'Envoy Extraordinaire, in charge of Economic Affairs'. This was an elevation from my less formal role that I had already discharged for Tajuddin as an extraordinary ambassador who was quite unsuited to the task of diplomacy.

17

Fulfilment: The Liberation of Bangladesh

The Campaign to Stop Aid to Pakistan

The Saxby–Church Amendment: Lessons on US Politics

I returned to London in August to find that the campaign by the local Bangalis was in high tide. A mammoth rally had been organized by them in Trafalgar Square. Press support was strong, spokesmen from all the British political parties were vocal in Parliament against aid to Pakistan and the Tory government was compelled to confirm their refusal to pledge new aid.

I had, earlier, been invited to address a meeting convened by the Royal Institute of International Affairs at Chatham House in London. This provided a rather prestigious audience for presenting Bangladesh's case before the British foreign policy establishment. I could not return in time to meet this commitment so that Salma spoke in my place along with the Labour MP Arthur Bottomley, who had just returned from a visit to Pakistan as head of a British Parliamentary delegation sent out to report on the situation. Salma gave a moving account of the situation, and along with Bottomley's first-hand report, the occasion proved a most effective forum for the Bangladesh cause. I subsequently was invited by Chatham House to address them in October.

From the UK, I moved back to Washington. Around August, the entire Bangali contingent in the embassies at Washington and in the UN had finally declared their allegiance to the Bangladesh government. It was a great diplomatic coup since they were a big group and had within their ranks some of the most able officers of the Pakistan Foreign and Civil Services. S.A. Karim, who was Deputy Permanent Representative at Pakistan's mission to the UN and the senior most among them, came in from New York and joined the group in a well-attended press conference held to announce their decision. Unfortunately, Enayet Karim had been hospitalized by a severe coronary attack and could not participate in this event but declared his solidarity with his colleagues from his sickbed.

On my return to New York in early September, I found that Ayesha and Karim had also moved into a smaller apartment in a less fashionable block in the Upper East 90s of Manhattan. When I eventually moved to Washington, I had expected to once again stay with Haroun but found that he had sent his German wife Marlene, and their four sons back to Germany as he felt unsure of his future. He had subsequently moved from his suburban home in McLean to a small apartment opposite the US State Department in downtown DC. However, when I reached Washington, Haroun was travelling abroad so that I was in need of accommodation. Muhith, who received me on my arrival, drove me to the home of Tom Dine who lived close to the US Congress in a somewhat downmarket neighbourhood. The Dines had generously agreed to host me until Haroun returned to DC. As they had limited accommodation, I had to sleep in their living room on a camp bed, which was put up for me before we retired. This generosity to someone who was a relative stranger to them was quite exceptional. We became good friends, and I attended the first-year birthday party of their daughter, Amy, who subsequently became the youngest campaigner for the Bangladesh cause and a media celebrity. Her mother, Joan, took her along in her pushchair to join a small demonstration, which was picketing the World Bank–IMF annual meeting at the Sheraton Hotel, seeking a stoppage of all aid to Pakistan.

Now that the Paris consortium had decided, in their Paris meeting, to suspend new aid commitments to Pakistan, our main target was to persuade the Nixon administration to stand by this decision and to also suspend their arms aid to Pakistan. There was some concern that given the special relationship of the USA to Pakistan, which had just surfaced following Kissinger's secret visit to Beijing via Islamabad, that the USA may feel compelled to bypass the consortium decision. To this end, it had been strategized by Bangladesh's friends on the Hill, led by Tom Dine and other aides, to move a special bill before Congress to compel the Nixon administration to suspend aid to Pakistan. A bill was accordingly tabled in the name of Frank Church, and Senator William Saxby, who had earlier been my lunch host.

Fortunately, by the time the bill was tabled in Congress, the Bangladesh movement in the USA had become more organized in their lobbying efforts. Support among the US public had crystallized in the form of a number of effective volunteer organizations made up of committed and idealistic Americans who were willing to volunteer their time and energies to work for the Bangladesh cause. One of the most effective of these groups was the Bangladesh Information Center (BIC), which was based in Washington. This group took on the task of coordinating the lobbying effort for the Saxby–Church amendment.

The newly established Bangladesh diplomatic mission and the BIC became focal points for the lobbying effort in Washington for the Saxby–Church amendment. The amendment sought to attach a rider on the US Foreign Aid Bill that all fresh commitments of US aid to Pakistan be cut off until they stopped their genocide and resumed a dialogue with the elected representatives of Bangladesh. This bipartisan group in the US Senate, led by a ranking Republican and a Democrat, had already attracted a large number of adherents within the Senate.

The political objective of the movement was to secure a majority vote for the amendment on the floor of the Senate. While the amendment had attracted very strong support, its supporters had to contend with strong counter-pressures from the US administration. They had moved to justify their support for the Yahya regime on the plea that they wished to retain leverage on the Yahya government and that any move to cut aid would prejudice their efforts to influence the Pakistanis. On this ground, they continued shipments of arms and spare parts to Pakistan, an exercise that had been exposed by Senator Kennedy on the floor of the Senate. An imaginative effort by a group of American supporters to organize a boat picket of a ship docked in Baltimore port for carrying the arms shipments to Pakistan attracted much public attention.

My own efforts on my return to Washington were thus concentrated on working on the Hill to secure support for the Saxby–Church amendment. In this task I worked closely both with the Bangladesh Mission and the BIC. The BIC had taken on the staff work for the lobbying. This consisted of a well-researched file index on each Congressman, which spelt out their reported political positions and phobias. An explicit lobbying instruction kit was prepared. Bangalis and sympathetic Americans, both from the Washington area and across the country at large, were persuaded to come into Washington to contribute some time to the lobbying exercise. This mobilization attracted quite extensive support. People took leave from their work to come into Washington and spent a few days in the task of lobbying. Americans were sent off to Senators from their respective states while Bangalis were each assigned specific members of the Senate to approach.

Being closely involved in this lobbying exercise, I came to acquire some insight into the intricacies of US politics and the ways in which political opinion is mobilized in the USA. The dedication with which some of the American friends in the group and our now widening circle of friends among the staff on the Hill, worked for the cause of Bangladesh will remain an abiding memory. I particularly remember the work of Joan Dine and David Weisbrod, who provided the core staff of the BIC. Weisbrod, a young graduate student, became the full-time secretary of the BIC. They were aided by a young Bangali, Kaiser Haq, who did good work in the office.

David Weisbrod was then a young, long-haired, Peace Corps alumnus of radical views. He usually accompanied me on my numerous forays on the Hill, where we tried to persuade Congressmen of quite diverse political persuasions to vote for the amendment. For each Congressman, we needed to devise a politically customized lobbying strategy so that I emerged out of the campaign with a sizeable file on the peculiarities of US politicians. I must have achieved some proficiency in my task as many years later, David Weisbrod, sporting short back and sides, and senior vice president at J.P. Morgan, appeared to remember my efforts with some awe. David accompanied me on various other safaris to media persons and public figures outside Congress so that we became good friend in the process. I was delighted when David along with Tom and Joan Dine were recently honoured by the Bangladesh government for their services to the Bangladesh liberation struggle.

On the Hill, Tom Dine, Gerry Tinker and Dale Diehan, who were our friends from the early days, were joined by Mike Gertner, aide to Senator Saxby. Ever since the lunch he hosted for me in May, Senator Saxby had become one of the staunchest supporters of the Bangladesh cause, as was evident from his willingness to co-sponsor an amendment to his own Administration's Foreign Aid Bill. In staying loyal to his commitment, he faced up to a lot of pressure from the White House. During this phase, his aide Mike Gertner, was an indefatigable source of advice and support.

One of our targets in the lobbying exercise was Senator Jackson, a Democrat with a hawkish disposition, who chaired the Senate Defence Committee. He was reputed to be strongly pro-Israel. I was sent by Tom Dine, to his chief aide Richard Perle, to persuade Senator Jackson to use his leadership of the Senate committee to stop ongoing US arms aid to Pakistan. Perle earned notoriety as a Republican ideologue of extreme right-wing and pro-Israel views who subsequently became Assistant Secretary of State under Reagan. Perle tried to persuade me to contact the Israel Embassy and seek arms for our war. I exercised my own judgement in rejecting this toxic suggestion. I do not recollect if Jackson voted for the amendment.

The lobbying effort behind the Saxby–Church amendment reached its climax at a debate on the floor of the Senate at the end of November. Here a peculiar coalition emerged, bringing together such liberal senators as Frank Church and Kennedy with the Southern conservatives. The liberals spoke of the misuse of US aid in supporting the genocide by Yahya Khan's hordes in Bangladesh. Virtually, all liberal supporters of the amendment spoke in this vein. They were however now joined by the conservatives who had been outraged by the public enthusiasm on the floor of the

General Assembly by some Third World countries over the recent admission of PRC to the UN. The year 1971 was indeed the year when Communist China displaced Taiwan from its seat in the UN some 22 years after the victory of the Communist Revolution. The whole episode in the UN rankled deeply among conservative Congressman, who saw this as a display of political ingratitude by many US aid dependant Third World countries. They were in the mood to strike at them through a cut-off in aid.

I sat in the Senate gallery listening, with some amusement, at the fulminations of some Southern Senators against foreign aid and recognized that the Foreign Aid Bill had no future. This was made evident when the objective of securing passage for the Saxby–Church amendment exceeded its own ambitions and ended in the defeat of the entire Aid Bill on the floor of the Senate. This had more far-reaching implications for the rest of the world. But it served as a victory of sorts for the Bangladesh lobbying effort as it effectively cut off all fresh commitments of US aid to Pakistan, among other US aid recipients.

This victory was however not enough to restrain the US administration from finding other loopholes to get their aid through to Pakistan. By then the Nixon administration had, among its North Atlantic Treaty Organization (NATO) allies, become the sole bulwark of support for the Yahya administration. The need to sustain our lobbying effort in Congress and among the US public was thus an essential component of the strategy to at least contain the excesses of the US administration on their commitment to the Pakistan junta. Gary Bass has cited in his book Nixon's compulsion to aid Pakistan and his frustrations at these setbacks to deliver aid to Yahya.

Encounters with World Finance

While the lobbying in Washington continued, the donors' aid consortium to Pakistan still remained an important arena of influence. The annual World Bank–IMF meeting held in October 1971 in the Sheraton Hotel in Washington became another target for our efforts. Although aid to Pakistan was not an item on the agenda of the meeting, we had been advised by our friends in the Bank that Pakistan would use the occasion to meet with the consortium to seek a rescheduling of its debt servicing obligations and once again attempt to line up fresh commitments. Muhith and I put together a fresh document spelling out Pakistan's circumstances and the case for refraining from any fresh relief to Pakistan just when the Liberation War was reaching a critical stage.

Muhith and I took on the task of tackling the different delegations from the consortium countries who were attending the meeting, to present our campaign literature to them and to talk with them. Our efforts inside were on one day assisted by Professor Nurul Islam, who flew in from Yale where he was based. Outside the Sheraton Hotel, the BIC group had organized a small demonstration. On one occasion, Muhith found himself linked with the demonstration outside the hotel and was evicted by the security guards from the premises of the Sheraton. Fortunately, I was at a distance from these proceedings and managed to rescue the bundle of literature with Muhith to resume our lobbying efforts within the hotel.

It was a challenging experience for us, trying to buttonhole delegates in the rooms and lobbies of the hotel, in order to press our case. While some gave us a hearing, others avoided us. We had some strange encounters. On one such occasion, I ran into an old classmate from Cambridge after all of 18 years, Shahpour Shirazi, who was then the Governor of the Bank Markazi in Iran. I remembered Shahpour as a party-loving playboy at St. John's College, so his transformation into a distinguished central bank chief was quite a change. Shahpour, however, remained no less amicable than he had been in Cambridge. When I questioned him on the subject of the Shah of Iran's military aid to Pakistan, he claimed that the Shah had interceded with Yahya to prevent the execution of Bangabandhu. I have no way of verifying the accuracy of this statement.

We also met another friend of mine from Cambridge, Lal Jayawardena, who was then the Secretary of Economic Affairs in the Government of Sri Lanka. Lal arranged a meeting for Professor Islam and me with the Trotskyite, Finance Minister of Sri Lanka, N.M. Perera. We took Perera to task for Sri Lanka's provision of landing rights to PIA and the Pakistan Air Force to facilitate their carriage of arms and troops to Bangladesh. Perera, rather unconvincingly, denied this and promised to see that landing rights were not thus abused. Again I cannot vouch for his success in making good on his promise.

Stopping Aid to Pakistan: The Last Round

Revisiting Paris

We had to the end maintained communications with the donors to see that they did not reopen the question of fresh aid pledges to Pakistan. This had meant a final visit by me to Paris in early November for a meeting of the Pakistan consortium. I had flown back from the USA to England towards the end of October to address a meeting at Chatham House on the Bangladesh liberation struggle. I had spent time with the family in Oxford before I flew over to Paris. On the morning after the meeting, I was once again treated to a luxurious breakfast by Cargill at the Royal Monceau Hotel. Here he confirmed that, in spite of some US pressure, the members of the consortium were inclined neither to extend new pledges of aid nor to commit themselves to a rescheduling of Pakistan's debt servicing liability. This stand had elicited a threat from Pakistan to declare a unilateral default on their debt service obligations. Such a development would of course have immediately invoked a total cut-off in aid in the pipeline by such countries as Japan that were bound by strong legislative constraints in responding to the threat of default. The World Bank at this stage felt that they may have gone too far and were active in trying to work out a compromise between Pakistan and the consortium, which would have averted any overt default by Pakistan.

The campaign to persuade donors to cut off aid to Pakistan must be viewed as a moderate gain for Bangladesh. From the initiation of the campaign by some of us in May, to the liberation of Bangladesh on 16 December 1971, none of the members of the consortium actually pledged any new aid to Pakistan. There were, however, pledges of relief supplies in the way of food and transport equipment that were presented by donors as a humanitarian gesture to avert famine in Bangladesh. In actual practice, Pakistan had a full pipeline of aid, its current import programme into the Bangladesh area had been drastically cut down, it had been eating into its foreign exchange reserves and it had slowed down on its debt service payments even before it had threatened an overt default. With resort to these expedients, it was not clear if Pakistan had as yet come to the point where their capacity to sustain an acceptable level of current imports and consumption, at least into West Pakistan, was at a critical point until the donors had addressed themselves to blocking the aid pipeline as well as withholding new aid pledges. But our attempts to convince donors to cut off already pledged aid was less successful as it was claimed by some donors that this raised various legal problems with potential suppliers.

Thus, the impact of our campaign on Pakistan was more political and psychological than a tangible restraint on their actions. But they were, all along, kept on a fairly tight leash on the economic front and made to feel that the noose around their neck was drawing tight as the days went by without any further aid pledges. Had the Liberation War been further prolonged, there is little doubt that Pakistan would have faced a sufficiently severe resource crunch that could have had a direct impact on the economy and people of West Pakistan.

Encounter with a Giant

On my last visit to Paris in November to monitor the final consortium meeting held there to service the 'old' Pakistan, I had the special privilege of meeting with the distinguished French Nobel laureate, André Malraux. We had earlier on read in the press that Malraux had publicly proclaimed his support for the Bangladesh cause and had pledged that he would mobilize some of his former colleagues from the French war of resistance against the Germans to join him in extending their services to the Mukti Bahini. Malraux was himself over 70 and not in good health, so it was not clear how far this offer had any practical possibilities. But Daniel Thorner felt that as an official representative of the Bangladesh government, I should at least call on him to communicate our appreciation for his gesture.

Daniel took me to Malraux's residence on the outskirts of Paris, where I had the privilege of meeting this great man for the first time. Malraux spoke with great passion. He indicated that since the Spanish Civil War, where he was a pilot who flew in the service of the Republic, he had never been so strongly moved over the affairs of a country other than his own. He felt so committed to the justice of the Bangladesh cause that in spite of his advanced years and ill health, he was willing to draw upon the services of ex-resistance fighters who had responded to his call to join him in fighting for Bangladesh. He indicated that they could provide valuable skills in matters of explosives and communications, which were an essential element in any guerrilla war. He was willing to take out such a team, fully equipped with explosives and communications equipment, to serve with the Mukti Bahini. He then involved me in an intensive, down-to-earth, technical discussion on the needs of the Mukti Bahini in this area and the practical problems associated with his involvement in the war. In this area, I was regrettably somewhat underqualified to advise him. But I extended the sincere gratitude of the people and Government of Bangladesh for his gesture and promised to convey his commitment to the Bangladesh government.

Apart from Malraux's pledge to intervene directly, he also promised to use his influence with his former colleagues in the Gaullist cabinet in ensuring that France supplied no further arms to Pakistan. This had already been suspended because of Pakistan's failure to service its debt. It would appear that in the matter of arms sales, the French were more likely to be moved by pressure on their pocketbook rather than on political grounds or issues of principle.

My visit to Malraux was not publicized but, much to our surprise, was reported in the 13 November issue of the daily *Paris Match*. The report stated that "André Malraux, last week, received in great secrecy, Rehman Sobhan, special envoy of Bangladesh. The meeting took place at his residence at Verrierers-de-Buisson. Malraux confirmed to the Bangladesh representative his decision to leave for Calcutta before the end of this month" (translated from French).

In the aftermath of Liberation, Bangabandhu, in recognition of Malraux's commitment to our cause, invited him to visit Bangladesh and be honoured by the government and people of Bangladesh. On the occasion of his visit, Professor Sarwar Murshed, the then VC of Rajshahi University, invested him with an honorary doctorate. Kamal Hossain hosted an intimate dinner for him at the State Guest House attended by both of us as well as Salma and Hameeda. Professor Anisuzzaman and Professor Razzaq may have also attended the dinner. Malraux, who was not too intimate with English, preferred to speak French. As Salma was the only one among us who spoke French, she played a critical role in our exchanges. I asked Malraux what he particularly remembered about the atmosphere in post-liberation Paris. He cryptically replied, "The lies." He was referring to the ambiguous role played by many French public figures who either collaborated with the German occupation of France or kept their distance from the Resistance, but later proclaimed their involvement in the struggle. Malraux's observations about the French resonated with our experience of our own post-liberation scenario.

The Campaign at the UN

Adventures as a UN Delegate

The other significant effort with which I came to be associated in 1971 was the campaign at the UN. The Bangladesh government had nominated a delegation to the UN General Assembly session beginning in October 1971, originally to be headed by Bangladesh's first Foreign Minister, Khondkar Mushtaq Ahmed. However, by the time the General Assembly was to meet, the political intrigues from Park Circus, in opening a line of communication with the Nixon administration, had come to the notice of the Indian intelligence agencies who passed on this information to Tajuddin Ahmed. It was apprehended by Tajuddin that Mushtaq might use his mission to the UN to connect with the US administration with a view to negotiating a deal with and within Pakistan. He therefore assigned the leadership of the UN delegation to Justice Abu Sayeed Chowdhury, who flew over from London to New York for this purpose.

As a fallout from this crisis, on the eve of the liberation of Bangladesh, Tajuddin replaced Mushtaq as Foreign Minister with Abdus Samad Azad. Mushtaq never forgave Tajuddin for his demotion and invested much effort after Liberation in sowing the seeds of discord between Bangabandhu and Tajuddin. Mushtaq's ultimate revenge was exacted on 5 November 1975 when he personally spoke over the phone to the Chief Superintendent of Dhaka Central Jail, ordering him to permit entry to Muslehuddin and other assassins sent from Banga Bhaban on their fatal mission to murder Tajuddin and his three other colleagues from the Liberation War who were at the time incarcerated there. By a strange irony, Abdus Samad, then also in custody, was spared but was fated to hear the death cries of his friend Tajuddin who was located in the cell next to him. Mushtaq subsequently died in his bed, in ignominy. Azad lived on to once again serve as Foreign Minister from 1996 to 2001 in the cabinet of Bangabandhu's daughter.

I was nominated as a member of the UN delegation, along with S.A. Karim; Ambassador K.K. Panni, who had defected from Manila; Ambassador A. Fateh, who had defected from Iraq; and a number of other delegates such as Dr A.R. Mallick, VC of Chittagong University, who had come over from Calcutta to join the delegation. The lobbying exercise at the UN turned out to be rather frustrating. Our immediate mission was to generate support for a resolution in the General Assembly to stop the genocide in Bangladesh. This issue may have provided occasion for some speeches in our favour on the floor of the Assembly and in some of the Committees, but not much more came of this largely because most UN members were reluctant to raise their voice against anything that appeared to interfere with the sovereignty of a member nation. As at that stage, none of the veto power States had sought to lend their public support to the cause of Bangladesh, the lobbying effort in this initial phase of the session tended to yield insubstantial results.

The lukewarm support in the UN to Bangladesh's liberation struggle remains a far cry from today's world where the Western powers feel free to sponsor even military action in support of various separatist insurgencies, usually directed against regimes that they deem to be strategically hostile to their interests. The support by Western powers for such insurgencies challenging an incumbent regime or with a separatist agenda in Afghanistan, Yugoslavia, Sudan, Libya and now Syria, provides telling evidence of the changed world order since the emergence of Bangladesh.

An Advocate for Bangladesh

During this period, I involved myself in a number of speaking engagements on behalf of Bangladesh. These included a well-attended meeting at the University of Philadelphia, again organized by Sultana Alam; another at the University of Syracuse; another at MIT in company with Justice Abu Sayeed Chowdhury and Dr Mohiuddin Alamgir; one at Williams College, organized for me by Professor Anisur Rahman who was based there; and one at Yale, organized by Professor Nurul Islam. In most of these functions, an occasional group of Pakistanis would turn up, perhaps to heckle, but at the end, to put a few plaintive questions, more in sorrow than in anger.

I also continued to make some TV appearances and to write occasionally for periodicals. Articles by me on the Bangladesh issue were carried by *The New Republic* and, the more radical, *The Nation*, based in New York. Two of my most interesting appearances on TV took place towards the end of my stay. The first of these was an appearance on public television in Boston. This programme, known as the *Advocates*, is organized around a court case based on some highly topical public issue where two lawyers act as counsel for the prosecution and the defence. Each is permitted to bring three witnesses to speak for their cause. If I recollect correctly, on this occasion, the issue was to discuss the case for the USA government extending support to the Bangladesh cause. I fail to remember the advocate for our cause. But the opposition was led by William Rusher, the proprietor of the *National Review*, one of the foremost conservative weeklies in the USA, edited by the well-known right-wing figure William F. Buckley Jr. Rusher was well to the right of Buckley and possibly to the right of Attila the Hun. His view of the subcontinent was frozen around the time of John Foster Dulles. He appeared to have difficulty in distinguishing the India of Indira Gandhi from that of her father in the 1950s and still seemed to think that Krishna Menon was Foreign Minister of India.

The programme did not have that large a TV audience but was interesting because it brought to the surface the various arguments for and against Bangladesh. Rusher had, for his case, sent out a television crew to Pakistan to interview Bhutto, whose highly tendentious and self-serving testimony was produced before us in the studio on a video screen. Rusher also lined up Congressman Freylinghausen from New Jersey and a former US Ambassador to Pakistan who was the Pepsi-Cola magnate. On the Bangladesh side, our advocate had lined up John Stonehouse, the Labour MP who had in England been one of the most eloquent campaigners for Bangladesh, who was specially flown in from London for the programme. There was, in addition, Ambassador M.K. Rasgotra, who was then number two to L.K. Jha in the Indian Embassy in Washington and who later became the Foreign Secretary in the Government of India. Rasgotra had been actively involved in presenting the Bangladesh case in Washington, so I had met him several times and had become very friendly with him. Finally, there was myself as the only Bangladeshi on the programme. We faced a full studio audience and, I am told, a small but enthusiastic audience of TV viewers.

The large studio audience included a young undergraduate student from Radcliffe, Benazir Bhutto. When years later as PM of Pakistan, Benazir encountered Salma's sister, Princess Sarvath, on a visit to Amman, she enquired about her family and was told that her sister Salma was married to someone from Bangladesh named Rehman Sobhan. Benazir paid me the ultimate compliment by exclaiming, '*the* Rehman Sobhan!'

My second TV appearance was at a more historic moment. Prior to this, all of us at the UN delegation had become more active as the Bangladesh issue finally came before the Security Council and General Assembly following the outbreak of open hostilities between India and Pakistan. The escalation in the Liberation War and the growing tension on the Bangladesh border, through direct military engagements between the Indian and Pakistan forces, had culminated, in an act of aggression by the Pakistan air force, through bombing attacks on targets in northern India on 3 December. Pakistan, which had hitherto been fully committed to keep the Bangladesh issue off the UN agenda, now became active in internationalizing it as part of an Indo-Pakistan threat to peace rather than as a liberation struggle. The subsequent successful advance of the Indian army into Bangladesh and the disintegration of the Pakistan army compelled Pakistan to seek international support for a ceasefire and a withdrawal of the Indian army back across the border. In this task, they were strongly supported by the USA and China. The latter's advocacy of the Pakistani case was their first public action since they had joined the UN a month earlier.

The move to secure passage of a ceasefire and withdrawal of forces resolution had irresistible support both in the Security Council and in the General Assembly. Apparently, most members can be moved to unite behind such a resolution lest they one day find themselves at the receiving end of a war. As a result, the relevant resolution, moved jointly by the USA and China, seeking a ceasefire secured a clear majority in the Security Council. Its passage was only frustrated by a Soviet veto.

To circumvent the veto, a similar resolution was brought before the General Assembly, where the members tend to be even more forthcoming in support of any resolution seeking a ceasefire. Such a resolution was thus assured an overwhelming majority. I subsequently analyzed all the speeches made on this debate on the floor of the Assembly and found that very few of the countries who voted for the resolution did so out of positive support for Pakistan. Most votes were cast in support of peace as a general principle of conduct in international affairs.

We Bangladeshis were spectators to this drama in the UN, which we witnessed from the galleries. Our efforts in the lobbies of the UN brought us much private sympathy for the cause of Bangladesh but little support on the floor of the Assembly. There, most speakers were inclined to forget the nine-month aggression and genocide by the Pakistan army on the people and land of Bangladesh and were inclined to concentrate on the immediate outbreak of war between India and Pakistan.

Apart from my shared efforts at lobbying the delegates to the Security Council, I was invited to make my second TV appearance through participation in a programme on New York public television, on a channel that is distinguished by the fact that it is the only one to feature the proceedings of the General Assembly and Security Council. Our programme was designed to coincide with the debate in the General Assembly on the Indo-Pakistan–Bangladesh war. There were two panels; one was made up of Americans. If I remember, this included Tom Dine, Arnold de Borchgrave of *Newsweek* magazine and one other well-known personality. They were followed by what was meant to be a three-cornered discussion between the Consul General for Pakistan in New York, Najmus Saqib Khan; the Consul General for India, Vishnu Ahuja; and myself, speaking for Bangladesh.

The Pakistani Consul General was instructed by his government to decline to appear on the same platform with me so that he and his Indian counterpart went on the screen together ahead of me. Thus, when I came on screen, it turned out to be a solo appearance. By a strange coincidence, I came on screen just as the tally of the vote count at the General Assembly was being announced. Just as I had launched myself into my statement, the cameras switched from the studio to the General Assembly to report on the massive vote there in favour of an immediate ceasefire and withdrawal of forces across national boundaries. The cameras then switched back to me and the interviewer invited me to give an instant reaction to what was clearly an event that did no service to the cause of liberating Bangladesh.

To the best of my recollection, I had to improvise very rapidly and stated that "Bangladesh, which was the centre of this war as a result of the genocidal action of the Pakistan army, was not invited to participate in this debate in the General Assembly. The people and government of Bangladesh are therefore not party to these resolutions and would continue our war of liberation until such time as the Pakistani aggression on the people of Bangladesh had been defeated." My statement and subsequent observations on the situation arising out of the UN debate and the situation in Bangladesh appeared to be well received. For days after my TV appearance, I was stopped on the streets of New York by strangers who had heard my piece on the subject and complimented me for my forthright statement.

Drama at the UN: Witness to the End Game

My role as TV celebrity was however ephemeral. The real drama was going on in Bangladesh and, more peripherally, in the UN. We had learnt that Mr Zulfikar Ali Bhutto, who had at the eleventh hour been inducted into the government by Yahya Khan, as Vice President and Foreign Minister, was coming to New York to argue the Pakistani case before the Security Council. However, Bhutto's flight to New York was being overtaken by events on the ground in Bangladesh. The spectacular advance of the Indian and Bangladesh forces and the imminent collapse of Pakistani defences were setting their own seal on the debate in the UN. From a Bangali cypher clerk who had, on our instructions, stayed on in the Pakistan UN mission, we learnt that top secret cyphers had been received on 10 December reporting that General Niazi had sought permission to surrender to the advancing forces. We also learnt that Paul Marc Henri, the UN representative in Dhaka, had relayed a message from Rao Farman Ali to the Secretary General seeking his good offices in securing a surrender that guaranteed the safe withdrawal of Pakistani forces from Bangladesh.

Bhutto was greeted at the airport with this, for him, alarming piece of news. His promised coup de théâtre in the Security Council was thus immediately in danger of being upstaged. Being quite unprepared for this development, Bhutto went to ground and spent the next few days in close confabulation with the US Representative to the UN, George Bush Senior, later President of the USA, and with the newly designated Chinese representative to the UN, Huan Huang. It is not clear what was discussed by them in these conclaves, but for a while, we heard no more of talks of surrender. It appears that Niazi and Farman Ali had been overruled by Islamabad and were advised that new help was on the way. This suggested that China from the north and the USA from the sea may have held out promise to Yahya and Bhutto of such an intervention. Suddenly, we found that another session of the Security Council had been convened that was to be addressed by Bhutto.

Again, the Bangladesh UN delegation remained spectators in the galleries of the Security Council to Bhutto's antics in the Security Council. We spent our time trying to get through to delegates from the member countries of the Security Council, to persuade them to moderate their position against demanding a ceasefire and impressing them with the inevitability of Bangladesh. In the lobbies, most of the spokesmen recognized that Bangladesh was a fact and that the best solution was the rapid victory of the allied forces leading to the early surrender of the Pakistan army. They conceded that the Security Council was a sideshow staged by the Americans and Chinese to create the impression that they were doing all they could in support of their friend, Yahya Khan.

In these meetings, Takeo Eguchi—an Oxford contemporary of Kaiser Morshed whom I had then come to know from my visits to Oxford—who was serving on the Japanese UN delegation and many years later became Japan's Ambassador to Bangladesh, regularly met me and kept us informed of the mood and developments within the Security Council. Another close friend of mine from childhood days, Sheel Haksar, who had also been at Oxford when

I was in Cambridge, and was now First Secretary in India's UN delegation, advised me that they had been assured that no action in the UN would frustrate the march of the Indian army to Dhaka as the Soviet Union had assured them of a veto on any such resolution in the Security Council.

It must have become apparent to Bhutto that the UN would be able to do nothing to stave off the inevitable surrender of the Pakistan army in Dhaka. Very likely, he also had intelligence from the USA and China, that whatever huffing and puffing they may do publicly, they would not intervene militarily to save Pakistan. Bhutto made the best of a bad hand by putting on a virtuoso performance that was climaxed by his tearing up the Secretary Council resolution and leading his delegation out of the hall, proclaiming to the bemused Council Members, "My people harken for me." These theatrics were presumably staged once the knowledge of the imminent surrender of the Pakistan army in Bangladesh was made known to him so his antics were targeted to his Pakistani constituency.

I witnessed the final debate in the Council on the eve of the surrender of the Pakistan army. While Bhutto was putting on his act in the Security Council, there were reports that the US Seventh Fleet had been ordered by Nixon to move to the Bay of Bengal for as-yet unspecified objectives. The US administration, under relentless pressure from President Nixon, had become more strident in its denunciations of India and it was not beyond imagination to visualize a last-minute intervention by the USA to bolster the fast depreciating position of the Pakistani forces in Bangladesh. The assumption was that had Niazi held out long enough, such an intervention could have been engineered and used as a basis for enforcing a ceasefire and settlement that preserved the 'integrity of Pakistan'. The Security Council drama was thus a sideshow to the bigger drama around Bangladesh.

It is as yet unrevealed whether the US Seventh Fleet would have intervened had the armies of General Niazi held out a bit longer or this was another exercise in public relations by Nixon to impress upon Pakistan that he was their true ally. Certainly, domestic political support within the USA for such an intervention was totally lacking. The media had been quite vocal on this issue, and Jack Anderson had already published his much quoted exposé of the leaked minutes of the National Security Council where Kissinger had reported on Nixon's instructions for the US State Department to take a strong stand against India. Members of Congress, led by Church, Kennedy and other friends of Bangladesh, had of course been active in mobilizing Congressional opinion against such an intervention. It may thus be speculated that had the US public, media and Congressional opinion been less sympathetic or even indifferent to the Bangladesh cause, the Nixon administration may well have gone much further in their support of Pakistan. To this extent, the intensive campaign to go over the head of the unsympathetic Nixon administration to the American people was not without significance to the Bangladesh cause.

The possibility of an intervention or a diversion by the Chinese in the north-eastern sector of India was also held out as an ancillary hope for the beleaguered garrisons of General Niazi. We had heard of Bhutto's air-dash to Peking on 5 November with a number of leading Generals of the Pakistan army to solicit such an intervention where the Chinese had confirmed their reluctance to directly intervene on behalf of Pakistan in any prospective war with India. This reaffirmed their earlier position to which I had been provided some insight at least two months earlier.

At the end of August, while I was at Oxford on my way back from Calcutta to the USA, I had received a message from Farooq in Paris that our uncle K.M. Kaiser, Pakistan's ambassador to China, urgently wished to meet me. Kaiser was attending a meeting of Pakistani ambassadors convened in Geneva on 24–25 August, where he had briefed the conclave on China's position on the crisis. He had indicated that China had advised for a political settlement with the AL and had expressed doubt over Chinese military support for Pakistan in case of a war with India.[1] After this meeting, Kaiser secretly flew over to Paris, where he met with me at Farooq's residence and reaffirmed, perhaps more categorically, what he had

[1] Srinath Raghavan. 2013. *1971: A Global History of the Creation of Bangladesh*. Cambridge: Harvard University Press.

presented at Geneva to his colleagues, that China would provide arms and diplomatic support, but was not going to intervene militarily to save Pakistan.

I was advised by Khwaja Kaiser to convey this critical intelligence to the Bangladesh government, which I duly did on my return to London. As I gathered later, I was not the only channel of such information on China's intentions as some of the Bangalis in the Pakistan Embassy in Beijing, led by Obaidullah Khan, had also managed to pass on this information to the Mujibnagar government. To what extent subsequent military strategies in the region were planned on this intelligence, I cannot say.

Given these tactics both within and outside the Security Council by the USA, China and Pakistan, the resolution of the tension rested on the capacity of the allied forces to secure a rapid surrender of the Pakistan army. This had been imminent around 10 December but had at the last minute been countermanded on orders from Islamabad in order to buy time for the outside manoeuvres to be played out. When I left New York for London on my way home, the atmosphere was surcharged with high tension.

Journey's End

Joyous Moments

As I prepared to leave the UN premises at the end of the Security Council debate around 7:00 p.m. on 15 December to board a bus to JFK on my way to London, I slipped on the escalator and tore a ligament in my leg. I managed to get to the airport and then from Heathrow to Oxford in a semi-crippled state, sustained by the elation that Bangladesh's liberation was near.

In the darkened airport bus that drove us to JFK, I reflected on the long journey I had travelled since I left my home on the morning of 27 March. My thoughts moved back to the night at the end of March I had spent on a nauka, carrying us along the river to Brahmanbaria when Bangladesh's and my own future were permeated with uncertainty. Yet within nine months, these tensions had abated and I could aspire to return to a liberated Bangladesh. This thought invested me with a unique sense of fulfilment that served as a balm to my tortured ligament.

Someone near me turned on a transistor that was playing *Spanish Harlem*, the hit song of 1971 sung by the irresistible Aretha Franklin. During the months I had spent in the USA, I had heard the distinctive strains of this song over the car radios of Haroun, Muhith, Razzaq Khan and sundry cab drivers as they drove me to various appointments in D.C. Ever since, *Spanish Harlem* has remained indelibly embedded in my mind as the sound of 1971. As the song faded to its end, I felt it provided a fitting coda to 1971 and an epic phase in my life.

I landed at Heathrow on the morning of 16 December and managed to reach Oxford with some difficulty. I arrived home in time for Salma and me to witness on television the exhilarating spectacle of the surrender of the Pakistan army to the combined forces of India and Bangladesh at the Dhaka Race Course Maidan.

Collaborators and Criminals

This historic moment had been clouded by the discovery of the mutilated corpses of some of my Dhaka University colleagues, on the eve of the surrender. This death list included Munier Chowdhury, one of the iconic literary figures of Bangladesh; Ghiasuddin Ahmed, a much loved teacher of history; Rashidul Hasan of the English Department who had contributed articles to *Forum*; and my good friend, the eminent journalist and writer Shahidullah Kaiser, among others, most known to me. These intellectuals, known for their progressive and secular views, had been abducted from their homes by cadres of the Jamaat-e-Islam and taken to a brick field in Rayer Bazaar on the outskirts of Dhaka, where they were brutally murdered. This terrible act was all the more heinous because it was committed by fellow Bangalis. Once again we were reminded that a small segment of our citizens had collaborated with the Pakistan army, served as informers and had actively joined in the genocide inflicted by the army on the Bangalis.

I remember the sense of outrage we experienced throughout the war whenever we read of such acts of collaboration by Bangalis. We were particularly incensed by the pro-Pakistan statements of such public figures as Fazlul Qadir Chowdhury, Hamidul Huq Chowdhury, Sabur Khan, Shah Azizur Rahman, Abdul Salam Khan, Farid Ahmed, Mahmud Ali, once a leader of the left, and Ghulam Azam, the Jammat leader. Such statements by these Bangali collaborators were designed to perpetrate the illusion before a global audience, that there was an alternative body of Bangalis fighting to preserve the integrity of Pakistan who thereby supported the atrocities of the then Pakistan army. We were no less angered when some of our academic colleagues such as Professor Syed Sajjad Hussain, a much respected Chair of the English Department at Dhaka University, and some other teachers not only spoke against the Liberation War but travelled abroad as advocates of the Pakistani genocide. Most Bangalis at that time felt that the most extreme measures against such collaborators would be justified. No tears were shed when we learnt that former Governor, Monem Khan, a strong loyalist of the Ayub regime, was assassinated at his Banani residence by members of the Mukti Bahini.

I remember coming across such Pakistani loyalists as Shah Azizur Rahman, moving furtively along the corridors of the UN, where they had been dispatched as members of the Pakistan UN delegation to counter our lobbying efforts. Shah Aziz and other Bangali collaborators looked deeply shamefaced and avoided conversations with us. Other such collaborators were less politely treated outside the UN. In one public function in the USA addressed by these collaborators of the Pakistan army, it was reported that Mahmud Ali was slapped on the face with a shoe by an enraged Bangali woman.

The final act of collaboration by the Jamaat, manifested in their murder of the intellectuals in the last days of the war, came as less of a surprise as the Jammat had been quite conspicuous in their open links with the Pakistan army. The Pakistan army had militarily trained and equipped Jammat cadres to serve as killer squads who were assigned historically inspired designations such as Al Badar and Al Shams. These squads had already been active as auxiliaries of the Pakistan army. It was reported that as Bangladesh's liberation became imminent, a Pakistani general, who had prepared a list of key Bangali intellectuals to be eliminated as part of a parting legacy for the independent State of Bangladesh, sent out these killer squads to do their dirty work. The murder of the intellectuals reinforced the almost universal belief among Bangalis that these Bangali assassins should be tried and punished not just for their collaborationist role but for being agents of genocide.

Returning Home to an Independent Country

The days following the surrender of the Pakistani forces were especially joyous moments for Salma and me. Not only were we together again as a family, but the perilous and uncertain journey on which we had embarked when I left our Gulshan home on the morning of 27 March appeared to be nearing its end. Bangladesh was now a liberated and independent country to which we could return together as a family. On 27 March, none of these possibilities appeared foreseeable. It was then winter in Oxford, with some snow on the ground and a fire burned in the hearth of our small house. The urge to prolong these precious moments was strong. Salma had built a cosy niche for the family in Wolvercote. She had a regular part-time teaching position and, in spite of our limited resources, teaching demands, mother care and running the household, had established a reasonably secure life for the family. I had a regular research position at QEH and could stay on so that the family could live a more predictable, if not overly comfortable, life at least for the next six to nine months. Salma was, thus, keen for me to remain in Oxford and discharge my responsibilities to QEH by writing a book on the emergence of Bangladesh, for which I had already been contracted by Penguin Books.

Salma's suggestion tantalized me. I had been unrelentingly active over the last eight and a half months and badly needed the rest. However, Bangladesh was now a nation. Those of us who participated as foot soldiers in its creation were now living to see the fulfilment of a dream. It is not often that one's most cherished aspirations are fulfilled in one's lifetime. While we had hoped such a day would one day emerge, none of us had imagined nine months ago, as copious blood was fertilizing our soil and flowing down our rivers, that this ordeal of terror would end so soon. What was relief for Salma was also exhilaration for me.

Eventually, the excitement of returning to an independent Bangladesh overwhelmed my urge for spending these tranquil months with my family, so once again, as in 1969 when I chose to abandon my pursuit of a PhD at the LSE so I could return to a post-Ayub Pakistan, I disappointed Salma and chose to rush back to Dhaka. As a compromise, I suggested that Salma stay on in Oxford with the boys until things were more settled in Dhaka not just for me but also for the country.

I flew to Delhi in the last week of December and thence to Calcutta. I sought out Mosharraf. He had worked hard with Kamruzzaman to prepare a resettlement and rehabilitation plan for the 10 million refugees who had already begun to return to Bangladesh. The Planning Board report was used as a basis for discussions with the Indian government that was committed to both fund and assist the Bangladesh government in the enormous tasks of rehabilitation. Mosharraf had flown to Dhaka with the first group of Bangladeshi officials who accompanied Tajuddin. The team was expected to host an Indian team of officials travelling to Dhaka to discuss the rehabilitation process. After meeting the Indian team in Dhaka, Mosharraf had recently flown back to Calcutta to assist Inari in packing up and arranging for the return of his family to Dhaka.

When I met Mosharraf in his Park Circus hovel, he said he had arranged to return to Dhaka on 31 December and suggested that I should accompany him. He had secured two seats for us aboard an old Dakota aircraft that had been specially arranged to take back Kamruzzaman and his family as well as Zohra Tajuddin and her children to Dhaka. Mosharraf, following his return to Dhaka, was somewhat more sceptical than I was on what lay before us in

Bangladesh. In the absence of Bangabandhu, whose fate in Pakistan was yet unknown, he feared that the various factional struggles of Mujibnagar would pose serious problems in a post-liberation Bangladesh. I spent a day or so connecting with my friends Monu Palchaudhuri and Dipankar Ghosh who were both back in Calcutta. They were fascinated by the narration of my adventures, which seemed so removed from our more carefree moments in Darjeeling and Cambridge.

The rather ancient Indian air force Dakota that flew us back to Dhaka aroused some insecurity in my mind as to its flight-worthiness. However, the flight was fuelled by our high spirits and we landed safely in Dhaka on a cold but sunny morning on 31 December. Tajuddin was there to receive his family. As we exchanged greetings, I sensed that Tajuddin had many problems on his mind. He suggested that once I settled in I should come and visit him in Banga Bhaban, where his government held office. A new year and a new life in a new country were opening up for us, and I at least, was full of hope and expectation.

As I had no idea what had happened to my home in Gulshan, once we had abandoned it, Mosharraf and I first decided to go to the house of our mutual friend Zeaul Huq Tulu in Dhanmondi. Tulu was overwhelmed to see us. We had last met at Baraid, nine months ago, before I embarked on my uncertain odyssey for a liberated Bangladesh. He immediately suggested I move in with him as my Gulshan house was reported to have been looted by the Pakistani army and was in an abandoned state. Mosharraf chose to return to his family home in Wari.

That night on New Year's Eve, Tulu hosted the first of his famous New Year's Eve parties, which remained a tradition until he passed away in 1997. That first celebration was very special. It was an open house and not just friends, but friends of friends dropped in to share a cup of cheer. Most had lived through these nine months not knowing who would be alive to greet the new year. Tears and laughter enhanced the flavour of our libations as we embraced each other in a spirit of hope and unity where none could anticipate the cruel and divisive days that lay ahead.

Annexure

DECLASSIFIED
Authority UND 32940

CONFIDENTIAL

NEA – Mr. Van Hollen May 14, 1971
NEA/INC – Anthony C.E. Quainton
Meeting with Bangla Desh Professor Rehman Sobhan

At the suggestion of Tom Dine of Senator Church's office, I had lunch with Professor Rehman Sobhan, of Dacca University. I had last met Sobhan briefly at a Pakistan Economics Association meeting in Peshawar five or six years ago when Sobhan gave a provocative paper on economic disparities between East and West Pakistan.

At the very start Sobhan made the vigorous assertion that the State Department did not have the facts of the situation because Consul General Blood's reports had been suppressed at the instigation of the Embassy in Islamabad. I told him that this was completely false and that all on-the-spot reports from Dacca had been received here and had been read with attention. We have fairly good information on what happened in March, particularly in Dacca, and were under no illusions about those events. Despite these assurances, Sobhan said he wanted to give me some additional background, particularly since he understood that M.M. Ahmed was putting about stories which were patently untrue. Sobhan said that prior to March 25 there was no breakdown of law and order, and indeed no breakdown of the political talks. He and M.M. Ahmed, among

The photo of this document has been taken by Mizanur Rahman Khan, Joint Editor, *Prothom Alo* on 26 December 2012.

others, had reached agreement on the six points and the Awami League had accepted several specific changes which had been suggested by Ahmed with respect to currency and banking. Agreement was not fully reached on the terms of the transfer of power and the end to martial law.

I asked Sobhan about the pre-March 25 communal incidents. He said that the only incident of a communal nature which had taken place was in Chittagong on March 1 and 2 when some 150 Biharis were murdered and about 200 Bengalis were killed in reprisals. Mujib had taken immediate actions to see that there were no further incidents. Sobhan acknowledged that there was a civil disobedience campaign directed against the Army and that no supplies of food were getting through. He did not regard non-cooperation as provocative, though he did think that Yahya had actively provoked a confrontation by trying to unload the ammunition in Chittagong in the face of the port workers' strike. Mujib had told Yahya that the campaign would be lifted as soon as a political settlement was reached.

Sobhan said that Mujib throughout had taken a very moderate stance as evidenced by his speech on March 7. Mujib regarded himself as the last hope for democracy in Bengal and for a peaceful democratic solution to the East Pakistan problem. Mujib had put this point to Yahya on a more or less take-it or leave-it basis. In Sobhan's view the Awami league had been acting on the political assumptions of the Indian Freedom struggle of the 1930s using the Gandhian techniques of non-violence and civil disobedience. They were the last of this generation, and when they were gone a new style of leadership would emerge within the Awami League, being more militant and more radical. He thought that the present Awami League leadership would last about six months before it was replaced by others.

I asked Sobhan whether he thought the attempt to discredit the Awami League as an Indian tool would succeed. He replied that this had been tried by right-wing Bengali politicians such as Farid

Ahmed in the last elections. These politicians had charged that Mujib was in Indian pay and had referred to the Agartala conspiracy. The elections results had demonstrated how effective the charges had been. They would be even less so now. In fact, he said, many East Bengalis could not understand why the Indians had done so little for them.

Sobhan also talked at some length about the allegation that Mujib had demanded that the National Assembly meet in two committees. This, he said, was absolutely false. The demand for two committees was made by Bhutto in order to consolidate his own power in the West Wing. Many of the politicians from the smaller provinces in West Pakistan were very bitter with the Awami League for agreeing to this proposal, since they felt it meant handing them over to Bhutto.

In talking about the future Sobhan was vague and imprecise. He said that the future depended on whether the US renewed economic assistance to Pakistan. I said I thought that it was not quite as simple as that, we were only one actor in the game, and that we had to consider the economic and political impact of a cessation of aid both in the East and the West.

I also mentioned the dangers of escalation and the possibility that the Chinese might intervene. He said he thought this was most unlikely and added that the Bengalis could not understand why China had taken such a strongly pro-Pakistani position. I said China had an important political, economic and air transit stake in Pakistan which they wished to preserve. Sobhan said that they could have maintained those interests with an independent Bangla Desh. An unarmed Bangla Desh would have wanted good relations with all major powers, particularly India and China.

Sobhan was less than his normally ebullient self. He was somewhat resentful that he had been unable to meet official Americans and noted that I was the first official of the US Government he had been able to see. He seemed at a loss as to how to get the Bangla

Desh story across to high levels in this country in the face of the misrepresentations of the Yahya Government. He indicated that he hoped to meet others in the Department at the working level. He said he thought the next four of five days would be critical and that all major decisions would be taken in that period. I said that I thought the process would be rather more drawn out. We had waited seven weeks without taking any major decisions and I assumed that future decisions would be spaced over a fairly long period of time. He would have to judge our policy on the basis of those decisions.

The essence of his pitch was a familiar one. The struggle will go on; the political process will become more radical; there will never be a settlement within the framework of a unified Pakistan; and the United States cannot achieve the peace and stability it desires for the region until Bangla Desh has come into existence. (This analysis when stripped of his personal biases and the rhetoric of his presentation seems very much on the mark.)

NEA/INC:ACEOusinton/emg

CC: NEA/PAF – Mr. Baxter
AID/NESA – Mr. Swayze
INR – Mr. Cochran
NSC – Mr. Hoskinson

Index

About the Author

Rehman Sobhan is a noted Bangladeshi economist and freedom fighter who played an active role in the Bangali national movement. He is currently the Chairman, Centre for Policy Dialogue, Dhaka, Bangladesh. He was educated at St. Paul's School, Darjeeling; Aitchison College, Lahore; and the University of Cambridge. He was one of the several economists whose ideas influenced the 6-point programme of Sheikh Mujibur Rahman, which became the basis for the struggle for self-rule for Bangladesh. A former Professor of Economics at Dhaka University, he has authored numerous books and articles on various developmental issues. The most recent of these, *Challenging the Injustice of Poverty: Agendas for Inclusive Development in South Asia*, was published by SAGE in 2010.

He served the first Government of Bangladesh as Envoy Extraordinaire with special responsibility for Economic Affairs, during the Liberation War in 1971. He was a member of the first Bangladesh Planning Commission, and in the 1980s headed the premier development research facility, BIDS. In 1990–91, he became a Member of the Advisory Council of the President of Bangladesh in charge of the Ministry of Planning and the Economic Relations Division. In 1993, he founded and became the Chairman of the Centre for Policy Dialogue (CPD), one of Bangladesh's most prestigious think tanks. He also headed the South Asia Centre for Policy Studies (SACEPS) from 2000 to 2005, one of the leading think tanks for promoting regional cooperation in South Asia.

